REAL EST

&
ASSET PROTECTION

For Texas Real Estate Investors

2020 Edition

By David J. Willis, J.D., LL.M.

First Edition Design Publishing
Sarasota, Florida USA

Real Estate Law & Asset Protection
For Texas Real Estate Investors
2020 Edition
Copyright ©2013, 2014, 2015, 2016, 2018, 2020 David J. Willis

ISBN 978-1506-908-70-0 AMZ
ISBN 978-1506-908-67-0 PBK
ISBN 978-1622-879-44-1 EBOOK

LCCN 201594404

January 2020

Published and Distributed by
First Edition Design Publishing, Inc.
P.O. Box 20217, Sarasota, FL 34276-3217
www.firsteditiondesignpublishing.com

Table of Contents

PREFACE

This book is a pragmatic and creative approach to legal and asset protection issues faced by investors in Texas real estate, particularly investors in residential and smaller commercial properties. If you are a real estate investor who owns (or aspires to own) 10, 20, or 50 or more properties, then you should consider reading this book. If you use creative methods such as wraparounds and "subject to" transactions then you may find this volume very useful indeed. If, however, your goal is to assemble an international consortium to purchase Rockefeller Center or Trump Tower, then this is probably not the book for you.

It is not my intention to offer a textbook or comprehensive academic treatise. Rather, this volume contains practical perspectives and techniques developed over the years in the course of advising and representing investors, both in transactions and in the courtroom. Since there are usually as many opinions as there are lawyers in a room, it should be no surprise if other lawyers disagree with at least some of my conclusions. In response, I would point out that there is nothing theoretical presented here. Every strategy I describe has been tried and has largely succeeded in the real world. Having said that, readers should consult an attorney prior to implementing any of my suggestions in order to insure compatibility with individual circumstances. Business plans vary and so do investments and asset protection strategies. Note also that the law changes and evolves, often rapidly. While cases and statutes are cited in this book, the reader should do independent research to ascertain the current status of the law before relying on any of these citations. I do not offer legal guidance to any particular person with regard to any particular case.

As you consult this book, I suggest that you make sure you have the latest edition. You can check on this by going to our website, www.Lone StarLandLaw.com.

All real estate investors should form the habit of doing thorough due diligence prior to investing in real estate. This includes consulting attorneys, accountants, insurance advisors, and other qualified professionals on overall methods and goals as well as specific transacttions. Every investor should have a team of seasoned professionals available to answer questions, offer input, and provide customized services. A professional investor will also acquire a basic level of competence in searching and obtaining information and copies from real property and appraisal district records.

On the subject of transactional documentation, I urge readers to avoid most standard forms, especially those obtained from the Internet, except for contracts and addenda promulgated by the Texas Real Estate

Commission and the Texas Association of Realtors. Consider others suspect.

There are many resources for investors, not the least of which is the Texas Property Code. I suggest that every investor have a paperback copy of the Code on his or her desk and refer to it regularly (go to www. JonesMcClure.com). There are also a number of quality educational opportunities in the marketplace, including real estate schools and mentorship programs, enough so that there is no excuse for an investor not to master the trade.

Since the Texas legislature meets every two years, it is also prudent to check for recent legislative changes that may affect the business of real estate investment. This is most easily done at the official website for the Texas legislature at www.capitol.state.tx.us. Also, all cases and statutes cited in this book should be read in full before relying on them in any particular case.

Lastly, it has been my experience that good ethics make for good business. Avoid any transaction that even hints of fraud or deception. If it appears too good to be true it probably is.

I welcome comments and criticism. I can most easily be reached by email at LoneStarLandLaw@aol.com.

David J. Willis

PART I

CONTRACTS & CLOSINGS

Chapter 1

RESIDENTIAL SALES CONTRACTS

The TREC One to Four Family Residential Contract

The most commonly used residential sales contract in Texas is the One to Four Family Residential Contract (Resale) promulgated by the Texas Real Estate Commission as form number 20-13. The blank form is available at www.trec.state.tx.us. I will refer to it as the "TREC 1-4 contract." All licensed brokers and agents are required to use this contract and other TREC promulgated forms when representing clients in the purchase and sale of real property. Non-license holders and attorneys may use any format they wish. Note that our comments in this chapter are not intended as comprehensive instructions on how to complete the TREC 1-4 contract or as a substitute for using the services of broker, agent, or real estate attorney. We merely touch upon the highlights.

Real estate investors will find that they are almost always better off using the TREC 1-4 contract with appropriate addenda rather than anything simpler that is supposedly designed or streamlined for investor use—and that includes the modified contracts that emerge from the multitude of real estate "guru" seminars. Accordingly, an experienced investor will become familiar with the various options and boxes to be checked in TREC forms and learn how to tailor a contract to his or her advantage.

The truth is, even when amicably conducted, the sale and purchase of real estate is by definition an adversarial transaction. From a lawyer's perspective, producing a contract and closing documents that advance the client's best interests is the whole point of the exercise. Experienced negotiators, however, know that it is better not to demand changes that you yourself would not be willing to grant if you were on the other side of the transaction.

Strike-Outs Versus an Addendum

Let's assume that you find the existing text and format of the TREC 1-4 contract to be inadequate for an upcoming transaction. How should revision of the TREC 1-4 contract be accomplished? One way is to make changes on the form itself—strike, insert, and initial with pen. This is legally valid although it can get messy if there are lots of alterations. It is often cleaner to attach a special provisions addendum that supersedes any printed form provisions that may conflict. Only items to be altered are mentioned in the addendum. This method of modifying the contract has an obvious advantage in negotiations: it is immediately apparent, on a single page or two, which terms are being changed and which are not. Another advantage to the addendum method is that brokers and agents are more comfortable with it, since the actual body of their familiar TREC contract has not been changed.

Another possibility is to design an entirely custom contract suited to the specific circumstances, but this seldom happens since non-standard contracts tend to push agents and brokers out of their comfort zone, at least in the residential arena. Custom contracts are much more common in large commercial transactions.

If your choice is to add a special provisions addendum, the wording "See Special Provisions Addendum attached hereto and incorporated herein" should be inserted in paragraph 11 (Special Provisions) of the TREC 1-4 contract. Also, in paragraph 22 (Agreement of Parties), the box "other" should be checked and "Special Provisions Addendum" inserted in the line that follows.

A further note as to paragraph 11 (Special Provisions): it is a blank space available for inserting extra comments, but its permitted use by brokers and agents is limited to "factual statements and business details applicable to the sale"—i.e., not modification of text or addition of provisions that are primarily legal in nature. It is therefore not the appropriate place for license holders to insert provisions that have legal implications (unless this insertion is suggested by an attorney for one of the parties) nor is it usually an acceptable substitute for a special provisions addendum when dealing with a creative or complex transaction. For one thing, the blank space offered by the form has been reduced over the years and is now too small to include much additional text. A special provisions addendum is usually the better way to go, whether one is a license holder or an unlicensed investor.

Caution: certain of the above customization methods are likely, at least in the case of substantive contract changes, to constitute the practice of law. While it is unlawful for anyone to practice law without a license, doing so is particularly problematic for real estate license holders, who may as a result incur both TREC sanctions and considerable liability to their clients. License holders should generally refer their clients to a real estate attorney if non-standard provisions or changes are contemplated.

Typical Concerns of the Seller

The seller usually has the simpler side of the transaction, at least when it comes to modifying the contract. First and foremost, the seller wants to make sure that a buyer is serious and capable of following through. For this reason, the seller may want to require that the buyer submit a pre-approval letter with the contract. Also, a contract should arrive with sufficient earnest money and show that the buyer will be making a substantial down payment. Other concerns of the seller include:

(1) *As Is.*" The seller usually wants to convey the property to the greatest extent possible "as is" without responsibility for repairs or any representations or warranties (other than warranties of title), particularly those that survive closing. This means checking the box at 7.D.(1). The latest TREC 1-4 contract includes a fairly good explanation of what it means to convey property "as is:" it "means the present condition of the Property with any and all defects and without warranty except for the warranties of title and the warranties in this contract." Not bad, but there are much better "as is" clauses available, for instance:

AS A CONSEQUENCE OF SPECIFIC NEGOTIATIONS BETWEEN THE PARTIES, AND AS A MATERIAL PART OF THE CONSIDERATION FOR THIS TRANSACTION, WITHOUT WHICH SELLER WOULD NOT AGREE TO SELL THE PROPERTY TO BUYER, SELLER AGREES TO SELL AND CONVEY TO BUYER AND BUYER UNCONDITIONALLY AGREES TO BUY AND ACCEPT THE PROPERTY (DEFINED TO INCLUDE THE SURFACE AND SUB-SURFACE OF THE REALTY TOGETHER WITH ALL IMPROVEMENTS) ENTIRELY "AS IS," IN ITS/THEIR PRESENT CONDITION, WITH ALL DEFECTS, KNOWN OR UNKNOWN, PATENT OR LATENT, AND WITHOUT REPRESENTATIONS OR WARRANTIES, EXPRESS OR IMPLIED, EXCEPT FOR SUCH WARRANTIES OF TITLE AS MAY BE EXPRESSLY SET FORTH AND/OR LIMITED IN THE DEED TO BUYER. THE CONSIDERATION TO BE PAID FOR THE PROPERTY REFLECTS THE "AS IS" NATURE OF THIS CONTRACT.

BUYER AGREES THAT BUYER HAS A DUTY OF THOROUGH DUE DILIGENCE. BUYER WILL RELY SOLELY ON BUYER'S INSPECTIONS AND OTHER DUE DILIGENCE IN DETERMINING THE PROPERTY'S CONDITION, SUITABILITY, AND ACCEPTABILITY TO BUYER.

**ANY AND ALL ORAL STATEMENTS CONCERNING THE
CONDITION, SUITABILITY, OR VALUE OF THE PROPERTY
OR THE IMPROVEMENTS, WHETHER MADE BY SELLER,
SELLER'S AGENTS, OR THIRD PARTIES, ARE EXCLUDED AND
DISCLAIMED AND ENTIRELY SUPERSEDED HEREBY.**

**AN "AS IS" CLAUSE DRAFTED BY SELLER WILL BE
INCLUDED IN THE WARRANTY DEED TO BUYER AND BUYER
WILL BE REQUIRED TO UNCONDITIONALLY CONSENT TO
THE "AS IS" CLAUSE BY EXECUTING AND ACKNOWLEDGING
THE WARRANTY DEED.**

In the case of contracts for the sale of commercial property, the "as is" clause in the earnest money contract should go on to extensively disclaim environmental liability. If the seller will require an indemnity on environmental issues, mention of this should also be included.

Care should then be taken to assure that the warranty deed presented to the seller at closing does in fact include "as is" language and require the signature of grantee as well as grantor. It is not sufficient to rely on contract language, since pursuant to the doctrine of merger the final closing documents (the deed, note, and deed of trust) usually control going forward.

Note: if the seller performs any repairs and treatments prior to closing, as paragraph 7.D.(2) may require, then the "as is" clause should specifically include these within its scope, thereby preventing the buyer from later claiming that such repairs were warrantied by the seller.

Lastly, if there are adverse conditions or defects known to the seller, the seller will want to use the contract as a means of fully disclosing these conditions, up front and in detail. In other words, the seller never wants to be in the position of being accused of withholding such information, or minimizing it, or glossing over it. Get it out there, in full. See chapter 2 for an explanation of why this is true.

(2) *Buyer Due Diligence.* The seller should make it clear that due diligence duties are the sole obligation of the buyer (including obtaining inspections, determination of square footage, an appraisal, a title commitment or policy, legal advice, and the like). Reliance on any statements by seller or seller's agents should be expressly disclaimed.

(3) *Existing Survey.* If an existing survey is supplied by seller to buyer, the survey should be supplied "as is" without warranties. If the buyer wants someone to hold liable for survey currency or

accuracy, then the buyer should be required to obtain a new one at the buyer's own expense. And there should be no automatic extension of the closing date for survey-related issues.

(4) *Curing Objections.* The TREC contract allows the buyer to submit objections to the survey or the title commitment which the seller "shall cure" so long as the seller does not have to incur any expense in doing so. The seller should want to make it clear that seller *may* but shall not have the *obligation* to cure any objections; further, in the course of attempting to do doing so, seller will not be bound to expend effort or expense. The seller probably does not, for instance, want to have to cure heirship objections to title and do so "within 15 days" as called for by the contract. Basically, the seller wants cure efforts to be entirely at its discretion. And the seller certainly does not want the failure to cure objections (or failure to even try) to be construed as a default that could result in a lawsuit from the buyer.

(5) *Specific Performance.* "Specific performance" is an equitable remedy available to a buyer who pleads and proves that he was ready, willing, and able to perform according to the contract— although actual tender of the purchase price is excused if it would be a useless exercise given the obvious default of the seller. *DiGiuseppe v. Lawler*, 269 S.W.3d 588, 593-594 (Tex. 2008). It is in the seller's interest to avoid the possibility of being sued for specific performance since this might result in a lis pendens (public notice of the suit) that could cloud the title and prevent sale of the property to anyone else (see chapter 6). Accordingly, specific performance as a buyer remedy should be struck. And since specific performance is generally an ineffective remedy for the seller, there is no reason from the seller's point of view not to agree to strike specific performance all around.

(6) *Content of Warranty Deed.* The seller should exercise at least some control over the content of the warranty deed that conveys title to the buyer instead of merely accepting a basic assembly-line version supplied by title company attorneys. As previously noted, the seller may want to require inclusion of comprehensive "as is" language along with the buyer's signature indicating the buyer's assent to this provision. The seller may also want to expand that section of the deed entitled

"Exceptions to Conveyance and Warranty" to include "all matters of which Grantee has actual or constructive notice and all matters excepted from coverage in any owner's title insurance policy issued to Grantee in connection with this conveyance." The seller generally pays for the warranty deed, so there is no reason why the seller should not have input into what it contains. This will require obtaining a copy of the proposed deed prior to closing.

(7) *Assumptions.* In assumptions, the seller should assure that there will be a mutually acceptable deed of trust to secure assumption (with a due-on-sale clause) as well as an assumption agreement that specifies when and to whom the buyer will make payments, how casualty insurance will be handled, and other oft-overlooked but important details. The assumption agreement should also include disclosure of the potential future impact of any existing due-on-sale clause and provide a course of action in the event due-on-sale is invoked by the lender.

(8) *Seller Financing.* If there is seller-financing, it is in the seller's interest to control the terms and conditions of the note and deed of trust beyond what is provided in the TREC Seller Financing Addendum—and then, ideally, obtain early approval from the buyer for all seller-financing documents. By early, we mean well before closing since last-minute disputes about the form and content of seller-financing documents have ended more than one transaction. Many attorneys like to attach the form of these documents to the contract as approved exhibits—a great practice, although this more commonly occurs in commercial transactions.

(9) *Wraparounds.* In the event the transaction is a wrap, there should be a wrap addendum that addresses pertinent details. Since there is no TREC or Texas Association of Realtors promulgated addendum for this, a custom addendum drafted by an attorney is needed. As is the case with assumptions and seller financing, early review and approval of legal documents is preferred. Again, the best way to do this is to attach the pre-approved legal documents to the sales contract itself, although this seldom occurs because the parties are usually in a rush and reluctant to pay an attorney to create documents at this early stage.

(10) *"Sub2" Transactions.* In the case of a "subject to" transaction, precise language to this effect should be included in a custom addendum to the contract since there is no TREC or TAR addendum for a sub2. As is the case with a special provisions addendum and a custom wrap addendum, drafting a custom sub2 addendum constitutes the practice of law.

(11) *Seller Representations.* These are generically referred to by lawyers as "representations and warranties" (or "reps and warranties" for short) and they occur in nearly every contract pertaining to the sale of real estate. Paragraph 19 states "All covenants, representations, and warranties survive closing." Really? Forever? This is clearly not in the seller's interest and should be struck and the change initialed. Just as the seller wants to convey the property "as is," at least to the maximum extent possible, a seller should also prefer to put a period on any ongoing liability. Note that the last sentence of this paragraph (allowing for back-up offers) should remain.

The foregoing is a partial list of seller concerns. There may well be other items to consider based on the unique nature of a particular transaction. Each item can be effectively addressed by a customized special provisions addendum that is brief and to the point.

As an aside, be cautioned that the TREC 1-4 contract should *never* be used as a substitute for a contract for deed or other executory device. Given changes to Section 5.061 et seq. of the Property Code, this practice, always dubious, is now out of the question.

Seller Disclosure

If a condition could reasonably affect the decision by an ordinary buyer to buy or not buy, then it should be disclosed, even if the conveyance is to be made "as is." That may mean going beyond the Seller's Disclosure if that form does not provide sufficient scope or detail. Failure to do so could violate the Deceptive Trade Practices-Consumer Protection Act ("DTPA"). See Tex. Bus. & Com. Code Sec. 17.41 et seq. and chapter 41 of this book. However tempting it may be for a seller to avoid disclosure of a material fact or condition, it is not worth risking a lawsuit that ends with a judgment for treble damages plus attorney's fees. More details on seller disclosure are found in the next chapter.

The Buyer's Side of the Transaction

A buyer's concerns are more complex. Generally, the buyer should want to know everything there is to know about the property, whether that information is derived from due diligence, a title commitment, a survey, disclosure by the seller, information provided by a broker, or even gossip from neighbors. "Buyer beware" still has considerable meaning in the purchase and sale of real estate.

There is no excuse for a buyer (particularly an investor) failing to do his or her homework on a property or failing to read documents before signing them. We live in an information society. Not putting forth a minimum effort to obtain information about a property one is buying (not having it professionally inspected, for instance) looks more and more . . . well, stupid—and judges and jurors are likely to see it that way. Yet there continue to be suits by buyers who claim they were absolved from their duty to inspect or read documents because they were rushed or pressured by the seller. Such a claim will likely not stand up in court.

Specific items of concern to the buyer:

(1) *Financing Contingency.* A buyer should want the third-party financing contingency to be a true contingency governed by specific parameters. The TREC Third Party Financing Addendum states: "Buyer shall apply promptly for all financing described below and make every reasonable effort to obtain credit approval for the financing, including but not limited to furnishing all information and documents required by Buyer's lender." Is this sufficiently specific to protect a buyer from accusations by a seller who argues that the buyer failed to "apply promptly" or make "every reasonable effort" to get a loan? Does "promptly" mean two days or twenty? Does "every reasonable effort" require application to one lender or four? The text is silent on these specifics. Moreover, nowhere in the contract or in the TREC Financing Addendum is it spelled out what constitutes adequate evidence of failure to get financing. Can the buyer be sure that the seller will take the buyer's word and agree to return the earnest money? These issues may not be so compelling if the earnest money is only $500 . . . but what if it is $5,000 or $15,000, amounts that are not uncommon in sales of higher-end properties? It is also to the buyer's benefit to specify that providing a "turn-down letter" shall be conclusive, indisputable evidence that financing was denied.

(2) *Assumptions, Seller Financing, and Wraps.* If the transaction involves an assumption, seller-financing, or wrap, there is always the issue of the specific content of legal documents that the buyer will be asked to sign at closing. We have discussed this from the seller's side, but in many cases it is just as important to the buyer. The TREC Loan Assumption Addendum and the TREC Seller Financing Addendum are reasonably detailed, but what if the seller's attorney includes unexpected or oppressive clauses in the note or deed of trust? Does the closing fail? Is there a breach? It is wise to anticipate and prepare for these issues well before closing. Again, a special provisions addendum may be useful. Even better, a careful buyer may want to see and approve the form of the warranty deed that the seller will deliver at closing.

As noted, there is no promulgated addendum for a wrap, yet many pesky details need to be addressed. Is the buyer fully informed about the particulars of the wrapped debt? Has the buyer seen copies of the existing note and deed of trust? How can the buyer be sure the seller will pass monthly payments along to the first-lien lender? Will the buyer have the right to contact the lender or receive written evidence from the seller that payments are current? What happens if the lender exercises due-on-sale and accelerates the wrapped note? What about casualty insurance? Wrap issues should be addressed in a custom wrap addendum to the TREC 1-4 contract, followed by a detailed wraparound agreement signed at closing. Additionally, wrap deals may include extra seller financing in the form of a second or third lien. The down payment on a wrap may even be financed by means of a down payment note. What will the seller-financed note and deed of trust look like? The buyer's attorney should see all this coming and insist on reading and approving draft legal documents early on. Ideally, no buyer should be ambushed at closing with documents that the buyer has neither seen nor agreed to.

(3) *Disclosure of Material Conditions and Defects.* Disclosure is often the buyer's biggest concern. A Seller's Disclosure (TREC form OP-H) is required by Property Code Section 5.008, which states that "[a] seller of residential real property comprising not more than one dwelling unit located in this state shall give to the purchaser of the property a written notice as prescribed by this

section or a written notice substantially similar to the notice prescribed by this section which contains, at a minimum, all of the items in the notice prescribed by this section." Section 5.008(d) goes on to say that the "notice shall be completed to the best of seller's belief and knowledge as of the date the notice is completed and signed by the seller." There are exceptions, notably as to previously unoccupied new homes.

The Seller's Disclosure has several problems from a buyer's point of view. First, the form states, right at the top, that "IT IS NOT A WARRANTY OF ANY KIND BY SELLER OR SELLER'S AGENTS." Why not? The form's utility as a disclosure tool is diminished by this statement. The buyer's attorney should consider using a special provisions addendum to convert the Seller's Disclosure into a set of express representations and warranties.

Second, disclosure of defects and conditions is limited to the seller's knowledge and awareness—not the highest standard. *What the buyer is concerned with is not what the seller knows or says he knows, but with what is actually true about the property.* It is just too easy for an unethical seller to later say, "Oh, I didn't know about that." Sometimes problems can be detected by inspections and other due diligence, sometimes not. Often, the truth is discovered only after subsequent conversations with neighbors—who may take perverse delight in reporting that not only did the seller know about water penetration behind that faux stucco, he *personally* patched and painted it to conceal the damage. The buyer should want to know about any such repairs and ask to see contractor paperwork to determine the extent of the work done, whether or not proper permits were obtained, and whether or not there is a transferable warranty. Broadly speaking, what a careful buyer wants is something stronger than what is offered by the Seller's Disclosure, namely an express representation and warranty by the seller that certain defects and negative conditions do not exist.

Finally, at no point does the seller expressly state, swear, or affirm that the Seller's Disclosure is true and correct. Most everyone assumes that this is so since the seller signs it. *But look closely—the form does not say that, merely stating that "This Notice is a disclosure of seller's knowledge...."* This is another disappointment for the buyer. From the buyer's point of view, there is no substitute for maximum, unconditional disclosure backed up by meaningful recourse against the seller that survives closing.

What about previous inspection reports? Neither the contract nor the Seller's Disclosure obligates the seller to provide them. The buyer should therefore always request copies of these.

(4) *Joint Tenancy with Right of Survivorship*. The buyer also has an interest in the wording of the warranty deed. For example, unless otherwise instructed, title company attorneys will list the grantee as "John Jones and wife, Mary Jones," creating tenancy in common. This form of co-ownership does not provide for the surviving spouse to automatically inherit the entire property when the other dies. Title to the property vests in the surviving spouse only if the property is community property and the deceased had no children or, if there are children, all of them are the result of the marriage between John and Mary. Accordingly, if it is the desire of the buyer to use the deed to do some basic estate planning, an entirely reasonable goal, then the grantee should be listed as "John Jones and wife, Mary Jones as joint tenants with rights of survivorship as provided by Texas Estates Code Sec. 112.051 et seq. and not as tenants-in-common," and both grantees should sign the deed—which will then constitute a written agreement in compliance with the statute. This adds value for the buyer at no cost to the seller.

(5) *Sub2 Transactions*. Investor buyers will often want to take title "subject to" existing indebtedness. Express language (both in the buyer's addendum and in the deed) to the effect that the buyer will not be assuming the obligation to pay the existing debt— and therefore the seller will not be released from the loan until it is paid—is essential in forestalling subsequent claims by remorseful sellers who suddenly realize that they remain on the hook for their old loan with no control over whether or not the current owner makes monthly payments.

(6) *Legal Description and Survey*. The contract must describe the property with reasonable certainty using lot-block-subdivision information or metes and bounds. It is not enforceable

otherwise. Note that the weight of Texas case law suggests that a mere street address is not enough.

The survey should be studied carefully to assure that it matches the legal description provided. Major variations are a problem. To the extent that there may be minor variations, use of a recent survey description is preferred over the legal description contained in the prior deed to the seller.

It is usually in the buyer's best interest to delete the "survey exception" to title insurance coverage by requiring that the standard printed exception as to discrepancies, conflicts, shortages in area or boundary lines, encroachments or protrusions, or overlapping improvements be amended to read "shortages in area." The TREC 1-4 contract offers offer a box at 6.A.(8) to be checked for this purpose. Although negotiable, the buyer usually pays for this.

While a new survey is almost always a good thing, a cash buyer may want flexibility as to whether or not to order a new survey if the seller does not have an existing survey or fails to deliver it pursuant to paragraph C(1). The alternative offered in C(2) states that the buyer *shall* order a new survey; but this mandatory language may not be necessary, and the buyer should not be compelled by contract to order a new survey if there is no lender involved that requires one.

(7) *Seller's Representations.* Because of concern with full disclosure, the buyer may not be satisfied with the language of paragraph 19 (Representations). This paragraph states that "If any representation of Seller in this contract is untrue on the Closing Date, Seller will be in default." Again, this merely provides grounds for a lawsuit; it does not facilitate the buyer's expedient termination of the contract and return of the earnest money plus out-of-pocket expenses, so a special provisions addendum should address this and other representations and warranties that may be desirable from the buyer's point of view.

For instance, what about asking the seller to declare that he or she has made full disclosure of any item that could materially affect the buyer's decision to buy or not buy? Or what about openly declaring that the Seller's Disclosure is true and correct?

Any deal where a seller refuses to agree to such terms should be avoided as if the property were radioactive (it just might be). There are many such "reps and warranties" a buyer may want from a seller that are not on the TREC forms. Here is one of my favorites: *Seller represents and warrants that: (i) the improvements on the Property have never been flooded or penetrated by water from any source, including roof leaks, wall leaks, or slab seepage; (ii) the lot or tract drains properly - no part of it experiences standing water after a rain; (iii) the Property is not with an area designated by H.U.D., the Army Corps of Engineers, or any governmental agency as having an increased likelihood of flooding; and (iv) there is not, nor was there ever, any evidence of mold in any of the improvements.* And where do these additional representations and warranties go? In a special provisions addendum.

(8) *Restrictions.* Applicable covenants and restrictions should not be overlooked as part of the buyer's due diligence. Title companies like to provide these at closing, if at all, but by then it may be too late for the buyer to back out. If a specific use of the property is vital to the buyer (for instance, a day-care center in a neighborhood that is transitioning out of exclusively residential use) then a request for a copy of the restrictions should be made *during the option period.* The specific use should also be expressly described in the blank at paragraph 6.D of the TREC 1-4 contract.

(9) *Final Walk-Through.* The buyer should have the unconditional right to do a final walk-through when the property is vacant and all furnishings removed. It is best to do this in the hours immediately prior to closing. If there is a material adverse change, the buyer should have the right to terminate and receive the earnest money as well as compensation for expenses.

(10) *Seller Default.* Just as the seller would prefer to eliminate specific performance (paragraph 15(a)), the buyer should want to retain the option to pursue this remedy if the seller decides not to close. Additionally, a buyer who invests a substantial amount in the due diligence process—reasonable and customary expenses such as inspection fees, appraisal fees, the cost of a survey, attorney's fees, travel expenses, and the like— may not be satisfied with simple a return of earnest money. A

prudent buyer will want the contract to provide for reimbursement of these pursuit costs. Lastly, it is in the interest of the buyer to strike out paragraph 16 (requiring mediation) in its entirety. A mediation (which can take months to arrange) often provides time and cover for a seller to convey the property to someone else. It is far more effective for a buyer to go directly to court and obtain a TRO against the sale.

(11) *Earnest Money Installments.* Brokers and agents typically encourage the buyer to put down substantial earnest money to demonstrate that he or she is serious. This is of course self-serving from the broker's point of view, because if the buyer is financially committed in a significant way, it is more likely that there will be a closing and a commission. However, rather than depositing say, $10,000, with the title company, a careful buyer may want to consider dividing the earnest money into two $5,000 installments, with the second installment being due at the title company upon expiration of the option period specified in paragraph 23. The earnest money paragraph (paragraph 5) easily provides for this.

(12) *Assignability.* It is entirely possible that an investor buyer will want to assign the contract, so the language of the "parties" paragraph should clearly state that the contract is assignable without seller consent.

(13) *Income Stream.* If the property is rented and the buyer is an investor, he or she will likely be seeking to ensure an income stream that produces an acceptable rate of return. Accordingly, the form and content of the lease, as well as the tenant's payment history, should be examined in the due diligence process. Also, if there have been recent substantial improve-ments to the property, it is worthwhile to check with the appraisal district to see if the property has been fully assessed in its present condition; otherwise, a tax increase may occur that could alter the investor's anticipated rate of return.

Negotiation of Representations and Warranties

Lawyers talk about certain issues being "heavily negotiated." For some reason, lawyer just *love* that term, probably because it sounds so invigoratingly physical for persons who generally spend their days sitting behind a computer. Still, the term has real meaning when using a special provisions addendum to the TREC 1-4 contract (or, in the case of commercial transactions, the TAR 1801). It will certainly be the case that the parties' representations and warranties will become the subject of intense back-and-forth between the lawyer for the seller and the lawyer for the buyer. If this is not the case, one of the two lawyers is not doing his or her job. So this wrangle over reps and warranties is expected and can be quite useful in revealing both the seriousness and candor of the parties.

Note, for legal scholars among our readers, that there is a conceptual difference between representations and warranties versus covenants and agreements. If you think about it for a moment, the distinction is apparent. A rep or warranty basically says "such and such is true about the property and/or me." A covenant or agreement is subtly different. It states an affirmative promise by the seller or buyer to *actually do* an act or thing—such as the seller agreeing to deliver good, indefeasible, and undisputed title at closing. There is also a difference in how these two categories of obligation are enforced in the event of default. Competent counsel should address both in the course of their negotiations.

Disclosure by Investors and License Holders

Whether in the capacity of buyer or seller, investors and real estate license holders should always disclose their status in the contract. They should also disclose if they are acting on behalf of a relative, a personal company, or a trust in which they have an interest. The appropriate place to do this is the special provisions paragraph (or in a special provisions addendum) by using language similar to the following: "Buyer is a real estate investor [and/or license holder] engaging in this transaction for a profit. Buyer has not given Seller real estate advice. Seller should obtain professional advice." This disclosure mitigates any subsequent claim by lay persons that their relative innocence was exploited by a predatory professional. As discussed later, judges and juries do not favor investors if the transaction contains any hint of unfairness.

Do you have a contract? What about electronic communications?

Since negotiations can become fast-paced and complex, utilizing multiple media, it is useful to know when you actually have a contract. Generally speaking, the Statute of Frauds set out in Business & Commerce Code Section 26.01 and 26.02(b) (explained in detail in chapter 12) requires a signed writing in order to have a valid contract for the conveyance of real property. Beyond that, however, there must be offer and acceptance that is clearly communicated—i.e., a meeting of the minds on material terms. For instance, if an offer is made containing specific terms and conditions, and the other party counters with a slightly different set of terms and conditions, then as a matter of law the original offer has been rejected. Why? No meeting of the minds on material terms, so the original offer is now effectively irrelevant. A counter-offer is now on the table, awaiting action. *G.D. Holdings, Inc. v. H.D.H. Land & Timber, L.P.*, 407 S.W.3d 856 (Tex.App.—Tyler 2013, no pet.).

Can emails or a sequence of emails taken together constitute a binding contract? Yes, if by reading all the emails together the intent of the parties to enter into a contract is clear. *Dittman v. Cerone*, No. 13—11—00196—CV, Court of Appeals of Texas, Corpus Christi—Edinburg, March 7, 2013. The principal statute affecting electronic communications is the Uniform Electronic Transactions Act ("UETA") which clearly states that a contract may be valid and enforceable even though it is in electronic form.

Electronic signatures are a related issue. Is a sender's name in the "from" line of an email the same as a signature? Can a person's standardized signature block at the end of an email have the same effect as a custom signature on a written contract? Yes to both, according to the 1st Court of Appeals in Houston: "A signature block from an email performs the same authenticity function as a "from" field. Accordingly, it satisfies the requirement of a signature under the UETA" as well as the Statute of Frauds. *Khoury v. Prentis Tomlinson Jr.*, No. 01-16-00006-CV (Tex.App.—Houston [1st Dist.] March 30, 2017). Although the 2nd Court of Appeals in Fort Worth reached a contrary result in a similar case, it is likely that *Khoury* charts the future direction of Texas law in this area.

Needless to say, an electronic contract that is intended to be signed and binding—such as one transmitted by DocuSign—is in fact no different in its legal effect than one that is on paper and executed by hand.

Online electronic notarization is now permitted in Texas. Chapter 406 of the Government Code discusses "regular notaries" (Subchapter A) and "online notaries" (Subchapter C) who have the same authority as traditional notaries. The online notarization process requires two-way video and audio conferencing and still requires that a signer produce valid, government-issued identification. The Secretary of State is tasked with developing rules and standards for this process.

Electronic signatures on real estate contracts and lender disclosures are common now, and electronic closing documents (including promissory notes) are next. Property owners may appear at appraisal board hearings and offer evidence electronically (see Tax Code Sec. 41.45). Clearly, future business transactions and agreements will dispense with the required presence of your biological organism—which is as it should be. A legal agreement is nothing more than information, consent to which is verifiable.

Amendments and Extensions

TREC form number 39-8 is customarily used to amend or extend contracts. Filling out the form is straightforward enough. But what about consideration? Say, for instance, the parties want to extend the closing date for 30 days. Does the buyer have to pay an extension fee for this to be legal? The answer is no, *not unless the parties clearly intend that payment and receipt of a fee is required as a condition precedent.* "The words the parties [choose] are the best indicators of an intent to create a condition precedent. To make performance specifically conditional, a term such as 'if,' 'provided that,' 'on condition that,' or some similar phrase of conditional language normally must be used." *KIT Projects, LLC v. PLT Partnership*, 479 S.W. 3d 519 (Tex.App.—Houston [14th Dist.] 2015, no pet.). In the *KIT* case, the court ruled that an extension agreement was valid even though the buyer's check for the extension fee bounced! Why? The required magic words were not used in the contract amendment.

Interpretation of Contracts

Texas law generally favors enforcement of express contract terms if they are clear and unambiguous, disallowing any "parol evidence" (oral comments by the parties) that would purport to change these express terms. However, contracts are occasionally ambiguous. Terms and conditions may even contradict one another. In such event, the court may look to extrinsic evidence (including oral statements) to clarify an ambiguity. There are also certain rules of construction that apply: for example, typewritten (or word-processed) terms prevail over any items that are hand-written, and words prevail over numbers. In one case a promissory note stated in words that the amount of the debt was "one million seven thousand." The printed numbers, however, were "$1,700,000." The lender lost, since words prevail over numbers. *Charles R. Tips Family Trust v. PB Commercial LLC*, 459 S.W.3d 147 (Tex.App.—Houston [1st Dist.] 2015, no pet.).

Closing Documents and the Doctrine of Merger

Prospective changes in an earnest money contract should be considered in light of the doctrine of merger, which provides that the closing documents (most especially the deed) supersede the provisions of the contract. "After delivery and acceptance, deeds are generally regarded as the final expression of the agreement of the parties and the sole repository of the terms on which they have agreed." *Smith v.*

Harrison County, 824 S.W.2d 788, 793 (Tex.App.—Texarkana 1992, no writ). This is the reason, for instance, that (from the seller's point of view) an "as is" clause should be included in the deed as well as in the earnest money contract. It also impacts the survival of any representations and warranties made by the parties.

The Role of the Real Estate Attorney

Negotiating a real estate transaction presents multiple opportunities to favor one side or another, and not just on price. This is where it may be advantageous to consult a real estate lawyer. A real estate investor should always have (at least) three professionals on call: a CPA, an insurance agent, and a real estate attorney.

Why, might one ask, involve an attorney in preparing or advising on a TREC form that is available online and which is often completed by agents and brokers who are trained and licensed to do the job? Because lawyers can (1) modify the actual language of the form and, if needed, (2) customize a special provisions addendum to favor a client. Brokers and agents cannot do either one. License holders are limited to checking appropriate boxes, filling in blanks, and attaching required promulgated addenda. They are not permitted to materially alter or supplement the contract text, or write custom addenda, which is considered the practice of law.

Another logical question: why alter these contracts at all, since they were prepared by a broker-lawyer committee composed of experienced, practicing professionals? The answer is that no standard form can anticipate every condition or circumstance; and while many transactions are similar, no two are ever identical. Goals of sellers and buyers vary. Every transaction is unique. While some may say, "It's just a standard form, it's OK to sign it," no investor, and certainly no attorney, should ever be satisfied with *any* standard form. Neutrality is not good enough. The goal is to negotiate and draft a contract that is in one's best interest.

Unfortunately, there is a common fear that bringing in an attorney will kill the deal. This is almost never the case with an experienced real estate lawyer, since lawyers know the difference between changes that are reasonable and those that are not—and they could not stay in business with a reputation for killing deals. Likewise, meticulous and ethical investors and realtors should see the wisdom of suggesting that an inexperienced person obtain legal advice, particularly when a transaction has non-standard aspects. This not only benefits the individual involved but shifts liability away.

A Buyer's Nightmare

A buyer goes to closing without doing a last-minute walk-through. When the buyer arrives at her new home, she finds that the seller removed all the shrubbery and rose bushes—that very morning—and took them with him.

Moreover, the buyer discovers that the seller had, when showing the house, strategically positioned his artwork and oriental rugs to conceal sheetrock and slab cracks. The foundation will cost $15,000 to repair. The seller has moved to Missouri. The inspector has no E&O insurance.

Although the seller indicated on the Seller's Disclosure that *the house itself* had never been flooded, he neglected to mention that during heavy rains the entire lot is 18 inches underwater, all the way up to the weepholes. And weep the buyer does.

The buyer decides to repaper the bathroom and discovers black mold under the old wallpaper. Astonishingly, the Seller's Disclosure did not ask specifically about mold—only about "water penetration" or "any condition that materially affects the physical health or safety of an individual." When confronted by phone, the seller replies, "That mold never bothered *my* health."

Even after all these challenges, the buyer settles in. Suddenly, the front door opens and in walks the seller's estranged common-law wife (whose existence was not disclosed by the seller) and shouts "Honey, I'm home!"

Chapter 2

SELLER DISCLOSURE

Three Rules: Disclose, Disclose, Disclose

As the previous chapter made clear, sellers and buyers have different needs and motivations when it comes to the transfer of real estate. One area that is often an issue is property condition. Sellers typically want to make the transfer "as is" without warranties and with no obligation for repairs. They naturally want to avoid being on the hook for future liability. Buyers, on the other hand, have an interest in acquiring property that is in the best condition for the price. They also want full disclosure of adverse conditions, defects, and needed repairs, since it is not possible to perform an accurate cost-benefit analysis of the investment unless all costs are known.

Residential Sales

TREC promulgates a Seller's Disclosure for use in residential real estate transactions (www.trec.state.tx.us/forms). This form (TREC OP-H) is filled out by the seller and attached to the TREC 1-4 contract. The form tracks Section 5.008 of the Property Code which states:

> **5.008(a) A seller of residential real property comprising not more than one dwelling unit located in this state shall give to the purchaser of the property a written notice as prescribed by this section or a written notice substantially similar to the notice prescribed by this section which contains, at a minimum, all of the items in the notice prescribed by this section.**

The purpose of the Seller's Disclosure is to make it clear what appliances, equipment, and features exist on the property; whether or not these items are working; if the seller knows of any defects or malfunctions in critical systems; if certain red-flag events like termite treatment, previous fires, or flooding have occurred; the need for repairs; and the existence of unpermitted additions, unpaid HOA fees, violations of deed restrictions, lawsuits, or conditions that "materially affect the health or safety of an individual." It should be "completed to the best of seller's belief and knowledge as of the date the notice is completed and signed by the seller." Prop. Code Sec. 5.008(7)(d).

In 2019, the Seller's Disclosure was expanded to include new and more specific questions regarding flooding, water penetration, and previously-filed insurance claims relating to both issues (What took the legislature so long?).

The Seller's Disclosure seeks to implement the core disclosure requirement in Texas, succinctly articulated in *Myre v. Meletio*, 307 S.W.3d 839, 843-44 (Tex.App.—Dallas 2010, pet. denied): "In the context of a real estate transaction, a seller is under a duty to disclose material facts that would not be discoverable by the exercise of ordinary care and diligence by the purchaser, or that a reasonable investigation and inquiry would not uncover. But a seller has no duty to disclose facts he does not know. Similarly, a seller is not liable for failing to disclose what he only should have known." Actual knowledge is thus required. A careless and neglectful seller who has not thoroughly acquainted himself with the condition of property he is selling may be off the hook—unless, of course, he encounters a skeptical jury that considers his conduct not just neglectful but dishonest.

Exceptions

Property Code Section 5.008(e) provides that the requirement that a Seller's Disclosure be provided does not apply to a transfer:

1. pursuant to a court order or foreclosure sale;
2. by a trustee in bankruptcy;
3. to a mortgagee by a mortgagor or successor in interest or to a beneficiary of a deed of trust by a trustor or successor in interest (which would include deeds in lieu of foreclosure);
4. by a lienholder who has either purchased at a foreclosure sale or a sale pursuant to a court order or accepted a deed in lieu of foreclosure;
5. by a fiduciary in the course of an administration of a decedent's estate, guardianship, conservatorship, or trust;
6. from one co-owner to one or more other co-owners;
7. made to a spouse or to a person or persons in the lineal line of consanguinity of one or more of the transferors;
8. between spouses incident to divorce, legal separation or a property settlement agreement;
9. to or from a governmental entity;

10. a new residence of not more than one dwelling unit that has not been occupied for residential purposes (this would include newly built homes);

11. of real property where the value of any dwelling does not exceed 5% of the value of the property (pure "tear-downs," in other words).

Penalty

If the seller does not give the Seller's Disclosure as required, Property Code Section 5.008(f) permits the buyer to "terminate the contract for any reason within seven days after receiving the notice." The statute does not address the legal consequences of the seller never giving the Seller's Disclosure at all. However, if the failure to give the notice is coupled with fraud or failure to disclose defects, then other laws and penalties may (and likely will) arise pursuant to the Deceptive Trade Practices Act and the Statutory Fraud Act (see below).

Commercial Sales

For commercial transactions, the Texas Association of Realtors has a Commercial Property Condition Statement that is an *optional* attachment to its standard commercial contracts. Its scope is broader than TREC's Seller's Disclosure since it addresses additional issues such as wetlands, underground storage tanks, toxic waste, and the like. Although the form is optional in commercial transactions, a careful buyer should always require that the seller provide it. Note that this and other TAR forms are available only to realtors.

Purpose of Disclosure Forms

The intent and purpose of both the residential and commercial disclosure forms is the same: to induce the seller to disclose material conditions, circumstances, and defects. For some reason, however, the drafters of these forms saw fit to insert a statement at the top to the effect that the contents of the form do not constitute a warranty by the seller. The TREC Seller's Disclosure states:

> **THIS NOTICE IS A DISCLOSURE OF SELLER'S KNOWLEDGE OF THE CONDITION OF THE PROPERTY AS OF THE DATE SIGNED BY SELLER AND IS NOT A SUBSTITUTE FOR ANY INSPECTIONS OR WARRANTIES THE PURCHASER MAY WISH TO OBTAIN. IT IS NOT A WARRANTY OF ANY KIND BY SELLER OR SELLER'S AGENTS.**

The TAR Commercial Property Condition Statement reads:

THIS IS A DISCLOSURE OF THE SELLER'S KNOWLEDGE OF THE CONDITION OF THE PROPERTY AS OF THE DATE SIGNED. IT IS NOT A SUBSTITUTE FOR ANY INSPECTIONS OR WARRANTIES A BUYER OR TENANT MAY WISH TO OBTAIN. IT IS NOT A WARRANTY OF ANY KIND BY SELLER, SELLER'S AGENTS, OR ANY OTHER AGENT.

What is the point of these disclaimers? Is the seller making disclosures but then warning the buyer not to rely on them? Apparently so, which makes for a mixed message. This should be unsettling from the buyer's point of view. A careful buyer should consider negotiating the inclusion of a contract clause (contained in a special provisions addendum) which makes it clear that the seller is standing behind the truth of these disclosures. Buyers, commercial or residential, will want to minimize a seller's wiggle-room on the disclosure issue with a simple requirement: *Tell me what you know. All of it.*

Ongoing Duty to Disclose

The Seller's Disclosure does not in and of itself impose an ongoing duty to disclose matters that may come to the seller's attention after the form has been signed and delivered to the buyer. *Bynum v. Prudential Residential Servs.*, 129 S.W.3d 781,795 (Tex.App.—Houston [1st Dist.] 2004, pet. denied). Although this may be strictly true as it relates to the promulgated form, it would be unwise for a seller to withhold material adverse information that is subsequently discovered. There are too many statutory and common law avenues for an aggrieved and angry buyer to pursue, most notably an action for deceptive trade practices (see chapter 41).

The case of *Comel v. Birdwell*, 2014 WL 4347815 (Tex.App.—Eastland 2014) imposes a duty on the seller to update the Seller's Disclosure under certain stated circumstances, namely, if a confidential or fiduciary relationship exists; when the seller has already disclosed part of the issue (then the rest of it must be disclosed); when a prior representation by the seller would be untrue or misleading without further explanation; and in the case of partial disclosure when that partial disclosure creates a false impression in the mind of the buyer. Practice note: silence may be considered misleading!

Two additional important points. Firstly, inclusion of an "as is" clause in the contract does not relieve a seller of the obligation to disclose material facts (*Ritchey v. Pinnell*, 357 S.W.3d 410 (Tex.App.—Texarkana 2012, no pet.); and second, merely giving the buyer a copy of an expert report on a certain condition (termites, for example) does not eliminate the requirement that the seller disclose what he knows about that condition (*Lawrence v. Kinser*, Tex.App.—Dallas 2011, no pet. h.).

Broker Liability for the Seller's Disclosure

Accurately completing the Seller's Disclosure is the responsibility of the seller, preferably in the seller's own handwriting—a good way for the seller's broker to avoid liability, since the seller's broker does not ordinarily become liable for the seller's wrongdoing in this regard unless the broker has actual knowledge of a defect and the failure to disclose it. Texas Occupations Code Sec. 1101.805 (e) states that a "license holder is not liable for a misrepresentation or a concealment of a material fact made by a party to a real estate transaction unless the license holder: (1) knew of the falsity of the misrepresentation or concealment; and (2) failed to disclose the license holder's knowledge of the falsity of the misrepresentation or concealment." Accordingly, a broker "would have a duty to come forward only if he had any reason to believe that the seller's disclosures were false or inaccurate, and the only way he could be held liable for [the seller's] statement in the notice is if it were shown to be untrue." *Sherman v. Elkowitz*, 130 S.W.3d 316, 321 (Tex.App.—Houston [14th Dist.] 2004, no pet.).

An agent working for Ebby Halliday in Dallas was relieved of any liability for failing to disclose prior flooding because it could not be conclusively demonstrated that she had actual knowledge of the condition. A special provisions addendum was involved, and the court emphasized that the agent merely passed this along but had no role in preparing it. *Sutton v. Ebby Halliday Real Estate, Inc.*, 279 S.W.3d 418 (Tex.App.—Dallas 2009). Similarly, a broker does not become liable for a defect or adverse condition (mold, for example) merely by transmitting a mold inspection report to the buyer. Handling and delivering such a report does not make the broker liable for its contents. *Arlington Home Week Inc. v. Peek Environmental Consultants, Inc.*, 361 S.W.3d 773 (Tex.App.—Houston [14th Dist.] 2012).

It should be clear at this point that a seller's agent should avoid participating in completing the seller's disclosure, except of course to advise the seller to complete it truthfully. If the seller confides in the agent (for instance) that flooding has occurred in the past, then the cat is out of the bag: the agent then has "actual knowledge" which could potentially result in liability on the part of the agent unless the condition is fully disclosed. Section 1101.652 of the Texas Occupations Code states that TREC "may suspend or revoke a license issued under this chapter or take other disciplinary action authorized by this chapter if the license holder, while acting as a broker or salesperson . . . fails to disclose to a potential buyer a defect . . . that is known to the license holder."

In order to help achieve the fullest level of disclosure, it is recommended practice that available relevant repair estimates, invoices, and receipts be attached as exhibits to the Seller's Disclosure.

Note that Article 1 of the National Association of Realtors Code of Ethics makes it clear that information about defects is not confidential. A broker has no obligation to become the accomplice of a dishonest seller. Disclosure of defects is in fact a duty for all members of the NAR.

The Deceptive Trade Practices-Consumer Protection Act (DTPA)

Have no doubt about it: the DTPA applies to real estate transactions. The cases consistently declare that real estate is a "consumer good" as that term is defined in the statute. *Chastain v. Koonce*, 700 S.W.2d 579, 582 (Tex. 1985).

Business & Commerce Code Section 17.46 declares that "false, misleading, or deceptive acts or practices in the conduct of any trade or business are hereby declared unlawful. . . ." Also expressly stated to be unlawful are misrepresenting the characteristics and uses of a particular item; representing that goods or services are of a particular quality and standard when they are not; advertising with intent not to sell as advertised; and failing to disclose information in an attempt to induce the consumer into buying.

"Mere puffing or opinion" expressed by a seller is carved out from most liability by DTPA cases. "Whether a representation is a warranty or merely an expression of [the seller's] opinion depends in part upon whether the seller asserts a fact of which the buyer is ignorant, or merely states an opinion or judgment on a matter on which the seller has no special knowledge and on which the buyer may be expected to have an opinion and exert his judgment." Also, a "general statement concerning a future event should be looked at differently than a statement concerning a past or present event or condition." *Humble Nat'l Bank v. DCV, Inc.*, 933 S.W.2d 224, 230 (Tex.App.—Houston [14th Dist.] 1996, writ denied).

Bottom line: affirmative misrepresentations or failure by a seller to disclose known material adverse conditions and defects are violations of the DTPA. The key question for a court that later looks at the case is whether or not the seller's misrepresentation or failure to disclose would have influenced an ordinary buyer's decision to buy or not buy.

Does it sound as though most any of the itemized grievances in the DTPA might form the basis of a lawsuit against a real estate investor? Count on it. But it does not end there when it comes to investor liability. Section 17.50 adds breach of warranty and "any unconscionable action or course of action by any person" to the list. "Any unconscionable action?" Seriously? Statutory language does not get any broader or more potentially damaging than that. Investor sellers beware: if you fail to disclose a material item, a jury can find that your action was "unconscionable" (an open-ended term by any definition) and award treble damages, attorney's fees, and court costs against you.

For more detail concerning the DTPA and its impact on real estate investors, go to the chapter 41.

Statutory Fraud

The Statutory Fraud Act (Tex. Bus. & Com. Code Sec. 27.01) is another potential pitfall for sellers who fail to make full disclosure:

> **(a)** Fraud in a transaction involving real estate or stock in a corporation or joint stock company consists of a
>
> > **(1)** false representation of a past or existing material fact, when the false representation is
> > > **(A)** made to a person for the purpose of inducing that person to enter into a contract; and
> > > **(B)** relied on by that person in entering into that contract; or
> >
> > **(2)** false promise to do an act, when the false promise is
> > > **(A)** material;
> > > **(B)** made with the intention of not fulfilling it;
> > > **(C)** made to a person for the purpose of inducing that person to enter into a contract; and
> > > **(D)** relied on by that person in entering into that contract.
>
> **(b)** A person who makes a false representation or false promise commits the fraud described in Subsection (a) of this section and is liable to the person defrauded for actual damages.
>
> **(c)** A person who makes a false representation or false promise with actual awareness of the falsity thereof

commits the fraud described in Subsection (a) of this section and is liable to the person defrauded for exemplary damages. Actual awareness may be inferred where objective manifestations indicate that a person acted with actual awareness.

(d) A person who (1) has actual awareness of the falsity of a representation or promise made by another person and (2) fails to disclose the falsity of the representation or promise to the person defrauded, and (3) benefits from the false representation or promise commits the fraud described in Subsection (a) of this section and is liable to the person defrauded for exemplary damages. Actual awareness may be inferred where objective manifestations indicate that a person acted with actual awareness.

(e) Any person who violates the provisions of this section shall be liable to the person defrauded for reasonable and necessary attorney's fees, expert witness fees, costs for copies of depositions, and costs of court.

The above language is tighter than that found in Property Code Section 5.008 or in the common law. The elements of statutory fraud under Section 27.01(a) are the same as the elements of common law fraud, except that Section 27.01(a) does not require proof of knowledge or recklessness as a prerequisite to the recovery of actual damages.

For greater clarity on what constitutes a misrepresentation, observe the language in *Coldwell Banker Whiteside Associates v. Ryan Equity Partners*, 181 S.W.3d 879, 888 (Tex.App.—Dallas 2006, no pet.): "A misrepresentation may consist of the concealment or non-disclosure of a material fact when there is a duty to disclose. The duty to disclose arises when one party knows that the other party is ignorant of the true facts and does not have an equal opportunity to discover the truth. A fact is material if it would likely affect the conduct of a reasonable person concerning the transaction in question."

Exemplary or punitive damages are available to plaintiffs who prevail. A plaintiff is entitled to recover exemplary damages in cases of statutory fraud if the false representation is made with actual awareness of the falsity of the representation. *Hines v. Hash*, 843 S.W.2d 464 (Tex. 1992).

Real estate brokers are liable under the DTPA only for intentional fraud.

Common-Law Fraud

The Statutory Fraud Act does not preclude a deceived buyer from filing suit on grounds of common-law fraud as well. In other words, the two causes of action can be pursued side-by-side. Any competent plaintiffs' attorney will include as many causes of action as possible in his lawsuit against a non-disclosing seller. This is known as the "shotgun approach" and is designed to insure that, when the dust settles, at least some lines of attack will have found their mark.

Additional Liability for Non-Disclosure in the Case of Real Estate License Holders

Agents and brokers who are also sellers or investors need to be especially concerned about failing to make full disclosure of material facts, conditions, and circumstances—or at least those that do not violate one's legitimate duty of confidentiality. Unlike unlicensed real estate investors, license holders are subject to the Real Estate License Act ("RELA," found in Occupations Code Section 1101.652), the rules of the Texas Real Estate Commission (Texas Administrative [TAC] Code Chapters 531-543), and the canons of professional ethics and conduct contained in TAC Chapter 531. The canons encompass the requirements of fidelity (the duty to act as a fiduciary); integrity, including the duty to use prudence and caution; competency, including not just the exercise of skill and judgment, but also being knowledgeable in the conditions of the market in which the license holder operates; the duty to provide relevant consumer information, specifically including methods by which a complaint may be filed with TREC; the duty of non-discrimination (more on this below); and the duty to provide the standard "Information About Brokerage Services" form, commonly referred to as the IABS.

The fiduciary requirement is particularly important. Being a fiduciary means that the license holder must place the interests of his or her principal above their own. This manifests in a variety of specific duties to disclose, inform, and perform at a knowledgeable and professional level. The rules also make it clear that a license holder has a duty of honesty and fair dealing with regard to everyone, not just clients. Given these standards, it is difficult to imagine *any* scenario in which a license holder would be justified in not making full disclosure to a potential buyer. A fiduciary's responsibilities are often summed up in the acronym "OLD CAR:" obedience, loyalty, disclosure, confidentiality, accountability, and reasonable care and diligence.

Could a license holder's failure to disclose be potentially linked to discrimination? It is certainly a possibility that could cross the mind of a plaintiff's attorney. The duty of non-discrimination is clear. TAC Section 531.19 states that "No real estate license holder shall inquire about, respond to or facilitate inquiries about, or make a disclosure of an owner, previous or current occupant, potential purchaser, lessor, or potential lessee of real property which indicates or is intended to indicate any preference, limitation, or discrimination based on the following: (1) race; (2) color; (3) religion; (4) sex; (5) national origin; (6) ancestry; (7) familial status; or (8) disability." Note, interestingly, that age is not on this list, but perhaps one day Texas will get there.

Then there is the issue of penalties. TREC may revoke or suspend the license of a broker or sales agent if the license holder is convicted of any offense involving fraud or engages in misrepresentation, dishonesty, or untrustworthy behavior. RELA Section 1101.652(b)(3) provides that a license holder may be sanctioned for making "a material misrepresentation to a potential buyer concerning a significant defect, including a latent structural defect." Section 1101.652(b)(4) specifically adds failure to disclose a significant defect to the list. Accordingly, investors who have a real estate license have a heightened level of duty and potential liability.

Suppose a broker fails to disclose an important personal fact—for instance, that she is the mother of the seller. Does this void the earnest money contract? Probably not, although the broker may be vulnerable to sanctions by TREC. *Goldman v. Olmstead* 414 S.W.3d 346 (Tex.App.— Dallas 2013, pet. denied). Note, however, that *Goldman* would likely not prevent a creative plaintiffs' attorney from alleging that the license holder acted in a civil conspiracy with the seller. Result? The broker must expend time and resources to defend against this charge. In the long run, license holders are always better off pursuing a policy of full disclosure that continues throughout the course of the transaction.

Standards of good conduct in any profession—real estate, law, or any other—are about trust. The profession as a whole has a vested interest in assuring that the public continues to place trust in its licensees. Behavior that has *even the appearance of impropriety* can result in sanctions, not to mention reputational damage, so license holders should consider it part of their professional duty to walk the extra mile when it comes to disclosure.

"As Is" Transactions

It is important to observe that the TREC 1-4 contract for residential transactions contains an optional "as is" clause, and the transaction becomes "as is" if the box at paragraph 7D(1) is checked. *Cherry v. McCall*, 138 S.W.3d 35, 39 (Tex.App.—San Antonio 2004, pet. denied). But is this sufficient? Some real estate attorneys think it may not be, at least not in every case. Yes, 7D(1) amounts to a very basic "as is" clause; problem is, not all "as is" clauses are equally thorough and effective. Some are far better and more comprehensive than others (see chapter 1 for an example of solid "as is" language that a seller could use in a special provisions addendum to the contract). In commercial transactions, the "as is" clause is often one of the most heavily-negotiated provisions. In certain residential transactions, particularly high-dollar ones, the "as is" clause may be no less important.

Consider the case of a leaky roof at a condominium building in *Birnbaum, et al vs. Atwell et al*, No. 01-14-00556-CV (Tex.App.—Houston [1st Dist.] 2015, no pet.). The seller disclosed the water penetration in an "as is" contract; the buyer, a commercial real estate broker with a law degree who was also represented by an experienced attorney, and who conducted thorough due diligence after being put on notice of the water leaks, *still sued the seller*, alleging that both the seller and the seller's realtor failed to *fully disclose* the recency and frequency of the leaks. Birnbaum ultimately lost, but only after putting the seller through expensive litigation all the way to the court of appeals.

If the transaction is "as is," must the seller still make full disclosure?

Here is the central question: Is it lawful to transfer property without disclosing material defects if the contract states that the transaction is "as is?" In other words, does use of the words "as is" or similar phraseology relieve the seller of the obligation to disclose? The answer, as is true in many areas of the law, is *it depends*—but probably not, unless the contract expressly states that the seller is declining to make any disclosures and the buyer agrees (in a residential transaction this likely would be unlawful, since delivery of a completed Seller Disclosure is usually a requirement under Property Code Section 5.008). There have been many seller disclosure cases in Texas in the last 25 years of so. Taken together, these cases suggest that avoiding disclosure in *any* real estate transaction, whether residential or commercial, is at best a risky strategy for the seller and, at worst, plainly illegal.

The root difficulty for many sellers is separating the concept of "as is" from avoidance of full disclosure. These are not inextricably linked. One does not necessarily imply the other.

The foundational case in this area is *Prudential Insurance Co. v. Jefferson Associates Ltd.*, 896 S.W.2d 156 (Tex. 1995), which upheld "as is" clauses in certain narrow circumstances. Two things are critical if such a clause is to be upheld: the specific wording and whether or not the buyer obtained an inspection. Also, in evaluating an "as is" transaction, courts look not just at these two factors but at the totality of the circumstances. Note that if the buyer consults an attorney before agreeing to an "as is" clause then a court is more likely to find the clause enforceable. Courts dislike situations where the parties are unequally informed of their rights. For this reason, it is more likely that an "as is" provision will be upheld in a commercial rather than a residential transaction since commercial buyers are presumed to be more sophisticated.

In 2007, the Dallas Court of Appeals said the following with regard to "as is" transactions involving residences: "The nature of the transaction and the totality of the circumstances surrounding the agreement must be considered. Where the 'as is' clause is an important part of the basis of the bargain, not an incidental or 'boilerplate' provision, and is entered into by parties of relatively equal bargaining position, a buyer's affirmative agreement that he is not relying on the representations of the seller should be given effect." *Kupchynsky v. Nardiello*, 230 S.W.3d 685, 690 (Tex.App.—Dallas 2007, pet. denied).

The commercial landlord-tenant case of *Italian Cowboy Partners, Ltd. v. Prudential Insurance Co. of America*, 341 S.W.3d 323 (Tex. 2011), involved the lease of a restaurant with a history of chronic sewage odor. The landlord's manager, who knew of the problem, fraudulently induced the tenant into a lease by orally declaring that the premises were in "perfect condition." Even though *Italian Cowboy* is a commercial lease case, it is highly likely that a similar theory of liability would be applied against a seller of residential property who made such false statements. It is worth noting that *Birnbaum* (a residential case) cited *Italian Cowboy* (a commercial case) with approval.

Also relevant is the 2014 case of *Harstan, Ltd. v. Kim*, 441 S.W.3d 791, 796-97 (Tex.App.—El Paso 2014, no pet.) which articulates the standard for the validity of an "as is" clause in an earnest money contract: "Courts assess the validity of an 'as is' agreement in light of three factors: (1) the sophistication of the parties; (2) the terms of the 'as is' agreement; and (3) whether there was a knowing misrepresentation or concealment of a known fact." Evaluation of these factors in a specific case can result in a court declaring an "as is" clause invalid as a matter of law. However, as discussed above, even if an "as is" clause is valid, it likely does *not* relieve a residential seller of the obligation to fully disclose defects and adverse conditions.

Willful Concealment and Fraudulent Inducement

The general take-away from this discussion is that "as is" clauses, when used in appropriate circumstances, are valid and binding in Texas. However, an "as is" clause will not protect a seller in a case of willful concealment, and it will certainly be no protection if the seller engages in fraudulent inducement. *Ritchy v. Pinnell*, 357 S.W.3d 410 (Tex.App.—Texarkana 2012, no pet.).

Example? A seller knows that there is foundation settlement because of cracks in the sheetrock and floor tile. So the seller positions a picture over the wall crack and a rug over the cracked tile (willful concealment) and then goes on to tell the prospective buyer that there are no serious defects in the condition of the house (fraudulent inducement).

"As Is" Clauses in the Deed

An "as is" clause should also be included in the warranty deed to the buyer in order to leave no doubt as to the intent of the parties. The buyer should then be required to sign and acknowledge the warranty deed, leaving no doubt as to the buyer's consent to and agreement with the "as is" clause.

To summarize, the optimal "as is" scenario for a seller would be to (1) make full disclosure of defects and adverse conditions; (2) avoid making any statements relating to property condition, value, or potential use, even those that could be considered sales puffing; (3) include effective "as is" clauses in *both* the earnest money contract and the warranty deed which are clear, conspicuous (bold and capitalized), and unequivocal; and (4) require that the buyer sign and acknowledge the warranty deed in order to *expressly accept* the property in its present state (This has the effect of making the deed a contract as well as a conveyance). Since most buyer lawsuits are based on allegations of fraud, following these guidelines will provide maximum protection for the seller.

The practical question, of course, is whether or not a buyer will be willing to accept such strict "as is" language. As is true with many contract terms, it may come down to price.

"As Is" in the Real World

Generally speaking, an "as is" clause (both in the earnest money contract and the warranty deed) is an extremely valuable, even essential, tool for the cautious seller, but it should not be used as a means of avoiding disclosure of defects or adverse conditions. No one, especially juries, likes a liar—whether the lie is by commission or omission. The best advice an attorney can give a seller is *disclose, disclose, disclose,* whether or not the contract contains an "as is" clause. If an "as is" clause is going to be included in a contract or deed, it should be in bold and all caps. The seller should get a real estate attorney to draft it so that it specifically fits the circumstances and meets the requirements of the case law.

Investor clients often ask, "Can they sue me if . . . ?" For lots of reasons, this is the wrong question, since anyone can sue anyone for anything and incur little or no liability for doing so, at least in this country. The better approach—since lawsuits are so very expensive—is to deter suits in the first place by being open and above-board.

Buyers confronted by a seller who insists on an "as is" clause while attempting to avoid disclosure should be suspicious. In such a situation, the best course of action for the buyer may be to walk away. *Not every deal can or should be made.* On the other hand, a tough "as is" clause may not be a problem for the buyer so long as he or she conducts thorough due diligence within the available time frame. Having said that, whenever a seller wants to include an "as is" clause in a sales contract, the buyer should respond by asking that a provision be included to the effect that such a clause does not relieve the seller of the obligation to disclose known material conditions and defects. If the seller balks at this, then it may be time for a prudent investor to look elsewhere for a deal.

Chapter 3

TITLE INSURANCE

Title Companies—a Blessing and a Curse

Title insurance is available to protect owners and lenders from loss resulting from defects in the title to real estate. Title policies and regulations are a complicated and evolving area and we are not offering a comprehensive treatise on the subject here. This chapter is designed only as an introductory overview for investors. Further information may be obtained at the websites for the Texas Land Title Association (www.tlta.com) and the Texas Department of Insurance (www.tdi. state.tx.us).

Closing at a title company that issues a title insurance policy to both buyer and lender is the usual way to do business in Texas, but it is not the only way. Closings can occur without title insurance—for example, in a lawyer's conference room or even at the kitchen table of one of the parties. There are good reasons, however, why obtaining title insurance is customary:

(1) The title company maintains a database of real estate resources that can be searched in order to produce a "title commitment," which is a review of the status of title and an important part of the pre-closing process. Why? Because "a purchaser is bound by every recital, reference and reservation contained in or fairly disclosed by any instrument which forms an essential link in the chain of title. . . ." *Wessels v. Rio Bravo Oil Co.*, 250 S.W.2d 668 (Tex.App.—Eastland 1952, writ ref'd).

(2) The title company acts as a clearinghouse for closing documents that need to be signed and recorded, as well as for funds to be collected and disbursed at closing. The "closer" is the contact person who creates the file (which is assigned a file number or "GF" number), assembles the closing disclosures, and supervises the execution and notarization of documents on the day of closing.

(3) The title policy provides an avenue of recourse and recovery in the event either lender or buyer sustains a monetary loss as a result of a title defect. What kind of monetary loss? Well, suppose the title company missed a valid lien and the lienholder comes to collect; or suppose there is a previously unknown heir who appears and claims an interest in the property. The title company will work to resolve such issues or, if appropriate, pay compensation. In many respects, a title company is like any other insurance company.

Does a title company have an obligation to produce good title?

No, that is a myth. A title company examines title but does so primarily for its own information and benefit in order to determine whether or not it will issue a title policy, not (strictly speaking) for the benefit of the buyer or lender to be insured by the policy. It is part of the insurer's own due diligence undertaken to minimize risk. Does the title company have a duty to at least point out issues that affect title? Again, no. "A title insurance company is not a title abstractor and owes no duty to examine a title or point out any outstanding encumbrances." *IQ Holdings, Inc. v. Stewart Title Guaranty Company*, 451 S.W.3d 861 (Tex.App.—Houston [1st Dist.] 2014, no pet.). A title company will produce a title commitment for a pending transaction, listing conditions that must be cured before a policy will be issued; but, if you think carefully about it, this is not the same as counseling either the buyer or the lender.

This raises the broader question, particularly relevant for real estate investors, as to how much reliance can be placed on a title company to look after the particular interests of the any of the parties to the transaction. The answer is short: *no such reliance is justified*. It is not the title company's job to cure title defects or cause legal documents to be prepared in any party's best interest. The only safe assumption that can be made is that the title company will look after itself. Involvement of a title company in a transaction is accordingly no substitute for the services of a real estate attorney specifically retained to protect one's interests— whether in connection with contract interpretation, curative issues, the effect of restrictive covenants or prior deed reservations, or the content of the closing documents.

What *does* the title company owe the parties? The *IQ Holdings* case states that a "title insurance company assumes a fiduciary duty to both parties when it acts as an escrow agent in a transaction"—i.e., when it collects and holds money. This consists of "(1) the duty of loyalty; (2) the duty to make full disclosure; and (3) the duty to exercise a high degree of care to conserve the money and pay it only to those persons entitled to receive it." Again, however, these duties pertain to funds in escrow, not the status of title. Beyond this fiduciary duty, the title company's only obligation is to honor the terms of its policy and indemnify the insured against covered losses.

The Title Commitment

The title commitment consists of Schedules A through D plus various notices and disclaimers. Schedule A indicates the type of transaction that will be insured plus the current owner of record and legal description of the property to be conveyed (lot and block or metes and bounds). It also lists the amount of the policy that will be issued at closing.

The examination of title referred to in the previous section is reflected in the title commitment, which is produced after the title company receives a copy of a signed sales contract and a check for earnest money. Schedules A through D of the commitment review the status of title, list title issues and defects that need to be addressed or cured before closing, and state any other preconditions to issuance of a title policy.

Schedule A indicates the type of transaction that will be insured plus the current owner of record and legal description of the property to be conveyed (lot and block or metes and bounds). It also lists the amount of the policy that will be issued at closing (for prospective owners, this amount should be the contract sales price). Schedule B lists exclusions and exceptions to coverage including such matters as restrictions, setback requirements, and utility easements. Items one through nine are standard exceptions and are general in nature. Any items which follow are special exceptions pertinent to the property being conveyed. Look for easements and mineral leases.

Note that the second item on Schedule B excepts (i.e., declares that the title policy will not cover) discrepancies, conflicts, or shortages in area or boundary lines, or any encroachments or protrusions, or any overlapping of improvements. By checking box 6.A.(8) on the TREC contract, the buyer may amend the commitment and delete this "survey exception"— except for the part that refers to "shortages in area," which will remain regardless of whether the survey exception is deleted or not. Why? Because title companies insure title, specifically the chain of title, not surveys.

Schedule C lists potential problem areas such as liens and judgments, and the title company will routinely require payment and release of these. Other miscellaneous requirements may appear on Schedule C, such as a marital status affidavit, a not-same-name affidavit if there is a judgment in a name similar to that of the seller, an affidavit as to debts and liens, and the like. If there are more serious issues like mechanic's liens, judgments against the seller, tax liens, lawsuits affecting title, heirship issues due to a previous owner dying without a will, or gaps in the chain of title, the commitment will indicate what must be done if title is to be insured in the name of the new owner. Specific curative action may be required.

Schedule D is usually of less concern. It discloses, among other things, the price of the policy and the parties who will receive any part of the title policy premium.

Role of the Earnest Money Contract

The title company's duties commence when it receives the executed sales contract and a check for earnest money. For residential transactions, Paragraph 6 of the TREC 1-4 contract entitled "Title Policy and Survey" applies. Although it is customary for the seller to pay for the title policy, this is not required, and paragraph 6 provides the opportunity to instead check the buyer as the paying party. The title company has 20 days to produce the commitment with an automatic 15-day extension if needed.

Paragraph 6.D provides a blank for insertion of a time period during which the buyer may object to issues raised by the commitment. The time period inserted in this blank is usually seven to ten days. If the buyer does not make timely objections, any such issues are waived. Despite the buyer's waiver, however, the title company may insist that Schedule C items be cured before a title policy issues. It is, after all, the title company's liability that is on the line. If the buyer raises timely objections, then the seller must cure them or the TREC contract terminates.

Policies of Title Insurance

As is the case with any insurance policy, a policy of title insurance is a contract between the insurer and the insured. "A title insurance policy is a contract of indemnity that imposes a duty on the insurance company to indemnify the insured against losses caused by defects in title. The alleged defect must involve a flaw in the ownership rights of the property to trigger coverage. An irregularity that merely affects the value of the land, but not the ownership rights, is not a defect in title." *McGonagle v. Stewart Title Guaranty Company*, 432 S.W.3d 535 (Tex.App.—Dallas 2014, pet. pending). In other words, a title policy makes no assurances as to value or price, present or future.

Two policies are usually issued: one for the buyer (the T-1 Owner Policy of Title Insurance) for the sales price of the land and improvements, which remains in effect so long as the new owner retains an interest in the property; and one for the lender (the T-2 Loan Policy of

Title Insurance, formerly called the "Mortgagee Policy") for the value of the property or the amount of its loan, whichever is less. The loan policy terminates when the note matures and the four-year statute of limitations for foreclosure on the lien expires. An investor will not get a loan on Texas real estate from an institutional lender without a T-2 loan policy, so plan on using a title company if the intent is to borrow purchase money from a bank. A private hard-money lender may do the deal without title insurance, however, since the private market is far less regulated.

A title insurance policy insures "good and indefeasible" title, which is a slightly lesser standard than the "good and marketable" standard that most people assume is the case. The distinction goes back to the Great Depression when many properties were sold at sheriffs' sales. Issues of marketability were raised, and this led to Texas adopting the "good and indefeasible" title rule—stating, in effect, that your title is better than anyone else claiming it, but we'll leave the marketing to you.

In the case of a construction loan, title companies do not cover mechanics' liens filed during construction, although one can and should request a down-date endorsement to the policy for an extra fee.

Remember, an owner policy is not required by law. It is always possible to do a title search or obtain a title report or abstract of title, thereby providing a comfort level regarding the status of title, the absence of liens, and the like—and then proceed on that basis. Many investors do just that and then close their deals.

Title Insurance Rates

The cost of title insurance is set by the Texas Department of Insurance which regulates this industry pursuant to Title XI of the Texas Insurance Code (the "Texas Title Insurance Act"). The form of a title insurance policy and the various available amendments are prescribed. The basic premium for a $100,000 policy is less than a $1,000, which is a one-time fee for coverage that lasts as long as the buyer has an insurable interest in the property. A formula applies for amounts higher than that. Hearings on rate increases occur biennially in even-numbered calendar years. Further information is contained in the Texas Title Insurance Basic Manual which can be found at www.tdi.texas.gov/company/title man.html.

It is customary in Texas for the seller to pay the cost of the owner's policy. However, this is negotiable. It is all a question of price.

Exclusions and Exceptions to Owner's Coverage

As with any insurance policy there are exclusions, exceptions, and conditions. The residential owner's policy expressly excludes such items as building and zoning ordinances; condemnation; title problems created by or undisclosed by the insured, or arising from fraud by the insured; title problems that result in no actual loss; access issues; refusal of anyone to lend money; and physical condition of the land.

Exceptions are specific limitations on coverage. These include standard printed exceptions on Schedule B—restrictive covenants and deed restrictions; the survey exception ("discrepancies, conflicts, or shortages in area") which can (and, for buyers usually should) be deleted for a fee; homestead, community, and survivorship rights; the exception for riparian rights, water-rights, and tidelands; the tax exception, including rollback taxes; the mechanic's lien exception; the exception for leases and subordinate liens; the rights of parties in possession; and, if there is no survey, easements and encroachments. The title company may also add special exceptions that it deems necessary after doing its research.

Title companies do not insure fraudulent conveyances or preferential transfers (transfers made to avoid payment of creditors). Excluded is "any claim, by reason of the operation of federal bankruptcy, state insolvency, or similar creditors' rights laws, that the transaction vesting the Title as shown in Schedule A is (a) a fraudulent conveyance or fraudulent transfer, or (b) a preferential transfer for any reason not stated in Covered Risk 9 of this policy." So if one is engaged in edgy asset protection, do not look to a title company for assistance.

Minerals

Title insurance companies are not required to insure the mineral estate. Tex. Ins. Code Sec. 2703.0515. Title companies have traditionally taken the view that the job of determining title to minerals belongs not to title insurers but to landmen and oil and gas attorneys, although the title company will provide copies of mineral leases and conveyances if a buyer or the buyer's attorney wishes to review them prior to closing (never a bad idea). Since minerals in producing regions have usually long-since been conveyed away (especially in the typical urban residential setting) the typical concern of a homeowner is damage to the surface of the land (surface estate) by a mineral-interest holder seeking to gain access to underground minerals. Optional endorsements are available that will protect against damage to the surface estate (T-19.2 or T-19.3). The Texas T2-R already protects lenders against such surface damage. This is an evolving area currently under review by the Department of Insurance.

Community Property and Heirship Property

Texas is a community property state and, as such, all property acquired by either spouse during marriage is presumed to be a community asset. Tex. Family Code Sec. 3.003. It is common for a title company to either require joinder of a seller's spouse on a deed or, in the alternative, a marital status affidavit and/or a non-homestead affidavit.

If someone in the chain of title died without a will, one should also expect that the title company will require a conveyance of some kind (usually a special warranty deed) from each and every heir and, if an heir is deceased, from the heirs of that heir. Alternatively, the title company may be satisfied with an affidavit of heirship if there are no other heirs and the circumstances of family history can be sufficiently well established. It can get complicated and expensive to cure defects in heirship property. See chapter 5 on the subject of affidavits of heirship.

Differences between Title Companies

Since rates are regulated, there is nothing to gain from comparing title companies for the cheapest policy. Title companies do, however, vary in at least two significant respects: first, in the level and quality of service they (or a particular closer) may provide; and second, in their willingness to "insure around" certain potential defects or insure non-standard transactions (wraparounds, trusts, and the like). Title companies are by nature conservative institutions. If a title company sets out requirements that are difficult or impossible to satisfy—and this happens—then it may be telling you something: their underwriter does not want to do this deal. The title company may in fact just plainly say so. Accordingly, it may be necessary to shop title companies until one is found that is willing to insure your transaction and other deals you may have that fall on the creative end of the spectrum.

Working with title companies to get deals closed is an inescapable part of being a real estate investor. In doing so, one learns a couple of important lessons. The first of these is respect for the chain of title. Grantor and grantees must form a sequential link that conveys the same property (correctly described) over the course of the property's history. The legal description must be consistent and correct. Spousal interests must be accounted for since Texas is a community property state. Owners in the chain who are deceased must have a will or an affidavit of heirship (at the very least). And so forth. Experienced professional investors are careful about all of these matters, preferring to use an attorney for most transactions rather than trying to DIY the legal documentation, which may require expensive clean-up later. There is a saying that when one acts as one's own attorney, one has picked the most expensive attorney there is—since the clean-up can be much more costly than doing the documentation correctly in the first place.

A second important lesson is to view every transaction from the perspective of a future title company and anticipate their objections. Underwriters will never admit it, but they just love to raise these, which is the primary purpose of Schedule C. Anticipate objections and eliminate them, in advance, by documenting the conveyance accordingly.

What is a fee attorney?

Some law firms enter into an arrangement with title underwriters to act as "fee attorneys," meaning that these attorneys are permitted to close transactions in their offices and issue title policies as an agent for the underwriter. While this may seem convenient, some argue that it is a conflict of interest—that the lawyer's job is to advocate for the buyer or the seller or the lender, not merely to act as neutral escrow officer in order to collect insurance premiums and fees. We agree. The interests of buyers and sellers differ, sometimes immensely, and lawyers should choose a side and represent it fully. Since real estate documents can often be highly customized to favor one party or another, a lawyer trying to represent everyone may mean that no one gets adequate representation.

The Title Company's Duty to Defend

If a title defect or lien appears after closing, the title company must investigate and:

1. commence legal proceedings to clear title;
2. indemnify the insured pursuant to the policy;
3. reinsure the title to the property at current value;
4. indemnify another insurer if another company does the reinsuring; or
5. cure the defect or obtain a release of the lien.

If the title company does not take one or more of the above actions, it can be sued by the insured for breach of contract. Note that the company's duty to defend against a claim is contingent upon and activated by the insured providing timely written notice of the defect or lien. The duty to defend is not triggered by demands for money and the like that do not constitute a true cloud on the title.

The Title Company's Liability for Damages

A title policy is like any other insurance contract in that it can be breached and, if a breach occurs, the title company may be liable for monetary damages. Recovery under an owner's policy is limited to the owner's actual money loss or the amount of the policy, whichever is less. "The only duty of a title insurer is to indemnify the insured against losses caused by a defect in title" states the court in the *McGonagle* case, in which the plaintiffs alleged liability on the part of Stewart Title for failing to point out the existence of restrictive covenants. In a judgment that might alarm many real estate investors, the court went on to conclude that Stewart had no such duty. Accordingly, it should be part of an investor's routine procedure to specifically request copies of any applicable restrictive covenants from the title company.

Making a Claim

In an insurance contract dispute, the initial burden falls on the insured to establish coverage under the terms of the policy. *Comsys Info. Tech. Servs., Inc. v. Twin City Fire Ins. Co.*, 130 S.W.3d 181, 188 (Tex.App.— Houston [14th Dist.] 2003, pet. denied). The insured must give the title company prompt notice and cooperate in furtherance of the claim. The old requirement that the policy itself be produced in order to recover has been eliminated. Payment must be made by the company within 30 days of determination of liability and the extent of the loss. If the title company settles a covered claim, it is subrogated to the rights of the insured as to that claim (i.e., it assumes the insured's right of recovery).

The usual four-year statute of limitations for written contracts applies, commencing when a claimant knew or, through the exercise of ordinary diligence, should have discovered the breach and ensuing injury (sometimes called the "discovery rule"). This places a duty upon policyholders to thoroughly read closing documents and discover obvious errors. In one case, the title company was supposed to insure title to both lots 8 and 9; however, the warranty deed and the deed of trust referred only to lot 9. The court ruled that the claimant should have reasonably raised this issue at closing and not waited over nine years to bring his claim. *Dunmore v. Chicago Title Insurance Company*, 400 S.W.3d 635 (Tex.App.—Dallas 2013, no pet.).

Chapter 4

EARNEST MONEY DISPUTES IN RESIDENTIAL

TRANSACTIONS

The Process for Release of Earnest Money

Disputes over earnest money usually arise when either buyer or seller perceive the other to be at fault for failing to close in a timely manner. The parties can be emotional, unreasonable, and determined to stand on principle, all common shortcomings in persons who may threaten to file lawsuits but are unacquainted with the costs and burdens of litigation. Usually "fault" is not the issue, at least as to earnest money, since its orderly disposition is expressly governed by the TREC 1-4 contract and its addenda. Problems and the potential for litigation most often arise when a party refuses to do what the contract says.

This chapter does not address what occurs when earnest money is not deposited at all, except to observe that this constitutes a breach (a default) by the buyer in the case of an otherwise valid and accepted earnest money contract. Failure of the buyer to perform in this regard does not, as many believe, cause the contract to fail altogether.

Buyer Withdrawal Because of Failure to Obtain Financing

A common area of dispute is the buyer's inability to obtain financing. Note that the TREC Third Party Financing Addendum contains a blank for a *specific time* during which the buyer must notify the seller of his inability to obtain financing. If this notice is not timely given, the contingency is waived. Buyers often miss this detail and insist on their continuing right to get their earnest money back if their loan application is denied, even after the specified time has run.

Sellers, on the other hand, may believe that the buyer did not make "every reasonable effort to obtain credit approval" (as required by the TREC addendum) and therefore should not be entitled to return of earnest money even if notice is given within the prescribed period. Unfortunately for this point of view, the addendum does not go into detail about what "every reasonable effort" means.

Contract Provisions Relating to Release of Earnest Money

Whatever the cause of the dispute, paragraphs 18.C through E address the procedure for release of earnest money:

> C. DEMAND: Upon termination of this contract, either party or the escrow agent may send a release of earnest money to each party and the parties shall execute counterparts of the release and deliver same to the escrow agent. If either party fails to execute the release, either party may make a written demand to the escrow agent for the earnest money. If only one party makes written demand for the earnest money, escrow agent shall promptly provide a copy of the demand to the other party. If escrow agent does not receive written objection to the demand from the other party within 15 days, escrow agent may disburse the earnest money to the party making demand reduced by the amount of unpaid expenses incurred on behalf of the party receiving the earnest money and escrow agent may pay the same to the creditors. If escrow agent complies with the provisions of this paragraph, each party hereby releases escrow agent from all adverse claims related to the disbursal of the earnest money.

> D. DAMAGES: Any party who wrongfully fails or refuses to sign a release acceptable to the escrow agent within 7 days of receipt of the request will be liable to the other party for liquidated damages in an amount equal to the sum of: (i) damages; (ii) the earnest money; (iii) reasonable attorney's fees; and (iv) all costs of suit.

> E. NOTICES: Escrow agent's notices will be effective when sent in compliance with Paragraph 21. Notice of objection to the demand will be deemed effective upon receipt by escrow agent.

The contract is clear. Upon failure of the contract for any reason, the party desiring the earnest money must make written demand upon the title company. A copy of the demand should be sent to the other party. The written demand triggers a 15-day window during which the other party may make written objection to the title company. Phone calls, almost always legally insufficient in real estate for notice purposes, will not meet the requirements of the contract. Fax? Maybe. Email or text might be sufficient, since Texas is gradually recognizing the legitimacy of these forms of communication, but certified mail to both the title company and the other party is always best, particularly if litigation is a possibility. There is nothing like being able to show a signed green card to a judge in order to prove that notice was given. Send another copy by first class mail.

The language of the contract is vague about *which* demand—demand from the party desiring the earnest money versus demand from the title company—triggers the 15- and 7-day periods, but it is prudent to be conservative and assume that these periods begin when the first party makes written demand.

What happens next?

The title company will follow up with a notice of its own that written demand has been made and enclosing a release form for signature. It must be signed by all parties and their brokers. Fifteen days are allowed for written objections to be made.

The TREC contract formerly made the choice of mediation elective in paragraph 16. There is no longer a "yes or no" box to check on the latest form of this contract, so mediation is now required as a means of settling disputes—unless this paragraph is either struck and initialed or a special provisions addendum is attached that deals differently with dispute resolution. Generally, including a mediation requirement is a favorable provision for the seller, less so for the buyer.

Lawsuit Remedy in Justice Court

Lawsuits may be filed in justice court so long as the total amount claimed (including attorney's fees) does not exceed $10,000. If total damages exceed that amount, then suit may be filed in the county court at law. Named defendants should include the party refusing to sign the release *and* the title company holding the earnest money. Title companies will usually respond by interpleading the earnest money (depositing it into the court's account) which removes them from the merits of the litigation. The title company may then seek dismissal from the case or decide to remain in an attempt to recover attorney's fees from the party at fault.

Before filing a legal action concerning earnest money, it is useful to consider the practical reality that attorney's fees and costs, once added up, can easily exceed the amount of earnest money in dispute. As a consequence, many earnest money disputes are resolved by the parties' splitting the funds and going their separate ways, respective claims of principle notwithstanding.

Can you avoid earnest money disputes by imposing a liquidated damages penalty?

The idea here is that the contract would contain a liquidated damages clause to be applied in the event the seller refused to release the earnest money, something sufficiently harsh to discourage a seller from withholding these funds. A clause such as this would have to be included in a special provisions addendum. In *Magill v. Watson*, 409 S.W.3d 673 (Tex.App.—Houston [1st Dist.] 2013, no pet.), the court disallowed such an arbitrary treble-damages penalty because it was not rationally related to any actual damages that the buyer would suffer. It left open, however, the possibility that such a clause would be enforceable if the provision reflected a reasonable assessment of what the buyer's damages would be.

Chapter 5

AFFIDAVITS OF HEIRSHIP

An Inexpensive Alternative to Probate

If a person dies without a will, and title to his or her property does not expressly include joint tenancy with survivorship language, then issues may arise as to which persons now have title and in what percentages. Such property is often referred to as "heirship property." It is essentially unsellable as it is, and a title company will not insure the title until heirship issues are addressed and resolved. This is usually accomplished by either a probate proceeding in county court, resulting in appointment of a personal representative of the estate and ultimately a judgment determining heirship, as provided in Estates Code Section 202; or by the less formal and expensive method of utilizing an affidavit of heirship (Est. Code Sec. 203.002) followed by a "curative deed" or "consolidation deed" (our terms) signed by the surviving heirs in favor of a new sole owner.

Even if the decedent had a will, an affidavit of heirship may be used. Reason? A last will and testament is not self-executing as to bequests of real property. It is merely a statement of the decedent's intent. The will must be acted upon in some manner, either by means of a formal probate proceeding (filed within four years of death) or by means of a recorded affidavit of heirship, the result of which is to declare as a matter of record the identity and interests of the heirs.

Note that this is not a chapter on probate law, although we occasionally refer to sections of the Estates Code. If an investor is faced with probate issues, then an attorney who is a board-certified specialist in that area should generally be consulted.

When is an affidavit of heirship required?

Schedule C of the title commitment may state: *We are to be furnished with an affidavit executed by an immediate member of the family and corroborated by at least two disinterested parties containing the marital history of the deceased and his spouse and a complete list of heirs, together with an original death certificate attached.*

The title company is asking here for an affidavit of heirship. The purpose of the affidavit in an intestacy case (no will) is to describe family history and circumstances and identify the likely heirs. Estates Code Section 203.001 states in part:

(a) **A court shall receive in a proceeding to declare heirship or a suit involving title to property a statement of facts concerning the family history, genealogy, marital status, or the identity of the heirs of a decedent as prima facie evidence of the facts contained in the statement if:**

    (1) the statement is contained in:

        (A) an affidavit or other instrument legally executed and acknowledged or sworn to before, and certified by, an officer authorized to take acknowledgements or oaths, as applicable; or

        (B) a judgment of a court of record; and

    (2) the affidavit or instrument containing the statement has been of record for five years or more in the deed records of a county in this state in which the property is located at the time the suit involving title to the property is commenced, or in the deed records of a county in this state in which the decedent was domiciled or had a fixed place of residence at the time of the decedent's death.

The affidavit must be signed under oath by a person familiar with facts relating to family circumstances and history, which is usually but not always a family member. Although the statute does not expressly require that the affidavit be attested to by disinterested witnesses (i.e., persons who have no personal or financial stake in the outcome), title companies routinely require two notarized signatures of disinterested persons—three is prudent.

After execution, the affidavit should be filed in the real property records of the county where the property is located. If the property overlaps county boundaries, then a separate affidavit should be filed in each county where the property makes an appearance.

Title Company Policy

Estates Code Section 203.002 provides a recommended format for the affidavit, although strict adherence to the form is not required. As a practical matter, it is more title company underwriting policy rather than the requirements of this statute that drive the content of such affidavits.

Individual title underwriters vary in their requirements. The following are among the rules that have been promulgated by American Title Company:

(1) the decedent must have died at least six months prior to the execution of the affidavit;

(2) a death certificate on the decedent must be furnished to the title company;

(3) the affidavit must be signed by at least two disinterested parties having personal knowledge of the family history of the decedent and having personally known the decedent for at least ten years (a disinterested party is one that will receive no benefit of any kind from signing the affidavit—so this would exclude a spouse or child of a person who expects to receive an heirship interest).

(4) in addition to bearing the signature of the affiant, the affidavit must also be executed by all adult heirs who are taking title pursuant to the intestacy statutes;

(5) if the disinterested parties are related to the decedent, then this must be disclosed;

(6) the title company's examination of title cannot reveal any discrepancy with the facts asserted in the affidavit;

(7) if there is a will that has not been probated, it must be attached to the affidavit and must support the facts asserted in the affidavit; and

(8) the following paragraph must be included:

"I am aware of the penalties of perjury under Federal Law, which includes the execution of a false affidavit, pursuant to 18 U.S.C.S., Section 1621 wherein it is provided that anyone found guilty shall not be fined more than $2,000 or imprisoned not more than 5 years or both. I am also aware that perjury in the execution of a false affidavit is a criminal act pursuant to Section 37.02 of the Texas Penal Code. Finally I am also aware that under Section 32.46 of the Texas Penal Code, a person commits an offense, if with intent to defraud or harm a person, he, by deception, causes another to sign or execute any document affecting property or service of the pecuniary interest of any person, and that an offense under such section is a felony of the third degree which is punishable by a fine of $5,000 and confinement in the Texas Department of Corrections for a term of not more than 10 years or less than 2 years."

Expect high-dollar transactions to receive extra scrutiny—and perhaps additional requirements.

Since other title companies may have additional or different requirements than those mentioned in this chapter, and these may change over time, it is nearly impossible to draft an affidavit of heirship that is guaranteed to be accepted by all title companies at all times in the future. The attorney's job is to get as close as possible. If the client wants a precise and reliable result, then the alternative is to seek a declaratory judgment from a court.

Applicable Case Law

How do affidavits of heirship actually play out in court? The following is a good example: under Estates Code Section 203.001, "the affidavit of heirship, having been on file in the deed records for more than five years, serves as prima facie evidence of the facts therein stated in a proceeding to declare heirship or in a suit involving title to real or personal property." Accordingly, the filed affidavit prevails unless other parties "produce summary judgment evidence sufficient to raise a fact issue on the matter." *Jeter v. McGraw*, 79 S.W.3d 211, 215 (Tex.App.—Beaumont 2002, pet. denied).

Intestate Succession

When a person dies intestate, the rules of intestate succession take over. Essentially, the State of Texas has, by means of Estates Code Chapter 201, made a will for intestate decedents.

If the intestate decedent is unmarried, then Section 201.001 applies, providing that property goes in equal shares to the children if there are any. If not, then the property goes in equal shares to the parents. If the decedent was married, then community property is involved and Section 201.003 applies:

§ 201.003. Community Estate of an Intestate

(a) If a person who dies intestate leaves a surviving spouse, the community estate of the

deceased spouse passes as provided by this section.

(b) The community estate of the deceased spouse passes to the surviving spouse if:

> **(1)** no child or other descendant of the deceased spouse survives the deceased spouse; or

> **(2)** all of the surviving children and descendants of the deceased spouse are also children or descendants of the surviving spouse.

(c) if the deceased spouse is surviving by a child or other descendant who is not also a child or descendant of the surviving spouse, one-half of the community estate is retained by the surviving spouse and the other one-half passes to the deceased spouse's children or descendants. The descendants inherit only the portion of that estate to which they would be entitled under Section 201.101. In every case the community estate passes charged with the debts against the community estate.

A well-drafted affidavit of heirship will thoroughly review relevant facts, refer to specific sections of the Estates Code, and reach a reasoned conclusion as to the identity of the heirs and the amount of their respective interests.

Two-Step Process: Affidavit then Deed

Curing title (resolving heirship issues) outside of probate court is usually a two-step process. First, the affidavit of heirship must be prepared and signed by someone with first-hand, personal knowledge of family history (marriages, births, and deaths). Crafting a thorough and effective affidavit is both art and science and should be left to an attorney who will assure that its contents are both admissible and persuasive in any future litigation. Accordingly, Internet forms should *never* be used for this or any other serious legal purpose.

The affidavit of heirship will generally be presumed to be true after it has been filed of record for at least five years, although no title underwriter is bound by this.

Preparation of the Deed

The second step in the process, after drafting, execution, and filing of the affidavit, is a deed transfer that focuses title into a single heir who may then keep the property or sell it. Alternatively, all heirs may (for example) sign conveying the property to a third-party buyer.

The deed is usually a special warranty deed or deed without warranties, but not a quitclaim deed, which is to be avoided because title companies may not insure it. All heirs named in the affidavit (or their legal guardians) must sign. Both documents are filed in the real property records in the county in which the property is located—the affidavit first, and then the deed.

What the Attorney Needs from the Client

The attorney needs basic information from the client in order to proceed, including:

(1) an explanation of family history and circumstances (e.g., who married whom and who had children, who died with a will or without, who got divorced and re-married, and so on);

(2) a copy of the existing recorded deed to the property and, if available, a copy of a title commitment;

(3) the names and addresses of all relevant parties; and

(4) an explanation of the client's intent. Is the goal to consolidate title into one or more heirs? Or sell the property to a third party?

In many cases heirs are spread across the country and may have lost touch. Some heirs may not sign unless they are paid to do so—and financial issues between family members can get ugly. Clients are often disappointed when they discover how difficult and expensive the process can be. Heirs may attempt to resolve heirship and title issues on their own, without an attorney (often using junk forms from the Internet), and are left with a result more confusing and chaotic than when they started. Affidavits and deeds may then have to be re-prepared and refiled in order to correct the record, prolonging the process and increasing expense.

Family Values

A prospective client calls an attorney and says "My mother died six months ago, and I need to get a deed to her ranch. How much do you charge for preparing a deed?"

The attorney needs to know a great deal more information before he or she can respond, starting with asking, "Did she die with a will?" The client admits that he hasn't seen his mother in ten years, but he believes there was no will. He goes on to ask, "But I can still get my deed can't I?" Further questions from the attorney reveal more information about the family. The mother was a widow. The father died two years earlier, also without a will. In addition, it turns out that the client has several siblings, one of whom was from the father's prior marriage. Another has dropped out of sight and has not been heard from in years. There are rumors he is homeless on the streets of Los Angeles. Another sibling recently passed away, leaving two small children who are currently in foster care because their remaining parent is in prison. Also, the youngest sibling was living with Mom and taking care of her at the time of Mom's death, and she continues to occupy the property, now claiming it as *her* homestead and threatening to use a shotgun on anyone who enters without her consent. She contends that Mom promised that the house would be hers in exchange for care during her final illness.

The attorney is forced to tell the client he is *not* going to get a deed, at least not until heirship issues are straightened out, beginning with the father and which persons were entitled to inherit from him, and then moving on to the mother and her heirs. The client is suspicious. He says, "Look, your secretary told me that the fee for a deed is $350. It sounds like you're just trying to charge me more money. I'm the oldest, and I was always told the property would be mine one day. I want my deed now!" Unfortunately, that is just not possible given the facts of the case. The attorney is not a miracle worker, nor is a law office a court of law where differences such as these can receive a binding adjudication.

Chapter 6

LIS PENDENS

Are These a Proper Device to Stop a Closing?

A notice of lis pendens indicates that a civil action is pending that pertains to the title to real property, the establishment of an interest in real property, or enforcement of an encumbrance against real property (Prop. Code Sec. 12.007(a)). The party filing the notice must claim an actual interest in the property, not merely monetary damages. "In evaluating claims pertaining to real property for purposes of the lis pendens statute, Texas courts generally have distinguished between claims in which a party asserts a direct interest in real property, which qualify for a lis pendens, and claims in which a party asserts only a collateral [monetary] interest in real property, which do not qualify for a lis pendens." *In re. Moreno*, No. 14-14-00929-CV, Mandamus Proceeding (Tex.App.—Houston [14th Dist.] 2015).

The requirement that there be an interest in the subject property, not just a monetary claim, means that the popular tactic of filing suit for breach of an earnest money contract by a seller, and then filing a lis pendens in the real property records to hinder the property's subsequent sale to another, is improper. A court is required to grant a motion to expunge a lis pendens if the plaintiff fails to establish by a preponderance of the evidence the probably validity of a real property claim. Prop. Code Sec. 12.0071.

The lis pendens itself takes the form of an affidavit filed in the county clerk's real property records announcing that a lawsuit involving local real estate is pending in a certain court. "Generally speaking, the purpose of a lis pendens notice is twofold: (1) to protect the filing party's alleged rights to the property that is in dispute in the lawsuit and (2) to put those interested in the property on notice of the lawsuit." *David Powers Homes, Inc. v. M.L. Rendleman Co., Inc.* 355 S.W.3d 327,336 (Tex.App.—Houston [1st Dist.] 2011, no pet.). A Houston appeals court case nicely summarizes the basic concept: "A properly filed lis pendens is not itself a lien, but rather it operates as constructive notice to the world of its contents. . . . [Property Code Sec. 13.004(b)] expressly provides that a property filed notice of lis pendens prevents a purchaser for value from acquiring property free and clear of the encumbrance referenced in the lis pendens." *Cohen v. Sandcastle Homes, Inc.*, 469 S.W.3d 173 (Tex.App.— Houston [1st Dist.]).

Applicable Law

The law applicable to lis pendens is found in Property Code Section 12.007 et seq.:

Sec. 12.007. LIS PENDENS

(a) After the plaintiff's statement in an eminent domain proceeding is filed or during the pendency of an action involving title to real property, the establishment of an interest in real property, or the enforcement of an encumbrance against real property, a party to the action who is seeking affirmative relief may file for record with the county clerk of each county where a part of the property is located a notice that the action is pending.

(b) The party filing a lis pendens or the party's agent or attorney shall sign the lis pendens, which must state:
    (1) the style and number, if any, of the proceeding;
    (2) the court in which the proceeding is pending;
    (3) the names of the parties;
    (4) the kind of proceeding; and
    (5) a description of the property affected.

(c) The county clerk shall record the notice in a lis pendens record. The clerk shall index the record in a direct and reverse index under the name of each party to the proceeding.

(d) Not later than the third day after the date a person files a notice for record under this section, the person must serve a copy of the notice on each party to the action who has an interest in the real property affected by the notice.

Sec. 12.0071. MOTION TO EXPUNGE LIS PENDENS.

(a) A party to an action in connection with which a notice of lis pendens has been filed may:
    (1) apply to the court to expunge the notice; and
    (2) file evidence, including declarations, with the motion to expunge the notice.

David J. Willis, J.D., LL.M.

(b) The court may:

    (1) permit evidence on the motion to be received in the form of oral testimony; and

    (2) make any orders the court considers just to provide for discovery by a party affected by the motion.

(c) The court shall order the notice of lis pendens expunged if the court determines that:

    (1) the pleading on which the notice is based does not contain a real property claim;

    (2) the claimant fails to establish by a preponderance of the evidence the probable validity of the real property claim; or

    (3) the person who filed the notice for record did not serve a copy of the notice on each party entitled to a copy under Section 12.007(d).

(d) Notice of a motion to expunge under Subsection (a) must be served on each affected party on or before the 20th day before the date of the hearing on the motion.

(e) The court shall rule on the motion for expunction based on the affidavits and counter-affidavits on file and on any other proof the court allows.

(f) After a certified copy of an order expunging a notice of lis pendens has been recorded:

    (1) the notice of lis pendens and any information derived or that could be derived from the notice:

        (A) does not:

            (i) constitute constructive or actual notice of any matter contained in the notice or of any matter relating to the action in connection with which the notice was filed;

            (ii) create any duty of inquiry in a person with respect to the property described in the notice; or

            (iii) affect the validity of a conveyance to a purchaser for value or of a mortgage to a lender for value; and

        (B) is not enforceable against a purchaser or lender described by Paragraph (A)(iii), regardless of whether the purchaser or lender knew of the lis pendens action; and

    (2) an interest in the real property may be transferred or encumbered free of all matters asserted or disclosed in the notice and all claims or other matters asserted or disclosed in the action in connection with which the notice was filed.

(g) The court in its discretion may require that the party prevailing in the expunction hearing submit an undertaking to the court in an amount determined by the court.

Sec. 12.008. CANCELLATION OF LIS PENDENS

(a) On the motion of a party or other person interested in the result of or in property affected by a proceeding in which a lis pendens has been recorded and after notice to each affected party, the court hearing the action may cancel the lis pendens at any time during the proceeding, whether in term time or vacation, if the court determines that the party seeking affirmative relief can be adequately protected by the deposit of money into court or by the giving of an undertaking.

(b) If the cancellation of a lis pendens is conditioned on the payment of money, the court may order the cancellation when the party seeking the cancellation pays into the court an amount equal to the total of:
(1) the judgment sought;
(2) the interest the court considers likely to accrue during the proceeding; and
(3) costs.

(c) If the cancellation of a lis pendens is conditioned on the giving of an undertaking, the court may order the cancellation when the party seeking the cancellation gives a guarantee of payment of a judgment, plus interest and costs, in favor of the party who recorded the lis pendens. The guarantee must equal twice the amount of the judgment sought and have two sufficient sureties approved by the court. Not less than two days before the day the guarantee is submitted to the court for approval, the party seeking the cancellation shall serve the attorney for the party who recorded the lis pendens a copy of the guarantee and notice of its submission to the court.

The specific statutory categories listed in Property Code Section 12.007(a) provide the sole and exclusive legal basis for the filing of a lis pendens. A close look at these categories indicate that the law will not support the filing of a lis pendens unless *the property itself* is truly the subject of the suit. A notice that only indirectly affects the property (or is merely "collateral" to it, in the parlance of the case law) is not valid. *Flores v. Haberman*, 915 S.W.2d 477, 478 (Tex. 1995). For instance, a suit seeking only monetary damages would not justify the filing of a lis pendens, nor would a suit to specifically enforce or set aside an earnest money contract, because neither of these pertain to the property itself— only to a breach of contract to convey the property, a subtle but meaningful legal distinction.

Section 12.0071 was amended in 2017 to clarify that after a certified copy of an order expunging a notice of lis pendens has been recorded, the previously filed notice of lis pendens no longer constitutes actual or constructive notice, creates any duty of inquiry, or affects the validity of any subsequent conveyance of the property. Query for the legislature: why does this provision apply only to a certified copy of an expungement order and not to an ordinary release and cancellation?

Duration of a Lis Pendens

A lis pendens has no life of its own apart from the lawsuit that underlies it. "A *lis pendens* operates only during the pendency of the [underlying] suit, and only as to those matters that are involved in the suit. It terminates with the judgment, in the absence of an appeal." *Rosborough v. Cook*, 108 Tex. 364, 367, 194 S.W. 131, 132 (1917). A timely appeal or motion for new trial extends the operative effect of the lis pendens. "Because the recording of a lis pendens is specifically authorized by statute and has no existence separate and apart from the litigation of which it gives notice . . . the filing of a notice of lis pendens . . . is a part of the 'judicial proceeding.'" *Kropp v. Prather*, 526 S.W.2d 283 (Tex.App.—Tyler 1975, write ref'd n.r.e.). In other words, a lis pendens does not represent a stand-alone claim. *Collins v. Tex Mall, L.P.*, 297 S.W.3d 409, 419 (Tex.App.—Fort Worth 2009, no pet.).

Cancellation of a Lis Pendens

If a notice of lis pendens is wrongfully filed, a court may order it canceled by means of a motion to expunge. In the hearing on the motion, "the court shall order the notice of lis pendens expunged if the court determines that . . . claimant fails to establish by a preponderance of the evidence the probable validity of the real property claim. . . ." (Prop. Code Sec. 12.0071(c)(2)). In other words, it can be expected that a lis pendens based on tenuous or bogus assertions regarding the subject property will not survive a challenge.

Section 12.0071 specifies that a "court shall order the notice of lis pendens expunged if the court determines that: (1) the pleading on which the notice is based does not contain a real property claim; (2) the claimant fails to establish by a preponderance of the evidence the probable validity of the real property claim; or (3) the person who filed the notice for record did not serve a copy of the notice on each party entitled to a copy under Section 12.007(d). Once a party seeks to expunge a lis pendens, the evidentiary burden shifts to the other party to prove by a preponderance of the evidence that its claim is probably valid. *In Re I-10 Poorman Investments, Inc.*, 549 S.W.3d 614 (Tex.App.—Houston [1st Dist.] 2017, no pet.).

If a motion to expunge a lis pendens is denied, the remedy for the movant is to seek a writ of mandamus, not to file an appeal. *In re. Howard Chong*, No. 14-19-00368-CV (Tex.App.—Houston [14th Dist.] 2019).

A court may not, on its own motion, cancel or expunge a lis pendens. There must be a motion made by one of the parties and then notice to all concerned.

With court approval, one may "bond around" a notice of lis pendens and obtain its cancellation by paying an adequate sum into the registry of the court. Prop. Code Sec. 12.008(b).

Rule Relating to Bona Fide Purchasers

Although a lis pendens is not a lien, it is a cloud on title and can therefore have the effect of stopping a sale. Why? Because constructive notice of litigation has now been given to potential buyers. ("Constructive notice" is the idea that we are all charged with knowledge of items filed in the public records, whether we have actually read them or not). Property Code Section 13.004(a) states that a "recorded lis pendens is notice to the world of its contents." If this were not the case, the rule regarding a bona fide purchaser ("BFP") would apply—i.e., a buyer who purchases real property for valuable consideration without notice of a disputed claim or prior interest does so free of that claim or interest. Accordingly, if a notice of lis pendens is properly filed, then a buyer (by definition) cannot be a BFP since constructive notice has been given by the filing; at best the buyer becomes a purchaser pendente lite, meaning that he or she would take title subject to the outcome of the litigation.

The closing of a transaction and the issuance of title insurance can be affected. A title company usually will not issue an owner's policy of title insurance to a buyer until a lawsuit is cleared up or the lis pendens is canceled. The practical result is that a seller involved in litigation concerning a property cannot easily get rid of the problem by selling that property to someone else. Without this rule, the parties could be prevented from justly resolving their litigation and the authority of the courts defeated.

Note that if a prospective purchaser has actual knowledge of a pending suit, then the lis pendens doctrine applies whether or not a statutory notice has been filed in the real property records. A buyer cannot know about a lawsuit (from whatever source) and still claim to be a BFP. *Sommers v. Sandcastle Homes, Inc.* 521 S.W.3d 749 (Tex. 2017).

Penalties for Wrongful or Fraudulent Filings of a Lis Pendens

The Property Code does not grant a penalty for filing a wrongful or fraudulent lis pendens. As a result, "courts have given a broad reading to § 12.008, so as to grant an effective remedy." *Prappas v. Meyerland Cmty. Improvement Ass'n*, 795 S.W.2d 794, 798 (Tex.App.—Houston [14th Dist.] 1990, writ denied).

The content of a lis pendens is considered to be privileged, just as all that is said in the underlying litigation is privileged. *Jetall Companies, Inc. v. Dyke*, No.14-19-00104-CV (Tex.App.—Houston [14th Dist.] 2019). A lis pendens is just a notice, even if filed with malice.

Note, however, that Rule 13 of the Texas Rules of Civil Procedure provides sanctions if lawsuits are "groundless and brought in bad faith or groundless and brought for the purpose of harassment . . . . 'Groundless' for purposes of this rule means no basis in law or fact and not warranted by good faith argument for the extension, modification, or reversal of existing law." So caution is in order: the filing of a frivolous lis pendens could easily fall within the definition of harassment and potentially open the door to Rule 13 sanctions in connection with the conduct of the lawsuit generally.

It is also worth looking at Civil Practice & Remedies Code Section 12.002 which addresses "liability related to . . . a fraudulent lien or claim filed against real or personal property." Since a lis pendens could be interpreted as a claim of sorts, or at least the memorandum of one, the filer could potentially incur liability under this statute if aspects of the lis pendens or the underlying suit are found to be fraudulent. A person who knowingly and intentionally files a fraudulent lien may be held liable in district court for the greater of $10,000 or actual damages, exemplary damages, and recovery of attorney's fees and costs. It is also a criminal offense. Penal Code Sec. 37.01. If applicable, a cause of action under Chapter 12 should be included in any suit against the filer of the lis pendens.

Additionally, the filing of a fraudulent lien or claim may under certain circumstances form the basis of a cause of action under the Deceptive Trade Practices Act, Bus. & Com. Code Sec. 17.44 et seq.

Lis pendens are a useful tool but are subject to abuse as well as potential consequences. They must be employed in strict compliance with the statute and not merely to gain advantage in a dispute over some monetary aspect of a real estate closing.

PART II

OWNERSHIP & TRANSFER OF TEXAS REAL ESTATE

Chapter 7

CO-OWNERSHIP OF PROPERTY

Including Comments on Joint Tenancy with Rights of Survivorship

For purposes of most investor transactions, co-ownership is generally "tenancy-in-common" although several other ownership regimes exist. Tenancy-in-common means that the interest of a co-owner, absent express provision to the contrary, passes directly to that person's heirs—who may or may not be the other co-owner(s). And, for purposes of this discussion, disregard the common meaning of "tenant" and "tenancy." Traditional legal language can be misleading. In this context, these terms refer to owners not renters.

Attorneys often face co-ownership issues when advising on inheritance and probate avoidance. Inheritance in such cases may be determined by express language in a deed or a last will and testament, or in the absence of either, by intestacy provisions of the Estates Code. In some circumstances a co-owner may have no survivorship rights at all, so assumptions should be avoided. "Why do I need a will?" many a husband has asked his wife. "We're married. You're going to get everything when I die." Well, maybe. See our discussion below.

Another commonly-encountered question in the area of co-ownership is how someone can be "added" to a deed (i.e., adding another person to the title to realty), which may not always be as simple as it sounds. This topic is also discussed below.

Co-Owners Who Are Spouses

Does a surviving spouse inherit the entire interest in the home when the other dies? Not necessarily. It is first necessary to determine if the deceased spouse died "testate" (with a will) or "intestate" (without a will). If a spouse dies intestate, property automatically vests 100% in the surviving spouse *only* if the property is community property *and* the deceased had no children—or, if there are children, all of them are the result of the marriage between these two spouses (i.e., there are no children from a prior marriage, an increasingly uncommon circumstance). See Estates Code Section 201.003 for further explanation.

Co-Owners Who Are Not Spouses

Texas law presumes that if two non-spouses are named as co-owners, and nothing more is said, then they are tenants-in-common (Est. Code Sec. 101.002). This means they each person owns an undivided one-half interest in the property *but there is no automatic right of survivorship.* When one co-owner dies, the interest of the deceased co-owner goes directly to that person's heir or heirs, either by will or by intestate succession. The line of succession is vertical, downward to the heirs of the deceased, rather than horizontal, across to the co-owner.

Joint Tenancy with Rights of Survivorship (JTWROS)

Joint tenancy with rights of survivorship has been dubbed the "poor man's will," since it eliminates the need for a last will and testament as to a particular piece of property (but not others, obviously). Again, it is ownership we are discussing here, not tenancy, but the legal acronym remains what it is. JTWROS comes up in two contexts, between non-spouses and spouses.

Estates Code Section 111.001(a) states the following as to non-spouses: "Notwithstanding Section 101.002, two or more persons who hold an interest in property jointly may agree in writing that the interest of a joint owner who dies survives to the surviving joint owner or owners." Accordingly, business partners, or perhaps a brother and sister, may agree in writing to establish JTWROS.

As to spousal community property, Section 112.051 applies: "At any time, spouses may agree between themselves that all or part of their community property, then existing or to be acquired, becomes the property of the surviving spouse on the death of a spouse." Section 112.052 further requires that such an agreement "must be in writing and signed by both spouses." So long as the statutory requirements are met, no action or intervention by a court of law is required (Est. Code Sec. 112.053)—which, of course, is the goal most people have in mind when establishing JTWROS.

The simplest way to accomplish JTWROS is to recite language in the deed which expressly declares survivorship rights. In order to make the intention of the parties plain on the face of the deed, this language should be included at the time that both spouses receive their interest in the property. An example of a grantee clause that creates joint tenancy is "John Smith and wife, Mary Smith, as joint owners with rights of survivorship as provided by Estates Code Section 112.051, and not as tenants-in-common." The deed should go on to state that it is the intention and agreement of the co-owners to establish an agreement concerning spousal survivorship. In order to comply with the requirement that the agreement be signed by both husband and wife, both spouses (i.e., both grantees) should sign and acknowledge the deed. Our opinion is that this satisfies Section 112.051.

Section 121.152 imposes a caveat: in order for a joint tenant to inherit, the survivor must survive the deceased by at least 120 hours. If this does not occur, then "one-half of the property shall be distributed as if one joint owner had survived, and the other one-half shall be distributed as if the other joint owner had survived."

Note that if property is currently held by two persons as tenants-in-common, they can convert this to joint tenancy by means of a survivorship agreement as provided in Estates Code Section 111.001(a) or Section 112.051 (depending on whether or not the property is community property). However, this method does not physically change the warranty deed, and many persons are looking for just that—a single title document that states both names and makes survivorship clear.

The Role of a Last Will and Testament

Even if a deed contains no survivorship language, each co-owner may make his or her wishes plain by executing a valid will that provides for inheritance of the deceased's interest (Est. Code Sec. 101.001). The Estates Code is a fallback that comes into effect by default, in the absence of a will. Failing to make a will is equivalent to asking the State of Texas to determine how your property will be disposed. Est. Code Sec. 201.001 et seq.

Deeds Prepared by the Title Company

It is rare for a title company to offer co-owners the opportunity to take title as JTWROS. When buyers arrive at a title company to close, they are often handed a minimalist deed that contains no extra clauses favorable or customized to them—unless, of course, their own attorney has negotiated the inclusion of such clauses in advance. This is unfortunate, since a warranty deed is qualitatively different from the routine forms and disclosures that title companies also prepare. It is the sole document that evidences title to the property and may also set forth significant conditions upon which the seller is selling and the buyer is buying. It is far more important than, say, a MUD disclosure. And yet too many investor buyers and sellers say "Just let the title company prepare the deed" and forgo any opportunity to have input regarding its contents. A missed opportunity, to say the least.

For investors especially, it is worth the effort to customize the warranty deed so that it suits one's purposes. Generally, one should not expect the title company to assist with this sort of customization, at least not without being grumpy about it and perhaps increasing the deed prep charge. Title companies are *insurance companies.* They and their attorneys look out for what is in their interests, not yours. It is astonishing how many people, even investors, naively believe that the title company is concerned with their best interests and will draft documents accordingly. *This is false.*

If buyers want to hold title as joint owners with rights of survivorship, they must specifically ask in advance of the closing that appropriate wording and signature lines be included in the deed. Ideally, this provision should be an item expressly negotiated with the seller and therefore reflected on the earnest money contract (or a special provisions addendum to the contract).

Heirship Property

What happens if a person dies both without a will *and* without a survivorship provision in their deed? Such property may be "heirship property" and, without curative measures, may be unsellable except perhaps privately by means of a deed without warranties or quitclaim.

A title company will not issue title insurance until heirship issues are first addressed and resolved (they will let you know about their requirements in Schedule C of the title commitment). An affidavit of heirship is often used for this purpose (Est. Code Sec. 203.001), followed by a consolidating deed signed by the heirs. The affidavit recites relevant facts concerning family history, identifies the heirs, and is usually signed by a family member with personal knowledge. The deed is then signed by the heirs with the goal of moving title into a single heir or perhaps a third-party buyer. Both documents should then be filed in the proper order in the local real property records.

Adding Someone to the Deed

Clients often ask that their spouse or other person be "added to the deed" so that the other person will have co-ownership and inheritance rights. Prior to adoption of the Estates Code, the old common law method was for the owner to transfer the property out to a third party (the attorney or some other trusted individual) who then transferred the property back into the two desired names with JTWROS language. Why this circuitous route? Because the common law required that JTWROS be established at the "inception of title"—i.e., at the outset, when title was first received from the previous owner.

Now, pursuant to Estates Code Section 112.051, the owning spouse may deed the property directly into his or her name together with the name of the receiving spouse (i.e., both spouses are listed as grantees with rights of survivorship) and, so long as both spouses recite terms and sign this "written agreement," the statutory requirements are satisfied and JTWROS is created, with the names of both spouses appearing on the same deed. Care needs to be used in drafting this instrument so that all statutory requirements are satisfied. In this circumstance, the deed is both a conveyance and an agreement between the grantees.

If one's goal is to add another person to the title, but *not* provide for JTWROS, then one can always convey a partial or percentage interest (undivided) in the property (e.g., 50%) to the other party, but this does not result in a single document reflecting both names.

Liability on the Loan

Regardless of whether the result is tenancy in common or JTWROS, a co-owner that has been added to a deed does *not* automatically become liable on the loan on the property. Liability on a loan occurs only when a note is signed. No signature on a note, no liability to the bank. As has been pointed out elsewhere, title and debt are distinct concepts and can be severed.

Similarly, if both co-owners have signed the note and one co-owner sells his ownership interest, the selling co-owner remains liable on the note. Here is a common inquiry received by real estate lawyers: "I bought a home with my girlfriend ten years ago. She paid down the down payment but I've made the monthly payments ever since, which add up to far more than the down payment. Can I sue her to recover my excess contribution?" The answer is probably not, unless the parties had previously agreed to be business partners pursuant to Section 152 of the Business Organizations Code. Why? Because both parties are jointly and severally obligated on the note that each of them signed. The boyfriend, in making payments, was just discharging his own legally enforceable obligation.

Percentage Ownership

Let's discuss percentage deeds for a moment. As an example, if one investor owns 60%, another owns 20%, and a third owns 20%, then it is appropriate to specify these percentages in the deed by which the property is acquired, resulting in undivided percentage ownership. Alternatively, the three owners could form an entity (an LLC or a trust) to hold title, and the records of the LLC would reflect the varying membership interests or, if a trust is used, the varying beneficial interests. An LLC would be preferred if the parties are concerned with potential liability associated with a rental property, since trusts do not have a liability barrier.

Percentage ownership is not available in the case of JTWROS.

The Living Trust Alternative

A living trust achieves the objectives of joint tenancy and more. It is designed to hold property (primarily real estate) during the life of the trustor (the person conveying the property into trust) in order to avoid probate and potentially reduce estate/inheritance taxes at the time of the trustor's death. See chapter 22 for details.

Chapter 8

DEEDS IN TEXAS

An Overview for Investors

What is a deed?

A deed is a written document that conveys legal and equitable title to real property—the legal term is a "fee simple" interest, meaning the highest level of ownership. "An absolute or 'fee simple' estate is one entitling the owner to the benefits of that estate during his life and descending to his heirs, devisees, and legal representatives on his death. One can own a fee simple estate in both legal and equitable property interests." *Jackson v. Wildflower Prod. Co.*, 505 S.W.3d 80, 88 (Tex.App.—Amarillo 2016, pet. denied).

It is difficult to imagine a more important document to the real estate investor, and yet its preparation is often left to a title company attorney who represents neither buyer nor seller and who, accordingly, has no incentive to produce anything other than an inexpensive, boilerplate form that may omit advisable or useful clauses (depending on your perspective as grantor or grantee). Property Code Section 5.022(b) expressly states that "the parties to a conveyance may insert any clause . . . not in contravention of law." Accordingly, a deed that is custom-drafted may and should recite certain critical deal points pertaining to the specific transaction, an obvious example of which would be an "as is" clause if you are the seller. Further, if the deed is then executed by both parties (not just the grantor), the document becomes a contract as well as a conveyance. This can have significant value if the transaction involves special provisions upon which the parties are relying.

A deed is to be distinguished from a promissory note (or real estate lien note) which is a promise to pay a sum of money, and from a deed of trust, which provides the lender with remedies (including foreclosure) if a borrower defaults on the note. A warranty deed, note, and deed of trust are the three principal documents in most Texas residential real estate transactions.

This chapter briefly describes different types of deeds commonly used in connection with real estate investment in Texas. It is deliberately organized in a pragmatic fashion that an investor will recognize and is not intended as a comprehensive academic review of the topic. If you are looking for the latter, then I suggest you acquire an academic textbook on property law. This volume does not attempt to fill that role.

Minimum Requirements

There is no standard form for a deed although Property Code Section 5.022(a) offers a simple form that may be used for fee simple conveyances. Texas does have certain rules that apply if a deed is to be valid. For instance, the parties should be named, the intent to convey property must be clear from the wording, the property must be sufficiently described, and the deed must be signed by the grantor and delivered. *Gordon v. W. Hous. Trees, Ltd.,* 352 S.W.3d 32 (Tex.App.— Houston [1st Dist.] 2011, no pet.). Having said this, it is not true that all deeds are created equal. In particular, when a grantor intends to accomplish a specific objective and limit liability in doing so, the wording of a deed can be critically important.

"For a deed or instrument to effect conveyance of real property, it is not necessary to have all the formal parts of a deed formerly recognized at common law or to contain technical words. If, from the whole instrument, a grantor and grantee can be ascertained, and if there are operative words of grant showing an intention of the grantor to convey title to a real property interest to the grantee, and if the instrument is signed and acknowledged by the grantor, it is a deed which is legally effective as a conveyance." *Harlan v. Vetter,* 732 S.W.2d 390 (Tex.App.— Eastland 1987, writ ref'd n.r.e.). If there is a signed written document that identifies a grantor and grantee, provides a reasonably accurate description of the property, and clearly contains the intention to convey, then that document is a "deed" under Texas law. *Green v. Cannon,* 33 S.W.3d 855,858 (Tex.App.—Houston [14th Dist.] 2000, pet. denied).

In the event of ambiguity or controversy, the goal of a court in interpreting a deed is "ascertaining and effectuating the parties' intent . . . by conducting a careful and detailed examination of the deed in its entirety." *Wenske v. Ealy.* 521 S.W.3d 791, 792 (Tex. 2017).

Property Description

The general Texas rule is that a property description in a deed is sufficient if it identifies the property with reasonable accuracy. *Morrow v. Shotwell,* 477 S.W.2d 538 (Tex. 1972). Having said that, no investor should be satisfied unless the legal description is precisely correct and corresponds to previous descriptions in the chain of title. In some cases lengthy metes and bounds are used to describe the property rather than the usual "lot and block" descriptions commonly found in residential subdivisions. If such a description is outdated, or if there is any doubt as to its present accuracy (e.g., it refers to an "old oak tree for corner" or a "stream for boundary"), then a new survey would be a good investment.

If the deed for some reason refers to more than one description of the property, and there is a conflict, then the more specific metes-and-bounds description controls. *Stribling v. Millican DPC Partners, LP*, 458 S.W.3d 17 (Tex. 2015).

It is not required that the street address of the property be included in the deed, but it is certainly the better practice to include it. As a practical matter, this makes it easier for investors with multiple properties to determine which deed goes with which property.

A caveat concerning "legal descriptions" obtained from the appraisal district: these are typically abbreviated and condensed and *not* the official legal description of the property as shown in the county clerk's real property records. Two different computer systems are involved. The legal description in a new deed should track the description (lot and block or metes and bounds) in the prior deed on file with the county clerk—corrected, if necessary—in order to preserve proper chain of title.

Implied Covenants in a Texas Deed

At common law, a deed was accompanied by six implied covenants: (1) the covenant of seisin (the grantor is the owner of the property being sold); (2) the covenant against encumbrances (the land is owned free and clear of liens); (3) the covenant that the grantor has the right to convey the property without joinder of others; (4) the covenant of quiet enjoyment, which represents an assurance by the grantor that the grantee's title will not be disturbed by third-party claims; (5) the covenant of warranty, obliging the grantor to defend title against challenges by others; and (6) the covenant of further assurances, meaning a promise by the grantor that will take such other and further actions in the future as may be necessary to vest title in the grantee.

The Property Code, without excluding the potential existence of the common-law covenants in any particular case, recites only two, an attenuated version of the covenant of seisin and the covenant against encumbrances:

Sec. 5.023. Implied Covenants

(a) Unless the conveyance expressly provides otherwise, the use of "grant" or "convey" in a conveyance of an estate of inheritance or fee simple implies only that the grantor

and the grantors heirs covenant to the grantee and the grantees heirs or assigns:

> **(1) that prior to the execution of the conveyance the grantor has not conveyed the estate or any interest in the estate to a person other than the grantee; and**

> **(2) that at the time of the execution of the conveyance the estate is free from encumbrances.**

(b) An implied covenant under this section may be the basis for a lawsuit as if it had been expressed in the conveyance.

The common-law covenant of seisin was a representation on the part of the grantor that the grantor was, in fact, the owner of the property. Section 5.023 changes this to mean that the grantor has not previously conveyed the property to someone else, which is not quite the same thing. It is unclear what advantage this more limited covenant may possess, except perhaps to make it slightly easier for a swindler to flim-flam a gullible grantee.

The law of implied covenants has been established in Texas law for quite some time. "[In] the absence of any qualifying expressions, [such implied covenants] are read into every conveyance of land or an interest of land except in quitclaim deeds." *Childress v. Siler*, 272 S.W.2d 417, 420 (Tex.Civ.App.—Waco 1954, writ ref'd n.r.e).

And then came *Cochran Investments, Inc. vs. Chicago Title Insurance Company*, 550 S.W.3d 196 (Tex.App.—Houston [14th Dist.] 2018, pet. pending). In *Cochran*, the court of appeals reviewed a special warranty deed conveying a duplex and found that it was indeed possible for a deed to imply the traditional covenant of seisin, but that "it [must be] so clearly within the contemplation of the parties that they deemed it unnecessary to express it, and therefore they omitted to do so. . . A covenant will not be implied simply to make a contract fair, wise, or just." The court (questionably) ruled that since the deed did not expressly recite that the grantor owned the property, no covenant of seisin can be implied—a ruling that does more than muddle the difference between express and implied covenants; it has the potential to turn warranty deeds into quitclaims, at least unless the grantor makes an express representation of ownership in the deed, something that occurs only rarely. Real estate professionals are eagerly waiting to see if traditional Texas law as exemplified in *Childress* will be reinstated.

To summarize: even though deeds may legitimately vary in form in Texas, the use of the traditional phrase "grant, sell, and convey" will always include the two statutory covenants contained in Section 5.023 unless they are waived by express language in the deed. Accordingly, even in the case of a deed without warranties (discussed below) a careful drafter will take pains to expressly disclaim these two statutory covenants.

An additional item: one occasionally hears about the implied covenant of habitability and the implied covenant of good and workmanlike construction. Both of these covenants exist in Texas, but apply *only* in the case of newly-built residences. *Centex Homes v. Buecher*, 95 S.W.3d 266, 273 (Tex. 2002).

Reservations and Exceptions

Property Code Section 5.001 provides that a deed conveys a fee simple interest in property (i.e., all of the rights to the property, without exceptions or reservations) "unless the estate is limited by express words or unless a lesser estate is conveyed or devised by construction or operation of law." Modern deed formats usually refer to whether or not there are reservations and exceptions. These should either be expressly mentioned or "none" should be inserted in that space.

A note on terminology: "The primary distinction between a reservation and exception is that a reservation must always be in favor and [held back] for the benefit of the grantor; whereas an exception is a mere exclusion from the grant. . . ." *Pich v. Lankford*, 302 S.W.2D 645 (Tex. 1957). In other words, a reservation retains a certain interest in the grantor (e.g., minerals, an easement, or a life estate); by contrast, an exception stipulates that a certain interest is simply not conveyed at all, regardless of who may be the owner of it. Such language must be clear—an implied exception or reservation is not good enough. *Griswold v. EOG Resources, Inc.*, 459 S.W.3d 713 (Tex.App.—Fort Worth 2015, no pet.). Reservations and exceptions affect the total package of rights and interests a buyer is getting, so investors should consult an attorney and place close attention to the wording.

Community Property Considerations

Texas is a community property state and it is good practice (but not required) to state the marital status of the parties in the deed, since not doing so may raise questions later. For instance, a title company involved in a subsequent transaction may want to resolve any potential community property issues by asking that a prior owner in the chain execute a marital status affidavit or take other action to assure that all community property interests are properly tied up and accounted for before title insurance is issued. So how does one do this for the grantor? Usually, by showing the grantor's name in the deed followed by (for example) one of the following phrases:

> an unmarried person;

> a married person not joined herein by Grantor's spouse as the property conveyed forms no part of the residence or business homestead;

> a married person not joined herein by Grantor's spouse as the property conveyed is his or her sole and separate property and forms no part of the residence or business homestead; or

> a married person, joined herein *pro forma* by Grantor's spouse even though the property herein conveyed forms no part of the residence or business homestead.

Choices for the grantee would include "an unmarried person" and "as grantee's sole and separate property."

Must deeds be recorded to be valid?

There is no requirement that a deed be recorded in the county clerk's real property records in order to be valid—only that it be executed and delivered to the grantee (this may be done privately), at which time the transfer is fully effective between the grantor (seller) and the grantee (buyer). As between a grantor and grantee, deeds are valid even if the signature of the grantor is not acknowledged before a notary. *Haile v. Holtzclaw*, 414 S.W.2d 916, 928 (Tex. 1967).

However, a deed must be property acknowledged and notarized if it is to be recorded in the county clerk's real property records (statutory recording requirements are found primarily in Property Code Chapters 12 and 13). Texas is considered a "notice" state, meaning that recording gives notice to the world of the transfer and, of course, establishes priority in the event an unscrupulous seller conveys the property twice. "Recorded instruments in a grantee's chain of title generally establish an irrebuttable presumption of notice." *Noble Mortg. & Invs. v. D&M Vision Invs.*, 340 S.W.3d 65, 76 (Tex.App—Houston [1st Dist.] 2011, no pet.). All of this of course assumes that the deed is properly filed in the records of the county where it is located.

Recording makes it easier for title companies to research and insure the chain of title. Title companies insist on recording for this reason. Recording also informs the taxing authorities where ad valorem tax bills should be sent.

Executing and delivering a deed without immediately recording it can be a useful, inexpensive estate planning device—sometimes called "the deed in the drawer." If, for example, a parent wants to insure that property is transferred to a child without probate or other difficulty, then he or she can sign and deliver a deed with the intention that it be held and not recorded until death. This is an entirely legal technique that has been used for ages. Note that there is now another option in this area— the transfer on death deed (TODD), explained below.

One more item relating to timing—the doctrine of "after-acquired title." If I give you a deed today to property that I do not yet own, it of course has no effect; but if I acquire that same property next week, then the deed I gave you comes to life and the property is yours.

Lost Deeds

A good reason for recording a deed is to preserve evidence of the transfer in the event the original document cannot be located. What happens when an unrecorded deed is lost or destroyed? "A deed or other document is not made ineffective by its destruction or loss. . . . Production of the original document is excused when it is established that the document has been lost or destroyed. . . . Other evidence of the contents of a writing is admissible if the original has been lost or destroyed. . . . Loss or destruction of the document is established by proof of search for this document and inability to find it." *Gause v. Gause*, 496 S.W.3d 913 (Tex.App.—Austin, 2016, no pet.).

Must deeds show the actual purchase price?

No. In fact, in Texas, it is customary to recite that the consideration paid is "ten dollars and other valuable consideration." Why? Confidentiality. While recording gives the public notice that a transaction has occurred, and therefore preserves the integrity of the chain of title, it is Texas tradition that it is not the public's business what the purchase price was. Of course, the parties can always choose to show the actual price if they wish.

Who signs the deed?

A recordable deed must be signed and acknowledged before a notary by the seller. The buyer's signature is not usually required, but it may be advisable to include it if the deed contains specific agreements on the part of the buyer. In order for these to be clear and enforceable in contract, they should be set out in the deed and the buyer should also execute the deed before a notary.

Sale of Property Subject to Existing Indebtedness

Can title to property be transferred if money is owed to a lender? Yes. Title and debt are different and divisible concepts.

A "subject to" deed refers to acquiring title to property while expressly providing that the buyer assumes no liability for existing debts and liens. It is a common device used by investors in order to buy property, fix it, and then flip it for a profit, all without promising to pay the existing debt or taking any liability for it.

The sub2 concept may be better understood by reading the following sample sub2 deed clause: "This conveyance is made subject to any and all indebtedness of Grantor and liens against the Property, including but not limited to that certain indebtedness and liens securing same evidenced by a note in the original principal amount of $\_\_\_\_\_$, dated _____, executed by Grantor and payable to the order of ___, which note is secured by a vendor's lien retained in deed of even date recorded at Clerk's File No. ___ in the Official Public Records of Real Property of _____ County, Texas, and is additionally secured by a deed of trust of even date to ___, Trustee, recorded at Clerk's File No. ___ in the Official Public Records of Real Property of _____ County, Texas. Grantee does not assume payment of this or any other indebtedness of Grantor."

Refer to chapter 18 which goes into detail on "subject to" transactions.

Sale of Property "As Is"

A grantor may be willing to sell only on an "as is" basis. In such a case, "as is" refers to the condition of the property rather than the condition of the title. In other words, an "as is" deed may also be a warranty deed. The two are not mutually exclusive. Express and implied warranties of title may be and usually are present; however, there are no warranties made in an "as is" deed as to the state or condition of the land or any improvements upon it.

Does the presence of an "as is" clause negate any duty on the part of the seller to disclose defects? The answer will almost always be *no*. Read chapter 2 on seller disclosure where "as is" transactions are discussed at length.

Note that a grantor may wish to sell and convey property by means of a deed without warranties, which is the effective equivalent of an "as is" clause in the context of title. If this is the objective of the parties, a deed without warranties is almost always a better choice than a quitclaim.

Additional Deed Clauses Reflecting Agreements between the Parties

Some lawyers take the view that a deed should be a pure conveyance, uncluttered by clauses and agreements that do not bear directly upon the transfer of title or warranties made by the grantor. The result of this approach is often to necessitate the preparation of one or more companion documents designed to contain additional items that have been agreed to between the parties. In other words, two or more documents are required rather than one. This may have value when the parties' side agreements are confidential (not to be reflected in the public record), but otherwise it may be simpler and more direct to include such agreements in a single comprehensive document. Both grantor and grantee then sign and acknowledge the deed, making it a contract as well as a conveyance.

An example would be the sale of a rental property from one investor to another. In this scenario it would helpful to include certain assignments in the deed – e.g., assigning the escrow account, any transferrable warranties, and so forth to the grantee. Such a clause might look like this:

> Grantor irrevocably, absolutely, and unconditionally grants, transfers, and assigns to Grantee, Grantee's heirs and assigns, all of Grantor's interest in and to the following: (1) all funds, if any, held in escrow by any lender for the purpose of paying taxes, insurance, association dues, assessments, and other charges arising from or relating to the use and occupancy of the Property; (2) all policies of casualty insurance pertaining to the Property including Grantor's interest in and to any payments made or to be made pursuant to said policies; (3) all warranties and guaranties pertaining to the Property and the improvements, including but not limited to warranties on the structure(s) generally, the foundation, the roof, the HVAC system, appliances, and pest control, to the extent that same are in force and assignable; (4) all funds on deposit, if any, with utility providers to the Property; (5) all contracts and agreements relating to the upkeep, repair, maintenance, and operation of the Property including any structures and improvements thereon; (6) all uncollected and unpaid rents deriving from the Property, if any, whether past due, currently due, or to fall due in the future; (7) existing leases, if any, arising from or relating to use and

occupancy of the Property, whether written or unwritten, pursuant to which Grantor is landlord (the "Leases"); and (8) all funds held as security deposit(s), if any, arising from or relating to the Leases. In connection with the foregoing assignments, and to effectuate same, Grantor gives and grants to Grantee a special power of attorney to receive, endorse, and deposit to its own account any checks, proceeds, disbursements, or refunds which arise from the assignments and relate to the Property. These assignments are made without representation, warranty, or recourse, and are made only to the extent that assignment of the foregoing items is lawful and consistent with existing contractual obligations and commitments of Grantor.

The following are general categories of deed types that are likely to be encountered by a Texas real estate investor:

General Warranty Deed

The term "warranty deed" refers to a deed that contains both express and implied warranties (There is also a deed without warranties, discussed below.) A general warranty deed is the preferred form of deed for a buyer because it expressly warrants the *entire* chain of title all the way back to the sovereign, and it binds the grantor to defend against title defects, even if those defects were created prior to the grantor's period of ownership.

Here is a sample general warranty clause: "Grantor binds Grantor and Grantor's heirs, executors, administrators, successors and assigns to warrant and forever defend all and singular the Property to Grantee and Grantee's heirs, executors, administrators, successors, and assigns against every person whomsoever lawfully claiming or to claim the same or any part thereof, except as to the Reservations from Conveyance and the Exceptions to Conveyance and Warranty."

General warranty deeds predominate in sales of residential property.

Special Warranty Deed

In a special warranty deed, title is warranted *only* from the grantor and no further back than that. The grantor's liability for title defects is therefore limited to his period of ownership up to and including conveyance to the grantee. Example: "Grantor binds Grantor and Grantor's heirs, executors, administrators, successors and assigns to warrant and forever defend all and singular the Property to Grantee and

Grantee's heirs, executors, administrators, successors, and assigns against every person whomsoever lawfully claiming or to claim the same or any part thereof, when the claim is by, through, or under Grantor, but not otherwise, except as to the Reservations from Conveyance and the Exceptions to Conveyance and Warranty."

Commercial properties are typically conveyed by special warranty deed. Deeds into an investor's LLC may be either with general or special warranty, depending on the circumstances. There is usually no reason not to use a general warranty deed for this purpose if the property is residential.

Deed Without Warranties

A deed without warranties is just that—a conveyance of real property without warranties, express or implied, as to any matters whatsoever. If one is the seller, then one cannot be too careful in assuring that all warranties are excluded. This is a sample no-warranties conveyance clause: "Grantor, for the consideration and subject to the Reservations from Conveyance and Exceptions to Conveyance and Warranty, grants, sells, and conveys to Grantee the Property, together with all and singular the rights and appurtenances thereto in any way belonging, to have and to hold it to Grantee and Grantee's heirs, executors, administrators, successors, and assigns forever, without express or implied warranty. All covenants and warranties that might arise by common law as well as the statutory implied covenants contained in Section 5.023 of the Texas Property Code are excluded and disclaimed."

Why would anyone make or accept such a conveyance? The usual case is when the parties are unsure as to the extent of the grantor's interest, and/or if the grantor is willing to enter into the conveyance only on the condition that there is no liability for doing so. A deed without warranties may transfer the entire interest in a certain property, or it may not. The parties assume the risk of this uncertainty. A deed without warranties is therefore considered a lower form of deed, but it nevertheless is effective in transferring title. As a form of transfer, it is certainly superior to a quitclaim, discussed next.

Quitclaims

Clients often call a lawyer's office and say they need a quitclaim deed. The lawyer's response should almost always be "No, you don't." Why? For one reason, a quitclaim is not a true deed at all since it is technically not a conveyance. It merely "quits" any "claim" by Grantor to any right, title, and interest that the grantor may have in a certain property, if any such interest exists. It does not "grant, sell, and convey" as does a deed. *Rogers v. Ricane Enterprises*, 884 S.W.2d 763, 769 (Tex. 1994). Secondly, from a practical standpoint, title companies disdain quitclaims and will frequently require that a proper deed be obtained instead. One does no favor to the chain of title by inserting a quitclaim into it. If the seller is unwilling to provide a conveyance with warranties, then a knowledgeable buyer should insist on a deed without warranties instead of a quitclaim.

A quitclaim contains no covenant of seisen or warranty of title. *Jackson v. Wildflower Prod. Co., Inc.*, 505 S.W.3d 80, 90 (Tex.App.—Amarillo 2016, pet. denied).

Assumption Deed

Assumption deeds are general or special warranty deeds of the usual type. The difference is that assumption deeds expressly provide, as part of the consideration, that the grantee will assume liability for existing indebtedness and promise to discharge one or more existing liens against the property. The consideration clause in an assumption deed might read as follows:

> "Ten dollars ($10.00) and other valuable consideration, the receipt and value of which is hereby acknowledged, including Grantee's assumption of and promise to pay, according to its terms, all principal and interest remaining unpaid on that certain note (the "Assumed Note") in the original principal amount of $____, dated _____, executed by_____ and payable to the order of ____ (said payee together with its successors and assigns being referred to herein as "Lender"), subsequently assigned to and now held by ___. The Assumed Note is secured by an express vendor's lien and superior title retained in deed of even date recorded at Clerk's File No. ___ in the Official Public Records of Real Property of_____ County, Texas, and is additionally secured by a deed of trust of even date (the "Deed of Trust") in favor of ___, Trustee, recorded at Clerk's File No. ___ in the Official Public Records of Real Property of _____ County, Texas. As further consideration, Grantee promises to keep and perform all of the covenants and obligations of the Grantor contained in the Assumed Note and the Deed of Trust and to indemnify, defend, and hold Grantor harmless from any loss, attorney's fees, expenses, or claims attributable to a breach or default of any provision of this assumption by Grantee. Grantee shall

commence payments on the Assumed Note on or before the next regular due date under the Assumed Note."

Again, separate the concept of *title* from the concept of *debt.* They are related but different, and they can be divided, at least when discussing respective obligations of grantor and grantee. One can take title to property without becoming liable to pay the underlying debt. Of course, debts secured by liens against the property remain in place even if title is transferred.

Under an assumption deed the grantee declares his assumption obligation to the grantor—but, it should be pointed out, *not* to the lender, since the grantee has not signed the lender's note. Similarly, the grantor has not been released from the existing note unless the lender has approved the assumption and expressly released the grantor in writing, which is so rare as to be nearly non-existent. As a practical matter, expect a release only in response to full payment.

An assumption deed may be accompanied by a deed of trust to secure assumption which enables the grantor to step in and make payments if the seller discovers that the buyer has failed to do so. The seller may then recover these "advancements" from the buyer. This enables the seller to proactively mitigate loss and preserve good credit. If reimbursement for advancements is not made, foreclosure may follow.

Can assumptions occur without the lender's consent? Yes, and they often do, in spite of the due-on-sale clause contained in paragraph 18 of the widely-used FNMA deed of trust, which gives the lender the option (but not the obligation) to accelerate the note in such cases. See chapter 20 on this subject.

Deed in a Wraparound Transaction

A wraparound transaction is a form of creative seller financing that leaves the original loan and lien on the property in place when the property is sold. The buyer makes a down payment and signs a new note to the seller (the "wraparound note") for the balance of the sales price. This wrap note, secured by a new deed of trust (the "wraparound deed of trust"), becomes a junior (subordinate) lien on the property. The buyer makes monthly payments to the seller on the wrap note and the seller in turn makes payments to the original lender. The original lender's note is referred to as the "wrapped note," and it remains secured by the "wrapped deed of trust." The buyer receives a warranty deed (general or special) which transfers title to the property into the buyer's name.

The consideration clause in a wraparound deed reads something like this: "Ten dollars ($10.00) and other valuable consideration, including execution of a note (the "Wraparound Note") of even date in the principal amount of $___, executed by Grantee, and payable to the order of Grantor. The Wraparound Note is secured by a vendor's lien retained in this General Warranty Deed and by a Wraparound Deed of Trust of even date from Grantee to ___, Trustee."

Lots of details need to be addressed, so a wraparound agreement should accompany the warranty deed and other wrap documents. Unlike the deed, the wraparound agreement is not recorded, so deal points that are confidential can be discussed there.

Trustee's Deed or Foreclosure Deed

A trustee's deed is delivered by a lender's trustee to the successful bidder at a foreclosure sale. The lender often bids the amount of the debt (plus accrued fees and costs) and acquires the property in this way. If the sale generates proceeds in excess of the debt, the trustee must distribute the excess funds to other lienholders in order of seniority and the remaining balance, if any, to the borrower.

Property Code Section 51.009 states that a buyer at a foreclosure sale "acquires the foreclosed property 'as is' without any expressed or implied warranties, except as to warranties of title, and at the purchaser's own risk; and is not a consumer." It is also certain that the trustee's deed itself will contain its own disclaimer along the following lines:

THE PROPERTY IS CONVEYED BY THE TRUSTEE AND ACCEPTED BY GRANTEE "AS IS," IN ITS PRESENT PHYSICAL CONDITION, WITH ALL FAULTS AND DEFECTS, LATENT OR PATENT, KNOWN OR UNKNOWN. THE TRUSTEE MAKES NO REPRESENTATIONS OR WARRANTIES, EXPRESS OR IMPLIED, ORAL OR WRITTEN, AS TO TITLE, POSSESSION, QUIET ENJOYMENT, MERCHANTABILITY, MARKETABILITY, USABILITY, HABITABILITY, FITNESS OR SUITABILITY FOR ANY PARTICULAR PURPOSE, OR ENVIRONMENTAL CONDITION OF THE PROPERTY OR AS TO ANY OTHER MATTER RELATING TO THE PROPERTY. IMPLIED WARRANTIES AND ORAL STATEMENTS ARE EXPRESSLY DISCLAIMED AND EXCLUDED. THE TRUSTEE SPECIFICALLY DISCLAIMS THE VERBAL OR WRITTEN STATEMENTS OR INFORMATION INCLUDING REPRESENTATIONS AND WARRANTIES THAT MAY HAVE BEEN MADE OR PROVIDED BY AGENTS, BROKERS, INVESTORS, OR OTHER THIRD PARTIES.

Even with these limitations, a foreclosure deed is probably the cleanest title obtainable, though it does not eliminate taxes owed.

Deed Incident to Divorce

A divorce deed is typically a special warranty deed that contains a clause similar to the following: "Consideration for this transaction is the division of property pursuant to a Final Decree of Divorce dated ___ entered in Cause No. ___, IN THE MATTER OF THE MARRIAGE OF _____AND _____, in the ___ District Court of _____ County, Texas."

The deed may also include an "owelty of partition" that creates a lien in favor of the grantor to secure payment of a certain sum from the other spouse. This is used to equalize the overall division of property.

The parties to a divorce should not rely on the final decree to transfer title to real property. A special warranty deed (often accompanied by a deed of trust to secure assumption) should be executed and recorded. Family lawyers not infrequently forget to do this.

Transfer on Death Deed (TODD)

In 2015 Texas joined more than 25 other states in allowing a transfer on death deed (TODD), which is an uncomplicated, non-probate method of transferring title to real estate when the owner dies. The Texas Real Property Transfer on Death Act is found in Estates Code Chapter 114. Section 114.051 states that "An individual may transfer the individual's interest in real property to one or more beneficiaries effective at the transferor's death by a transfer on death deed. . . ." Moreover, a transfer on death deed is effective without consideration and without notice or delivery to or acceptance by the designated beneficiary during the life of the grantor (Sec. 114.056). All in all, a good basic estate planning device.

The instrument must be recorded and must otherwise comply with the usual legal formalities of a deed. A TODD cannot be revoked by a last will and testament but can be revoked by a recorded revocation. In fact, a TODD is revocable (by statute) even if the instrument states otherwise. Also, if the grantor sells the property by means of a recorded transfer subsequent to executing a TODD, then the TODD is automatically revoked: "If a transferor during the transferor's lifetime conveys to any person all of the transferor's interest in real property that is the subject of a transfer on death deed, the transfer on death deed is void as to that interest in real property" (Sec. 114.102).

Can a living trust be a "person" for purposes of being a beneficiary of a TODD? Yes, since in this context the term person has the meaning assigned by Government Code Section 31.005. In most situations, however, it would make more sense just to convey the property into the living trust contemporaneously, without waiting for the death of the grantor. Take a look at chapter 22 for more details on living trusts.

The TODD effectively replaces the former use of "Lady Bird Deeds" which are revocable deeds retaining a life estate. LBDs were designed to avoid recovery against the grantor's probate estate by Medicaid pursuant to the Texas Medicaid Recovery Program. This issue is clearly addressed by Sec. 114.106(b) which provides that real property transferred by means of a TODD is not considered to be a part of the grantor's estate. Texas law thus pushes back against the federal government's tendency to reach all of one's assets in exchange for its beneficence.

For those attempting to do some basic estate planning, it is possible to combine joint ownership with a TODD, so that (for example) parents now have an inexpensive alternative method to pass real property to a child upon the death of the last parent.

Deed in Lieu of Foreclosure (DIL)

A traditional deed in lieu of foreclosure is a specialized instrument designed to transfer property to a lender in satisfaction of a debt and in exchange for a full and complete release. The clauses contained in DILs can be quite technical. They begin with a general statement such as "This Deed is executed and delivered by Grantor and accepted by Grantee in lieu of Grantee demanding and collecting the Indebtedness and in lieu of the necessity for Grantee to give notice of default, notice of intent to accelerate, notice of acceleration, notice of posting for foreclosure, and conduct of a foreclosure sale of the Property." Much additional verbiage is then added.

Few institutional lenders today accept DILs as a means of avoiding foreclosure. The reason is that the foreclosure process itself is usually advantageous to the lender since it cleans up title by eliminating junior liens and clearly establishes a deficiency amount (the difference between the price at foreclosure and the balance on the note) for which the lender can then sue the borrower. Under certain circumstances, however, it may be useful to consider a unilateral DIL (i.e., without the lender's consent). Read chapter 10, *Deeding Property to the Lender*.

Correction Instrument under Property Code Sec. 5.027

The Texas Supreme Court case of *Myrad Properties, Inc. v. LaSalle Bank N.A.*, 300 S.W.3d 746 (Tex. 2009), provided guidelines for what would be considered "correctable," including errors in a metes and bounds description or an erroneous description of a party's capacity. According to the court, other more substantive items (adding or deleting a parcel, for instance) could not be cured by a correction instrument. This case prompted the Texas legislature to enact Property Code Sections 5.027 et seq., which add considerably more detail and differentiate between material and non-material corrections.

Instruments of this type used to be loosely referred to as "correction deeds." Under Property Code Section 5.027 et seq., a correction deed is now more properly called a "correction instrument." It may take a form similar to the old correction deed or it may be in the form of an affidavit that recites the correction. Either way, a correction instrument is a supplementary filing that relates back in time to an original deed that contained some error or mutual mistake. It corrects the mistake but leaves other terms of the conveyance intact. No new consideration is required.

The first step is to make sure one is looking at an instrument of conveyance (e.g., a warranty deed, not an affidavit or the like). The second step is to examine the instrument and determine if the error is non-material or material. Section 5.028 deals with correction instruments that make non-material corrections to instruments of conveyance—the classic scrivener's error, in other words. Perhaps a distance or an angle in the legal description was misstated, or the name of a party misspelled. A person with personal knowledge of the facts may execute this type of correction instrument without joinder of others, but a copy of the correction instrument must be sent to each party to the original instrument.

Material corrections are a more serious issue and are addressed by Section 5.029. Examples are the conveyance in the original instrument of the wrong property (lot 5 instead of lot 6 for example) or conveyance of property to the wrong entity. A correction instrument effecting a material correction such as these must be executed by each party to the original recorded instrument.

It is the better policy in practice to have any correction instrument executed by all parties.

Correction instruments are appropriate for addressing errors only. If the parties intend to alter fundamental terms of the original conveyance, then a new instrument—*not* a correction instrument—is required.

Statute of Limitations in Deed Correction and Reformation Cases

The usual four-year statute of limitations for written documents commences on the date the deed is signed and delivered, or when a claimant discovers, or through the exercise of ordinary diligence, should have discovered the alleged error or defect (the discovery rule). There is, however, a rebuttable presumption that the respective parties know the contents of the deed at the time of closing, particularly if clearly stated, since it is the basic due diligence obligation of nearly everyone to read a document before signing or receiving it at a real estate closing. *Trahan v. Mettlen*, 428 S.W.3d 905 (Tex.App.—Texarkana 2014, no pet.). Waiting to take action does not work to the benefit of the plaintiff. In *Jarzombek v. Ramsey* (534 S.W.3d 534 (Tex.App.—San Antonio [4th Dist.] 2017, pet. denied), the court declined to reform a deed seven years after closing, stating that the discovery rule is not intended to extend the statute of limitations for the purpose of correcting conspicuous and plainly-evident mistakes.

Deeds Involving Co-Ownership

This topic has already been extensively covered. The primary point to remember is that co-ownership in Texas is presumed to be as tenants-in-common, meaning that heirs of each owner will inherit that owner's respective interest upon death. The decedent's interest (likely) passes vertically. This is contrasted with JTWROS which provides that a co-owner will inherit the other co-owner's interest upon death—a horizontal transfer. JTWROS must be expressly created by specific wording when the property is acquired and a written agreement must be signed by both parties (Est. Code Sec. 111.001(a) and 112.051). Married buyers should consider taking title as JTWROS as basic estate planning. We suggest reading chapter 7 for more detail on JTWROS and the requirements for implementing it.

Deeds with Life Estate Reserved

It is possible that an investor may encounter a situation where an older person is willing to sell but wishes to retain the right to reside in the property until his or her death. This may be an excellent investment if the property is likely to appreciate. A deed with life estate reserved should contain wording substantially similar to the following: "Grantor reserves, for Grantor and Grantor's assigns, a legal life estate in and to the Property for the remainder of Grantor's life, including rights to full possession, benefit, use, rents, revenues, and profits of and from the Property, until the death of Grantor (the "Life Estate") at which time full legal and equitable title to the Property shall automatically vest in Grantee, free of any interest of Grantor, Grantor's successor, heirs, and/or assigns. Grantor shall have the right to reside in the Property without rent or charge during the Life Estate."

Fraudulent Deeds

A fraudulent deed is a void deed, but action must generally be taken in order to establish that the deed is fraudulent. It does not happen automatically, merely upon allegation. Section 51.901 of the Government Code requires a county clerk to act if there is "a reasonable basis to believe in good faith that document or instrument previously filed or recorded or offered or submitted for filing or for recording is fraudulent." One way to trigger such action is for an aggrieved party to file an affidavit which includes the property's legal description, send a copy of the affidavit to the perpetrating party, and demand that the fraudulent deed be canceled. If this strategy is unsuccessful, a suit alleging fraud (both common-law fraud and statutory fraud under Business & Commerce Code Section 27.01) and requesting rescission and a declaratory judgment should be filed.

Note also that Civil Practice & Remedies Code Section 12.002 provides that a person who knowingly and intentionally files a fraudulent lien or claim against real property may be held liable in civil district court for the greater of $10,000 or actual damages, exemplary damages, and recovery of attorney's fees and costs.

Deeds and the Earnest Money Contract

The variety of deeds along with the choice of different clauses that can affect the conveyance and alter the liability of the parties make it advisable to a consult a real estate attorney, and do it early in the process. If an investor seller knows in advance that certain wording will be required in a deed (an "as is" clause, for example) then a provision to that effect should be expressly included in a special provisions addendum to the earnest money contract. Otherwise, the wording of the "as is" clause (or any other custom clause) may become a matter of last-minute negotiations with potential to cause the closing to fail.

What the Attorney Needs from the Client

When a client needs a deed prepared, the existing warranty deed to the property should be provided to the attorney along with a copy of the sales contract and relevant names and addresses. And, since Texas is a community property state, the client should supply the marital status of the parties and the names of spouses. The client should also tell the attorney if there will be any exceptions or reservations from the conveyance (e.g., mineral interests). If the property will be deeded into a series LLC, then the attorney will need to know which series (Series A or B, etc.), since the specific series should be stated as grantee. And, as referenced above, the attorney will need to know if the proposed deed should be drafted to include special provisions, disclosures, disclaimers, or conditions that would make the signature of both grantor and grantee advisable.

Chapter 9

DEEDING PROPERTY TO AN LLC

An Essential Step in Asset Protection

A primary purpose of an LLC, whether a traditional LLC or a series company, is to provide protection from personal liability for its members. For this reason, any property that could potentially generate a lawsuit or other liability, especially investment and rental property, should be held in the name of an LLC—*not* in a personal name and preferably *not* reflecting personal information such as the homestead address.

Ideally, property ownership should reside in a dedicated holding company while management functions (entering into contracts, collecting rent, payment of expenses, and the like) are performed by a separate, shell management LLC. This accomplishes separation of assets from activities, a core principle of asset protection derived from the legal concept of privity.

General Theory of Asset Protection

A sound asset protection structure (1) creates barriers to personal liability with one or more LLCs, at least one of which should be a series company if multiple properties or assets are involved (we prefer Texas and Nevada, two top asset protection states with similar statutes); (2) maximizes anonymity in the public records; (3) utilizes homestead protections afforded individuals by the Texas Constitution and Property Code; (4) deters lawsuits and judgment creditors; and, (5) in the event of suit, exhausts their determination and resources. Planning ahead is critical, particularly in the context of property ownership, since the range and benefit of asset protection measures decrease significantly after suit is threatened or filed.

Deeding Property to an Investor's LLC

If possible, rental or investment property should be acquired directly in the name of an investor's LLC. In a two-company structure, the optimum plan would be to acquire properties in the name of the management company and then, after closing and rehab, transfer them into individual series of the holding company (i.e., each property in its own series). Lenders, however, often require that an investor take title to the property in his or her personal name for underwriting reasons. If that is the case, property should nonetheless be moved *without delay* into the investor's series holding LLC after closing.

The series LLC is now the holding vehicle of choice for many real estate investors. Unlike a traditional LLC (which owns its assets in a single pool) a series company permits the LLC to hold multiple properties in separate, insulated compartments—Series A, Series B, and so forth. The assets and liabilities of each series are confined to that series only and are segregated from the assets and liabilities of other series. So if there is a lawsuit or a foreclosure that affects property in Series A, then other series (Series B, Series C, and so forth) *are not affected or liable for the outcome.*

The Series LLC as Grantee

The power of a series to hold title to property is expressly granted by Business Organizations Code Section 101.605(3). When deeding property into a series, the deed should specifically reflect which series the property is going into—for example, "ABC LLC—Series A." Failure to do this will result in the property being acquired as an asset of the company at large, thereby losing series insulation and protection.

Care should be taken to correctly show the name of the LLC. For example, if the name of the company as shown on the Secretary of State's Certificate of Filing is "Alamo Investments LLC," then listing "Alamo Investments, L.L.C." as grantee would be incorrect, since the addition of a comma and three periods means that this is a different company name. The same is true of capitalizations that do not correspond exactly to the official name. Think of it this way: the name of a registered entity as shown on the certificate of filing is like a screenshot; it must appear *exactly that way* on a deed in order to avoid the possible necessity of filing a correction instrument later.

Similar issues arise when designating a particular series of a series LLC as grantee. This must be done correctly in order to convey the property as intended and avoid a correction instrument. Firstly, the company name must conform exactly to the certificate of filing as discussed in the previous paragraph; secondly, the series must be clearly and correctly indicated. The company agreement may establish the naming regime for series in any way that is reasonable, but series are most commonly alphabetical (Series A, B, C, etc.) or numerical (Series 1, 2, 3, etc.). It is also possible to name a series after the property that it contains, such as the "Oak Street Series." But this is problematic; what happens if the LLC sells the Oak Street property? Is action then necessary to change the series name so it can accommodate a new property with a different address? Clearly, it is more practical to list the series in the form of letters or numbers.

Although series LLCs have been in use in Texas since 2009, one still sees errors in how series are reflected as the grantee on a deed. If Alamo Investments LLC is a series company, and the intention is to convey property into series A, then the correct formulation would be "Alamo Investments LLC—Series A, a series of a Texas series limited liability company." A common miswording would be "Alamo Investments—Series A LLC," which is incorrect. A series is *not* an LLC and should not have these letters after its name.

What happens if Alamo is a series company but no series is indicated on the deed—i.e., the conveyance is into "Alamo Investments LLC" with no mention of a series? In that case, the property is conveyed into the company at large and *not* into an individual series of Alamo. Series LLCs can own property both ways. Of course, transferring property into the company at large defeats the purpose of having a series LLC in the first place, so this usually indicates that an error has been made.

Due-on-Sale Issues

Will the lender call the note due if the property is transferred into an investor's LLC? There are two points to note on this subject. First, the standard due-on-sale clause contained in the Fannie Mae deed of trust *prohibits nothing*; it merely gives a lender the option to accelerate a note if a transfer of title occurs, so it is *not* correct to say that such a transfer "violates" or "breaches" the due-on-sale clause. Lenders may choose whether or not to act under this clause—that is all.

Second, lenders seldom act when property with a performing loan is transferred into the borrower's personal company and in any case they are far more concerned with loans that are in monetary (rather than technical) default—although, as pointed out, transferring title is *not* a default, not even a technical one. Some lenders will send a threatening letter, but little will likely come of it so long as the note remains current.

What should be done with the homestead?

It is neither necessary nor advisable to transfer a homestead into an LLC that holds investment properties. As a general rule, homestead-exempt assets should be kept separate from investment assets. Why? First, the homestead is already protected by the Texas Constitution and Property Code against forced sale or execution upon a judgment. Second, mixing the homestead with investment assets that are prone to incur liability and lawsuits is just not a good idea. The homestead should be kept out of the line of fire.

Our recommendation is to transfer the homestead into a living trust (also called an inter vivos trust). Trusts do not provide a liability barrier, but this is not a problem because the homestead is already protected. What the living trust accomplishes is probate avoidance (since the trust cannot die), providing for automatic transfer of the beneficial interest in the property without delay or expense. Even considering that Texas has expedited probate procedures, this is a real benefit. There is nothing to lose and everything to gain from using such an arrangement. A pour-over will should be executed along with the living trust to complete the picture.

General Warranty Deeds Versus Special Warranty Deeds

Deeds into an LLC may be made by deed with either general or special warranties, depending on the situation. In most cases, there is no reason for an investor not to use a general warranty deed when conveying property into a personal company. Under no circumstances, however, should a quitclaim be used, since these can create problems with the chain of title. If one is determined to avoid warranties, use a deed without warranties rather than a quitclaim.

Assumption or Subject to?

Most investment properties have at least a first-lien with outstanding debt. What should be said about this when deeding the property into an investor's LLC? The choice has both legal and accounting implications. If nothing is mentioned about the debt, then the result by default is that the property has been conveyed subject to the debt. But it is important to be deliberate and intentional in drafting real estate documents, so the better practice is to expressly state whether the LLC will be assuming the existing indebtedness or taking the property "subject to."

Other Clauses in the Deed

It is also advisable to include an "as is" clause in the deed—in bold and in all caps. This should be routine for all business transactions in which an investor is the seller, even if the transfer is being made into one's own company. If the property is rented it may also be appropriate to assign the escrow account, the seller's interest in the casualty insurance policy, and the tenant's security deposit to the LLC. If so, assignment clauses should be included addressing these issues.

For married investors, it is the preferred practice for both spouses to sign the deed into an LLC, since Texas is a community property state. If that is not done, it is possible that a future title company will ask for a marital status affidavit, non-homestead affidavit, or even a spousal signature—which could be awkward if the marriage is no longer solvent.

Transfers Made for the Purpose of Defrauding Creditors

It is preferable to transfer assets into an LLC *before* trouble arises. Otherwise the usefulness of doing so may be limited by rules against fraudulent transfers that reach back up to two years. Such transfers are generally indicated by so-called "badges of fraud" including:

1) transfers to a family member;

2) whether or not suit was threatened before the transfer occurred;

3) whether the transfer was of substantially all of the person's assets;

4) whether assets have been removed, undisclosed, or concealed;

5) whether there was reasonably equivalent consideration for the transfer; or

6) whether or not, after the transfer, the transferor became insolvent as a result (made his cash disappear).

Texas law recognizes that life goes on, even after a lawsuit is threatened or filed. Even, in fact, after a judgment. People still buy and sell assets, move residences, and so forth in the ordinary course of life and business, and this is allowed. What is not permitted (and what is subject to being set aside by a court) is the making of such transfers for the blatant purpose of assuring that a judgment creditor does not get paid. Fortunately, the transfer of an investment property into an investor's LLC for purposes of asset protection is so sensible and routine that it should be relatively easy to justify in the event of a challenge.

Chapter 10

DEEDING PROPERTY TO THE LENDER

The Merits of Strategic Default and Transfer

Foreclosure is the involuntary transfer of property from a borrower, usually to the lender. But what about relinquishing property voluntarily and unilaterally? Since a lender cannot be forced to foreclose (and some lenders drag their feet) an option may be for the owner to unilaterally deed the property to the lender and walk away. It may be more cost-effective to let an underwater or underperforming property go and instead direct resources to profitable investments, a cheaper housing alternative, or toward paying off homestead-exempt assets.

Effects of Foreclosure

So what are the potential benefits of a unilateral DIL? To answer, one must consider the alternative and examine the negative after-effects of foreclosure. These include adverse credit impact for seven or more years; the potential for a deficiency lawsuit by the lender; and the prospect that the IRS will deem the deficiency amount to be ordinary income taxable to the borrower. That could be a whopping number (deficiencies in the $100,000 range are not uncommon) and the borrower must take that amount as ordinary income all in one year. For an investor, the IRS consequences may be the worst aspect of the foreclosure process.

In 2008 Congress made homestead deficiencies exempt from the IRS deemed-income problem, but that does not help investors who may be looking at numerous underwater investment properties.

Effects of *Non*-foreclosure: Zombie Titles

Surprisingly, a significant percentage of banks are choosing *not* to foreclose after borrowers default. Why? These lenders have considered the negative factors involved in taking foreclosed properties into inventory (maintenance and insurance costs, carry time, etc.) and decided that it is more financially favorable to sell the defaulted note to a collector and write off the loss. These lenders walk away, effectively dumping the abandoned property onto the local municipality. The nightmare result for the homeowner (who was under the impression from lender notices that a foreclosure was imminent) is that he or she is relentlessly pursued by a third-party collector who now owns the note, by local taxing authorities seeking unpaid ad valorem taxes, and by cities and homeowners associations who either sue or impose liens for trash removal, health and safety code violations, and demolition. After all, since the lender decided not to go through with the foreclosure sale, the homeowner *still owns title* and is therefore responsible for the property. In this scenario, the best option may be a unilateral DIL to the lender enabling the borrower to assert non-ownership of the property as a defense against circling vultures.

What is a deed in lieu of foreclosure?

Executing and delivering a deed from the owner of real property to the lender-lienholder has traditionally occurred in the context of a bilateral DIL, which is designed to transfer property to the lender in satisfaction of the debt and in exchange for a release of lien. The customary DIL occurs when both parties expressly consent to the mutual benefits of this arrangement. *Morission v. Christie*, 266 S.W.3d 89 Tex.App.—Ft. Worth 2008, no pet.). The problem is that few lenders nowadays will agree to accept a DIL and give a release in exchange. They would rather use the foreclosure process to wipe out junior liens and acquire a deficiency judgment, which then appears as an asset on the lender's books. So a traditional, bilateral DIL is often not an available option.

This chapter examines the benefit to deeding property to the lender *anyway*—even if the lender has not expressly agreed to discharge and release the debt in exchange. What happens if a borrower executes a unilateral DIL, records it, and then sends a copy to the lender saying "Here, the property is yours now, and by the way, I consider the debt paid in full?"

Conveyance to the Noteholder

A DIL should convey the property to the current owner and holder of the note. This can be confusing, since ownership of the note is often split from the servicing function. In order to maximize the unilateral DIL strategy, the homeowner should deed the property to the actual holder of the note, not the servicer.

The 80-20 Problem

What if there are two liens against the property and two different lienholders? There is no perfect solution in such a case, but the most effective strategy is to give a DIL to the senior lienholder since it likely holds the largest debt. If one must choose, it makes sense to defend against the more significant threat, especially the possibility of IRS deemed income on a large deficiency.

Presumption of Acceptance

When a grantor transfers property, title to the property vests in the grantee upon execution and delivery of the deed. The grantee's acceptance is not usually indicated anywhere on the document. Acceptance is generally presumed. A showing that a deed was executed and delivered with an intent to convey the property is sufficient to establish that the deed vested title in the grantee. *Stephens County Museum, Inc. v. Swenson*, 17 S.W.2d 257, 261-62 (Tex. 1975). Proof that a deed was recorded creates a presumption of and establishes a prima facie case of delivery and intent by the grantor to convey the land. *Troxel v. Bishop*, 201 S.W.3d 290, 297 (Tex.App.—Dallas 2006, no pet.). Both cases are cited with approval in *Watson v. Tipton*, 274 S.W.3d 791 (Tex.App.—Fort Worth 2008, pet. denied).

Notwithstanding the foregoing, the weight of authority is that the presumption of acceptance does not apply if a title transfer is accomplished without the knowledge or agreement of the grantee. *Aguilar v. Sinton*, 501 S.W.3d 730 (Tex.App.—El Paso, 2016, pet. denied). This nonetheless leaves a lender who receives a unilateral DIL in a possibly hazardous position. If enough time goes by without action by the lender, is this still true? What if the lender, after receiving such a deed, takes possession or refrains from filing a foreclosure or a deficiency suit—might not this inaction be construed as implied agreement with the stated terms of the deed (i.e., discharge of the debt)? After all, courts widely recognize the concept of an implied agreement based on conduct of the parties.

Property Code Section 51.006

What sort of instrument must the lender file if it wishes to reject a deed? Property Code Section 51.006 may offer guidance. This statute "applies to a holder of a debt under a deed of trust who accepts from the debtor a deed conveying real property subject to the deed of trust in satisfaction of the debt." It expressly provides that a lender may record an affidavit voiding such a deed within four years if the grantor-debtor did not disclose liens of which the lender hand no personal knowledge. But this is narrowly focused. It applies only to this specific non-disclosure scenario.

The practical question is, if a lender already has a DIL in hand, will it expend time and money to formally reject it and proceed with foreclosure? Perhaps, perhaps not. Lenders vary in their response to this. Some (the minority) simply send the deed to their loss mitigation or REO department with instructions to list the property for sale and not bother with foreclosure. Others (the majority) continue with foreclosure in spite of having been given a DIL. Property Code Section 51.006 expressly permits that "[i]f a holder accepts a deed in lieu of foreclosure, the holder may foreclose its deed of trust as provided in said deed of trust without electing to void the deed."

Potential Benefits Even if There is a Foreclosure

Accordingly, it is unlikely that deeding property to an unwilling lender will result in avoidance of foreclosure. But even if foreclosure occurs, might there be other significant benefits to executing a DIL? Given the potentially severe effects of both foreclosure and non-foreclosure, does the borrower have anything to lose by giving this method a try?

The first effect—the effect on credit—will not be avoided by executing a unilateral DIL if the lender chooses to go ahead and conduct a foreclosure sale anyway. That much is clear.

The second effect—avoiding or defending against a deficiency suit—presents more interesting possibilities. Say that the DIL contains language reciting that it was being executed and delivered in satisfaction of the debt. If the lender sues for the deficiency but has never filed anything of record rejecting the deed, might not the borrower be able to assert the deed as a defense (an "accord and satisfaction")? Essentially, the borrower could argue that *no deficiency exists*. It would be a creative argument.

Similarly, if the IRS declares that the deficiency amount is ordinary income and then demands that tax be paid, the borrower could produce the DIL and declare that since the lender accepted it (or, more precisely, never rejected it) there is *no* deficiency and therefore *no* taxable income. Would this argument prevail? No cases yet. However, it certainly has a fighting chance, which is a good deal more than most taxpayers have in this circumstance.

Lastly, in a non-foreclosure scenario (where the lender threatens to foreclose but then does not), the former homeowner can use the DIL to defend against suits from third parties who are trying to collect taxes or enforce liens that have accumulated against a neglected property.

It goes without saying that a unilateral DIL must contain specific statements and recitals if it is to have any effect. A simple warranty deed to the lender will not do the job.

This Is *Not* Your Parents' Default

Texans are inclined by nature to honor their word and are reluctant to default on any obligation. However, consider that the world has changed; the top 1% of Americans now controls 80% of the wealth. The CEO of the bank holding the note you can no longer afford may be sitting on his yacht in the Bahamas, toasting his fellow Wall Streeters on their obscene new wealth—*unprecedented in human history*—and laughing at poor souls who continue to make payments on their underperforming properties.

Executing a unilateral DIL is not a perfect technique but it may have interesting and potentially rewarding benefits in certain limited cases. Even so, this strategy remains in the experimental category.

PART III

NOTEWORTHY
STATE & FEDERAL LAW

Chapter 11

EXECUTORY CONTRACTS IN TEXAS REAL ESTATE

A Snake Pit for Investors

Contracts for deed, lease-purchases, and lease-options have long been traditional tools of Texas residential real estate investors. Why? Because it was easy to induce tenant-buyers into such arrangements with a minimal down payment and easy to evict them using the forcible detainer process if they defaulted. No longer. Since 2005, these "executory contracts" are heavily regulated under Chapter 5 of the Property Code. Many requirements now apply, and the burden is on the seller to meet these. Also, the existing lender, if any, must give consent. Violation may entitle the purchaser to cancel and rescind the contract and receive a full refund of payments made to the seller. That is not all, since a claim may also be made under the Deceptive Trade Practices-Consumer Protection Act ("DTPA") which can result in treble damages plus attorney's fees. Add up the numbers and one can easily see that the potential downside is significant. Note that the statute contains *no significant defenses* for well-meaning sellers who thought they were giving the buyer a fair deal, even if the whole arrangement was the buyer's idea in the first place.

Accordingly, the risks to an investor of engaging in executory contracts have nearly eliminated their use in the residential context, at least as to contracts exceeding 180 days.

What exactly is an executory contract?

Executory contracts include any transaction that defers material action by either party that pertains to ownership or possession of real property into the future. Think of it this way: an executed contract is one that is fully performed at closing. It is done, finished. An executory contract, on the other hand, leaves something dangling—usually the most important item of all, the delivery of title (a deed) to the buyer. The classic executory contract is the contract for deed (or land sales contract), which provides that the buyer gets title after making payments over a period of years.

"In a typical real estate contract, the seller and purchaser mutually agree to complete payment and title transfer on a date certain, the closing date, at which time the purchaser generally obtains both title and possession. By contrast, in an executory contract, the purchaser is usually given immediate possession, but is required to satisfy numerous obligations over an extended period of time before the seller has an obligation to transfer title. Under an executory contract, the buyer has the right, but not the obligation, to purchase. . . . But, in a typical real estate contract, the buyer must complete the purchase." *Bryant v. Cady,* 445 S.W.3d 815, 822-23 (Tex.App.—Texarkana 2014, no pet.).

Contracts for deed, lease-purchases, and lease-options for longer than 180 days are unambiguously defined as executory contracts subject to Property Code Sections 5.061 et seq. Look closely at Section 5.062(a)(2): "An option to purchase real property that includes or is combined or executed concurrently with a residential lease agreement, together with the lease, is considered an executory contract for conveyance of real property." The "180 days or less" exemption exists as an accommodation to real estate brokers, because otherwise the TREC 1-4 contract could violate this provision when combined with a TREC temporary lease.

Options that are not combined with a residential lease as well as options on commercial property are *not* affected by Property Code Section 5.061.

Changes to the Investor Environment

Why does the Texas legislature continue to reform the law relating to executory contracts? In order to balance the equities. Executory contracts had traditionally given a tremendous advantage to the seller, who technically retained "legal title" to the property. The buyer, on the other hand, had only "equitable title"—a fuzzy concept that arises by operation of law and requires filing an expensive lawsuit to enforce. A buyer under financial pressure was therefore more likely to abandon the property, forfeit money paid, and move on. Unscrupulous sellers and investors used this situation to their advantage, disregarding buyers' equitable rights and representing to justices of the peace (the authority in eviction cases) that such buyers were ordinary tenants subject to ordinary leases. Evictions were obtained for minor or technical defaults and down payments were confiscated in the process, freeing the seller to move on to the next victim. The legislature rightly acted to stop such abuse.

Executory Contracts: Requirements for Validity

Make no mistake, one can still do a transaction by means of an executory contract, but many requirements now exist that did not apply before 2005. Property Code Sections 5.069 and 5.070 contain a number of these requirements, which must be met *before* the executory contract is signed by the purchaser (i.e., before and not at closing).

5.069(a)(1) requires that the seller provide the purchaser with a survey which is no older than a year, or a current plat. Subsection (a) also requires the seller to notify the buyer that there "are no restrictive covenants, easements, or other title exceptions or encumbrances that prohibit construction of a house on the property." An additional notice is required advising the buyer to "obtain a title abstract or title commitment covering the property and have the abstract or commitment reviewed by an attorney before signing a contract of this type, and purchase an owner's policy of title insurance covering the property."

5.069(a)(2) requires that the seller provide the purchaser with copies of liens, restrictive covenants, and easements affecting title to the property.

5.069(a)(3) requires that a statutory disclosure be given to the buyer addressing such pragmatic issues as whether or not the property is in a recorded subdivision; if water, sewer, and electric power are available; if the property is in a floodplain; who is responsible for maintaining the road to the property; and the like. An affirmative statement is required to the effect that no one but the seller owns or claims to own the property or have an interest therein.

5.069(b) states that if "the property is not located in a recorded subdivision, the seller shall provide the purchaser with a separate disclosure form stating that utilities may not be available to the property until the subdivision is recorded as required by law."

5.069(c) pertains to advertising the availability of an executory contract. It requires that the advertisement disclose information regarding the availability of water, sewer, and electric service.

5.070(a)(1) requires the seller to provide the purchaser with a tax certificate from the collector for each taxing unit that collects taxes due on the property.

5.070(a)(2) requires the seller to provide the purchaser with a copy of any insurance policy, binder, or evidence that indicates the name of the insurer and insured; a description of the insured property; and the policy amount.

Cancellation and Refund

What happens if the foregoing requirements are not met? First, failure to do so is defined by Section 5.069(d)(1) as a "false, misleading, or deceptive act or practice" pursuant to Section 17.46 of the DTPA; second, the purchaser is entitled under Property Code Section 5.069(d)(2) to "cancel and rescind the executory contract and receive a full refund of all payments made to the seller." That includes the down payment plus any money expended by the buyer on permanent improvements to the property. What about monthly payments? Not included. "While the buyer remains entitled to a 'full refund of all payments made to the seller,' cancellation and *rescission* of a contract also requires that the buyer restore to the seller the value of the buyer's occupation of the property." *Morton v. Nguyen*, 412 S.W.3d 506 (Tex. 2013).

Also, Property Code Section 5.074(a) entitles a purchaser to cancel an executory contract for any reason within 14 days of signing, even if all statutory requirements have been met.

Financial Disclosure Required

An additional pre-closing requirement is imposed by Property Code Section 5.071, which requires a seller to provide financial information similar to a RESPA disclosure:

> *Before* [italics added] an executory contract is signed by the purchaser, the seller shall provide to the purchaser a written statement that specifies:
>
> (1) the purchase price of the property;
> (2) the interest rate charged under the contract;
> (3) the dollar amount, or an estimate of the dollar amount if the interest rate is variable, of the interest charged for the term of the contract;
> (4) the total amount of principal and interest to be paid under the contract;

(5) the late charge, if any, that may be assessed under the contract; and

(6) the fact that the seller may not charge a prepaying penalty or any similar fee if the purchaser elects to pay the entire amount due under the contract before the scheduled payment due date under the contract.

There is some slight relief under this section (if you want to look at it that way) in that a violation by the seller is not defined as a DTPA violation.

The Seven-Day Letter

Another, related pre-closing requirement is contained in Property Code Section 5.016: "A person may not convey an interest in or enter into a contract to convey an interest in residential real property that will be encumbered by a recorded lien" without giving a seven-day notice to both lender and purchaser. The statute sets out the required content of this notice, which is quite technical, although no real penalties are imposed other than allowing the buyer a pre-closing right of rescission. After closing, there is no buyer remedy and no liability on the part of the seller. Result? The seven-day letter requirement is widely ignored. Anticipate that a future legislature may revisit this statute and insert penalties for non-compliance.

Punitive Fees and Clauses

Property Code Section 5.073 prohibits these. Excessive late fees are banned, as are prepayment penalties and any clause that "prohibits the purchaser from pledging the purchaser's interest in the property as security to obtain a loan or place improvements." This codifies the traditional view from the justice court bench: exorbitant late fees are almost never allowed in an eviction judgment.

Recording Requirement

In the past, lease-options and other executory contracts did not need to be recorded. No longer. Section 5.076(a) states that "the seller shall record the executory contract, including the attached disclosure statement . . . on or before the 30th day after the date the contract is executed." Additionally, any instrument that terminates the contract must be recorded.

In 2017, Section 5.079(a) was amended to provide that a "recorded executory contract shall be the same as a deed with a vendor's lien. The vendor's lien is for the amount of the unpaid contract price, less any lawful deductions, and may be enforced by foreclosure sale under Section

5.066 or by judicial foreclosure. A general warranty is implied unless otherwise limited by the recorded executory contract." It would not be prudent practice, however, to take the statute's word for it and simply assume that a recorded executory contract is as good as a deed. Basically, nothing is as good as general warranty deed that conveys a fee simple interest.

Annual Accounting Statement

Section 5.077 requires an annual accounting statement every January, which must include amounts paid, the remaining amount owed, the number of payments remaining, the amount paid in taxes, the amount paid for insurance, an accounting for any insurance payments by the insurer, and a copy of the current policy—a comprehensive status report to the buyer, in other words. There is no requirement that this be recorded.

What if the seller makes a good-faith error in the annual accounting statement? Does that trigger Draconian statutory penalties? Is that a DTPA violation? Probably not, "unless the statement is so deficient as to be something other than a good faith attempt by the seller to inform the purchaser of the current status of their contractual relationship." *Morton v. Nguyen*, 369 S.W.3d 659 (Tex.App.—Houston [14th Dist.] 2012). The Texas Supreme Court, when it later reviewed this case, left this part of the appeals court opinion in place, so this is the law.

A 2015 appeals court case further discussed the issue of damages for failure to provide an annual accounting statement. The court noted that Tex. Civ. Prac. & Rem. Code Sec. 41.008 limits the amount of exemplary damages that a plaintiff can recover in lawsuits generally. The issue was whether or not this statute specifically applies in the context of failure to provide the required accounting under Property Code Section 5.077. Why is that relevant? Because in this case, the plaintiff failed to show actual damages. The court ruled that Chapter 41 applies in these situations. In other words, to recover the exemplary damages provided by Section 5.077, actual damages in more than a nominal amount must be proven by clear and convincing evidence. *Smith v. Davis*, 462 W.W.3d 604 (Tex.App.—Tyler 2015, pet. denied).

Buyer's Right to Convert to a Deed

The buyer has an absolute right "at any time and without paying penalties or charges of any kind" to convert an executory contract to "recorded, legal title" under Section 5.081. That means a deed, probably a general warranty deed, but no less than a deed without warranties. The seller has no choice in the matter so long as the buyer tenders the balance owed under the contract. This is true whether or not the executory contract was recorded.

The SAFE Act Licensing Requirement

Executory contracts are a form of owner financing and, therefore, both the federal Secure and Fair Enforcement for Mortgage Licensing Act ("SAFE Act") and the Texas version ("T-SAFE") apply. However, the seller is required to be licensed only if the property is not the seller's homestead and/or the sale is not to a family member. The Commissioner of the Texas Department of Savings and Mortgage Lending ("TDSML") has ruled that T-SAFE will *not* be applied to persons who make five or fewer owner-financed loans in a year. Note that the T-SAFE licensing rule applies only to residential owner financing.

Dodd-Frank Law (Mortgage Reform and Anti-Predatory Lending Act)

Dodd-Frank and the SAFE Act were both born of the real estate collapse. Dodd-Frank generally requires that a seller-lender in an owner-financed transaction involving a residence make an informed determination that the buyer-borrower has the ability to repay the loan. Most sellers are therefore obligated to qualify the buyer-borrower in the same way any regular lender would. This law also has a de minimis exception that excludes persons doing no more than three owner-financed transactions per year, at least so long as the seller-lender is not in the building business. Although Dodd-Frank is roundly criticized by some politicians as an example of over-regulation, there is no doubt that corrective action was necessary in order to avoid another epidemic of toxic loans.

Termination of Executory Contracts

It is not permissible to simply evict a buyer under an executory contract if there is a default. Why? Because the buyer has equitable rights and is more than a mere tenant. The Property Code therefore requires ample notice and opportunity for the buyer to cure the default. Sections 5.063 and 5.064 specify the content of the default notice, which must be followed *to the letter* if it is to be valid. The buyer must be allowed a 30-day unconditional right to cure the default before an eviction can be filed. If the judge grants possession to the seller at the eviction hearing, then and only then is the buyer's down payment forfeited.

There is also the "40 or 48 Rule" contained in Property Code Section 5.066(a): if the buyer has paid in 40% or more of the purchase price, or the equivalent of 48 monthly payments, then a 60-day notice is required and, if the default is not cured, a traditional foreclosure (*not* an eviction) must be used to regain title. Clearly, the intent is to keep sellers from unfairly confiscating down payments and buyers' equity.

The Reality of the Courtroom

Why not just ignore the executory contract rules and march merrily forward? The reason is that courts and juries do not favor investors and landlords, who are often perceived as profiteers preying upon the weak and helpless. It does not matter how clever the investor's legal argument is. If a transaction does not pass the "smell test" a seller-landlord will likely lose. Even if the executory contract rules are found not to apply, the court can look to the laundry list of offenses under the DTPA, which prohibits "any unconscionable action or course of action by any person"—a very large hammer a jury can use against investors they do not like.

Note that pretending an executory contract is something else by renaming it will fool no one. A judge and jury may even be angry with an investor-seller who tries to pull a fast one with overly clever verbiage—and therefore more inclined to consider a finding of fraud, which brings the prospect of treble damages plus attorney fees.

Property Code Section 5.073(a)(4) prohibits forfeiture of a buyer's down payment or option fee if a monthly payment is late. This is an important change, because it codifies what judges and juries have been telling lawyers for quite some time. They *hate* forfeitures. The trend in the law is to view any substantial forfeiture as unreasonable and unconscionable, whether within the context of an executory contract or not, if it results in a buyer losing either a large down payment or the home itself.

Landlords and sellers should generally avoid residential executory contracts lasting more than 180 days because of the numerous requirements and potential liability for doing them improperly. Penalties fall entirely upon the seller, even if the purchaser was a willing participant in the transaction, and there are no significant defenses. Accordingly, such contracts are generally inadvisable unless the property is paid for or used exclusively for commercial purposes.

Chapter 12

THE STATUTE OF FRAUDS

The Requirement of a Writing in Real Estate

This chapter addresses the requirement that agreements relating to real property be in writing, a requirement known generically as the "Statute of Frauds." To satisfy the Statute of Frauds, a contract "must furnish within itself, or by reference to some other existing writing, the means or data by which the property to be conveyed may be identified with reasonable certainty." If a contract does not meet this standard, it is void under the Statute of Frauds. *Long Trusts v. Griffin*, 222 S.W.3d 412 (Tex. 2006).

Most investors are aware that they need a written contract when real estate is bought or sold. The issue of whether or not a signed writing must exist most often arises in connection with oral modifications, amendments, and extensions to a written contract. As an example, a lawyer may be asked if a handshake agreement to add thirty days to a designated closing date is binding. Generally, the answer is *no*, but there may be exceptions.

Applicable Law

Provisions of the Statute of Frauds applicable to real estate are found in Business & Commerce Code Sections 26.01 and 26.02(b):

26.01. Promise or Agreement Must Be In Writing.

(a) **A promise or agreement described in Subsection (b) of this section is not enforceable unless the promise or agreement, or a memorandum of it, is**

(1) **in writing; and**
(2) **signed by the person to be charged with the promise or agreement or by someone lawfully authorized to sign for him.**

(b) **Subsection (a) of this section applies to:**

(1) a promise by an executor or administrator to answer out of his own estate for any debt or damage due from his testator or intestate;

(2) a promise by one person to answer for the debt, default, or miscarriage of another person;

(3) an agreement made on consideration of marriage or on consideration of nonmarital conjugal cohabitation;

(4) a contract for the sale of real estate;

(5) a lease of real estate for a term longer than one year;

(6) an agreement which is not to be performed within one year from the date of making the agreement;

(7) a promise or agreement to pay commission for the sale or purchase of:
  (A) an oil or gas mining lease;
  (B) an oil or gas royalty
  (C) minerals; or
  (D) a mineral interest; and

(8) an agreement, promise, contract, or warranty of cure relating to medical care or results thereof made by a physician or health care provider as defined in Section 74.001, Civil Practice and Remedies Code.

26.02. Loan Agreement Must Be in Writing

(b) A loan agreement in which the amount involved in the loan agreement exceeds $50,000 in value is not enforceable unless the agreement is in writing and signed by the party to be bound or by that party's authorization.

Section 26.02(b) is particularly important when those seeking loan modifications find themselves unwittingly foreclosed upon, despite an alleged oral agreement. These unfortunate homeowners likely have no recourse unless a written agreement signed by both borrower and lender was in existence at the time of the foreclosure.

Additional Statute of Frauds provisions are found in Business & Commerce Code Section 2.201, but these apply to the sale of goods, not real estate.

Although not labeled as such, there is another important Statute of Frauds in Texas, Property Code Section 5.021, which is sometimes referred to as the "Statute of Conveyances:"

5.021 Instrument of Conveyance

A conveyance of an estate of inheritance, a freehold, or an estate for more than one year, in land and tenements, must be in writing and must be subscribed and delivered by the conveyor or by the conveyor's agent authorized in writing.

What does the statute of frauds require of a contract at a practical level? How complete must the written document actually be? "The statute of frauds requires that a memorandum of an agreement, in addition to being signed by the party to be charged, must be complete within itself in every material detail and contain all of the essential elements of the agreement so that the contract can be ascertained from the writings without resorting to oral testimony." *Sterrett v. Jacobs*, 118 S.W.3d 877, 879-80 (Tex.App.—Texarkana 2003, pet. denied). Note, however, that the contract need not be contained with the four corners of a single document. "A valid memorandum of the contract may consist of numerous communiques [or emails] signed by the party to be charged...." *Key v. Pierce*, 8 S.W.3d 704, 708 (Tex.App.—Fort Worth 1999, pet. denied).

Exceptions to the Statute of Frauds

A discussion of the requirement of a signed writing would not be complete without addressing the equitable exceptions. "Equity" is that branch of the law which provides relief in cases where strict application of a statute or common-law rule would result in unfairness or injustice. In the case of the Statute of Frauds, the following exceptions apply:

(1) when enforcement of the Statute of Frauds would itself amount to an actual fraud (but not a mere wrong);
(2) when the doctrine of "promissory estoppel" applies, the three elements of which are
   a. a person makes a promise that he or she should have expected would lead another person to sustain some definite and substantial damage or injury;
   b. such damage or injury occurred; and
   c. the court must act to relieve or avoid the damage or injury; or

(3) when significant partial performance of an oral agreement has occurred and denying enforcement of the agreement at that point would amount to an actual fraud.

Circumstances constituting partial performance are particularly common in real estate transactions. "Under the partial performance exception to the statute of frauds, contracts that have been partly performed, but do not meet the requirements of the statute of frauds, may be enforced in equity if denial of enforcement would amount to a virtual fraud." *Hairston v. SMU*, 441 S.W.3d 327, 336 (Tex.App.—Dallas 2013, pet. denied). A Texarkana case involving an oral agreement to take over payments on a property provides an excellent summary of the specific items required in order to successfully argue for the partial performance exception: "In order to establish the partial performance exception, [the buyers asserting the exception] had to show that (1) they had performed acts unequivocally referable to the agreement; (2) that the acts were performed in reliance on the agreement; (3) that as a result of the acts they had experienced substantial detriment; (4) that they have no adequate remedy for their loss; and (5) that [the seller] would reap an unearned benefit such that not enforcing the agreement would amount to a virtual fraud." *Thomas v. Miller*, 500 S.W.3d 601 (Tex.App.—Texarkana 2016, no pet.). In this case, the seller tried to convey the property to someone else after the buyers had been making the mortgage payments for an extended period—and the court declined to let him get away with it.

Exceptions to the Statute of Frauds are not found in the Property Code but in case law. Their use is strictly limited since widespread allowance of these exceptions would effectively void the rule and result in significant chaos in the world of real estate transactions. See *Nagle v. Nagle*, 633 S.W.2d 796, 799-800 (Tex. 1982); *Birenbaum v. Option Care, Inc.*, 971 S.W.2d 497, 503 (Tex.App.—Dallas 1997, pet. denied); *Exxon Corp. v. Breezevale Ltd.*, 82 S.W.3d 429, 438 (Tex.App.—Dallas 2002, pet. denied).

Mineral Interests and Easements

Oil, gas, and other mineral interests "constitute real property; therefore, an agreement for the transfer or assignment of a mineral interest must comply with the Statute of Frauds." *Anderson Energy Corporation v. Dominion Oklahoma Texas Exploration & Production, Inc.*, 469 S.W.3d 280 (Tex.App.—San Antonio 2015, no pet.).

Easements are real property interests subject to the Statute of Frauds, even if their location and terms of use are less than clear. "If an easement, though uncertain, is susceptible to a reasonable construction as to its true intent and meaning, the easement satisfies the Statute of Frauds. *Fuqua v. Oncor Elec. Delivery Co.*, 315 S.W.3d 552 (Tex.App—Eastland 2010, pet. denied).

Occurrence of Statute of Frauds Issues

Lawyers tend to encounter Statute of Frauds issues in two contexts: first, when a client inquires whether or not a certain oral agreement is legally enforceable; and second, in litigation, when a plaintiff seeks to enforce an oral agreement and the Statute of Frauds must be raised by the defendant as an affirmative defense. If the Statute of Frauds is so raised, then the burden shifts back to the plaintiff to demonstrate how one of the exceptions would apply—a difficult task, inasmuch as these exceptions are narrowly construed.

Alleged subsequent oral modifications are a particularly common issue for attorneys. "Generally, if a contract falls within the statute of frauds, then a party cannot enforce any subsequent oral material modification to the contract." *SP Terrace, L.P. v. Meritage Homes*, 334 S.W.3d 275,282 (Tex.App.—Houston [1st Dist.] 2010, no pet.).

An example of the strictness of the Statute of Frauds in Texas is found in a Fifth Circuit case where the court denied enforcement of a written contract merely because exhibits to the contract (describing oil and gas leases to be conveyed) had not been finalized. See *Preston Exploration Co. v. PEC P'ship*, 669 F.3d 518 (5th Cir. 2012). On the other hand, a Texas appeals court concluded that the failure of one party to sign a lease did not cause the lease to fail under the Statute of Frauds. *Thomas P. Sibley, P.C. v. Brentwood Inv. Dev. Co.*, 356 S.W.3d 659 (Tex.App.—El Paso 2011, pet. denied).

Property Description Issues

A real estate contract must sufficiently describe the subject property. How is "sufficient" defined? A property description is sufficient if the writing furnishes within itself, or by reference to some other existing writing, the means or data by which the particular land to be conveyed may be identified with reasonable certainty. *General Metal Fabricating Corp. v. Stergiou*, 438 S.W.3d 737, 753 (Tex.App.—Houston [1st Dist.] 2014). This is Texas' reasonable certainty standard, in effect since at least 1945.

What about situations where a contract makes references to other documents? Again, the courts are strict. Only in limited circumstances may extrinsic evidence be used and then "only for the purpose of identifying the [property] with reasonable certainty from the data in the [writing]." *Pick v. Bartel*, 659 S.W.2d 636, 637 (Tex. 1983), "The written memorandum, however, need not be contained in one document." *Padilla v. LaFrance*, 907 S.W.2d 454, 460 (Tex. 1995) (citing *Adams v. Abbott*, 254 S.W.2d 78, 80 (Tex. 1952)). The Texas Supreme Court has repeatedly held that multiple writings pertaining to the same transaction will be construed as one contract. *Owen v. Hendricks*, 433 S.W.2d 164 (Tex. 1968); *Fort Worth Indep. Sch. Dist. v. City of Fort Worth*, 22 S.W.3d 831, 840 (Tex. 2000).

Trusts

Since land trusts are discussed in this book, we should point out that there is a statute of frauds that pertains to trusts found in Property Code Section 112.004: "A trust in either real or personal property is enforceable only if there is written evidence of the trust's terms bearing the signature of the settlor or the settlor's authorized agent." Accordingly, the common (but careless) practice of showing a trust as grantee in a deed, without an underlying written trust agreement, is insufficient as a matter of statute.

Get it in Writing

"Get it in writing" is not just valid folk wisdom, it is a baseline of Texas law when it comes to the purchase and sale of real property. There are very limited exceptions. A proper contract is best, but even an informal scribbling signed by the parties can be sufficient depending on the circumstances.

Chapter 13

MORTGAGE LOAN FRAUD

Where There's a Way, There's a Crook

Mortgage loan fraud, on the decline after the Great Recession due to more intense monitoring by lenders and regulators, is again on the rise. Title Insurer First American Financial Services estimates that fraud in mortgage loan applications increased nearly 10% between January 2018 and January 2019. Interest rates were low a decade ago, and refinance loans were dominant in the mortgage marketplace until rates gradually began increasing in 2016. As rates increased, the relative percentage of refinance loans—typically safer and better collateralized than purchase-money loans—began to decline.

Purchase-money loans generally have a higher potential for fraud in the application and documentation process, largely because there are more commission-driven individuals in the loan supply chain. As a new kind of crisis has emerged—the affordability crisis—banks have been under pressure to loosen their credit and underwriting standards, which in turn has led to more fraudulent activity . . . and so the cycle begins again.

Everyone involved in real estate sales and closings is a potential subject of scrutiny. And prosecutions are not limited to actual mortgage and bank fraud. There are also related prosecutions for conspiracy, mail and wire fraud, identity theft, and money laundering. An example of the latter is the 2019 mortgage fraud conviction of Paul Manafort, who formed a shell company to buy an expensive Manhattan condominium for the purpose of laundering money on which income taxes had not been paid. Manafort later applied for a cash-out refinance loan and stated on his application that his daughter lived in the condo. This was false, since the truth was that he was renting the property on Airbnb. Manafort's classic error? Greed, of course. Not satisfied with merely transforming untaxed income into legitimate loan proceeds, Manafort also wanted income from the property, running afoul of the old saying: "You can make money being a bull, and you can make money being a bear, but you can't make money being a pig."

Regulation and Enforcement

The Financial Institution Fraud Unit of the FBI investigates and prosecutes criminal loan fraud, particularly where mortgage industry professionals and insiders are involved, proceeding on the basis of suspicious activity reports ("SARs"). The FBI uses two categories: "fraud for housing," which occurs when a single borrower misrepresents assets and/or liabilities in order to purchase a home, and "fraud for profit," which occurs when mortgage professionals act collectively to defraud a lender to collect fees.

The 2007 Texas Residential Mortgage Fraud Act changed the legal landscape at the state level. The Act amended certain sections of the Finance Code, the Government Code, and the Penal Code to address mortgage fraud. It also created a Residential Mortgage Fraud Task Force under the direction of the attorney general, which includes a range of state officials—the consumer credit commissioner, the banking commissioner, the credit union commissioner, the commissioner of insurance, the savings and mortgage lending commissioner, the presiding officer of the Texas Real Estate Commission, and the presiding officer of the Texas Appraiser Licensing and Certification Board. Although the Task Force was abolished in 2017, the interlinked bureaucratic machinery remains, and these agencies continue to share information and resources.

Criminal prosecution is not the only risk. There is also the matter of civil liability. Lenders commonly file civil suits against perpetrators of mortgage fraud. In recent years, it has also become more common to see attorneys who assist in or facilitate the fraud sued as co-conspirators.

What does mortgage fraud look like?

Examples of fraudulent schemes include flipping based on false loan applications and inflated appraisals (this category does *not* include buying property at a bargain price and then selling it for fair market value for a profit, which is entirely legal); nominee loans using the name and credit of straw buyers; equity skimming in "subject to" transactions; phony second liens to contractors who never perform any work; "silent seconds" that involve concealing the loan of a down payment to a borrower, when the down payment was supposed to come from the borrower's own funds; concealing other indebtedness of the borrower; the use of fictitious or stolen identities; and "stop foreclosure" schemes that mislead homeowners into paying fees and signing the property over to a crooked investor. Common to most of these schemes are inflated appraisals that create phantom equity, illegal kickbacks (payments not shown on the closing statement), and falsified loan applications.

One can be reasonably sure that loan fraud has occurred when it is clear that a lender would not have made a particular loan if it had known all the facts, and the lender was prevented from knowing the facts by means of misrepresentation and concealment. Putting it another way: inducing a lender to make a loan based on false pretenses is fraud.

Many transactions, while not plainly illegal, fall into a risky gray area. The popularity of no-money-down investment programs and guru seminars has added huge numbers of people to the investment game and resulted in intricate get-rich-quick strategies. The FBI attitude toward these schemes (and to real estate investors generally) is openly disdainful. One official was heard mocking real estate entrepreneurs as "entremanures." So if the FBI comes calling, even legitimate investors should assume the FBI's intent is hostile. Saying nothing and immediately contacting a white-collar crime defense attorney is probably the best course of action.

One can nonetheless be sympathetic toward the FBI's attitude, since the lender is not the only victim of mortgage loan fraud. It is easy to feel antipathy toward banks, but most home loans nowdays are either securitized or sold, meaning that others in the chain of ownership (including pension funds and the like) may be subject to loss. Also, many loans are sold to Fannie Mae, Freddie Mac, and Ginnie Mae, which are quasi-public entities. If there is a loss connected with these loans, it is the taxpayer who gets the bill. Finally, if loan fraud results in a foreclosure, then that has the potential to depress property values, so everyone in the neighborhood suffers. Mortgage loan fraud is definitely not a victimless crime.

Temptations of the Investment Business

A visit to the courthouse on foreclosure day is akin to watching sharks being fed at the aquarium. The problem, of course, is that it is impossible for *all* fledgling investors to become overnight millionaires. Real success involves hard work over time. Unfortunately, intense competition in the real estate investment business can lead impatient and unethical investors to look for profits in ways that cross the line.

Legitimate investors should avoid investment plans that sound too good to be true, either to the investor or homeowner. Programs that ask a homeowner to sign incomprehensible documents with weird names often involve fraud. If a deal is just too complicated for the average person to understand, it may well involve fraud. If it involves several people signing interests back and forth to one another and not recording anything, it is probably fraud. Payments made off the closing statement are almost certainly fraud.

Some perpetrators believe that giving their documents creative names will exempt them from the law. The problem for con artists who dream up these documents is that courts look to substance over form, and prisons are now offering long-term housing to these clever folks. Juries may not always understand the technicalities of mortgage finance but they intuitively understand fraud. Here are some other tip-offs that you may be dealing with a real estate con artist:

"This is a great investment! You'll make great money with no effort."

"There's no need to talk to a lawyer. These are all standard forms."

"Just sign this blank loan application here. We'll do all the paperwork."

"We put the property in your name. You're totally secure."

"We pay all the costs and you get half the profit! Easy money!"

"We'll pay you a bonus at closing. You'll have cash in your pocket and instant equity."

"We're going to manage and sell the property and then split all the profits with you."

"God has sent us to give you abundant wealth."

The Straw Buyer

The straw buyer scenario was more common before the bust, but it is becoming fashionable again. Here's how it works:

1. A crooked investor generally looks for two categories of homes, those owned by distressed sellers who are behind on payments and new-home builders who have unsold inventory that is draining them because of the interest carry.

2. The perpetrator recruits straw purchasers-borrowers who are willing to allow their names and credit to be used in exchange for an up-front, off-the-closing statement kickback (often $10,000 or more) and then buys the property in their names. The note, deed of trust, and other loan documents, including an affidavit of intent to occupy, are all signed by the straw purchasers at a title company closing that appears legitimate.

3. A real estate broker accomplice may be involved to make this easier and eventually collect a commission from a "client" the broker never met, never obtained a buyer's

representation agreement from, and never gave an IABS to.

4. A mortgage broker accomplice submits a fraudulent loan application and supporting documents that show the straw buyer as having significantly higher income than is actually the case.

5. An appraiser accomplice inflates the value of the property, often by $100,000 or more.

6. The amount of the loan applied for exceeds the true market value of the house.

7. A title company may be complicit in this process in order to facilitate a smooth closing with no questions.

8. All the various accomplices and co-conspirators get paid large fees at closing, either on the closing statement for vague and unspecified charges, or off the closing statement altogether.

9. The house is placed on the market but does not sell because its value is grossly inflated.

10. The lender forecloses, taking a loss (part of which is passed on to HUD or a mortgage insurer) and ruining the credit of the straw purchaser. By then, the con artists have left with profits in hand.

Looking closely, it is clear that the whole transaction has been concocted so that the co-conspirators can generate large up-front fees for themselves, something that should always set off alarm bells.

Interestingly, straw buyers often allege that they were wronged. They even file lawsuits. It is difficult to feel sorry for them, however, since they willingly signed blank documents and gladly received an under-the-table payoff at closing. They cooperated in the fraud and benefited from it.

In the past sub-prime lenders were complicit in this process. Eager to make loans and collect fees, many did not supervise the underwriting process as thoroughly as they should.

Applicable Law

In addition to the usual civil statutes that may be violated (statutory fraud, deceptive trade practices, etc.), numerous federal criminal statutes may be involved:

FEDERAL CRIME	LAW	PENALTY
False statement on a HUD loan	18 U.S.C. § 1012	1 year, fine, or both
False statement to obtain credit	18 U.S.C. § 1014	2 years, $5,000, or both
Mail/wire fraud	18 U.S.C. §§ 1341, 1343	5 years, $1,000, or both
Concealment	18 U.S.C. § 1001	5 years, $10,000, or both
Conspiracy	18 U.S.C. § 371	5 years, $10,000, or both
Racketeering	18 U.S.C. §1961	20 years, $25,000, or both
Money laundering	18 U.S.C. § 1956	20 years, $25,000, or both
Aggravated identity theft	18 U.S.C. § 1028	20 years, $25,000, or both

At the state level, the Residential Mortgage Fraud Act amended Texas Penal Code Section 32.32(b) to state: "A person commits an offense if he intentionally or knowingly makes a material false or misleading written statement to obtain property or credit, including a mortgage loan." If the value of the property or amount of the loan exceeds $200,000, which is the case with the median-priced family home, then the offense is a first-degree felony punishable by 5 to 99 years in prison and a fine of $10,000.

Also, Finance Code Section 343.105 requires that lenders and mortgage brokers give the following notice in 14-point type to residential borrowers at closing:

> **WARNING: INTENTIONALLY OR KNOWINGLY MAKING A MATERIALLY FALSE OR MISLEADING WRITTEN STATE-MENT TO OBTAIN PROPERTY OR CREDIT, INCLUDING A MORTGAGE LOAN, IS A VIOLATION OF SECTION 32.32, TEXAS PENAL CODE, AND DEPENDING ON THE AMOUNT OF THE LOAN OR VALUE OF THE PROPERTY, IS PUNISHABLE BY IMPRISONMENT FOR A TERM OF 2 YEARS TO 99 YEARS AND FINE NOT TO EXCEED $10,000.**
>
> **I/WE, THE UNDERSIGNED HOME LOAN APPLICANT(S), REPRESENT THAT I/WE HAVE RECEIVED, READ, AND UNDERSTAND THIS NOTICE OF PENALTIES FOR MAKING A MATERIALLY FALSE OR MISLEADING WRITTEN STATE-MENT TO OBTAIN A HOME LOAN.**
>
> **I/WE REPRESENT THAT ALL STATEMENTS AND REPRESENTATIONS CONTAINED IN MY/OUR WRITTEN HOME LOAN APPLICATION, INCLUDING STATEMENTS OR REPRESENTATIONS REGARDING MY/OUR IDENTITY, EMPLOYMENT, ANNUAL INCOME, AND INTENT TO OCCUPY**

THE RESIDENTIAL REAL PROPERTY SECURED BY THE HOME LOAN, ARE TRUE AND CORRECT AS OF THE DATE OF LOAN CLOSING.

The borrower must sign this notice. However, "[f]ailure of a lender, mortgage banker, or licensed mortgage broker to provide a notice complying with this section to each applicant for a home loan does not affect the validity of or enforceability of the home loan by any holder of the loan." Tex. Fin. Code Sec. 343.105(d). So the loan is valid without the notice, but it may still constitute fraud.

FinCen and Money Laundering

The Financial Crimes Enforcement Network ("FinCen") resides within the U.S. Treasury Department and is responsible for enforcement and rule-making in the area of money laundering, something that occasionally pops up in real estate investing. Why? Because buying and selling real estate is probably the best way to legitimize ill-gotten gains other than using the services of a casino to transform questionable cash into clean cash—and a lot less risky. FinCen imposes due diligence obligations on financial institutions, sometimes referred to as the "know your customer" or KYC rules. These have only expanded over the years, both in response to the Great Recession and as part of the worldwide effort to clamp down on international tax evasion. The "beneficial ownership rule," effective in 2018, obligates banks to inquire into and report on who actually owns or controls the entities they deal with, specifically persons who (a) own 25% or more of the equity of any entity that is borrowing money, and/or (b) have significant control or management responsibility with respect to the entity. This clearly impacts an asset protection strategy that seeks to achieve anonymity (or even a low profile) for principal investors in a borrowing entity. And, of course, any attempt to avoid or evade disclosure under the beneficial ownership rule is now a federal crime.

Email and Wire Fraud

This is a growing area of potential risk and liability for title companies, escrow agents, lawyers, and yes—even real estate investors who do business by email and wire transfer. The FBI reports that nearly one billion dollars of closing funds were the object of criminal intent in 2017, meaning that criminals attempted to divert or actually succeeded in diverting this amount from pending closings. Consider the magnitude and audacity of this. Wire fraud usually has small, unobtrusive beginnings; often there is an apparently harmless email (ostensibly from the seller) to the escrow agent, informing of a last-minute change in wire instructions and providing new bank account information. The closing is funded and funds which are wired to the new bank are immediately moved elsewhere, which means the money is likely gone forever. Conclusion: any emailed instructions concerning the electronic transmission of funds, particularly changes in those instructions, should be viewed skeptically.

Knowledgeable escrow agents (or anyone handling and wiring funds, including attorneys) are now refusing to accept such email changes in funding instructions, requiring either a telephone confirmation or even demanding that the seller come in person to the office and confirm the change.

It all begins with hacking into a victim's email, called an "email account compromise" (EAC) in the trade. Title companies, banks, and real estate lawyers are under continual attack. Some EACs are laughably foreign in origin; but others appear legitimate, at least on the surface. They provide the name of a seller or an address to property and say that attached closing documents are attached for review. Sometimes the email comes from a familiar address, but with just one or two letters slightly altered. And, of course, it's always urgent. Once you click on the attachment, you're done.

Our firm has been berated on more than one occasion by outraged parties who claim that, by asking for double confirmation and verification, or perhaps as a result of a request by us that the party come to the office to deliver a change in financial instructions personally, we are holding up the closing or even killing the deal. Tough. We will not allow ourselves to be on the hook for lost closing proceeds because a party foolishly disregards risk. The best practice for title companies and closing attorneys is to have a written policy that wire instructions are to be provided at the inception of the transaction, preferably from the client in person and in his or her own handwriting. Such instructions should not be subject to any change whatsoever without a personal visit by that party to the office. Staff should be thoroughly trained in these and other authentication procedures.

Confidential financial information of any important kind should be sent only by encrypted email. Failing to do this, even if it involves extra cost, will provide a cause of action for negligence if you are sued in the event of a loss. That is an easy case that most plaintiffs' lawyers would be willing to take on contingency.

Broad Potential Liability for Fraud

Let's return to the subject of fraud generally and its impact on investors. There are so many definitions of fraud in various statutes that prosecutors have little trouble finding one that can be used against an investor. The Residential Mortgage Fraud Act added another by amending Section 402.031 of the Government Code, which now defines fraud as "any act that constitutes a violation of a penal law and is part of an attempt or scheme to defraud any person." Moreover, this section imposes an affirmative duty to report fraudulent activity to "an authorized governmental agency" if "a person determines or reasonably suspects that fraudulent activity has been committed or is about to be committed." Loan officers, escrow officers, realtors, and attorneys all have this duty. Compliance results in immunity for the reporting individual. Failure to comply makes one a potential co-conspirator.

Mortgage loan fraud seldom occurs in a vacuum or in isolation. More than one perpetrator is usually involved. As a result, conspiracy has become something of a catch-all allegation that is available to both criminal prosecutors and civil plaintiffs. Even if it cannot be plausibly shown that a real estate investor directly engaged in unlawful or wrongful acts, he or she may nonetheless be forced to defend against charges or allegations of conspiring with others—which in terms of the legal consequences can be just as serious. The elements of civil conspiracy are (1) two or more persons (2) who have an unlawful or wrongful objective they intend to accomplish, (3) who have a meeting of the minds on the objective or course of action to be pursued, (4) followed by the occurrence of one or more overt unlawful or wrongful acts, (5) which result in damages as a proximate result. The king of conspiracy statutes is RICO (Title 18 of the U.S. Code) which targets a pattern of wrongdoing. Predicate crimes that contribute to establishing such a pattern include not just the obvious infractions of mail and wire fraud but can extend to mortgage loan fraud as well. Even an email can connect you to an underlying conspiracy. RICO is available not just for criminal prosecutions but also to civil plaintiffs.

State and federal conspiracy laws cast a wide net. Accordingly, the most prudent approach is to keep one's distance (and plenty of it) from any suspicious parties or transactions.

The laws discussed in this chapter make sobering reading for anyone involved in the sale, purchase, financing, and closing of residential home transactions. Who is affected? *Any* person (not just the primary wrongdoers) with actual knowledge of the fraud can be indicted for a felony criminal offense, all the way down to the notary. Moreover, culpable mental intent can be inferred from the circumstances, a relatively light burden for prosecutors.

Much of fraud prevention is common sense. If you suspect fraud in a transaction, immediately remove yourself from involvement and report the activity. Always read documents thoroughly before signing them. Do not sign blank documents. Check out the people you're dealing with. Be alert for irregularities. Ask questions. If the answers are overly complex or outright ridiculous, consider walking away from the deal.

Chapter 14

SAFE ACT AND DODD-FRANK

Federal Efforts to Promote Responsible Lending

The SAFE Act and Dodd-Frank rose from the ashes of the Great Recession in an effort to achieve better consumer protection by regulating careless and abusive lending practices. When these federal statutes and their state counterparts are considered alongside the 2005 amendments to the Property Code (regulating executory contracts) it is clear that the status of Texas as a free-wheeling haven for residential owner finance is now history.

SAFE Act and T-SAFE

The SAFE Act is a federal consumer protection law that each state is required to implement. Licensing and registration are a major emphasis of the SAFE Act. On the national level, the Nationwide Mortgage Licensing System and Registry was created under the supervision of the Conference of State Bank Supervisors and the American Association of Residential Mortgage Regulators. On the state level, individual states were required to devise their own licensing and registration regimes. Texas accomplished this in 2009 with the passage of T-SAFE.

T-SAFE contains tighter rules than the federal law by placing a licensing requirement on certain types of residential owner financing provided by professional investors. Since traditional owner finance transactions, wraps, and land trusts are forms of owner finance, T-SAFE applies to all of these; however, a seller is required to be licensed only if the property is not the seller's homestead and/or the sale is not to a family member. For example, if the subject property is a rental house being sold to a non-family member, a strict reading of the law would mean that the seller is required to have a residential mortgage loan origination ("RMLO") license from the Texas Department of Savings and Mortgage Lending in order to complete this transaction. RMLOs, who are trained in compliance with both federal and state law pertaining to mortgage loan origination, are intended to function as a buffer against recurrence of the abuses of the past.

State agencies typically have the power to issue rules and regulations designed to clarify and implement acts of the legislature. This is true both at the federal and state levels. In the case of T-SAFE, TDSML has ruled that the Act will not be applied to non-professionals—persons who make five or fewer owner-financed loans in a year, thus preserving the de minimis exemption under Finance Code Section 156.202(a)(3).

Intermediary Agents under T-SAFE

Does T-SAFE effectively shut the door on non-homestead owner finance for persons who do more than five such deals per year? Not if an investor utilizes the services of an RMLO. These intermediary agents charge fees (usually ranging from half a point to a one percent of the loan amount) in order to insure that federal and state legal requirements are satisfied. The RMLO supplies the new form of Good Faith Estimate, the Truth-in-Lending disclosures, orders an appraisal, gives state-specific disclosures, and the like, and requires that "cooling periods" be observed in the loan process. So, while it is true that unlimited non-homestead owner-finance transactions can still be done by professional investors, it is only with the assistance of these licensed individuals. The practical result? Owner financing deals remain feasible but at a higher net cost. Investors should probably look at the extra cost as a kind of premium that (at least potentially) reduces their future liability.

There has been a proliferation of RMLOs as a result of T-SAFE. Note that there is an exception to the licensing requirement for attorneys who as part of their drafting duties provide loan terms to the buyer, but most attorneys are steering clear of this loophole because of potential liability. And why not? Attorneys are already exposed to considerable liability and should be happy to offload at least a portion of that burden onto an RMLO. It therefore appears that RMLOs are here to stay.

Who is a loan originator?

Who is a loan originator? Anyone who takes a loan application, arranges credit or helps a consumer apply for credit, offers or negotiates loan terms, or even refers someone to a loan originator or creditor falls within the definition of "loan originator" or "mortgage originator." Quite a broad definition, which obviously includes mortgage brokers but would seem to be broad enough to include certain support personnel as well, even though persons who perform purely administrative or clerical tasks are expressly excluded (Note that it would be risky for a professional investor to rely on this loophole by delegating duties to his or her staff).

Real estate brokers are expressly excluded from the definition of a mortgage originator and may engage in these activities so long as they are not specifically compensated for doing so.

There are complex new rules relating to how loan originators are compensated. Also, mortgage originators are prohibited from steering borrowers to particular mortgage products in exchange for hidden fees (a popular practice before the bust) and this is backed up by a treble-damages penalty. Additionally, the previous practice by some refinance lenders of encouraging default on an existing loan before extending a new loan is banned.

Are real estate attorneys "loan originators?"

Real estate attorneys should be careful to avoid negotiating loan terms in residential owner financing cases since attorneys are *not* exempted from the definition of a "loan originator." Expect to see clauses in attorney engagement letters stipulating that they have not participated in loan negotiations—which is a bit strange, is it not, since this is traditionally part of what attorneys are expected to do when negotiating? Not any more, at least for lawyers who are careful about their liability. A more prudent approach is to require investor clients who are offering residential owner financing to arrive with their financial deal points essentially complete, a significant break from past practice.

Penalties for Violation of T-SAFE

The TDSML may enforce T-SAFE by a variety of measures, including license suspension, a fine of up to $25,000, and an order to make restitution to the buyer. What does restitution mean? Likely a refund of the down payment and all monthly payments that were made. Case law will eventually clarify this.

Dodd-Frank Wall Street Reform and Consumer Protection Act

The Dodd-Frank Wall Street Reform and Consumer Protection Act is a massive piece of legislation passed by Congress in 2010 as part of comprehensive reform of financial regulation. Our focus is Title XIV, entitled "The Mortgage Reform and Anti-Predatory Lending Act," which pertains to residential loans and lending practices. Title XIV will be referred to simply as "Dodd-Frank" or the "Act." The broad intent is to put an end to predatory lending practices, particularly the extension of loans to those who cannot afford to pay them back. Among other things, more lender disclosures and borrower protections are now involved.

Dodd-Frank achieves many of its reforms by means of amendments to the Truth-in-Lending Act ("TILA") and the Real Estate Settlement

Procedures Act ("RESPA"). The Consumer Financial Protection Bureau (the "CFPB," an active federal agency abundant in its regulatory tendencies) is charged with issuing regulations to implement Dodd-Frank. Regulations and must-use forms, as they continue to flower forth from the CFPB, are presenting as great a compliance challenge as the provisions of the Act itself. Some of these are complex, if not outright baffling.

Dodd-Frank overlaps the federal SAFE Act, formally known as the "Secure and Fair Enforcement for Mortgage Licensing Act of 2008." As mentioned above, the SAFE Act is implemented as "T-SAFE" in Texas. The intent of the law is to achieve better consumer protection by inserting a residential mortgage loan originator (RMLO) into the process. In other words, the seller must be an RMLO or there must be a person involved in the transaction who has an RMLO license—except, as noted, in sales of the seller's homestead and sales to immediate family members.

Broad Definition of "Owner Finance"

Note that the term "owner finance" includes the traditional version (sometimes called a "classic" owner finance, where the seller delivers a warranty deed to the buyer who then executes a note in favor of the seller secured by a first-lien deed of trust); wraparounds (the buyer executes a subordinate wrap note and makes payments to the seller who then pays the underlying lender); as well as various forms of land trusts. *Dodd-Frank applies to all of these.* An investor who argues that whatever creative device he or she has come up with or found on the Internet is not actually a form of owner financing will almost certainly lose the argument, given the way these laws are written and interpreted.

Summary of Dodd-Frank

Title XIV Subchapter B, Section 1411 of Dodd-Frank requires that a seller-lender in a residential owner-financed transaction determine at the time credit is extended that the buyer-borrower has the ability to repay the loan. Specifically: "A creditor shall not make a loan that is a covered transaction unless the creditor makes a reasonable and good faith determination at or before consummation that the consumer will have a reasonable ability to repay the loan according to its terms" (12 C.F.R Sec. 1026.43(c)(1)). The lender is obligated to investigate eight specific factors relating to the borrower:

1. current income or assets;
2. current employment status;
3. credit history;

4. monthly mortgage payment;
5. other monthly mortgage payments arising from the same purchase;
6. monthly payment for other-mortgage-related expenses (e.g., property taxes);
7. the borrower's other debts; and
8. borrower's debt-to-income ratio (DTI).

This is a non-exclusive list, *a minimum standard* that lenders must follow. Prospective lenders should also consider how much a borrower will have left over for life's necessities at the end of the month, after all bills have been paid. All of this must be based on verified and documented information in the loan file. This is referred to as the "ATR" (ability to repay) requirement." Result? "No doc," "low doc," and other "liar loans" are effectively banned. So are teaser-rate loans.

Additionally, an owner-financed note must have a fixed rate or, if adjustable, may adjust only after five or more years and be subject to reasonable annual and lifetime limitations on interest rate increases. If the interest rate is adjustable, the lender must consider the highest rate the borrower will have to pay in order to establish compliance with the ATR rule. Negative amortization loans (always risky) must be accompanied by disclosure and counseling for first-time buyers. Prepayment penalties are banned.

Mandatory arbitration provisions in loan documents (which always, in practice, favor the creditor) are prohibited.

Regulations Issued by the CFPB

Complex laws such as Dodd-Frank are nearly always passed in bare-bones form. They are skeletal structures requiring the appropriate administrative agency to issue rules and guidance in order to implement the law. The CFPB derives its authority to do this from Section 1053 of the Dodd-Frank Act, 12 U.S.C. 5563(e), as well as its general rulemaking authority to promulgate rules necessary or appropriate to carry out federal consumer financial laws (12 U.S.C. 5512(b)(1)).

The CFPB has been aggressive about rulemaking and has taken significant liberties in its interpretation of both the statute and the intent of Congress. For example, Subtitle B, Sec. 1411(a)(2) appears to frown on "non-standard loans" such as balloon notes. The CFPB, however, has focused on the ATR rule as the heart of the owner financing part of the law, rather than deciding that any particular type of loan (balloons for example) should be prohibited. Note that certain types of loans—home equity lines of credit, timeshare plans, reverse mortgages, and temporary or bridge loans—are exempt from the ATR rule.

De Minimis Origination Exception to Dodd-Frank

CFPB Regulations Sections 1026.36(a)(4) and (5) provide a de minimis exception for individuals who do only one transaction in any twelve-month period; and for entities (such as LLCs) who do three or fewer owner-financed transactions in any twelve-month period. (Recall that, legally speaking, entities are also considered "persons."). The exception is accomplished by stating that such "persons" are not included within the definition of "loan originators:"

4. SELLER FINANCERS; THREE PROPERTIES.

A person (as defined in § 1026.2(a)(22)) that meets all of the following criteria is not a loan originator under paragraph (a)(1) of this section:

The person provides seller financing for the sale of three or fewer properties in any 12-month period to purchasers of such properties, each of which is owned by the person and serves as security for the financing.

The person has not constructed, or acted as a contractor for the construction of, a residence on the property in the ordinary course of business of the person.

The person provides seller financing that meets the following requirements:

The financing is fully amortizing.

The financing is one that the person determines in good faith the consumer has a reasonable ability to repay.

The financing has a fixed rate or an adjustable rate that is adjustable after five or more years, subject to reasonable annual and lifetime limitations on interest rate increases. If the financing agreement has an adjustable rate, the rate is determined by the addition of a margin to an index rate and is subject to reasonable rate adjustment limitations. The index the adjustable rate is based on is a widely available index such as indices for U.S. Treasury securities or LIBOR.

The important item to note about this exemption is that the lender, exempted or not, must *still* comply with the ATR rule.

Since the foregoing exception applies only if the seller has not constructed a residence on the property in the ordinary course of business, professional builders who want to owner finance their new homes do *not* fall within the scope of the exception, no matter how many or how few homes they build.

Integrated Disclosures (the TRID Rule)

The CFPB is now the common regulator for Truth in Lending (TIL) and the Real Estate Settlement Procedures Act (RESPA), prescribing the form and content of the Loan Estimate and the Closing Disclosure, which have replaced the Good Faith Estimate and HUD-1 forms. The forms now used—a significant advance in simplicity—are sometimes referred to as "know before you owe."

The Loan Estimate (LE), which describes the proposed loan's costs and terms, must be provided to the borrower within 3 days of receipt of the application. There is now a disclosure of the "estimated cash to close." Also, itemization of all loan origination charges is required.

The Closing Disclosure (CD) which combines the old HUD-1 and final TIL is 5 pages long and designed to track the format of the Loan Estimate in order to make side-by-side comparison easier. Separate Closing Disclosures must be given to buyer and seller. There are a couple of other significant changes from past practice: the Closing Disclosure is now prepared by the lender (not the title company, as was the case with the HUD-1) and it must be received by the borrower at least 3 business days prior to closing, giving the borrower ample time to review (and perhaps question) what it says. Lenders must also offer a borrower a list of Settlement Services Providers.

Investors who seller-finance 5 or fewer properties per year are exempt from the TRID rule.

Qualified Mortgages ("QMs")

Loans have been divided into two groups, with "qualified mortgages" (considered to be more stable loans) in the first group; and all others in the second group, which would include any loan with "risky" features. QMs (or at least those that are not "higher-priced") are expressly designed to be a safe harbor from lender liability. ATR compliance, a landmine of liability in this context, is presumed.

What disqualifies a loan from being a QM? Examples would be interest-only provisions; negative amortization; higher than average interest rates; balloon payments; loan terms longer than thirty years; and loans with points and fees that exceed 3% of the loan amount. *These riskier loans are not banned, but the ATR rule must be strictly applied.* Any lender offering such non-qualified mortgages should, as a liability-avoidance strategy, literally stuff its loan file with documentary evidence that the borrower can in fact repay the debt as provided in the note. This file must be kept for a minimum of three years. Five is better.

The CFPB website states "Qualified Mortgages generally require that your monthly debt, including the mortgage, isn't more than 43% of your monthly pre-tax income. In some circumstances, certain small lenders may also decide that debt of more than 43% is appropriate."

HUD and FHA loans are automatically considered to be QMs.

It is not only stability and low risk that allow classification as a QM. Loans made in certain designated rural areas of the country qualify. The CFPB publishes a list of eligible counties on its website.

Lenders are categorized, with "creditor" and "small creditor" being defined terms. "Creditors" are those who make 5 or more home loans per year, unless the loan in question is a higher-priced mortgage loan (HPML), in which case the lender is a creditor regardless. "Small creditors" are those who make 500 loans or less per year and do not have more than two billion dollars in assets. Different rules apply.

Even persons knowledgeable in the lending industry can be forgiven for being confused about the rules around Dodd-Frank. It is suggested that, before deciding which rules apply in any given case, one should consult the CFPB website as follows:

Go to consumerfinance.gov
Click on "Law and Regulation"
Click on "Regulatory Implementation" on the drop-down menu
Click on "Title IV Rules"
Scroll down to a chart entitled "Rule/Compliance Guide"
Click on "Ability to Repay/Qualified Mortgage"

Investors and the Balloon Problem

Dodd-Frank, at least as interpreted and implemented by the CFPB, does *not* ban balloon mortgages. The CFPB website states "You can still opt for a balloon-payment mortgage when the lender meets the requirements to be considered a 'small creditor,' and your mortgage meets other criteria." For those concerned with the potential liability of making a risky loan and/or violating the ATR rule, this is rather vague; it creates a significant challenge for investors who want to include balloon provisions in their owner-financed notes.

Balloon notes originated by small creditors are classified as qualified mortgages only if the small creditor does business primarily in rural or "underserved" areas. All other balloon notes will be strictly subject to the ATR rule.

Until the CFPB rules reach a higher level of clarity, investors should be wary of selling properties using balloon notes.

Higher-Priced Mortgage Loans (HPMLs)

Owner-financing investors should not push the envelope on interest rates, even if a proposed loan is otherwise a QM. Higher-priced loans only receive a rebuttable presumption that the loan is a QM—not an absolute certainty. And there are extensive pre-loan disclosures required. The borrower must also get a certification from a housing counselor that he or she has received counseling on the high-cost mortgage being offered.

The CFPB offers two criteria for what constitutes an HPML: "a first-lien mortgage for which, at the time the interest rate on the loan was set, the APR was 1.5 percentage points or more over the Average Prime Offer Rate (APOR);" or "a subordinate-lien mortgage with an APR that, when the interest rate was set, exceeded the APOR by 3.5 percentage points or more." So the days when an owner-financing seller could determine the note's optimal interest rate solely by reference to the market and the state usury rate are behind us.

Dodd-Frank 2.0 - The Economic Growth, Regulatory Relief, and Consumer Protection Act

Signed into law in 2018, "Dodd-Frank 2.0" contains six titles which modify the original Dodd-Frank. Generally, the Act is (unsurprisingly) mostly about reducing regulations on banks and mortgage lenders. Lenders under $10 billion in assets are now exempt from the Volcker Rule based on the theory that these institutions are too small to cause the entire system to fail. This is a dubious conclusion, especially considering that $10 billion is not really a "small" number, nor does this approach take into account the tendency of failing institutions to cascade.

Two titles, however, Title III and Title IV, actually expand consumer protections in the areas of credit reporting and student loans. Even so, it is difficult to see Dodd-Frank 2.0 as anything other than a gift to big banks.

An Approaching Tide of Lawsuits?

Violation of the ATR/QM rules allow a consumer to sue for actual damages, statutory damages (including all finance charges and fees), attorney's fees and court costs. The burden of proving that the ATR determination was reasonable and made in good faith falls upon the lender. Consider this: if the borrower defaults early in the loan, but not as a result of a serious financial or other setback, then this is considered possible evidence that the lender was unreasonable!

The statute of limitations is three years from the date of the violation by the creditor. A defense to foreclosure in the form of a set-off is also provided. After three years, the consumer can bring ATR claims only as setoff/recoupment claims in a defense to foreclosure.

Investors should anticipate that borrower suits against lenders based on the evolving CFPB rules (the ATR/QM rules specifically) will be a growth industry in the next decade, particularly since lenders are now prohibited from including mandatory arbitration clauses in their notes. Prudence dictates that one avoid being on the wrong side of that trend, so owner financing of all types should be approached with caution and strict compliance.

There is also the possibility of enforcement by regulators. Even though the CFPB under Republican leadership backed off its more aggressive rulemaking and enforcement actions, state attorneys general are more and more stepping into the gap.

Real estate investors are often viewed by jurors as unscrupulous predators. It is a safe bet that future juries will, on the whole, not hesitate to find investors who are also lenders to be "unreasonable" under Dodd-Frank and therefore liable for substantial verdicts.

Service Providers

Among regulations issued by the CFPB is the requirement that those who provide services in connection with residential real estate loans be subjected to scrutiny as to qualifications, character, and E&O insurance coverage. Lenders are effecting this requirement by means of increased vetting of all participants in the loan process, including real estate lawyers who act as fee attorneys in the closing of transactions.

Borrower Defense to Foreclosure

Subchapter B Sec.1413 permits the borrower to assert a defense to foreclosure if the lender or mortgage originator violated the anti-steering rules or the ability-to-repay provisions of the law. This is clearly designed to penalize the formerly-widespread practice of putting under-qualified borrowers into loans that they could not afford to repay.

A Final Word about Dodd-Frank and Owner Finance

Dodd-Frank is an extremely complex law that is being subjected to substantial evolution by the rules that are intended to implement it. The text of the original statute is easy to find online. It can be a challenging read. The ensuing regulations (both existing and proposed), which are at least as convoluted as the statute, can be examined at the website of the CFPB (www.consumerfinance.gov/regulations). The reader should check current regulations before relying on any information provided in this chapter. Consult a real estate attorney who is specifically knowledgeable about Dodd-Frank before entering into a sales contract calling for owner finance. Your attorney may want to get on the phone with a CFPB attorney to clarify compliance (one must email them first). And never use seminar forms from non-lawyer "gurus" or forms off the internet to document such transactions. These are likely to be non-Texas specific and inadequate under the many state and federal laws and regulations that now pertain to owner financing.

Chapter 15

HIGHER-PRICED MORTGAGE LOANS

Escrow Requirement in Certain Owner-Financed Transactions

Certain home loans have been defined by the Federal Reserve as being "higher-priced mortgage loans" because (in part) the annual percentage rate charged on such loans exceeds the average prime rate by 1.5% for a first lien or 3.5% for a subordinate lien. Rules in this area are particularly important to owner-financed transactions since the APR is often higher than in conventional or FHA financing.

How can you determine if the HPML rules apply to your transaction? If the loan will be a first or subordinate lien on a one-to-four family residence; if the property will be owner occupied; and if the APR exceeds the amounts stated above, then such a loan is classified as a higher-priced mortgage loan and this law applies.

Applicable Law

Applicable law here is Regulation Z, 12 C.F.R. pt. 226, specifically Section 226.35. Higher-priced mortgage loan regulations are sometimes referred to as "HPML regs," and such loans are often called "Section 35 loans" or "HPML loans." Section 226.35, entitled "Prohibited Acts or Practices in Connection with Higher-Priced Mortgage Loans," became effective October 1, 2009 except for rules requiring collection of an escrow which became effective April 1, 2010.

Laws Impacting Owner Finance

The HPML regs exist alongside Dodd-Frank, which requires that a residential seller-lender in an owner-financed transaction perform affirmative due diligence in order to determine that the buyer-borrower can repay the loan; the federal SAFE Act (T-SAFE in Texas), which requires that a frequent seller-lender of one-to-four family residences in an owner-financed transaction have an RMLO license issued by the TDSML; a Texas requirement that the seller give both the existing lienholder and the buyer a seven-day written notice prior to closing a transaction with an existing loan in place; and burdensome rules relating to contracts for deed and other executory contracts contained in Property Code Sections 5.061 et seq. All of the foregoing are part of a wave of federal and state regulation designed to curb abuses in owner finance which contributed to the accumulation of bad loans and the subsequent collapse of the real estate market.

HPML Escrow Requirement

The seller in an owner-financed transaction subject to the HPML regs *must* establish an escrow account. Title 12 C.F.R. Sec. 226.35(b)(3)(i) states that "a creditor may not extend a loan secured by a first lien on a principal dwelling unless an escrow account is established before consummation for payment of property taxes and premiums for mortgage-related insurance required by the creditor, such as insurance against loss of or damage to property, or against liability arising out of the ownership or use of the property, or insurance protecting the creditor against the consumer's default or other credit loss."

This regulation requires that an escrow account be established before "consummation for payment of property taxes and premiums." When does such consummation occur? The language is unclear, but it is reasonable to interpret "consummation" in this context as the shift to the buyer of the obligation to pay ad valorem taxes and insurance premiums—and this occurs at closing.

A common practice is to provide for an escrow that commences with the first monthly payment. This may not comply with Section 226.35(b)(3)(i), however, since the escrow is generally not established at the closing itself. Since an escrow account cannot be commenced with a zero balance, it may therefore be necessary to open an escrow at closing with a deposit by the buyer of an initial escrow amount, even if that amount is nominal.

What if a buyer wants to terminate the required escrow? This appears to be permissible according to Section 226.35(b)(3)(iii), which states that a "creditor or servicer may permit a consumer to cancel the escrow account required in paragraph (b)(3)(i) of this section only in response to a consumer's dated written request to cancel the escrow account that is received no earlier than 365 days after consummation." Must a seller-lender comply with such a request? The statute's use of the word "may" rather "must" suggests that the seller may decline a buyer's request to terminate the escrow.

Escrow and Third-Party Servicers

The traditional owner-financed transaction contemplates that the seller will receive and handle both payments of principal and interest as well as an escrow. There are, however, potential problems with this approach. Will the seller report the amount of interest paid to the IRS? Will the seller have the capability of generating an escrow analysis if required? Does the seller report timely payment history to the credit bureaus? Most individual sellers are neither equipped nor inclined to perform these functions.

There is also the matter of trusting the seller on certain key items—for example, timely payment of taxes and insurance premiums. What if the seller fails to do this and instead mishandles the funds? Another example of trust occurs in wraparound transactions, in which the buyer agrees to make payments to the seller and the seller, in turn, promises to make payments to the first lienholder. What if the seller defaults on this obligation?

One solution to these issues is to engage a third-party servicer who will collect payments from the buyer (including by electronic means) and see to it that any escrow or secondary payments are properly made.

The HPML regs are, along with the SAFE Act and Dodd-Frank, part of a federal trend to impose nationwide regulations upon certain lending practices as they relate to owner finance. Texas, once the haven for easy money, now finds itself in the same highly-regulated environment as everyone else.

PART IV

CREATIVE TRANSACTIONS

Chapter 16

LEASE-OPTIONS, LEASE-PURCHASES, AND RIGHTS OF FIRST REFUSAL

Are They Still Useful in Texas?

Lease-Options

Lease-options have always been a favorite tool of Texas real estate investors—one of the "Big Three" alongside contracts for deed and lease-purchases—all of which are creative devices for getting under-qualified buyers into a home immediately. However, the Property Code now defines residential lease-options for longer than 180 days as executory contracts subject to strict regulation and penalties if not done exactly right. *Exactly right.* Specific requirements must be observed and the burden is entirely on the seller to do so. Violation incurs not only penalties under the Property Code (return of payments made by the buyer) but potential liability under the dreaded DTPA, which can involve treble damages plus attorney's fees.

The Pure Option to Purchase

Before continuing our discussion of lease-options, it is worth remembering that there *is* such thing as a stand-alone option to purchase, disconnected from a lease. It consists of a contractual right granted to a potential buyer which may be exercised in writing, at a time of the buyer's choosing, without the requirement of a triggering event, to purchase the property at a pre-determined price. It is not sufficient, however, to say "I have the option to purchase 123 Oak Street for $250,000" and let it go at that. How long does this option last (what is the option term, in other words)? Is it a one-time right or a continuing right? Is the option assignable? Just as important, what are the terms of the prospective purchase—cash, third-party financed, or seller-financed? How long will the buyer have to close after notice of the exercise of the option is given? When you think about it, *a well-written option agreement is going to contain all the key points and material terms that are usually found in an earnest money contract.* So beware the "one-liner" option, since it often raises more questions than it answers.

Buying and Selling Options

There is a notable change in this area, effective in 2017, which directly affects investors. Property Code Sec. 5.086 requires a disclosure for all persons who sell options or assign contracts: "Before entering into a contract, a person selling an option or assigning an interest in a contract to purchase real property must disclose to any potential buyer that the person is selling only an option or assigning an interest in a contract and the person does not have legal title to the real property." Failing to make this disclosure triggers a requirement in the Occupations Code that such transfers constitute real estate brokerage and therefore require a broker's license. The usual penalties apply. While not specified, it is likely that future cases will also deem failure to include the disclosure to be a deceptive trade practice.

What are executory contracts and why do lease-options fall within this category?

Another area that should be explored is the connection between any preferential right to buy real estate and executory contracts, since the latter are now so heavily regulated.

Executory contracts include any transaction that defers some material action by either party that pertains to real property ownership or possession into the future. So why do lease-options fall within this definition? Because the Property Code says so. Section 5.062(a)(2) states: "An option to purchase real property that includes or is combined or executed concurrently with a residential lease agreement, together with the lease, is considered an executory contract for conveyance of real property." There is an exception for lease-options for 180 days or less under Section 5.062(c)—otherwise, the TREC 1-4 contract would violate this provision when combined with a short-term lease. Commercial lease-options are not affected.

A case from the Texarkana court of appeals provides a good definition of an executory contract: "In a typical real estate contract, the seller and purchaser mutually agree to complete payment and title transfer on a date certain, the closing date, at which time the purchaser generally obtains both title and possession. By contrast, in an executory contract, the purchaser is usually given immediate possession, but is required to satisfy numerous obligations over an extended period of time before the seller has an obligation to transfer actual title." *Bryant v. Cady*, 445 S.W.3d 815, 822-23, (Tex.App.—Texarkana 2014, no pet.).

Executory Contracts: Requirements

Just for the record, one can *still* do a long-term lease-option or other types of executory contracts—but consider the requirements. The landlord-seller must provide the Buyer with a recent survey or a current plat; copies of liens, restrictive covenants, and easements; a statutory disclosure; a disclosure for non-subdivision properties stating utilities may not be available until the subdivision is recorded; tax certificates; a copy of the insurance policy showing the name of the insurer and insured along with a description of the insured property and the policy amount; a seven-day notice letter; and an annual accounting that includes amounts paid, amounts owed, payments remaining, taxes paid, and the amount paid for insurance premiums plus an accounting for any insurance proceeds. All of this must be done *before* the contract is signed. Prop. Code Sec. 5.069 et seq.

Additionally, it is required that sales advertisements disclose the availability of water, sewer, and electric service. The seller must provide a thorough disclosure of the financial terms of the transaction, including the interest rate, amount of interest charged for the term of the contract, the total amount of principal and interest to be paid, and the non-existence of a prepayment penalty. Excessive late fees and prepay-ment penalties are banned.

Even if all the foregoing statutory requirements are met, the buyer may *still* cancel an executory contract for *any reason* within 14 days of signing. Prop. Code Sec. 5.074.

The Short-Term Lease-Option

It is nonetheless true that lease-options may be useful if the term is 180 days or less *or* if the property is paid for (meaning a lender's consent will not be needed). Accordingly, an investor should not avoid utilizing a 180-day (or less) lease-option if it is appropriate under the circumstances, particularly if there is a fair possibility that the option may be exercised during that period. Also, if the parties decide in good faith to renew the option for another short term, they should not hesitate to do so. We recommend using a 179-day option term just to avoid any issue about whether or not the statute has been violated, since it is never a good idea to cut matters too closely when dealing with legal limits or deadlines—not just this time limit, but all of them, across the board.

A Month-to-Month Lease Combined with an Option

What if the lease is month-to-month? If it includes an option to purchase, do the requirements and penalties of Property Code Sections 5.062 et seq. apply? The answer is likely yes, so long as the term of the option fails to be expressly limited to 180 days or less. Since the lease can easily extend for longer than 180 days, the option can as well. Accordingly, a court would most likely find this arrangement to be an executory contract.

Potential Solution: Stacking Short-Term Options

What about the possibility of stacking six-month option contracts—i.e., allowing the option to expire and then renewing it again and again? This would appear to be a loophole, making stacking a possible way for a very aggressive investor to still do a lengthy lease-option without complying with the executory contract rules, although at some risk. If challenged by the tenant-buyer, a judge may examine the totality of the circumstances, including the intent of the parties, and declare that the arrangement is a de facto executory contract. It all comes down to whether or not the tenant-buyer becomes disgruntled and decides to (1) challenge the transaction with a lawsuit, or (2) resist an eviction based on an executory contract defense. No challenge, no issue. There are no executory contract police. Having said that, lease-option arrangements that endure in the aggregate for longer than 180 days are perilous. The legislature clearly intended to discourage their use in residential transactions and deliberately imposed significant liability on landlord-sellers for doing them improperly.

Lease-Purchases

A lease-purchase is conceptually different from a lease-option. In a lease-purchase or rent-to-own, a portion of each monthly rent payment is set aside and credited toward the tenant-buyer's down payment. It is common, but not universal, for a lease-purchase to provide that after a certain amount is paid in, the tenant-buyer is able either (1) to convert the transaction from a lease to an owner-financed sales transaction in which the tenant gets a warranty deed and gives back a note and deed of trust to the seller, or (2) the seller agrees that the tenant-buyer may show the accumulated down payment on a loan application to a third-party lender and thereby qualify for financing.

Are lease-purchases executory contracts? Yes, since fulfillment of a material term is deferred into the future.

Lease-Purchase-Option Hybrids

Lease-purchases may provide that once a sufficient down payment is paid, the tenant-buyer will have an option to purchase the property at a certain price. Result? The lease-purchase becomes tangled up with a lease-option. It becomes become a hybrid "lease-purchase-option." What if the lease-purchase provides that payments will continue over a number of years until the property is paid for? In such a case it may not be a lease-purchase at all but an old-fashioned contract for deed.

Two points are worth noting. The first is that each of these devices—lease-options, lease-purchases, and contracts for deed—can, if only slightly modified, become hybridized with something else, sinking the transaction deeper into the executory contract hole. The second point is that regardless of the ultimate form such hybrid contracts take, they remain executory contracts for purposes of the rules and penalties of Property Code Sections 5.061 et seq.

Recording Requirement

All residential executory contracts must now be recorded. Property Code Section 5.076 states that "the seller shall record the executory contract, including the attached disclosure statement . . . on or before the 30th day after the date the contract is executed." Additionally, any instrument that terminates the contract must also be recorded.

Lease-Purchases in the Real World

Residential lease-purchases for longer than 180 days are no longer a feasible strategy for investors because of the multitude of requirements and the potential liability for doing them improperly. There is really no way to use a stacking technique here. Add the fact that the Property Code declares open season on the investor-seller whenever a tenant-buyer becomes disgruntled with an executory contract, and there are more reasons to avoid lease-purchases than there are to do them—especially since loss of an executory contract lawsuit (and the ensuing punishing damage award) could present an extinction event for a small investor.

The Right of First Refusal ("ROFR")

A right of first refusal ("ROFR") is a preemptive right to purchase specific real property at some future time upon defined terms and conditions. *ROFRs do not specify a price.* Circumstances vary, and therefore the language of a ROFR clause may vary as well. For example, a ROFR may be triggered by an offer received by the owner from a third party; in such a case, the owner is obligated to first offer the property for sale to the holder of the ROFR at the same price and upon the same terms. Another scenario may occur if the owner makes the decision to sell the property but does not yet have a buyer; the ROFR may obligate the owner to first offer the property to the holder of the ROFR.

The principal benefit of a ROFR is that it is not an executory contract, even when combined with a lease. Caution: as soon as a specific price is included, it is likely that a ROFR will be transformed into an option and become an executory contract. ROFRs are therefore not an effective tool for the investor-seller who wants to preset an above-market price in order to lock in a long-term profit.

ROFR Versus Options

Certain characteristics are shared by ROFRs and options. Both are exercisable in the future. The validity of both can be limited to certain time periods or terms, i.e., either may expire before it is exercised. They can occur in both residential and commercial situations. Also, both ROFRs and options grant the holder the *power* but not the *obligation* to act. There is generally no breach or liability for damages if the holder of an option chooses to do nothing.

However, a ROFR differs from an option in that it is conditional, not fixed, and does not specify a dollar price. An option to purchase, on the other hand, is a unilateral contract which gives the holder the right to compel sale of property at a certain price within a certain option term. When an owner gives notice of intent to sell, the ROFR matures or ripens and then becomes enforceable.

The terms of an option consist of the contractual provisions granting the option along with the terms and conditions of any third-party offer. Once the property owner has given the holder notice of his intent to sell, the terms of the option cannot be changed for as long as the option is binding on the owner. *City of Brownsville v. Golden Spread Elec. Coop., Inc.,* 192 S.W.3d 876 (Tex.App.—Dallas 2006, pet. denied).

What if an investor-seller gets creative with document wording and deletes the word "option" from the document, substitutes ROFR language in its place, and then goes on to specify a dollar price? Under the *Brownsville* case, once price is specified, it is likely that the ROFR becomes an option and therefore an executory device. Further, courts are more likely to interpret a contract clause in light of what it *actually is* rather than what it *pretends to be* (the "quacks like a duck" rule). The result could be a finding that executory contract rules have been violated, or worse, that fraud has been committed by the investor.

Drafting ROFR Language

All of this presents an interesting challenge when attempting to draft a ROFR. Here is one example:

> In the event Owner offers the Property for sale, then Holder [of the ROFR] will have the right (but not the obligation) to purchase the Property under the following

terms and conditions: (1) Once Owner has established an asking or listing price for the Property, Owner must first notify Holder in writing of Owner's intent to sell and shall then offer the Property for sale to Holder at this price. Holder will have 10 days from receipt of such notice to consider this offer, and if Holder accepts, Holder will have 45 days to close. Consideration may be cash or third-party financing or, if agreed between Owner and Holder, by assumption, wraparound, or owner finance. (2) If Holder declines or fails to purchase the Property at the listing or asking price, Owner will be free to offer the Property for sale to others. However, if a bona fide offer is received from a third-party prospective buyer, then Owner must again notify Holder in writing and offer the Property to Holder at the price and upon the same or better terms as named by the prospective buyer. Holder will have 10 days from receipt of such notice to consider this offer, and if Holder accepts, Holder will have 45 days to close. Holder may shorten or eliminate any applicable time periods in this paragraph by waiving or declining in writing to exercise Holder's right of first refusal. The right of first refusal described in this section shall entirely expire on _____202__.

The advantage of the foregoing method is that the ROFR sales price is ultimately set by a third-party buyer. However, what if the ROFR as drafted merely gives the holder a general right? Some method has to be found to establish price. In the following instance, value is determined by reference to prevailing fair market value:

In the event Owner intends to offer the Property for sale, Owner must first offer the Property for sale to Holder at a price equivalent to prevailing fair market value. Terms of sale shall be cash or third-party finance, and closing shall be within 45 days.

If the parties cannot agree on what constitutes fair market value, then two appraisers shall be promptly selected, one by Owner and another by Holder. The two appraisers selected shall proceed to promptly determine the fair market value of the Property, taking into consideration its condition, comparables, and any outstanding indebtedness, liabilities, liens, and obligations relating to the Property. The appraisers shall deliver their respective reports within thirty (30) days. If the two appraisers arrive at different valuations, then these two valuations shall be averaged in order to produce a final valuation. The final valuation shall be binding on both parties. Each party waives the right to contest the final valuation in court. The costs of the appraisals shall be split equally between Owner and Holder.

The ROFR is a useful tool which stops short of being an executory device, but only so long as one does not try to stretch the language in order to make it an option by a different name.

Other Preferential Rights

There are similar preferential rights that also fall within this general category. One is a right of first negotiation ("ROFN," sometimes called a right of first opportunity) which means exactly what the title suggests and no more. The seller is obligated to notify the holder of a ROFN of his intention to sell, and the holder will then have the right to negotiate and make an offer, which the seller is not obligated to accept. There is no mention of price and no obligation to conclude a deal. Another somewhat lesser right is a right of first offer ("ROFO") which obligates the seller to notify a potential buyer of his intention to sell and the buyer will then have the right to make an offer, the terms of which are not specified in advance. There is no right to negotiate. ROFRs, ROFNs, and ROFOs are potentially useful substitutes for a lease-purchase, but they must be carefully structured and worded so as not to fall into the executory conveyance trap.

Statute of Frauds Applies

All preferential rights to real estate must be express (not implied) and must be in writing in order to comply with the Statute of Frauds. Provisions of the Statute of Frauds applicable to real estate are found in Business & Commerce Code Sections 26.01 and 26.02(b): "[A] contract for the sale of real estate is not enforceable unless the promise or agreement, or a memorandum of it, is (1) in writing; and (2) signed by the person to be charged with the promise or agreement. . . ."

There is another statute that is applicable: Property Code Section 5.021, sometimes referred to as the "Statute of Conveyances," which states: "A conveyance of an estate of inheritance, a freehold, or an estate for more than one year, in land and tenements, must be in writing and must be subscribed and delivered by the conveyor or by the conveyor's agent authorized in writing." For more detail on the requirements of the Statute of Frauds, see chapter 12.

Preferential Rights and the Leasing of Real Estate

It should be noted that certain of the preferential rights discussed in this chapter also apply to the leasing of real property, although these are more commonly found in the world of commercial leasing and are thus less relevant to an investor in single family residences.

Preferential Rights and Executory Contracts in the Real World

Preferential rights often cross the line into the zone of executory contracts, and the result has been to greatly inhibit their use in buying and selling residential real estate. Burdensome requirements and stiff penalties applicable to executory contracts cause sensible investors to avoid them. Many real estate lawyers will not do them at all, since failure to comply with even the smallest requirement may trigger significant liability not just for the seller but also for the attorney preparing and filing the various disclosures and documents.

Caution to Investors: Avoid the Courtroom

Lease-options, lease-purchases, and other devices that fall within the realm of executory contracts present worrisome prospect of litigation with limited or no defenses for the investor, who is seldom the most admired person in the courtroom. Even if executory contract rules are inapplicable, a court can still look to DTPA Section 17.50(a)(3) which prohibits "any unconscionable action or course of action by any person"—a multi-edged weapon to say the least. Investors should find a good real estate lawyer, one with courtroom experience, and pay attention to what he or she says about how a judge or jury may react to a proposed deal and the documents that underlie it, particularly if there are executory contract implications. A good lawyer knows that real estate documents should always be drafted as if one will someday have to defend them in court.

Chapter 17

WRAPAROUND TRANSACTIONS

A Form of Owner Finance Leaving Existing Loan(s) in Place

A wraparound transaction is a form of creative seller financing that leaves the original loan and lien in place when a property is sold. The buyer usually makes a down payment, gets a warranty deed, and signs a new note to the seller (the "wraparound note") for the balance of the sales price. This wrap note, secured by a new deed of trust (the "wraparound deed of trust"), becomes a junior lien on the property behind the existing first lien. The buyer makes monthly payments to the seller on the wrap note and the seller in turn makes payments to the first-lien lender. The original lender's note is referred to as the "wrapped note" and it remains secured by the existing "wrapped deed of trust." It is possible to wrap more than one prior note (e.g., an 80/20).

Often the principal of the wrap note to the seller exceeds the amount of the payoff on the wrapped note. This is seller profit. Alternatively, the buyer may make a cash payment to the seller for the seller's equity, and the wrap note payment will then be structured to correspond closely to the amount of the payment on the wrapped note (a mirror wrap).

Specific wrap terms can vary, but the principle remains the same. Wraps may be done on both residential and commercial properties. Wrap paperwork begins with the earnest money contract, which should include an addendum setting forth the terms of the wrap. At closing, details of the wrap should be contained and summarized in a comprehensive wraparound agreement.

Alternatively, if the parties are clear on terms and ready to move forward immediately, they can skip the contract phase and request that an attorney prepare wrap documents for immediate closing.

If and when the buyer gets a refinance loan, the wrapped loan is paid and released, and the seller keeps any cash that exceeds the payoff amount of this first lien. The main difference between a wrap and a conventional sale is that the seller must wait until the wrap note is paid in order to receive the full sales proceeds.

Wraparound financing is sometimes referred to as subordinate-lien financing.

Wraparound Documentation

Wrap documents should, at minimum, include:

1. a wrap note signed by the buyer;
2. a wrap deed of trust securing payment of the wrap note;
3. a warranty deed with vendor's lien conveying title to the buyer; and
4. a wraparound agreement covering miscellaneous details.

A short-term note for part of the down payment may also be included. For example, the seller might agree to accept $20,000 down—$10,000 at closing and $10,000 paid over the next 6 months. For this, you would need to add a down payment note to the above list.

The interest rate on the wrap note is often higher than that on the wrapped note since seller financing usually carries a rate slightly higher than market. Typical amortization is 15 or 30 years. In the past, most wrap notes were ballooned in 3 to 7 years, giving the investor a reasonably short time horizon for realizing a profit; however, Dodd-Frank now requires that the seller affirmatively determine that the buyer has the ability to repay before a balloon may be used (see chapter 14).

Other Forms of Seller Financing

Wraps are a form of seller financing. There is no disputing it. Dodd-Frank and the SAFE Act apply.

As noted in the previous chapter, residential lease-options and contracts for deed were both restricted by executory contract provisions incorporated into the Texas Property Code in 2005. Because there are severe penalties on sellers if strict, burdensome rules are not followed, investors have moved away from lease-options and contracts for deed. Only a few types of residential owner financing remain practicable and reasonably low-risk: traditional owner finance, used when residential property is paid for (i.e., no existing liens); exit land trusts, which involve temporarily deeding the property into a trust until a credit-impaired buyer can obtain financing; and wraparounds.

How is a wrap different from a contract for deed?

A wraparound is not an executory contract. It is an "executed" (complete) transaction as opposed to an "executory" (incomplete or unfinished) transaction. The buyer gets a deed to the property at closing, not at some future time, so the executory contract rules in Property Code

David J. Willis, J.D., LL.M.

Sections 5.061 et seq. do not apply. In the event of default, the seller must foreclose in order to get the property back. This is usually not an undue hardship since Texas has one of the fastest non-judicial foreclosure statutes in the country.

What about doing a wrap but delaying delivery of the deed to the buyer?

Some wraparound arrangements provide that the deed to the buyer will be held in escrow (perhaps by a lawyer) as security for a period of time—until the buyer pays in the full down payment, for instance. The wrap paperwork then states that the buyer is only leasing until the deed is delivered out of escrow. This is generally a bad idea. A material item of the transaction—the *most* material term, in fact—is unexecuted. Since the deal is unfinished, it qualifies as an executory contract and is subject to Property Code requirements and penalties, along with a nasty tie-in provision that makes violations of Section 5.061 et seq. also violations of the DTPA.

There is another version of this practice, the "security deed" technique. A security deed is a deed back from the buyer to the seller that is intended to be filed by the seller only if the buyer defaults—i.e., in lieu of going through foreclosure. This can legally be done but it is risky since a future court may disapprove of deliberately avoiding statutory foreclosure procedures. Remember, real estate investors are not the most beloved of persons in the hallowed halls of justice. The common perception is that investors are greedy predators exploiting the unfortunate. Juries are often happy to award treble damages and attorney's fees against investors, so caution is in order.

Isn't a wrap the same thing as an assumption?

No. In an assumption, the buyer formally assumes the legal responsibility for paying one or more existing notes. Sometimes this is done with the approval of the seller's lender, paying an assumption fee, and signing onto the debt; more often, the promise to assume the existing debt is made directly (and only) to the seller by means of an assumption deed. Either way, it is expressly stated that the buyer is taking on the legal obligation of paying the first-lien note. This is not the case in a wrap, which is a kind of "subject to" transaction. The wrapped first-lien note is the exclusive responsibility of the seller.

In a wrap, therefore, the first-lien note and the deed of trust securing it remain undisturbed. A new note (the wrap note) secured by a new wrap deed of trust is created. In other words, there are two separate and independent sets of payment obligations. The seller is obligated on the

156

wrapped first-lien note until it is paid and released; and the buyer is obligated to the seller on a new wrap note and wrap deed of trust. These obligations coexist.

How can I be sure a wrap is legitimate?

Wrap transactions *are* legitimate, primarily because there is nothing that says they are not. There are numerous Texas cases in which wraparound transactions have been upheld. Even the State Bar of Texas, in its Real Estate Forms Manual, publishes suggested forms for wrap documents.

Are there recent laws affecting wraparounds?

There are recent laws affecting *all* forms of owner-financed transactions. These laws include the SAFE Act, or T-SAFE as implemented in Texas, and Dodd-Frank.

The SAFE Act imposes a licensing requirement on certain types of owner financing extended by persons who are regularly engaged in selling owner-financed residences. A seller is required to be licensed as an RMLO if the property is not the seller's homestead and/or if the sale is not to a family member. So, if the property is a rental house being sold to a non-family member, then the seller *is* required to have an RMLO license, which requires training, a background check, and an exam. Note that the licensing rule applies only to residential wraps and is not applied to persons making five or fewer owner-financed loans in a year.

Dodd-Frank overlaps the SAFE Act in regulatory intent and effect. It requires that a seller-lender in a residential owner-financed transaction (including wraps) determine at the time credit is extended that the buyer-borrower has the ability to repay the loan (the ATR rule). The seller is obligated to investigate the buyer's credit history, current and expected income, financial obligations, debt-to-income ratio, employment status, and the like in order to make this determination. Dodd-Frank provides for a de minimis exception for persons doing no more than three owner-financed transactions per year (so long as the seller-lender is not in the building business)—but (1) the seller must take thorough steps to determine that the buyer has the ability to repay; and (2) the note must have a fixed rate or, if adjustable, may adjust only after five or more years and be subject to reasonable annual and lifetime caps. See CFPB reg. Sec. 1026.36(a)(4).

Dodd-Frank is a hugely complex law and continues to undergo interpretation and rule-making by the Consumer Finance Protection Board. Their rules are a challenge to understand, interpret, and apply— even for experienced real estate attorneys.

What if there is more than one existing lien?

It is not uncommon to wrap more than one note and lien (e.g., a first and a second). The prior liens may even be to different lenders. The principle is the same: the buyer pays the seller on the wraparound note, and the seller then pays both prior notes. The lien securing the wraparound note is subordinate to both of the prior liens.

Example of a Wrap

Consider the example of 123 Oak Street which is valued at $100,000 but has been slow to move. There is a first lien in the amount of $50,000 to Apple Bank and a second lien in the amount of $25,000 to Orange Bank which, taken together, result in $25,000 equity. In the usual case, a purchaser would make a down payment and obtain third-party institutional financing, allowing the seller to receive his equity at closing and go happily on his way. But what if the buyer is unable to get traditional financing? The solution is a seller-financed wrap note that may be in a premium amount—say $110,000—which is subordinate to the notes due Apple and Orange Banks. The wrap note will likely bear a higher than market rate of interest. It will be secured by a wrap deed of trust that enables the seller to foreclose if the buyer defaults on the wrap note.

Is a wrap a device to get sub-prime buyers into homes?

Perhaps, but prudent investors will require the buyer-borrower to have a substantial down payment. The seller-lender should evaluate and approve the buyer's qualifications just as any other lender would. In fact, Dodd-Frank requires this. The wraparound should be viewed as a legiti-mate device to sell property to reasonably qualified buyers who have money to put down and can afford the monthly payments.

Can wraps be used in conjunction with land trusts?

Yes. There may be circumstances where it may be a good idea to first transfer the property into a land trust and then do a wrap, but this requires more complex documentation since a trust agreement will also have to be prepared. Expect higher attorney's fees.

Are wraps just for homes?

No. Both residential and commercial wraps are possible. Commercial deeds of trust are more likely, however, to contain provisions that actually prohibit any transfer of title without prior lender consent. In all cases, but especially in commercial cases, one should carefully review the deed of trust securing an existing loan before proceeding with a wrap.

Why would a seller do a wrap?

The wrap seller can unload property at full market price (or even higher)—property that might otherwise have to be discounted or sit idly on the market. The seller gets at least some cash today (the down payment) which either goes into the seller's pocket or is used to reduce principal on the wrapped note (or a negotiable combination of both). The seller is then out from under the payment burden, although he or she must continue to be involved in collecting and forwarding payments to the first lienholder—unless a third-party servicer is used. The seller also gets the benefit of any spread between the interest rate on the wrapped note and wraparound note.

Why would a buyer do a wrap?

That is an easy question. The buyer does not have to apply and qualify for a new loan, at least not immediately. The buyer gets title to the property and immediate possession without lengthy delays, expensive loan fees, and closing costs.

Why would a broker encourage a wrap transaction?

Aside from meeting objectives of the broker's client, the buyer's down payment supplies cash for the broker's commission to be paid at closing, just as with any other transaction.

Is title insurance available?

Yes, but availability may be limited. Some title companies are more inclined to insure wraps than others. Certain underwriters are not comfortable with the wraparound process for reasons of their own. It may be necessary to shop title companies until a wrap-friendly title company is found. Be prepared to meet any additional underwriting requirements they may impose.

If a title company is issuing insurance, then closing will be held at the title company. However, most wraps are closed without title insurance in a lawyer's office based on an informal title search or a title report.

Isn't a wrap a breach of contract with the lender? What about the due-on-sale clause?

A wrap transaction is neither a breach of contract nor a violation of the most commonly used due-on-sale clause, which can be found at paragraph 18 of the FNMA deed of trust. This clause merely gives the lender an option to take action if it chooses. In other words, it says that a lender *may* (not must) accelerate.

Mortgage lenders are not usually interested in foreclosing upon a performing loan on merely technical grounds such as transfer of title by the borrower. However, some will send irate letters demanding that the new owner apply and qualify to assume the loan, threatening that the property will otherwise be posted for foreclosure. Even so, statistically speaking, actual acceleration of a performing loan based on due-on-sale seldom happens.

Isn't there some kind of notice requirement before doing a wrap transaction?

Yes. Property Code Section 5.016 requires that the seller (1) give seven days' notice to the buyer before closing that an existing loan will remain in place; (2) inform the buyer that buyer has this same seven-day period in which to rescind the earnest money contract without penalty; and (3) also provide a seven-day notice to the lender. These notices are all the obligation of the seller and must be in the form prescribed by the statute. Actual lender consent, however, is *not* required, which makes this a rather odd law. Lender notices, often sent to the loan servicer, generally produce no response.

Note that the buyer's opportunity to cancel is an exclusively pre-closing remedy. There is no right of rescission after closing has occurred.

Property Code Section 5.016(c)(10) provides an exception to the notice requirement when "the purchaser obtains a title insurance policy insuring the transfer of title to the real property." Thus if you are able to get a title company to insure your wrap, you may dispense with seven-day notices.

This is a law that has no teeth to speak of. As a consequence, it is widely disregarded. For now, it has not had a significant restraining effect on owner-financed transactions.

What kind of down payment should the seller get on a wrap?

Down payments are an underwriting issue. In the case of a wrap, the seller is also the lender and (like any lender) should carefully consider the risks inherent in the transaction as well as the borrower's creditworthiness and ability to repay—all of which should be examined before determining the amount of down payment and what interest rate to charge. Dodd-Frank requires such due diligence. Regardless of the borrower's qualifications, it is likely that a down payment of 5% or less will nonetheless fall within the risky category.

Can part of the down payment be financed? Yes. There is no prohibition against it. Typically, the buyer would pay part of the down payment at closing and then promise to pay the balance within a short period—say 30 to 90 days—utilizing a second wrap note (a down-payment note). Again, this is an underwriting issue for the seller but it is a common enough practice.

What if both notes are due on the first of the month?

The timing of payments is an issue and should be addressed in both the wrap note and the wraparound agreement. It is a good idea to schedule payments on a wrap note seven to ten days before payments are due on the wrapped note, to allow time for the seller to collect payments from the buyer and then forward them on to the wrapped lender in a timely manner.

What about casualty insurance on the property?

Sellers in wrap transactions nearly always want to cancel their casualty insurance policy. This is inadvisable. The wrapped lender, which usually collects an escrow or at the very least is named as additional insured, will be notified of the cancellation. The seller will then get a default letter from the wrapped lender who will likely "force place" another policy (usually a more expensive one) at the seller's expense. The existing policy should therefore be left alone *and* the buyer should obtain his own policy. This is an imperfection in the wrap process.

There is also an issue relating to insurable interest. What happens if there is a loss? Collecting on the seller's insurance policy can be problematic after a wrap since title to the property has changed hands. Even if the seller agrees to make a claim on behalf of the buyer, the insurer may refuse to pay it, asserting that the seller no longer owns the property. Worse, this could potentially be construed as insurance fraud. Therefore, the buyer should procure separate casualty and contents insurance, and claims should be made pursuant to the buyer's policy. It is unfortunate that this results in two policies, but there may be no reliable way around it. Insurance issues should be thoroughly addressed in the wraparound agreement.

If there is no escrow for insurance being collected by the wrapped lender, then it is in the seller's best interest to collect one from the buyer.

What about "double wraps"?

So long as the wrap deed of trust permits it, a wrapped loan can be wrapped and wrapped again, although the documentation can become prolific. This permits an investor to purchase property on a wrap and then sell it the same way (at a higher price and interest rate, of course), collecting a down payment (the investor's front-end profit) from a new buyer in the process. Usually, this new buyer commits to go through credit repair with the goal, but not the requirement, of paying off the wrap note early. The investor then gets his back-end profit.

Substitution of Collateral Clauses

An additional, advanced trick: some investor-buyers on a wrap include a "substitution of collateral" clause in their wrap notes that allows the property to be freed from the wrap lien so long as property of reasonably equivalent value is substituted in its place. If the buyer is an investor with multiple properties this could be a useful strategy.

What if the buyer defaults on the wrap note?

Let's review: the seller receives a wrap deed of trust that enables the seller to foreclose if the buyer defaults in paying the wrap note. The seller can also seek and obtain a deficiency judgment if the sales price at foreclosure is insufficient to discharge the wrap note plus accrued interest and fees. Accordingly, the seller has the same ability to enforce the wrap note and lien as does any other lender. The foreclosure of a wrap is no different from foreclosing on any other ordinary deed of trust lien.

Texas is fortunate to have an expedited non-judicial foreclosure process. Property Code Section 51.002 requires that a homeowner be given at least a 20-day notice of default and intent to accelerate the note if the default is not timely cured. If the deed of trust is on the FNMA form (which would be unusual for a wrap) then a 30-day notice and opportunity to cure is required. The default notice must be followed by a second letter stating that since the default was not cured, the note is accelerated and the property is being posted for foreclosure. This second notice must be given at least 21 days before the first Tuesday of the month in which the foreclosure will be held. So most Texas residential foreclosures take a minimum of 41 days—51 days if a FNMA deed of trust is involved—although, to repeat what we have said elsewhere, one should avoid cutting it close when it comes to legal notices. It is prudent to allow a cushion. Refer to chapter 39 on foreclosures.

What if the seller defaults by not paying the wrapped lender?

The wrap agreement should provide that if the seller fails to make payments to the wrapped lender, the buyer may do so and receive credit against the wrapped note. The buyer should also have the power to request documentary proof from the seller that the wrapped note is current.

Two related situations are of interest: what happens if the seller (1) files bankruptcy and seeks discharge of the wrapped debt, or (2) dies leaving the wrapped debt unpaid? In either case, the buyer could be forced to refinance the debt on short notice, which may be challenging. In the case of seller bankruptcy, the seller should agree in the wrap agreement to execute a reaffirmation agreement on the wrapped debt rather than surrendering the property to the lender. As for premature death, the buyer should check to see if the seller has or can add term life protection (payoff insurance). If not, the buyer might consider obtaining a term life insurance policy on the seller in the amount of the balance on the wrapped debt.

What about the interest deduction?

The seller continues to be able to deduct interest paid on the wrapped loan. Nothing has changed there. As to interest on the wrap note, interest received by the seller must be reported as income, and interest paid by the buyer is deductible.

What are the disadvantages of a wrap?

There are shortcomings to a wrap. For instance, the seller has to wait until the wrap note matures in order to receive the full proceeds of the sale. Also, the wrapped loan is frozen in place and cannot be refinanced for the duration of the wrap. Unless the seller utilizes a third-party servicer, the seller must collect and remit payments, which requires ongoing involvement. If the wrap borrower defaults, the seller must foreclose. In the unlikely event a loan is accelerated, the buyer may have to quickly secure traditional financing, so the wraparound agreement should specify the amount of time in which this must be done. The parties may also be carrying duplicate casualty insurance policies.

Some caution is in order as to the duration (term) of the wraparound note. Statistically, the wrap is more likely to be successful the longer the time the borrower has to find substitute financing. Wraps with a two-year balloon have a high mortality rate.

Wraps are useful devices, but they are not perfect.

Going Forward with a Wrap

A properly drafted wraparound transaction will include at least four documents—a warranty deed, a wraparound deed of trust, a wrap note, and a wraparound agreement to address the details. There may also be a down-payment note involved. These are sophisticated documents that should be highly customized for the specific transaction. Only a qualified real estate attorney experienced in preparing wrap documents should be used to draft this paperwork. There are no forms available from any source that are adequate to the task. Also, because there is no TREC or

TAR promulgated wrap addendum, the TREC earnest money contract should include an attorney-prepared custom addendum. Accordingly, attorney fees for wrap documentation may be somewhat more expensive than for the average closing.

Chapter 18

"SUBJECT TO" TRANSACTIONS

Buying Property without Accepting the Obligation to Pay the Debt

In order to understand "subject to" transactions, one must separate the concept of title from the concept of debt. They are divisible. A deed is a signed and acknowledged document that conveys legal title to real property. A note is a signed document promising to repay a debt. The two *can* be split and frequently are. Transferring title to real property without transferring the obligation to pay the debt associated with it is a "subject to" transaction.

Mechanics of a Sub2

In a sub2, an investor-buyer takes title but makes no promises (either to the lender or to the seller) about assuming the existing debt. In fact, a properly worded sub2 deed expressly states that the buyer is *not* assuming any such responsibility. Sub2s are often used by investor-buyers in order to buy, fix, and flip for a short-term profit, all before the loan gets so far in arrears that a foreclosure occurs. Presumably, upon resale, the buyer's new loan eliminates any existing arrearage or default.

Core sub2 documents include a sub2 addendum to the TREC 1 to 4 contract; a sub2 agreement (details below); and sub2 deed (either general or special warranty).

Form of Sub2 Deeds

There is no standard form for a sub2 deed although Texas does have certain rules that apply if any deed is to be valid (refer to chapter 8). This is a sample sub2 clause in warranty deed:

> This conveyance is made subject to any and all indebtedness of Grantor and liens against the Property, including but not limited to that certain indebtedness and liens securing same evidenced by a note in the original principal amount of $___, dated ___, executed by Grantor and payable to the order of ___, which note is secured by a vendor's lien retained in deed of even date recorded at

Clerk's File No. ___in the Official Public Records of Real Property of ___ County, Texas, and is additionally secured by a deed of trust of even date to ___, Trustee, recorded at Clerk's File No. ___ in the Official Public Records of Real Property of ___ County, Texas. Grantee does not assume payment of this or any other indebtedness of Grantor.

Must the buyer sign a sub2 deed? Usually not. Most often, the investor-buyer is accepting title and making no promises or agreements at all, so there is no reason for a signature. However, if there are additional points of agreement, then these may be inserted into the deed and accompanied by the investor-buyer's signature, making the deed serve the dual purpose of a conveyance and a contract. If these additional points are lengthy (or perhaps better kept confidential) then it is advisable to create a stand-alone unrecorded sub2 agreement, which is similar in many ways to the side agreement that is often executed as part of an assumption package—except, of course, for the obvious difference that in the case of a sub2 transaction the existing indebtedness is *not* being assumed.

As with other deeds, the sub2 deed need not reflect cash paid by the investor-buyer (presumably a buyout of the seller's equity in the property, if any). It is customary for confidentiality reasons to recite that consideration paid is "ten dollars and other valuable consideration" although the actual amount paid can always be shown if the parties desire to make that information part of the public record.

Recording

As with any other deed, there is no requirement that a sub2 deed be recorded in the county clerk's real property records in order to be valid—only that execution occur before a notary followed by delivery to the grantee. When this is done, the title transfer is effective between the parties. It is nonetheless in the buyer's interest to record the deed, not just to preserve the record chain of title but to avoid the possibility that the grantor may sell the property twice.

General Warranty Deeds versus Special Warranty Deeds

The term "warranty deed" is loosely used to refer to a deed that contains both express and implied warranties. There is also a deed without warranties. A general warranty deed is the preferred form of deed for a buyer because it expressly warrants the *entire* chain of title, whereas a special warranty deed warrants title *only* from the grantor. Although special warranty deeds are more common in commercial transactions, receiving a sub2 deed with special warranty should not trouble an investor, particularly since the last transaction involving the property likely encumbered it with a purchase-money lien and therefore a title policy was issued at that time.

Sub2 Versus Quitclaims

Some investors consider it adequate to acquire a quitclaim from a seller rather than a sub2 deed with either general or special warranties. This is not the best practice. Why? A quitclaim is the weakest form of transfer and title companies often decline to insure a chain of title containing a quitclaim. A title company may ask that a deed with general or special warranties be obtained to replace the quitclaim. If a grantor is unable or unwilling to provide any warranties then a deed without warranties should be used.

Seven-Day Notice Requirement

As with wraparounds (chapter 17) a Section 5.016 seven-day notice is required. Specifically, the seller must: (1) give seven days' notice to the buyer before closing that an existing loan will remain in place; (2) inform the buyer that buyer has this same seven-day period in which to rescind the earnest money contract without penalty; and (3) also provide a seven-day notice to the lender. Lenders do not usually respond to Section 5.016 notices, nor is lender consent required under this law. As a consequence, the seven-day notice requirement is widely disregarded in sub2 transactions. However, when representing sellers, we always advise full compliance.

Due-on-Sale Issues

As emphasized elsewhere in this book, there is no such thing as breaching or violating the usual residential due-on-sale clause. Transferring title without prior lender consent does not constitute an offense—moral, civil, or criminal. Due-on-sale merely enables the lender to *choose* to act—if the borrower transfers title then the lender *may* demand immediate payment in full, but the lender would have to decide that such action is in its best interest, and most lenders will balk at accelerating an otherwise performing loan. Experience shows that the risk of acceleration is small while the loan remains current. This will likely continue to be the case so long as interest rates remain on the low side historically, since the lender lacks incentive to incur foreclosure costs solely for the purpose of lending those same funds out again at a relatively low rate. A significant rise in interest rates could alter this environment.

What is a Sub2 agreement and why is it advisable to have one?

A sub2 agreement goes beyond the other documents and addresses specifics of the transaction, for example, the details of the existing note or notes; representations and warranties by seller (it is always a good idea to have these if you are the buyer); investor disclosures to the seller that the loan may go unpaid and that there is a due-on-sale clause; matters relating to Dodd-Frank and the SAFE Act; the mechanics of obtaining an eventual release of lien; an assignment of rents, escrow, and security deposit; and other important items. Any of these issues could become problematic later and create a headache for the investor.

If you are the buyer, a sub2 agreement is also a good place to include the online access information for the loan account. Sooner or later, the investor will want to sell the property and it will be necessary to get a loan payoff. If the investor is not the original borrower, then the lender's privacy policies will prevent disclosure of this information.

Hybrid Agreements

As stated above an investor-buyer generally makes no promises about assuming the existing debt. But is this a rigid rule? Not at all, as it turns out. Recall, if you will, that sub2s fall into the category of creative transactions, meaning that all sorts of variations are possible. For example, the investor-buyer may make an agreement with the seller to catch up on part or all of any arrearage that may exist. Other options include a pledge to make payments until the property re-sells, or even to split gross profits upon resale, which incorporates elements of a joint venture. Extensive additional agreements of this nature are best placed in a stand-alone unrecorded sub2 agreement.

Resale of Sub2s

A sub2 may be resold several different ways. First, having put a property under contract, an investor may simply assign the contract to a new buyer. For this reason, the sub2 contract should be expressly made assignable without requirement for the seller's prior consent. Another method is for the investor to close and then flip the property for a sum of cash, transferring the property on a sub2 basis to the new buyer. A third option is for the investor to close and then resell the property by means of selling financing, i.e., collecting a down payment and transferring the property utilizing a warranty deed, promissory note, and deed of trust. The latter option obviously involves a long-term commitment by the investor.

Contract Note

Generally speaking, the TREC 1-4 contract should be used for acquiring sub2s, but it should be accompanied by a "Subject To Addendum." Since neither TREC nor TAR offer such an addendum, a custom addendum drafted by an attorney will be needed.

A sub2 deed is a useful device that should be part of any investor's tool kit, ready to be deployed when the opportunity arises. Sub2 documents, like other creative real estate documents, are not created equal. Consult a real estate attorney. Never use seminar forms, forms from other states, or Internet junk to do a sophisticated transaction like a sub2.

Chapter 19

ASSUMPTIONS

Picking up the Note

The essential features of an assumption are that the buyer (1) takes title to property by assumption deed (usually with a vendor's lien) that contains either general or special warranties; and (2) promises to pay the balance of the indebtedness being assumed, a promise that may or may not be secured by a deed of trust to secure assumption (which gives the seller a non-judicial foreclosure remedy in the event of default).

Additional documents such as an assumption agreement may also be needed. If the buyer is an investor, some sort of authority—either a special power of attorney or a property management letter—should be secured so that the investor can obtain payoff information upon resale.

Having said the foregoing, there are assumptions and there are assumptions, meaning that there are minimalist approaches that incur the least potential liability for the investor-buyer; and there are fully-secured approaches that maximize protection for the seller.

Is the lender's permission required for an assumption?

No. An assumption may be accomplished with or without consent of the lender. What is an assumption, after all? Merely a title transfer (in which the lender has no participation) and a promise to take over payments on an existing debt. This promise is between buyer and seller. So there is no point in the assumption process where a lender can intercept and prevent the deal, nor is there a means by which a lender can command that an assumption be unwound.

Although a small due-on-sale risk may exist if title to property is transferred without lender consent (and it remains small so long as the note is kept current), the vast majority of assumptions occur "unofficially," that is, without consent from the lender.

What about the assuming buyer's liability on the assumed note? There is none, at least to the lender. Promising to pay the assumed indebtedness is a pledge from buyer to seller, not to the lender. *The only way one becomes obligated to a lender is to sign a note to that lender.* Similarly, the only way one is released from the obligation to pay a note is for the lender to cancel the note and sign a release of lien.

What is the difference between an assumable and a non-assumable loan?

Most all loans today are referred to as non-assumable. This is contrasted with certain loans in years past that could be assumed merely by paying an assumption fee and notifying the lender of the new owner.

But is the term "non-assumable" accurate? Not really. As stated earlier, the concept of title is separate from the concept of debt. An owner of property is normally entitled to transfer title whenever and to whomever he or she wishes. Doing so, however, does not relieve the seller from responsibility to pay the note (since the seller signed it), nor does it automatically obligate the buyer to pay the note (since the buyer did not sign it). A typical deed transfers title—that's all.

The assumability issue is relevant in determining whether or not the lender will allow substitution of one obligor on the note for another. In other words, will the lender let the seller off the hook for the debt and replace him under the note with the borrower? The answer is usually *no*. Lenders want a new buyer to apply, qualify, pay fees, and get a new loan. That is, after all, the nature of their business.

More about the Due-on-Sale Clause

If an owner transfers title without consent, has the owner breached the covenants of the deed of trust? Committed an illegal act? No, at least not under the commonly-used FannieMae deed of trust. Lenders would of course *prefer* to be notified if a loan is going to be assumed by a third party, so they can impose costs and conditions to their benefit—and, in fact, the seven-day notice rule in Property Code Section 5.016 applies for this purpose, but without any stated penalty. The practical result is that in a post-transfer scenario lenders are generally left with only an option to accelerate—a choice not an obligation—and, as noted, this rarely happens when payments are kept up to date. What would your business decision be if you were a lender? Foreclose on a performing loan merely because there was a change in title? Maybe, but probably not.

Is an assumption the same thing as a wrap?

No. In a wrap, a new debtor-creditor relationship between seller and buyer is created. The buyer becomes obligated to the seller on a new wrap note secured by a new wrap deed of trust. The wrap note is the key: no wrap note, no wrap. As to the existing note (which is "wrapped"), the seller remains obligated to continue monthly payments until it is paid and released. The wrap and the wrapped obligations coexist. By contrast, in an assumption, the buyer expressly assumes responsibility for paying the existing note. There is usually no new note (unless, for instance, there is a short-term subordinate note executed for part of the down payment).

What is the difference between an assumption and a "subject to" transaction?

In an assumption, the buyer promises to pay the existing debt. By contrast, in a "subject to" deal, the buyer takes title but *expressly disclaims any obligation to pay the seller's debt*, even though that debt is secured by an existing lien on the property. The buyer might make payments or might not. This is a typical assumption clause in a warranty deed:

> As further consideration, *Grantee promises to keep and perform all of the covenants and obligations of the Grantor contained in the Assumed Note* and the Deed of Trust and (subject to any non-recourse provisions that may apply) to indemnify, defend, and hold Grantor harmless from any loss, attorney's fees, expenses, or claims attributable to a breach or default of any provision of this assumption by Grantee. Grantee shall commence payments on the Assumed Note on or before the next regular due date under the Assumed Note.

This is a typical "subject to" clause:

> This conveyance is made subject to any and all indebtedness of Grantor and liens against the Property, including but not limited to that certain indebtedness and liens securing same evidenced by a note in the original principal amount of $_____, dated _____, executed by Grantor and payable to the order of _____, which note is secured by a vendor's lien retained in deed of even date recorded at Clerk's File No. _____in the Official Public Records of Real Property of _____ County, Texas, and is additionally secured by a deed of trust of even date to _____, Trustee, recorded at Clerk's File No. _____ in the Official Public Records of Real Property of ___ County, Texas. Grantee does not assume payment of this or any other indebtedness of Grantor. Grantor indemnifies and holds Grantee harmless from any and all

liens, liabilities, debts, causes of action, damages, or claims
of any kind that exist or may arise against the Property.

See the difference?

Assumptions are appropriate for those who intend to hold a property for a while. "Subject to" transactions, however, are usually entered into by investors who want to do a short-term flip to a new buyer for a quick profit, perhaps after doing some rehab work first, without incurring any responsibility for the existing note in the process. The objective is to sell the property to a new buyer who will then pay off the note.

Can title insurance be obtained on an assumption transaction for which lender approval was not obtained?

Sometimes but usually not. Title companies are conservative institutions that avoid potential liability, so most assumptions will need to be closed in the office of an attorney familiar with creative transactions. If a buyer is curious about the status of title, and an investor-buyer should *always* be curious about title, then a title report (cheaper than title insurance) can always be obtained.

What if there is more than one existing loan—an 80-20 for example?

It is not uncommon for a buyer to assume more than one note (e.g., a first and second lien). The notes may even be payable to different lenders. The principle is the same, only the assumption deed will recite that the buyer is now obligated to pay two notes rather than one.

The more complicated the assumption, the more important it is to have a separate assumption agreement which covers the details.

Can an investor-buyer make a limited agreement to pay the note until the house is flipped?

Yes. This is an interesting hybrid, not a true assumption but not a true "subject to" either. An investor-buyer may (either in the deed from the seller or in a side agreement) contractually agree with the seller to make loan payments for a limited time—say, a year, or perhaps until the property is resold to a third party. The wording might look like this: "Although buyer does not formally assume any legal obligation to pay the existing indebtedness, it is agreed between buyer and seller that buyer will commence making monthly payments directly to the lender on ____, 202_ and continue timely making such monthly payments for a period of up to 12 months or when the property is resold to a buyer who discharges the existing indebtedness, whichever is less." In this way, the seller may feel safer about doing the deal, while the investor-buyer has effectively limited his or her liability.

What documents are involved in an assumption?

At the contract stage, one should use the TREC 1-4 contract with the Loan Assumption Addendum attached. This Addendum unfortunately does not have a special provisions section that would allow for creative approaches discussed in this chapter, so customization by an attorney may be necessary.

Post-contract, there are two approaches to the documentation: the first is seller-oriented, since it includes security for the seller, namely the right to foreclose upon the buyer non-judicially and take the property back if the buyer does not comply with the assumption terms. Documents required are a warranty deed with vendor's lien and a deed of trust to secure assumption. Additional documents—a separate assumption agreement, a property management letter sent to the lender, and a power of attorney in favor of the buyer—may be included. These supplementary documents are advisable, if for no other reason than it may become necessary for the buyer to inquire about payoff, and without legal authority (i.e., a document signed and acknowledged by the original borrower) a lender will not supply this confidential information. An effective alternative might be to obtain the seller's online login information so as to access the lender's website.

The second, simpler documentation option is more favorable to an investor-buyer. It is used when the seller does not require, or perhaps even care about, taking security for the assumption. This might be true if the seller's credit is already in poor shape. The seller may just want to sign the property over to an investor and never hear another word about it. For this option, one document—an assumption deed—is sufficient to transfer title and complete the transaction. This should always be an investor-buyer's preferred approach. Quick, simple, and easy.

What if the buyer defaults on the assumption?

If the seller received a deed of trust to secure assumption at closing, then the seller may foreclose on the courthouse steps if the buyer defaults. Texas has an expedited non-judicial foreclosure process set out in Property Code Section 51.002. This statute requires that a homeowner be given at least a 20-day notice of default and intent to accelerate the note if the default is not timely cured.

If, on the other hand, the seller merely signed an assumption deed without a vendor's lien and without a deed of trust to secure assumption, then the seller is out of luck when it comes to a quick remedy. Even if the seller did not get a deed of trust to secure assumption for the buyer, the seller may foreclose on the vendor's lien retained in the deed—but this is a judicial process (a lawsuit), not something that can be accomplished expeditiously on the courthouse steps.

Order of Preference—Creative Approaches to Assumptions

From the point of view of an investor-buyer, there is a definite order of preference when it comes to structuring and documenting assumptions:

1. take title to the property by means of a "subject to" deed, which is of course not an assumption at all;

2. take title by means of a hybrid deed—basically a sub2 deed which promises to assume payments for, say, six months, or perhaps until the property is re-sold—so the assumption portion of the document is strictly limited in duration;

3. take title by means of a stand-alone assumption deed without a vendor's lien (and unsupported by a deed of trust) which promises, as part of the consideration for the transfer, that the investor-buyer will assume the entire existing debt, and then begin making monthly payments on a certain date, creating a contractually enforceable promise on the part of the buyer to the seller to fully pay the assumed indebtedness;

4. take title by means of a stand-alone assumption deed with a vendor's lien (and unsupported by a deed of trust);

5. take title by means of an assumption deed with vendor's lien, secured by a deed of trust to secure assumption, and supported by an assumption agreement along with a special power of attorney in favor of the buyer (for purposes of dealing with the lender)—all of which incur or increase the possibility of foreclosure in the event of buyer default.

Risk Management

Understand that every real estate investment entails an element of risk. Otherwise, why would there be a reward? Sensible risk management means tailoring each transaction so as to maximize the potential for a positive return while minimizing the downside. Here is just one example: every transaction in which debt is involved should ideally include a non-recourse clause against the general assets of the investor debtor. Memorize these words and repeat them like a mantra to your lawyer: *non-recourse clause.* Such an approach requires intelligent customizing of documents and is another reason to avoid forms from the Internet or anywhere else.

Chapter 20

DUE-ON-SALE

"There is no due-on-sale jail"—Attorney Bill Bronchick

We have touched upon due-on-sale in previous chapters, but it is time to look at this subject in detail. One consideration in using creative methods to convey real estate is whether or not such methods will enable a lender to accelerate the existing loan using the due-on-sale clause in the deed of trust. There are a variety of contractual and statutory factors that need to be considered. However, the fundamental fact is this: if a transaction involves a title transfer without prior consent of the lender, then the risk of acceleration (however small) *is* present if the lender's deed of trust contains a due-on-sale clause. And nearly all of them do. So the focus shifts from inquiring whether or not a lender *can* call a note due to how *likely* that is to take place.

Historically and generally speaking, mortgage lenders are not inclined to foreclose upon a performing loan on merely technical (non-monetary) grounds such as transfer of title by the borrower. However, some will send irate letters demanding that the new owner apply and qualify to assume the loan, threatening that the property will otherwise be posted for foreclosure. Whether or not that threat is real or just a bluff may be a gamble, depending on the deed of trust involved and the lender's practices in this area. The spread between the note rate and the current prevailing rate is also a factor. Even though acceleration of a performing note may be unlikely, it is nonetheless clear that acceleration *can* happen. The risk cannot be reduced to zero.

Due-on-Sale and Executory Contracts

Due-on-sale has become a more important consideration since lease-options, long a mainstay of residential investor portfolios, are now defined as executory contracts subject to burdensome restrictions and requirements. Especially problematic is Property Code Section 5.085(b)(3)(C) which requires in the case of an executory contract that "the lienholder consents to verify the status of the loan on request of the purchaser and to accept payment directly from the purchaser if the seller defaults on the loan." This means that the lienholder must be informed of *and* consent to an executory transaction, which is unlikely to ever occur as a practical matter. Accordingly, residential executory contracts longer than 180 days are effectively limited to paid-for properties. Residential investors owning property subject to a lien now tend to look to other alternatives—wraparounds, land trusts, or leases with a right of first refusal—all of which still require consideration of due-on-sale.

Due-on-Sale and Non-Executory Contracts

Property Code Section 5.016 attempts to deal with the issue of due-on-sale by (1) requiring seven days' notice to the buyer before closing that an existing loan is in place; (2) giving the buyer this same seven-day period in which to rescind the contract to purchase; and (3) also requiring that a seven-day notice be sent to the lender, theoretically giving the lender an opportunity to accelerate and call the loan due. Lender consent is not required. Clearly, this statute is designed to discourage transaction structures that separate title from debt and result in a lender losing control over its loan. Still, there is nothing illegal or even unethical about doing this. It happens often, most notably in "subject to" and wraparound transactions.

Section 5.016(c) lists 11 express exceptions to the seven-day notice rule:

(c) This section does not apply to a transfer:

(1) **under a court order or foreclosure sale;**

(2) **by a trustee in bankruptcy;**

(3) **to a mortgagee by a mortgagor or successor in interest or to a beneficiary of a deed of trust by a trustor or successor in interest;**

(4) **by a mortgagee or a beneficiary under a deed of trust who has acquired the real property at a sale conducted under a power of sale under a deed of trust or a sale under a court-ordered foreclosure or has acquired the real property by a deed in lieu of foreclosure;**

(5) **by a fiduciary in the course of the administration of a decedent's estate, guardianship, conservatorship, or trust;**

(6) from one co-owner to one or more other co-owners;

(7) to a spouse or to a person or persons in the lineal line of consanguinity of one or more of the transferors;

(8) between spouses resulting from a decree of dissolution of marriage or a decree of legal separation or from a property settlement agreement incidental to one of those decrees;

(9) to or from a governmental entity;

(10) where the purchaser obtains a title insurance policy insuring the transfer of title to the real property; or

(11) to a person who has purchased, conveyed, or entered into contracts to purchase or convey an interest in real property four or more times in the preceding 12 months.

The most obvious available exception between non-family members is a transaction where title insurance is issued (an odd exception, actually, since it was never the purchaser's *title* that was in doubt).

Transfers into a trust do *not* constitute an exception, although transfers by an existing trustee are excepted. So creating a land trust is not a means around the seven-day notice requirement.

No time period is specified during which a lender must act on the notice, if at all. The actual effect of this statute remains to be seen, particularly since the only sanction is to allow a prospective purchaser to back out of a contract before closing (not after).

Effect of the Texas Residential Mortgage Fraud Act

The Residential Mortgage Fraud Act requires virtually anyone connected with a real estate transaction (including real estate brokers, mortgage brokers, escrow officers, attorneys, etc.) to report to an authorized government agency suspicious activity that may involve real estate fraud. Tex. Gov't Code Sec. 402.031. Question: is failure to give the seven-day notice required "suspicious?" Future cases may answer this question in the affirmative. While Property Code Section 5.016 may be largely toothless, fraud sanctions can be severe. Accordingly, as a matter of best practice, the seven-day notice should be given unless there is a specific statutory exception available.

The Wording of the Due-on-Sale Clause is Critical

Even if seven-day notice must be given, it is not necessarily true that a lender *will* accelerate and foreclose; nor is true that a lender always *may* take such action. As noted above, lenders are generally loathe to accelerate a performing loan in a low interest rate environment.

The wording of a due-on-sale clause is critical in this context, and one should carefully examine the deed of trust before transferring title to property without the lender's permission. Take a look, for instance, at the language of the Fannie Mae/Freddie Mac Uniform Deed of Trust, which is the instrument most commonly used to secure institutional residential loans. It contains the following due-on-sale clause:

> 18. *Transfer of the Property or a Beneficial Interest in Borrower.* As used in this Section 18, "Interest in the Property" means any legal or beneficial interest in the Property, including, but not limited to, those beneficial interests transferred in a bond for deed, contract for deed, installment sales contract or escrow agreement, the intent of which is the transfer of title by Borrower at a future date to a purchaser. If all or any part of the Property or any interest in the Property is sold or transferred (or if Borrower is not a natural person and a beneficial interest in Borrower is sold or transferred) without Lender's prior written consent, Lender *may* [italics added] require immediate payment in full of all sums secured by this Security Instrument. However, this option shall not be exercised by Lender if such exercise is prohibited by Applicable Law.

Conveying title without lender consent is not a crime or a "violation" of this clause. It only provides that the lender "may" choose to accelerate the loan if the borrower does so. Secondly, paragraph 18 expressly states that a lender may not act if such action is "prohibited by Applicable Law." What is that? In a nutshell, it is a federal law that allows transfer of the property to a family living trust (see below).

The FHA deed of trust is worded differently:

> 9(b) Lender *shall* [italics added], if permitted by applicable law . . . and with the prior approval of the

Secretary, require immediate payment in full of all sums securing this instrument if : (i) all of part of the Property, or a beneficial interest in a trust owning all or part of the Property, is sold or otherwise transferred (other than my devise or descent, and (ii) the Property is not occupied by the purchaser or granter as his or her principal residence...."

Clearly, a transfer of title without an FHA lender's permission in this circumstance would be problematic, since acceleration is mandatory.

Transfer to a Living Trust—the Exception Provided by "Applicable Law"

The federal Garn-St. Germain Depository Institutions Act, 12 U.S.C. § 1701j-3, is among the applicable law that limits lenders' ability to act in matters of due-on-sale:

(d) Exemption of specified transfers or dispositions:

With respect to a real property loan secured by a lien on residential real property containing less than five dwelling units, including a lien on the stock allocated to a dwelling unit in a cooperative housing corporation, or on a residential manufactured home, a lender may not exercise its option pursuant to a due-on-sale clause upon—

> **(1) the creation of a lien or other encumbrance subordinate to the lender's security instrument which does not relate to a transfer of rights of occupancy in the property;**
>
> **(2) the creation of a purchase money security interest for household appliances;**
>
> **(3) a transfer by devise, descent, or operation of law on the death of a joint tenant or tenant by the entirety;**
>
> **(4) the granting of a leasehold interest of three years or less not containing an option to purchase;**
>
> **(5) a transfer to a relative resulting from the death of a borrower;**

(6) a transfer where the spouse or children of the borrower become an owner of the property;

(7) a transfer resulting from a decree of a dissolution of marriage, legal separation agreement, or from an incidental property settlement agreement, by which the spouse of the borrower becomes an owner of the property;

(8) a transfer into an inter vivos trust in which the borrower is and remains a beneficiary and which does not relate to a transfer of rights of occupancy in the property; or

(9) any other transfer or disposition described in regulations prescribed by the Federal Home Loan Bank Board.

Subsection (8) usually gets the most attention. This exception was intended to allow individuals to create family trusts for estate-planning purposes, especially probate avoidance, without worries about due-on-sale.

Are investor land trusts a solution to due-on-sale risk?

Subsection (8) is also the exception relied upon by many investors who use land trusts with the intention of avoiding the applicability and enforceability of due-on-sale. As stated above, this was not the purpose of the exception; however, setting that point aside, there remain an obvious pitfall to this approach: such trusts make use of a lease, lease-option, or other document allowing the buyer-beneficiary to move into the property immediately—which clearly "relates to a transfer of rights of occupancy." So while land trusts may in the right circumstances be effective creative vehicles, it cannot be claimed that they are a surefire method of dodging due-on-sale under Garn-St. Germain.

Other "applicable law" exists. For instance, the FDIC has promulgated 12 C.F.R. § 591.5(b)(1) which is unfortunately even more restrictive than Garn-St. Germain. It requires that in order for a land trust to avoid enforcement of a due-on-sale clause, the property must continue to be owner-occupied—something which is almost never true in the typical investor case. This rule reads:

§ 591.5 Limitation on exercise of due-on-sale clauses.

(b)(1) A lender shall not (except with regard to a reverse mortgage) exercise its option pursuant to a due-on-sale clause upon:

> **(vi) A transfer into an inter vivos trust in which the borrower is and remains the beneficiary and occupant of the property, unless, as a condition precedent to such transfer, the borrower refuses to provide the lender with reasonable means acceptable to the lender by which the lender will be assured of timely notice of any subsequent transfer of the beneficial interest or change in occupancy.**

Investor and seminar gurus often make extravagant claims that their complex and expensive forms provide immunity from due-on-sale issues, ironclad asset protection, expedited eviction in event of default, and other proprietary strategies that will lead an investor along the gold brick road to prosperity. Such claims are usually false. Few of these packages are customized for Texas, nor do they take into account the executory contract rules, violations of which are defined to be deceptive trade practices. Seminar guru forms can now get investors in real trouble.

Transfers to an Investor's Personal LLC

Transferring title of an investment property into an investor's personal company for asset protection purposes seldom results in the lender accelerating the note. In fact, this author has never seen that happen.

Note on Earnest Money Contracts

Consideration of due-on-sale begins with the earnest money contract, although TREC promulgated forms are less than adequate in dealing with the subject. It is a good idea to consult a real estate attorney to obtain a suitable special provisions addendum that addresses the non-standard nature of any creative transaction, including due-on-sale issues.

Chapter 21

LAND TRUSTS

A Form of Creative Ownership and Finance

In Texas, a "trust may be created for any purpose that is not illegal" (Tex. Prop. Code Sec. 112.031). There are many kinds of trusts and most of them can be adapted to hold real estate, whether investment property or the homestead. The difference between types of trusts revolves around their intended purpose, so one needs to be clear about goals before setting out to utilize a land trust. Is the trust being used to acquire and then flip property? Is anonymity a concern? Or is the primary purpose the transfer of property to a credit-impaired borrower? And what about duration—short term versus long term?

The scope of this chapter is limited to living trusts (meaning trusts formed during the lifetimes of the participants) for the purpose of holding investment real estate. Testamentary trusts, which take effect upon the death of the person creating the trust, are usually part of the estate planning process and can be substantially different, often because of tax issues—so consult an appropriate expert for advice on those. Living trusts designed specifically for the homestead are the focus of the next chapter.

Trust Basics

While land trusts can be used flexibly, there are certain structural items that do not change:

> (1) The *trustor* (sometimes called the settlor or grantor) is the current title-holder to the property. The trustor is therefore the person or entity who transfers property into the trust.
>
> (2) The *trust corpus* (or *trust estate*) is the real property or other asset that is conveyed into the trust.
>
> (3) The *trustee* controls the trust with authority to manage, maintain, lease, and sell the trust property. An LLC cannot usually be designates as trustee.

(4) The *successor trustee* serves if the trustee dies, resigns, or cannot otherwise serve.

(5) The *beneficiary* is the ultimate party in interest, the one with "ownership" to use that term loosely. An LLC can be a beneficiary.

(6) The *contingent beneficiary* acquires the beneficial interest if the primary beneficiary dies (note that there would be no need for a contingent beneficiary if the beneficiary originally named is an LLC).

In order for an attorney to draft a land trust, the client needs to specify which persons or entities will be acting in each role. Note that "a trust terminates if the legal title to the trust property and all equitable interests in the trust become united in one person," known as the doctrine of merger found both in common law and in Property Code Section 112.034. So the person or persons acting in each of the three main roles cannot exactly match. As a practical matter, particularly when dealing with lenders and title companies, it is better if these actors overlap as little as possible. This enhances the perceived legitimacy of the trust.

Once an investor identifies the persons who will be principals in the trust, then the next steps are to: (1) formally establish the trust by means of a signed trust agreement, and then (2) convey the property into trust by means of a warranty deed (usually a general warranty deed).

Duties of a Trustee

An examination of trusts of any type would be incomplete without mentioning the legal duties of a trustee, so we will pause our discussion for a moment to examine these. When serving as trustee for others, a trustee is a fiduciary and has certain duties with respect to both the beneficiaries and the property held in the trust, and these are significant, as is the potential liability for failing to perform these duties. Fiduciary standards may not be very important if the trustee is also the sole beneficiary of the trust (*not* a recommended set-up), but otherwise such considerations are very relevant indeed.

Duties include:

(1) a duty of loyalty;
(2) a duty of competence;
(3) a duty to exercise reasonable discretion;
(4) a duty of disclosure with respect to the beneficiaries; and

(5) a duty to comply with the prudent investor rule contained in Property Code Section 117.003.

While a trust agreement can attempt to reduce or mitigate some of these duties, it cannot eliminate them entirely, at least not as to intentional, bad faith, or reckless actions by the trustee (Trust Code Sec. 114.007).

Law Applicable to Trustees

The law in this area is found in a mixture of that portion of the Property Code known as the "Texas Trust Code;" the Restatement of Trusts (second and third versions), a body of academic literature that states common-law principles applicable to trusts; and case law as it is reported from the Texas courts. All of these sources make it fearfully easy for a beneficiary to sue and win against a trustee for breach of duty, especially in cases of trustee self-dealing, which is a breach of the duty of loyalty.

Section 113.053 of the Property (Trust) Code provides that except in limited circumstances "a trustee shall not directly or indirectly buy or sell trust property from or to: (1) the trustee or an affiliate; (2) a director, officer, or employee of the trustee or an affiliate; (3) a relative of the trustee; or (4) the trustee's employer, partner, or other business associate." An old supreme court case puts this succinctly: "[A] trustee, or person occupying a fiduciary relation to another, is incapacitated, in equity, to buy from himself property committed to his care, or secure to himself an advantage in a purchase of such property by another from him." *Tenison v. Patton*, 67 S.W. 92, 93-94 (Tex. 1902). Note that in cases where this duty is breached, it falls to the beneficiary (and really no one else) to raise the issue. *Harvey v. Casebeer*, 531 S.W.2d 206, 208 (Tex.App.—Tyler 1975, no writ).

As to real estate investing in particular, the law makes it clear that a trustee has an *active duty* to take reasonable measures to protect trust property and make it productive. The exact extent of this duty can be argued in any particular case; however, at the very minimum, a trustee is obliged to ensure that property belonging to the trust is not subject to unnecessary waste, loss, or other diminishment. Central to this is the "prudent investor rule" found in the Restatement (Third) of Trusts which sets forth core principles: (1) a preference for lower risk to achieve a beneficial rate of return, (2) applied as an overall strategy (which does not mean that any single investment needs to comply with this concept); plus (3) reasonable diversification to manage risk and avoid unnecessary loss; along with (4) a view toward increasing returns over time if that is reasonably feasible; (5) and, having said the foregoing, a trustee should nonetheless retain flexibility to actively take advantage of unique or special opportunities as they may arise.

A "Uniform Prudent Investor Act" is included within the Texas Trust Code (Chapter 117 of the Property Code). This law takes the general principles of the Restatement of Trusts and gets more specific, stating that "a trustee shall invest and manage trust assets as a prudent investor would, by considering the purposes, terms, distribution requirements, and other circumstances of the trust. In satisfying this standard, the trustee shall exercise reasonable care, skill, and caution." Prop. Code Sec. 117.004(a). The same section goes on to list specific items that a trustee should consider: "(1) general economic conditions; (2) the possible effect of inflation or deflation; (3) the expected tax consequences of investment decisions or strategies; (4) the role that each investment or course of action plays within the overall trust portfolio, which may include financial assets, interests in closely held enterprises, tangible and intangible personal property, and real property; (5) the expected total return from income and the appreciation of capital; (6) other resources of the beneficiaries; (7) needs for liquidity, regularity of income, and preservation or appreciation of capital; and (8) an asset's special relationship or special value, if any, to the purposes of the trust or to one or more of the beneficiaries."

Finally, note that if a real estate investor has considerable experience and knowledge of the business, then he or she will be held to a *higher standard* when acting as trustee for another: "A trustee who has special skills or expertise, or is named as trustee in reliance upon the trustee's representation that the trustee has special skills or experience, has a duty to use those special skills or expertise." Prop. Code Sec. 117.004(f). All of this should highlight the liability risk involved in anymore acting as trustee.

Lawyers are often asked to act as trustees for their clients trusts (for free, of course). Considering the extensive duties and liabilities outlined above, it is not surprising that lawyers are reluctant to do so without substantial compensation, especially since trustees are sued all the time. In fact, when the trust is sued, it is the trustee who is named as the defendant.

Types of Land Trusts

There is a wide variety of trusts that involve acquiring, holding, or selling real property. The following are the main categories:

entry trusts, used by an investor to acquire a property, usually with the intention of flipping using an assignment of beneficial interest;

exit trusts, used by an investor to transfer limited rights in a property to a buyer who is working to restore credit and obtain traditional financing;

living trusts for the homestead, principally for purposes of probate avoidance; and

anonymity trusts, which endeavor to conceal the principal or principals behind the trust.

Clients often ask attorneys for a "standard" trust (or worse, a fill-in-the-blank form they can use themselves) neither of which exists at any acceptable level of quality. There is no substitute for the analysis and drafting expertise of a competent professional in this complex area. Because trust agreements can be written in so many different ways, the challenge for the attorney is to discover what the client is trying to achieve and then tailor a custom document to suit specific needs.

The Entry Trust (Investor Acquisition of Property in Preparation for a Flip)

In the case of an entry trust, an investor coaxes a (usually) distressed seller into transferring property by recorded deed into an irrevocable trust. This is often done with a foreclosure looming. However, such trusts do not delay or stop foreclosure unless the investor is willing to promptly reinstate the loan and then continue payments until the property can be sold.

As for the trust itself, it has either been previously established by the investor or is created just for the specific transaction. In the latter case, there are two options: one names the seller as beneficiary, after which the seller immediately executes an unrecorded assignment of beneficial interest to the investor. Another version utilizes the seller as trustor (so the seller actually signs the trust agreement), the investor as trustee, and the investor's LLC as beneficiary. The latter option is much better, since it does not allow the seller ever to be in a position of asserting the rights of a beneficiary, even if the window for doing so is brief. It is better for the investor's potential liability if the seller is never given a beneficial interest at all. Why? Firstly, because courts tend to be sympathetic to trust beneficiaries and are more likely to go out of their way to preserve a beneficiary's rights; and secondly, if the seller never holds a beneficial interest, then he or she can never argue that he or she was duped out it by a sly investor. It is thus preferable to arrange for the seller to transfer a 100% fee simple interest to the trust by general warranty deed and then be entirely dismissed from the investment equation.

An entry trust should always be carefully-crafted document. And, as noted, the trust should be irrevocable, since allowing a seller the opportunity to experience remorse and revoke the trust is not a good idea. This is a bedrock principle, yet lawyers see revocable land trusts all the time.

Another bad idea is allowing the original seller to retain a beneficial interest that allows the seller to share in profits when the property is flipped. It is almost always the best policy to make a clean break so there is no further participation by the seller.

Other trust agreements permit the seller to have a power of direction over the trustee, an even worse idea.

Steps in the Process

The following are the steps involved in an entry trust if there is no trust in existence at the time of the transaction (i.e., if a new trust must be established for the transaction to take place):

> 1. the investor-buyer's LLC enters into an earnest money contract for the purchase of 123 Oak Street;
> 2. the contract lists the buyer as the investor's LLC and/or its assigns;
> 3. a trust agreement is executed showing the seller as trustor, the individual investor John Jones as trustee, and the investor's LLC as beneficiary;
> 4. at closing, the seller conveys the property to The 123 Oak Street Trust.

The foregoing should be closed as a stand-alone severable transaction. Subsequent assignment of the beneficial interest to an end-user should also be structured as a separate, stand-alone transaction. Do *not* attempt to collapse these two transactions into one. The potential liability of the investor (or the investor's LLC) goes up substantially if this is done. Courts are more inclined to pull apart a complicated collapsed transaction and find that fraud occurred somewhere in the process.

Note that using the investor-buyer's LLC as trustee is not an option because of the burdensome regulatory requirements that must be complied with in order for a registered entity (corporation LLC, or limited partnership) to qualify as a trustee.

Sale and Assignment of the Beneficial Interest to an End-User

Transfer of the beneficial interest in the trust to an end-user can occur in one of two ways: (1) by means of an assignment, as discussed above, in which case the trust will continue to exist; or (2) by means of a warranty deed from the trustee to the end-user, after which the investor's trust terminates. Again, this all depends on the circumstances.

If the assignment is for cash, then the document required is an irrevocable assignment of a 100% beneficial interest to the end-user, and that is all. To limit liability, the assignor should be the investor's LLC. If the assignment to the end-user is financed, then the investor will need to ask the attorney to prepare the assignment plus a secured note for the amount financed and a security agreement that imposes a lien on the assignment, allowing it to be cancelled and revoked in event of default. It is also useful for the investor to require the end-user to execute an assignment back to investor's LLC, to be held in reserve by the investor as security if the end user defaults on the secured note. The "assignment back" should include full release language for the benefit of the investor.

Note that if the assignment is financed, it is advisable that financing be short-term only, in order to limit ongoing liability. The note can be amortized over a longer term (even 30 years), but if so then it should balloon (all principal and interest due and payable) in no more than five years. One to three is better. This pressures the end-user to secure alternative financing.

Assignments of beneficial interest should be recorded in the real property records.

The Exit Trust (Transfer to a Trust Pending Credit Repair)

Exit trusts are created for the purpose of selling a specific property to an end-user. They involve a calculation on the part of the investor that it is better to utilize a trust than a wraparound, usually because there is some hesitation about giving the end user a deed and fee simple title. The property is conveyed into trust by general warranty deed and the buyer takes immediate possession pursuant to a lease or equivalent document. The buyer is given either a beneficial interest (in some percentage, not necessarily 100%) or an option to purchase a beneficial interest when certain minimum requirements (often credit repair) are completed. Upon becoming beneficiary of the trust, the buyer can decide if he or she wants to keep the trust in place or take a deed outright.

The trust acts as a temporary parking place for title to the property while the buyer works to obtain financing in order to purchase the property outright at a specified price. Sound similar to an ordinary lease-option? It is, except that beneficial interests in a trust are personal property, not real property, and therefore one can plausibly argue that they do not fall under the executory contract provisions of the Property Code.

In the exit trust scenario, there is no deed, recorded or unrecorded, into the name of the buyer, since the buyer is *not* acquiring actual title to the property at the time the trust is created and the deal is closed—only the option to buy a beneficial interest. The only warranty deed being executed is the deed into the trust.

Creation of an exit trust is a private transaction except for the recording of the warranty deed. The trust agreement is not recorded. In order to achieve maximum anonymity, the name of the trust should be generic, e.g., "The 123 Oak Street Trust."

There are no published cases on the success or failure of the exit trust as a long-term investment strategy, but there is an obvious degree of risk. A judge looking carefully at the transaction could use the sword of justice to slice through the trust verbiage and find a de facto executory contract that fails to comply with Property Code Section 5.061 et seq. For this reason, the best strategy is to keep the term of the trust as short as possible.

Are Exit Trusts a Form of Seller Financing?

The executory contract rules of Property Code Sections 5.061 et seq., the SAFE Act, and the Dodd-Frank law have combined to make seller financing of residential real estate a challenge for Texas investors. Is an exit trust a form of seller finance? The answer is debatable. If challenged, the investor will need to fall back on the argument that trust beneficial interests are personal and not real property; and even though an option is part of the trust agreement, the option is to purchase a beneficial interest rather than an option to purchase the real property itself. We make no prediction as to how that argument will fare before a discerning judge.

Use of an LLC in Combination with a Trust

Trust law in Texas falls under the Property Code while the law of business entities (LLCs and corporations) falls under the Business Organizations Code.

Trusts can hold property, of course, but there is no liability barrier against lawsuits as with registered entities formed under the BOC. Even if property is held in an anonymity trust, the trust—including the trustee as well as other participants in the trust—are still individually and personally exposed, an undesirable result given the propensity of plaintiffs' attorneys to sue every name they can find that is connected to a transaction. Utilizing an LLC as beneficiary (and as assignor if a beneficial interest is transferred to an end user) inserts a valuable layer of liability protection. One should recall that asset protection is about the combination and layering of incremental measures. Inserting an LLC into the transactional mix almost always helps.

The Anonymity Trust

Use of an anonymity trust (our term) is an edgy technique that must be implemented carefully and by planning ahead. The scenario goes like this: a trust agreement is executed along with a warranty deed conveying real property into the trust. The traditional way for a trust to hold property is by expressly stating the name of the trustee, e.g., "John Jones, Trustee of the 123 Oak Street Trust;" however, it is possible to list the grantee as only the trust—e.g., the "123 Oak Street Trust"—with no reference to a trustee. Anyone seeking to know who the principals are and what assets they have has their work cut out for them since trust agreements are generally private, unrecorded documents. County clerks will accept such a deed for filing in the real property records so long as it is properly executed and acknowledged by the person conveying the property into the trust. But filing is not the problem. Issues arise later when the investor decides to transfer the property *out* of trust, since no trustee was named in the deed who can now sign as grantor.

Accordingly, users of anonymity trusts should anticipate legitimate objections from a future title company based on the proposition that a trust is not a legal entity—which it technically is not, even though trusts often act as if they are in the real world. Texas subscribes to the entity theory of transactions, meaning that the grantee in a deed must be a legal entity or the conveyance is void.

A trust is actually a contractual relationship, not an entity. Accordingly, one should be prepared to record a second deed which properly *includes* the name of the trustee. A wise alternative would be to expect this obstacle and have such a deed already signed and notarized, previously held back in reserve (a version of the deed-in-the-drawer technique), but now ready to hand to the title company upon demand. Filing this second deed cures the "trust-is-not-an-entity" objection while having preserved anonymity in the interim.

Property Code Section 113.018

A development in favor of anonymity is Property Code Section 113.018, added in 2017, which permits a trustee to appoint an agent and grant the agent powers "to act for the trustee in any lawful manner for purposes of real property transactions." The agent can be anyone so long as the appointment is in writing and notarized (there is no requirement that it be recorded). The appointment—or "delegation" as the statute puts it—can be supplied on demand to third parties as evidence of authority. It is valid for six months.

The Title Company and the Trust Agreement

When trust property is sold, it is likely that the title company will want to see the trust agreement, so expect that this will occur. A written trust agreement must therefore exist. It must also be properly drafted and executed so that it will be accepted as valid. Otherwise, a title company may choose to ignore the trust altogether (act as if it never existed in the chain of title) and require signatures from all persons having an actual or potential interest in the property. One should also anticipate a requirement that any assignments of beneficial interest executed along the way will have been recorded.

Be aware that since the real estate crash, title companies have become suspicious, if not outright hostile, to land trust transactions, so this is a factor that must be considered when considering the use of land trusts (anonymous or not) as a principal feature of an investor's business model.

Certification of Trust

If for privacy reasons an investor is reluctant to show the entire trust agreement to the title company, then Property Code Section 114.086 provides for an alternative: a "certification of trust" (also commonly called a memorandum of trust) that is a concise summary of material trust terms. So long as the information required by the statute is contained in the certification, "A person who acts in reliance on a certification of trust without knowledge that the representations contained in the certification are incorrect is not liable to any person for the action and may assume without [further] inquiry the existence of the facts contained in the certification." Tex. Prop. Code Sec. 114.086(f). A title company is not compelled under this law to accept a certification of trust in lieu of the actual trust agreement, but liability to third parties may be avoided if the title company chooses to do so.

Due-on-Sale

It is widely advertised by seminar gurus that land trusts prevent a lender from exercising due-on-sale. However, Garn-St. Germain (the federal living trust exception) was intended to create an exception for transfers of property to family living trusts designed to avoid probate. It was not intended to provide a safe haven for investors seeking to use trusts as part of their business plan. *The truth is that an investor land trust does not defeat due-on-sale because it invariably contemplates a transfer of rights of occupancy—so due-on-sale provisions remain effective and enforceable.* Nonetheless, so long as monthly payments remain current, the discussion may be academic since lenders are generally hesitant to foreclose on performing loans. This could change, however, as interest rates rise and lenders perceive an opportunity to upgrade their portfolio of low-rate loans.

Conclusion

Not all land trusts are created equal. There are a myriad of trusts available on the Internet that purport to be good in all fifty states. *This is false.* A principal defect of trusts marketed over the Internet is failure to consider or comply with Property Code Section 5.061 et seq. pertaining to executory contracts. Construal of a trust transaction as an executory contract would be disastrous for an investor because of the various penalties for seller non-compliance.

Many Internet and guru trusts involve complex, exotically-named transactional documentation with fill-in-the-blank forms, a sure indicator that they are junk. The place to get a valid Texas land trust is from an experienced Texas asset protection lawyer who knows what he or she is doing in this area.

Chapter 22

LIVING TRUSTS FOR THE HOMESTEAD

Avoiding Probate

The living trust is a tried and true means of avoiding probate of the homestead. A trust of this type should be distinguished from other kinds of land trusts—for example, an anonymity trust that has no probate objectives, or an investor trust that contemplates a transfer of underlying ownership by means of an assignment of beneficial interest (described in the previous chapter on land trusts as entry trusts and exit trusts, respectively).

A Living Trust as Part of an Estate Plan

A living trust that includes the homestead should be considered, along with a pour-over will, as part of most middle-class estate plans. Note that the emphasis here is on probate avoidance and not asset protection. Why? Because homesteads are already protected in Texas from forced sale to satisfy judgments. Tex. Const. Art. XVI, Sec. 50; Tex. Prop. Code Chs. 41, 42. So it is useful to generally distinguish between homestead-exempt assets (protected) and cash or investment assets (unprotected).

Should living trusts be used for the long-term holding of rental properties and other investments? Probably not, because trusts have no liability barrier as do LLCs, and a liability barrier should be a priority for real estate investors—which makes an LLC the preferred choice. Also, an LLC, in particular the series LLC, is better suited to holding multiple investments.

Creating the Trust

There are three steps in the process of creating a probate-avoidance plan that includes a living trust for the homestead: (1) establishing the trust with a signed trust agreement; (2) executing and filing a warranty deed conveying the home into the trust; and (3) executing a pour-over will to move miscellaneous assets into the trust upon death.

As with other trusts, a trustor establishes the trust and conveys property into it. A trustee (or co-trustees if husband and wife) directs trust affairs on behalf of the beneficiaries (usually the children). Since title remains in the trust, and the trust does not die, the surviving beneficiaries "inherit" the trust property but without probate or other involvement by courts or lawyers.

The doctrine of merger (Prop. Code Sec. 112.034) was discussed in the previous chapter and applies equally to living trusts for the homestead. *Basically, the law does not allow you to convey your own property into trust to be managed by you for your own benefit.* If the purported trustor, trustee, and beneficiary are all identical, then as a matter of law it is not a trust at all. This should be kept in mind when drafting the trust agreement.

The trust agreement should state the trust's purpose in general terms along the following lines: "to hold, preserve, maintain, and distribute the Trust Property for the benefit of the Beneficiaries, including but not limited to payment of expenses for their respective health, education, maintenance, and support as the Trustee, acting in his or her sole discretion, deems reasonable, prudent, and necessary." Texas law confers wide powers upon a trustee including selling and purchasing trust property but imposes a fiduciary duty in the management of the trust and its assets.

The trustor usually reserves the right to revoke or amend a living trust for the homestead, so what we are discussing is considered a revocable living trust. The terms of the trust are therefore not finally fixed until the trustor dies (or, in the case of husband and wife co-trustees, usually when the surviving spouse dies) at which time most living trusts become irrevocable. No deed or probate is required at the time of the trustor's death. Even though Texas has an expedited probate process, the result may be a considerable saving of time, effort, and attorney's fees.

The trust agreement, unlike the warranty deed that follows it, should not be recorded. It is a private and confidential document, the terms of which need not even be disclosed to the beneficiaries.

A spendthrift clause should be included that prohibits a beneficiary from assigning his or her interest in the trust to creditors.

Trust Property

Trust property may be of any type, whether personal or real, tangible or intangible, and wherever located. Additional property may be transferred into trust at a later date after the trust is established.

The trust need not formally assume existing liabilities on trust property in order for the transfer to be effective. Property can be taken "subject to" existing indebtedness (i.e., without the trust or trustee taking any liability for the debt), or the debt can be assumed or wrapped. "Subject to" is more common in the trust context.

Real property is conveyed into trust by general or special warranty deed recorded in the county clerk's real property records. The deed should make certain specific recitals concerning the homestead nature of the property. *Conveying the property by deed into the living trust is an essential part of the process since the trust agreement, by itself, does not transfer title.*

Transferring property into a revocable living trust does not reduce a trustor's assets for Medicaid purposes. Trust property is still counted by Medicaid as belonging to the trustor.

Preserving the Homestead Tax Exemption

The trust agreement should contain language that preserves (1) homestead protections available to the trustor pursuant to Texas Constitution Article XVI, Section 50 and Property Code Chapters 41 and 42; and (2) any available homestead tax exemption whether currently on file or not. It is prudent to make express recitals to this effect in the trust agreement even though Property Code Section 41.0021 states that transfer of a homestead into a "qualifying trust" retains the homestead character of the property. Similar language should also be recited in the deed into the trust so as to make it clear to the local taxing authorities that a qualifying living trust has been established for the homestead. It is common for appraisal districts to require that the trust agreement or the deed contain a provision that the trustor may continue living in the property without paying rent.

Mixing Anonymity Techniques with Living Trusts

It is generally not advisable to utilize anonymity techniques when deeding property into a living trust for the homestead. Why? Because such matters are likely to become an issue only after the trustor or trustee is deceased and therefore unavailable to sign any curative deed that a title company may demand. Accordingly, a trustee should always be named in any deed associated with a living trust. The principal trust asset—the homestead—is protected anyway.

Due-on-Sale

Unlike investment land trusts, federal law creates a living trust exception to the enforcement of due-on-sale clauses on homesteads that remain owner-occupied. Garn-St. Germain Depository Institutions Act, 12 U.S.C. Sec. 1701j-3. Due-on-sale is therefore not a factor when contemplate-ing a living trust for the homestead, so long as the trustor intends to continue living there.

Pour-Over Will

It is good practice for the trustor to execute a last will and testament that contains pour-over provisions designed to include in the trust estate any property or assets that were not previously designated. Such assets "pour over" into the trust. In this way, the trust and the will work together as part of an overall strategy. It is also possible to have life insurance paid directly to the living trust. This may be advantageous for purposes of promptly paying off liens on the homestead.

The Title Company

If and when the property is sold out of the trust, a title company will probably want to see the trust agreement, or at least a memorandum of it (see Property Code Sec. 114.086 for the information this "certification of trust" should contain). What if the trustor used a junk form from the Internet? Following the real estate recession, title companies acquired an almost automatic resistance to any transaction with the word "trust" connected to it, so it is possible that a title company will ignore a suspect trust altogether and either require a deed from all heirs or a judicial determination of heirship—either of which can defeat the purpose of creating the living trust in the first place. So the trust agreement needs to be a solid, proper document.

To facilitate a title company's cooperation, the trust agreement should include release and indemnity language that a title company may rely upon in issuing title insurance. In rare cases, if all of the foregoing measures have been unsuccessful in obtaining a title company's cooperation, it may be necessary to change title companies.

Drafting and Maintaining the Trust

The purpose of a living trust is serious business and should never be relegated to fill-in-the-blank or Internet forms, most of which are not specifically designed to comply with Texas law. Additionally, it may be necessary to make amendments to the trust agreement over the years, especially if one homestead is exchanged for another or if the names of beneficiaries' change. Amendments are usually easy to do. Trust maintenance can be as important as trust formation.

Chapter 23

ADVERSE POSSESSION

Is This a Creative Investment Strategy?

Legitimate adverse possession claims are rare. Rather than happening as a singular event, they tend to accrue incrementally over the years without notice or fanfare. Classic adverse possession claims include the family that gradually takes over the empty lot next door to their home, or the rancher who has fenced an adjoining tract and pastured his cattle there for a decade.

Adverse possession refers to circumstances under which one may lawfully lay claim to ownership of property not originally one's own. The statute governing adverse possession is Civil Practices & Remedies Code Sections 16.021 et seq. The Code defines adverse possession as "an actual and visible appropriation of real property, commenced and continued under a claim of right that is inconsistent with and is hostile to the claim of another person." Case law adds that it must be true that the possessor of the property *actually does* openly possess it (the belief of entitlement to possess is insufficient), has in fact possessed it *continuously* for the statutory period (sporadic possession is insufficient), and *peaceably* asserts a claim of right *adverse* to and *exclusive* of all others (possession shared with an owner is insufficient). All of these are fact issues for a court to decide. *Kinder Morgan N. Tex. Pipeline, L.P. v. Justiss*, 202 S.W.3d 427, 438 (Tex.App.—Texarkana 2006, no pet.).

Adverse possession "requires an actual and visible appropriation of real property, commenced and continued under a claim of right that is inconsistent with and is hostile to the claim of another person." The "possession must be of such character as to indicate unmistakably an assertion of a claim of exclusive ownership in the occupant." *Hardaway v. Nixon*, 544 S.W.3d 402 (Tex.App—San Antonio 2017, pet. pending).

In order "to establish a claim for adverse possession, a claimant must prove: (1) actual possession of the disputed property, (2) that is open and notorious, (3) peaceable, (4) under a claim of right; (5) that is consistently and continuously adverse or hostile to the claim of another person for the duration of the relevant statutory period. *Estrada v.*

Cheshire, 470 S.W.3d 109, 123 (Tex.App.—Houston [1st Dist.] 2015, pet. denied).

It is not enough to be merely caring for property temporarily, or even paying the taxes on it, until the owner reappears. One can pay taxes on someone else's property for years, but if other requirements of a lawful adverse possession claim are not met, then those payments are nothing more than a gift to the owner.

Finally, it goes without saying that a mistaken belief that one owns property is nothing more than that—a mistake.

Intent is Important

In order to become a successful adverse possessor, actual possession must occur along with an unambiguous intention to appropriate the property from the record owner. The phrase occasionally used in the case law is "hostile intent" which connotes both a state of mind and a range of actions that are clearly designed to claim the land and exclude all others. If such factors are uncertain or difficult to prove, then a claim of adverse possession will almost certainly fail. *Nac Tex Hotel Co., Inc. v. Greak,* 481 S.W.3d 327 (Tex.App.—Tyler 2015, no pet.).

Property Description

So you want to make an adverse possession claim to the west forty acres north of the railroad tracks? Not good enough. The location and boundaries of land claimed must be determinable with reasonable certainty, and that means there must be a known legal description (lot and block or metes and bounds). This may necessitate a survey, especially in the case of rural property. One alternative is to obtain such a survey first and then file an affidavit of adverse possession with the survey attached as an exhibit; another option—if it is urgent to put an instrument on record immediately—is to file the affidavit with the property description as it is currently available and then later amend the affidavit to include the proper metes-and-bounds description.

Strict Rules Apply

Adverse possession rules are specific for a reason. As the Texas Supreme Court has stated, the adverse possession "doctrine itself is a harsh one, taking real estate from a record owner without express consent or compensation." *Tran v. Macha,* 213 W.W.3d 913, 914 (Tex. 2006). The statute sets forth rules and conditions under which the doctrine applies, and these must be conclusively met. Close enough is not good enough. In the event adverse possession is litigated, all issues become questions of fact to be decided by the court.

The statute is structured in such a way as to require affirmative action by the record owner to reclaim the property within certain periods of time, referred to as statutes of limitation. If the record owner is prevented from taking the property back by means of peaceable self-help, then he or she must file a trespass to try title suit to establish legal ownership and reclaim possession. If the record owner does not act, then the claim is barred and the adverse possessor prevails. Note that the doctrine of adverse possession does not apply to public lands or against a government entity.

The Various Statutes of Limitation

Adverse possession law is based on notice along with the opportunity for the record owner to respond to that notice. The legitimacy of an adverse possession claim is established when circumstances are such that it is visible to others—meaning others are or should be on actual notice that the possessor is asserting a claim of right to the property which is actual, open, notorious, exclusive, adverse, hostile, continuous, and uninterrupted for the applicable statutory period. Recording an affidavit of adverse possession adds to these actions and makes the adverse possessor's case more compelling.

The burden here is on the record owner. Once an owner discovers the presence of a potential adverse possessor or is otherwise put on notice of an adverse possession claim, he or she *must* act to defeat the adverse possessor's claim within the period prescribed by one of three statutes of limitation—or lose title.

The Three-Year Statute

Tex. Civ. Prac. & Rem. Code Sec. 16.024 (the three-year statute) states:

> **A person [i.e., the original owner] must bring suit to recover real property held by another in peaceable and adverse possession under title or color of title not later than three years after the day the cause of action accrues.**

Under this section, the possessor must actually have title (i.e., a deed as part of a regular chain of title) or at least "color of title," which refers to a claim to title that has a reasonable basis but for some legitimate reason does not fit within the usual chain of title. So, the possessor must be able to produce conveyance or title paperwork to support the claim if it is to be successfully asserted under the three-year statute.

The Five-Year Statute

Tex. Civ. Prac. & Rem. Code Sec. 16.025 (the five-year statute) states:

(a) A person [i.e., the original owner] must bring suit not later than five years after the day the cause of action accrues to recover real property held in peaceable and adverse possession by another who:

(1)cultivates, uses, or enjoys the property;

(2)pays applicable taxes on the property; and

(3) claims the property under a duly registered deed.

(b) This section does not apply to a claim based on a forged deed or a deed executed under a forged power of attorney.

This is self-explanatory. Note that under this five-year statute, some sort of deed of record is still required.

The Ten-Year Statute

Tex. Civ. Prac. & Rem. Code Sec. 16.026 (the ten-year statute [the "bare possession statute"]) states:

(a) A person must bring suit not later than 10 years after the day the cause of action accrues to recover real property held in peaceable and adverse possession by another who cultivates, uses, or enjoys the property.

(b) Without a title instrument, peaceable and adverse possession is limited in this section to 160 acres, including improvements, unless the number of acres actually enclosed exceeds 160. If the number of enclosed acres exceeds 160 acres, peaceable and adverse possession extends to the real property actually enclosed.

(c) Peaceable possession of real property held under a duly registered deed or other memorandum of title that fixes the boundaries of the possessor's claim extends to the boundaries specified in the instrument.

The 10-year provision is the catch-all. A deed or other memorandum of title is not necessary so long as the elements of adverse possession are met. However, such documentation may be useful to establish the boundaries of the claimed tract; otherwise the key to determining boundaries may be whether or not there is a "designed enclosure"—not just a "casual fence." *Rhodes v. Cahill*, 802 S.W.2d 643, 646 (Tex. 1990).

The designed enclosure rule from *Rhodes* appears in a later case concerning the grazing of cattle. "Under Texas law, use of land for grazing cattle fails to establish adverse possession as a matter of law unless the fence used is a 'designed enclosure' as opposed to 'casual fences'. . . . Unless the claimant establishes he erected the fence with the purpose of enclosing the property at issue, the fence is a casual fence rather than a designed enclosure." A casual fence is not good enough to win an adverse possession claim. *Anderton v. Lane*, 439 S.W.3d 514 (Tex.App.—El Paso 2014, pet. denied).

Other Statutes of Limitation

Two other sections, Section 16.027 and Section 16.028, are less commonly applied. The first provides a 25-year limitation "regardless of whether the person is or has been under a legal disability." The second allows a 25-year limitation based on a title instrument, even if that instrument is void on its face or in fact.

Statutes of limitation do not include any periods of disability (minority, insanity, or service in the armed forces) on the part of the original owner.

Statutes of limitation may be tacked or combined by various successive possessors of the property so long as there exists "privity of estate" (a direct legal connection by means of the chain of title) between these persons.

Co-Owners

A cotenant (the legal term for co-owner) may not adversely possess against another cotenant unless the claimant clearly repudiates the title and claims to be holding adversely to that title. *Dyer v. Cotton*, 333 S.W.3d 703 (Tex.App.—Houston [1st Dist.] 2010, no pet.). Moreover, a cotenant claiming adverse possession against another cotenant must affirmatively show that all other cotenants have been unequivocally ousted from the property. *Villarreal v. Guerra*, 446 S.W.3d 404 (Tex.App.—San Antonio 2014, pet. denied). Accordingly, an affidavit of adverse possession, or a deed based on adverse possession, puts cotenants on notice of an adverse possession claim only if that instrument is recorded prior to the other cotenants acquiring their interest.

Generally speaking, there is a higher standard for adverse possession in the case of cotenants. In *Hardaway*, cited above, the court explained that "Cotenants are required to surmount a more stringent requirement .

. . the burden is more onerous because cotenants have rights to ownership and use of the property a stranger would not have. . . . Thus, a party claiming adverse possession as to a cotenant must not only prove his possession was adverse, but must also prove some sort of ouster—actual or constructive." What is meant by "ouster?" Well, it may mean exactly what it implies, in the physical sense. It may also be "constructive" as evidenced by decades of exclusive possession without challenge from other co-owners. A reasonableness standard applies: "[Ouster] is nothing more than an application of the rule of circumstantial evidence that the existence of certain facts tends to support a reasonable inference that the record owner has been put on notice that the tenancy has been repudiated . . . . Thus acts which are inconsistent with the original use of the property may be sufficient to put the owner on notice that the tenancy has been repudiated. The same has been held to be true in cases of long-continued possession by the tenant under claim of ownership where the [claimant] has failed to assert any claim." *Tex–Wis Company v. Johnson,* 534 S.W.2d 895 (Tex. 1976).

The Special Case of Cotenant Heirs

It makes for an interesting case when a possessor stakes an adverse possession claim against family members in an heirship situation—for example, a son wants to claim the family farm after his parents died without wills, and his siblings show no interest or have long since disappeared. Previously, adverse possession against cotenant heirs was accomplished in the same manner as against any other cotenants (see previous paragraph). However, in 2017, Sec. 16.0265 was added to the Civil Practice & Remedies Code in order to govern the process as to "cotenant heirs." Who are cotenant heirs? Subsection (a) of the statute defines these as "one of two or more persons who simultaneously acquire identical, undivided ownership interests in, and rights to possession of, the same real property by operation of the applicable intestate succession laws of this state or a successor in interest of one of those persons." A ten-year possession period is required followed by a five-year waiting period commencing after a cotenant heir files an affidavit of heirship and claims adverse possession. Newspaper notice is also required and a limit of 160 acres is imposed.

The Burden on the Record Owner to Initiate Litigation

What sort of action should the owner take to defeat a claim of adverse possession? The most obvious option is to physically displace the interloper, if that can be accomplished peaceably, or file a suit for forcible detainer and treat the whole matter as if it were an eviction. If neither is effective, or if the adverse possessor asserts a title claim, then the owner's remedy is litigation in the form of a trespass-to-try-title action and request for a declaratory judgment.

Litigation by the Adverse Possessor

Alternatively, an adverse possessor may be the one to file suit to establish title. To do so, the possessor must prove (1) a visible appropriation and possession of the land, sufficient to give notice to the record titleholder (2) that is peaceable, (3) under a claim of right hostile to the title holder's claim, and (4) that continues for the duration specified in the applicable statute. What is a "visible appropriation?" The possessor must "visibly appropriate the property as to give notice to any other person that they claim a right to the property." *Perkins v. McGehee*, 133 S.W.3d 291, 292 (Tex.App.—Forth Worth 2004, no pet.). Many people accomplish this by fencing the property and otherwise asserting clear dominion over it.

Section 16.034 provides that the prevailing party in a suit for possession of real property may receive an award of costs and reasonable attorney's fees.

Judgment Liens against Adversely-Possessed Property

What happens if the land adversely possessed has one or more judgment liens that have attached to it? A San Antonio appeals court has held that the judgment liens are extinguished. "The parties have stipulated that Jones had a valid lien on the two parcels of property, and that he complied with the statutory prerequisites to foreclose his lien. The parties have also stipulated that, to the extent they apply, Harrison and Stephens have complied with the prerequisites of the three and five-year adverse possession statutes. . . . Under the facts of this case, the central issue is whether a limitations title by the adverse possession of the successor of title of the judgment debtor extinguishes a judgment lien. We hold that it does under Tex. Civ. Prac. & Rem. Code § 16.024 (Three-year Statute of Limitations), § 16.025 (Five-year Statute of Limitations), and § 16.030. . . . We further hold that limitations commenced to run against judgment lienholder, Jones, from the time of the entry into possession by the respective appellees who purchased from the judgment debtor." *Jones v. Harrison & Stephens*, 773 S.W.2d 759 (Tex.App.—San Antonio 1989, writ denied).

Creative Approaches: The Affidavit of Adverse Possession

What should an adverse possessor do who believes that one of the above statutes of limitation allows him to claim ownership? The first and best option is to file a trespass-to-try-title action. However, if a lawsuit is not affordable, a second choice is to file an affidavit of adverse possession in the county real property records which contains specific wording asserting the various elements of an adverse possession claim. Such an affidavit acts as a marker that commences notice, thereby providing a fixed point for the running of applicable statutes of limitation. As the affidavit matures over time without opposition, it gradually acquires increased credibility.

Note that it is possible to file an affidavit before the applicable statute of limitation has fully run. The affidavit may assert a date when adverse possession commenced (which may even be dated several years in the past) and state that should current circumstances continue and the entire limitations period expire, then the claimant will become the fee simple owner.

The dispute over whether or not county clerks have an obligation to accept property executed and acknowledged affidavits of adverse possession for filing was effectively settled by a Texas General Attorney's opinion (numbered KP-0165) issued in 2017. The question was answered in the affirmative, citing Local Government Code Sec. 192.001: "The county clerk shall record each deed, mortgage, or other instrument that is required or permitted by law to be recorded." Also cited was Property Code Section 12.001(1)(a): "An instrument concerning real or personal property [such as an affidavit of adverse possession] may be recorded if it has been acknowledged, sworn to with a proper jurat, or proved according to law." Attorney General Ken Paxton further states in his opinion that "A county clerk may not impose filing requirements beyond those set forth in [Property Code] Section 12.001." After all, he reasons, "The mere filing of an affidavit asserting an adverse interest in another's property does not vest the filer with legal title." If county clerks wish to have a remedy for suspicious documents, their recourse lies with Government Code Section 51.901 (a)(2) which pertains to the filing and recording of documents which the clerk has a reasonable basis to believe in good faith are fraudulent. But clerks cannot discriminate against an entire class of documents per se.

Title Research

It is a good idea to research title to determine if there are known owners who can be located. Title companies will issue a relatively inexpensive title report or an online service can be used. The title report can provide useful information in drafting the affidavit. If the title report reveals owners of record that can be located, a potential adverse possession claimant may be better advised to contact them and attempt a deal that preserves the existing chain of title. Unfortunately, this will likely involve payment of money for their interests.

Hybrid Affidavits

If heirs exist (whether they can be found or not), then an affidavit of adverse possession may be combined with an affidavit of heirship— entitled "Affidavit of Heirship and Adverse Possession." The heirship portion of the hybrid affidavit should include a recitation of family circumstances along with a statement of who the heirs are believed to be, in light of Estates Code Section 203.001. The adverse possession section would make the usual assertions as to actual and peaceable possession, etc. At least two disinterested witnesses should sign. Three is better.

Paying Taxes

Clients routinely inquire about payment of back taxes on land they want to adversely possess. "Should we pay the taxes?" they ask. Well, *yes*; otherwise the taxing authorities will eventually conduct a tax sale and title will be acquired by someone else. Clients also ask "Can you guarantee that if I pay the taxes, I won't lose my money?" The answer is of course *no*. Firstly, lawyers never guarantee anything. Secondly, it is always possible that the true owner of the property will appear and demand possession. If that occurs, then the client has made a gift to that person by paying back taxes.

The affidavit of adverse possession is a creative device that is inexpensive and often effective. The process is not, however, without a measure of risk and uncertainty.

Creating a New Chain of Title

As an additional creative step, the affidavit of adverse possession may be followed by a deed out of the adverse possessor (to a third-party trustee, for instance) and then another deed back into the name of the adverse possessor. The objective is to give the adverse possessor an actual recorded deed in his or her own name, in order to create a new chain of title. Such deeds should contain specific and appropriate language pertinent to adverse possession and the previously recorded affidavit with the ultimate goal of passing muster with a title company down the road. If the ten-year statute has run, one can use special warranty deeds for this purpose; if not, then deeds without warranties should be used. An appropriate indemnity provision should be included to protect the middleman.

This approach is designed to provide the adverse possessor with credibility as his claim to title seasons over a period of time. Since this method does not produce instant results, it is *not* suited for investors who want to adversely acquire property and then promptly flip it.

Do-it-yourselfers beware. These transactions should be handled only by a capable real estate attorney in order to avoid doing more damage than benefit when it comes to the adverse possession claim. There is an additional caution here: the 84th legislature amended Business & Commerce Code Chapter 27 to include real estate transfer fraud as a deceptive trade practice under the DTPA. The amendment also expressly permits prosecution of such fraud—so use of any creative technique to establish a new chain of title must be soundly based on the facts and the law.

Remedies for the Record Owner

What should an owner do who is put on notice that someone else is making a claim of adverse possession? There are a couple of options, but *doing nothing is not one of them,* since the statute of limitations will eventually run and the claimant may succeed in acquiring legal title. One possibility is to file an opposing affidavit in the real property records expressly rejecting the adverse possessor's claim; in certain circumstances this may be enough to end the matter. Otherwise, the only safe course of action is for the owner to file a suit known as "trespass to try title."

What does the attorney need from the client?

Circumstances vary, of course, so the client should be prepared to explain the nature of his or her adverse possession claim. Has the client fenced it? Erected a structure? Does the client mow and maintain the property? Pay taxes on it?

A proper legal description is essential. It does little good to make an adverse possession claim if the boundaries of the property are uncertain. In many cases, the client is best advised to get a survey before proceeding. The client should also provide a copy of the last recorded deed to the property so the affidavit of adverse possession can contain an express, direct link to the existing chain of title (note that an abbreviated legal description from the appraisal district, which uses a different computer than the real property records, is generally not sufficient).

Finally, if the case involves potential heirs, and the likely strategy will be the filing of a hybrid affidavit, then the client will need to do some research on who the heirs are and where they can be found. Obtaining a title report from a title company is a good idea in these more complex cases.

A Note on Illegality

Real estate lawyers are regularly approached by persons who wish to undertake a campaign of asserting adverse possession as to properties (sometimes dozens of them) that they perceive to have been "abandoned." These are often foreclosed houses owned by lenders that are currently sitting idle. Courts have tended to protect the interests of these absentee lenders/now owners.

The take-away is that the statute does not contemplate or condone the use of the adverse possession rules as a business plan for aggressive investors. In fact, such a strategy expressly involves breaking and entering, filing false instruments, slander of title, and fraud. District attorneys in Texas have begun prosecuting these actions as criminal offenses. In the aforementioned AG Opinion, Attorney General Paxton states: "Fraudulent affidavits are criminal and county clerks have a duty to notify property owners when a fraudulent affidavit is filed." Accordingly, affidavits of adverse possession should be used prudently and only in legitimate circumstances.

PART V

ASSET PROTECTION

STRUCTURING

Chapter 24

LLC FORMATION

A Basic Step in Asset Protection

This chapter discusses forming traditional and series LLCs. We favor LLC formation in Texas and Nevada, which have similar statutes and are both among the best states for asset protection.

What is an LLC?

How is an LLC different from a partnership? A corporation? A Houston appeals court case gives a good answer to these questions: "We conclude that [an LLC] does not fall within the ordinary meaning of 'partnership' even if the [LLC] elects to be treated as a partnership for federal-income-tax and state-franchise-tax purposes. Though an [LLC] may have some characteristics similar to a partnership in calculating its tax liability, [an LLC] also has characteristics similar to a corporation regarding civil liability. An [LLC] is a separate type of . . . entity and is not included in the ordinary meaning of the word 'partnership.'" *SJ Med. Ctr., L.L.C. v. Estahbanati*, 418 S.W.3d 867, 873 (Tex.App.—Houston [14th Dist.] 2013, no pet.). In other words, although members of an LLC may loosely refer to themselves as partners, that is not quite correct, even though an LLC offers an informal form of management similar to a partnership. But unlike a general partnership, an LLC has a liability barrier protecting the members from personal liability. This makes it an excellent vehicle for investing in real estate.

Another difference from a general partnership is that LLC members do not actually have a direct ownership interest in the company's property. "An LLC is considered a separate legal entity from its members. And . . . [Business Organizations Code Sec. 101.106] provides that a member of [an LLC] does not have an interest in any specific property of the company." *Spates v. Office of Atty. Gen.*, 485 S.W.3d 546, 550-51 (Tex.App.—Houston [14th Dist.] 2016, no pet.).

Chapter 101 of the Texas Business Organizations Code ("Limited Liability Companies") is the operative statute in the case of LLCs. The statute governing partnerships can be found at Chapter 152.

Why form an LLC?

There are lots of good reasons to form an LLC including (1) using the liability barrier to minimize personal exposure and maximize asset protection; (2) organizing and managing one or more businesses; (3) tax benefits including pass-through taxation; (4) achieving a measure of anonymity; (5) investor credibility in marketing and doing creative transactions; and (6) in the case of a series company, compartmentalization and insulation of assets and liabilities within separate series. This last item provides significant benefits to investors who own multiple properties.

Separation of Business from Personal Affairs

An LLC is a useful device in separating business from personal affairs. Failing to do this is a common mistake of novice investors. Running business income and expenses through one's personal account may not be illegal, but it can complicate your defense if you are sued. It will be alleged that you "commingled funds" which may arouse the suspicions of the judge and jury and result in your failing the "smell test." This sort of error can result in an investor being held personally liable for damages.

Why risk it? Set up an operating account in the name of your LLC in which all income and related expenses are clearly shown, coded separately for each series or property. In the case of investors who are landlords, a separate account for tenant security deposits is always the best practice. If suit is filed, a plaintiff will likely demand an accounting and production of bank statements. Be prepared to show a sound business structure that functions with integrity. This is an essential part of any investor's asset protection strategy.

Anonymity

Anonymity, at least in a certain amount, is a key aspect of asset protection and a primary reason for forming an LLC. Ideally, your personal name should *never* appear on any deeds or leases, and a tenant should *never* write a check to you personally. There is an old rule that people tend to sue whomever they write their checks to. Make sure that is never you.

It has been reported that a new lawsuit is filed every 1.3 seconds. Literally millions of lawsuits will be filed this year. At least some courts will award huge damages for such things as serving coffee that is too hot. In this legal environment, asset protection is a serious matter, and an LLC is an excellent tool for achieving it.

Asset Protection

Although there is no such thing as a bulletproof plan to avoid personal liability or protect assets, one can get close. Forming an LLC is an important step.

Asset protection is like a cross-country horse race: the more fences a plaintiff and his attorney have to jump, and the more effort and money they have to spend in order to get to you personally, the better protected you are. One way or another, plaintiffs have to pay their lawyers, and that means either cash or contingent fee—and lawyers may hesitate to take a real estate fraud case on a contingent fee if they know they will have to penetrate a bona fide LLC before getting to any real assets.

Setting Up an LLC

In forming a Texas LLC, one of the first things to consider is a company name, including whether or not it is available. The easy names tend to be taken, so one needs to be creative. Name availability information is available by calling the Texas Secretary of State at (512) 463-5555. In any case, do not be distressed if a favorite name is unavailable, since the better strategy is to use a generic name for the LLC and an assumed name ("DBA") for day-to-day company operations. Also, avoid using one's personal name for the company—"John Jones Investments LLC," for instance. Why make it easier for potential plaintiffs to know who owns the company? Better to seek out preferred DBAs for everyday use.

The old requirement was that a proposed LLC name could not be "deceptively similar" to an existing entity's name, presumably to avoid confusing the public. The new requirement is that the name of a new entity must be "distinguishable" from the names of other entities in the Secretary of State's database—an apparent loosening of the rules to more effectively compete with Nevada and other jurisdictions. Nonetheless, one should probably not expect a significant change in the Secretary of State's willingness to approve a new name that is very close to that of an existing entity. The agency has administrative discretion, and habits die hard.

After determining that a name is available, let your attorney know who the original members are going to be and what percentage of ownership each will have. Generally, LLCs have a managing member or co-managing members (common for husband and wife teams), although it is also possible to hire a manager who is not a member. An LLC may also have officers if the company agreement so provides. Who will be serving in these capacities? The client will also need to choose a registered agent with a physical street address, which can include a suite number but *not* a reference to a P.O. Box, PMB, Box, or other obvious indication that the address is not a physical office or residence. The Secretary of State occasionally googles a submitted address and may reject it if they think it is a POB.

The registered agent will receive and forward official company mail from the Secretary of State, the Comptroller, and anyone who is putting the company on formal legal notice. The registered agent is also the person who is served with process by the constable if the company is sued. For privacy reasons, listing the home address as the registered address is not recommended. Use of a physical office address is a better alternative. Note that the certificate of formation in Texas also requires listing the initial managers and their addresses. These addresses *may* (and should) be a POB rather than a home address.

All LLCs Are Not Created Equal

Basic one-pager, no-frill filings do *not* contain key asset protection provisions and should never be used by a serious investor. One's goal should not be to merely "set up an LLC" and consider the job done. *The goal should be to establish an LLC that includes sophisticated asset protection provisions beginning with the very first documents filed with the state* (the certificate of formation in Texas or the articles of organization in Nevada). The need for quality documentation continues with the company agreement, the minutes of the first meeting, and so forth. These documents work together to build a wall against lawsuits and creditors. The company should also have a formal record book with a seal and membership certificates that are dated and issued.

Clients sometimes report that "I already have an LLC." Often, they mean that the minimum initial paperwork has been filed (by an Internet service), the filing fee paid, and nothing else done. In terms of sound business practices and thorough record keeping, this is obviously insufficient; also, legally speaking, a minimalist filing may not be sufficient to maintain the company's liability barrier if the LLC is challenged in court. If the LLC is not sufficiently independent and fully established, a court could use its discretion to find fraud and "pierce the corporate veil," holding individual members personally liable despite Texas's rather tough rules on the issue of piercing. See chapter 28 on this subject.

Clients will go on to say the following about the formation of their LLCs: "I just filled out and filed the standard forms." That is the point. *There are no "standard forms" for establishing and properly documenting an LLC,* regardless of what Internet services may say or imply in promotion of their highly simplistic products. Even the very basic forms that are available at the Secretary of State's website are of minimal use—

they will get you a file number, minimal legal status, and that is about all. Will they get you real asset protection? Will they document the establishment of your business and your relationship with your partners in a clear way? Do not count on it.

Internet Services

If it is worth setting up an LLC in the first place, then it should be done with maximum effectiveness relative to the company's purpose and the desire of its members for asset protection. As for Internet forms, an entire chapter could be written on how they often do more harm than good. Here is what Internet services do not provide:

> NO comprehensive advice on how to structure business and investments to achieve an overall asset protection plan;

> NO attorney to serve as organizer, initial member, and/or registered agent in order to maximize anonymity;

> NO sophisticated company agreement that deters creditors from taking control of your company;

> NO advice on how to move property into the LLC after it is formed;

> NO advice on how to use the LLC in conjunction with a land trust;

> NO advice on how to set up and arrange the LLC's finances, including LLC accounts, injecting capital, or loaning money to the LLC;

> NO advice on how to maintain the LLC liability barrier to prevent a plaintiff from piercing the veil; and

> NO follow-up questions answered by a lawyer after the LLC is formed.

The documents provided by such services are so simplistic as to be barely above the level of junk. Business lawyers spend a fair percentage of their time cleaning up inadequacies in companies formed this way and offering asset protection guidance that the client should have received from the beginning.

The Series LLC

The series LLC allows an investor to hold assets and liabilities within separate compartments or series which effectively operate as sub-companies. It shares characteristics with the traditional Texas LLC, including the benefit of informal management, an effective liability shield, and pass-through taxation; but the series format also adds the unique ability to segregate assets and insulate them from liabilities arising from other assets within the same company.

Member-Managed vs. Manager-Managed LLCs

The better choice is almost always to be manager-managed, for a number of practical reasons. If the LLC is managed by its members, then any member may contractually bind the company—even if that member owns only a 1% interest—since each member-manager (or managing member) is considered to have full agency authority to act on behalf of the LLC (Tex. Bus. Orgs. Code Sec. 101.254). This means that third parties are entitled to rely upon what a member-manager says and does, at least for purposes of company business, even if the company agreement provides otherwise. A second practical reason to favor the manager-managed format is that it more readily accepted in business transactions to execute documents in the capacity of manager. Lenders and title companies prefer this. A lender will occasionally require than an LLC convert to manager-managed (requiring a certificate of amendment with the Secretary of State) before it will extend a loan to the company.

The certificate of formation must state which type of management will occur. Texas requires that the managers and officers of a company ("governing persons" in Texas terminology) be a matter of public record, both in the COF and for purposes of annual reporting (in the Comptroller's Public Information Report). Even foreign companies that register to do business in Texas must disclose this information. However, neither the Secretary of State nor the Comptroller collect *ownership* information. To the extent that certain members of an LLC wish to remain in the background, then a manager-managed LLC is a better choice for this reason as well.

Alternative Business Structures

Clients occasionally ask if they should form a corporation instead of an LLC. While the corporate format is still available, it has been declining in use, a trend that can be verified by examining the filings at the Secretary of State's office. The LLC combines the best of a corporation and a partnership. Generally, a corporation should be considered in the case of real estate investing only if an investor eventually plans to take the company public.

General partnerships, including a variation called "TICs" (for tenants-in-common), are also the subject of inquiry by clients. So are trusts. These may be useful structures in the right circumstances, but should be generally be used in conjunction with an LLC. Why? Because an LLC has a liability barrier. General partnerships, TICs, and trusts do not.

Limited partnerships (usually with a shell corporation or LLC as general partner) have an effective liability shield but are more complex structures commonly used for commercial transactions—acquiring shopping centers, apartment buildings, and the like—rather than residential flips or rentals. The general partner, who is supposed to be the only person running things, has sole full liability. The limited partners are at risk only for the amount of their contribution to the LP, but over-active limited partners can lose this protection. "Personal liability attaches to a limited partner when he takes part in the control and management of the business." *Thompson v. Flintrock Feeders*, Ltd., No. 2:09-CV-0010-J, 2010 WL 11561929 (N.D. Tex. May 10, 2010).

Fiduciary Duty of the Entity's Governing Persons

Managers and officers are fiduciaries, meaning they have an obligation to act ethically, with respect to the company and its members. *Super Starr Int'l, LLC v. Fresh Tex Produce, LLC*, 531 S.W.3d 829 (Tex.App.—Corpus Christi 2017, no pet.). Breach of fiduciary duty (usually involving an alleged misappropriation of funds or assets) is a common cause of action in litigation involving the break-up of small business LLCs.

Separating Assets from Activities: The Two-Company Structure

If an investor has (or intends to acquire) five to ten properties or more, a two-company structure is recommended. This should consist of a shell management company to interact with the public and a separate, stand-alone holding company to own hard assets. The fact that the holding company exists quietly in the background and does not enter into contracts or business dealings makes it nearly impossible to sue successfully. Few investors or business persons need anything more exotic than this.

Company Documents

It is critical that your attorney draft LLC governing documents so that they discourage creditors from even contemplating going after your membership interest. Asset protection provisions should be included from the outset in the certificate of formation and then extensively set out in the company agreement. See chapter 25, *LLC Governing Documents.*

Classes of Members

The owners of an LLC are referred to as members rather than share-holders or partners. We suggest establishing two classes of members and announcing this fact in the company's certificate of formation. Class A members are "regular" members who have full ownership and voting rights; Class B members are those who acquire their membership interest by some unfriendly or coercive means, including debt collection. They cannot vote and are not entitled to distributions except with the unanimous approval of the Class A members. How better to deter adversaries than to make it clear from the outset that any interest they obtain (or obtain influence over) may be nearly worthless?

Company Maintenance

In order to properly document your business and maintain the company as a separate legal entity that provides a liability barrier for its members, a certain amount of maintenance is advisable. The members should meet at least once a year. The first meeting of members (also called the organizational meeting) should include approval of the details of the certificate of formation and the company agreement. Annual meetings in successive years should review and ratify the preceding year's actions, recognize unusual events or circumstances, and elect new managers. It is also a good idea to hold special meetings to approve major decisions, the purchase or sale of real property, a loan to the company, or acceptance of new members and the associated realignment of percentage interests.

An LLC, like a corporation, is a distinct legal entity with its own rights, duties, and remedies. It has its own employee identification number ("EIN"), although the LLC's tax return is combined with the members' personal return (similar to a partnership). However, an LLC requires continued respect for its independence in order to maintain its separate status. It may be *your* company, but it should still be treated at arm's length for legal purposes. This is important if one wishes to avoid personal liability for the actions of the company or its agents and employees. Unless the company pays its state and federal taxes, maintains a bank account, conducts regular meetings, keeps records, and the like, then in the event of a lawsuit alleging fraud, a court could possibly decide an LLC defendant is not a "real" company—and allow the plaintiff to proceed directly against the members-owners personally. It will be alleged that the company is a sham and nothing but the personal alter ego of its owners, designed to shield them from the consequences of their wrongful conduct. Needless to say, this could be a disaster and entirely defeats the purpose of forming an LLC in the first place.

Remember, plaintiffs' lawyers are looking for deep pockets and hard assets wherever they can be found. If there is a hole in your company's liability shield, an aggressive lawyer will likely find it.

What if an investor operates with an LLC but is still sued personally?

Even if one has a properly constituted and operating LLC, it is still possible to be sued in a personal capacity. In fact, this happens alarmingly often in spite of the Texas bias against piercing in the absence of actual fraud. Unless one has personally guaranteed indebtedness of the company or engaged in wrongful or illegal conduct, this is a form of lawsuit abuse—yet plaintiffs' lawyers commonly do it anyway. The defense attorney should respond by sending out written discovery (including interrogatories and requests for production) to find out if the other side has any basis for insisting on personal liability. If no basis can be shown, a motion for partial summary judgment should be filed to have personal names removed as defendants. The LLC's attorney should also ask for fees and costs for having to go through this process. If the LLC has been properly maintained and there is no evidence of wrongdoing or actual fraud, then the motion should be successful. If not, this defense can be reasserted at trial.

The presence of fraud or a statutory violation changes things. A manager or officer may be held liable in his or her individual capacity based on conduct involving wrongful or illegal actions. *State v. Morello*, 2018 WL 1025685, ___ S.W.3d ___ (Tex. 2018). This is true even if the manager or officer was acting in furtherance of official duties. As is observed elsewhere in this book, operating with an LLC provides an effective liability shield only if one acts legitimately.

Moving Property into the LLC

Any and all investment property acquired or currently held in a personal name should be moved into the LLC by means of general or special warranty deed without delay. It is not necessary or advisable to transfer a Texas homestead into an LLC since the homestead is already protected by the Property Code and Texas Constitution. Keep in mind the general rule: personal and homestead-exempt assets should be kept separate from investment assets, and an LLC is a good mechanism for doing this.

Chapter 25

LLC GOVERNING DOCUMENTS

Building a Solid Foundation for Asset Protection

Asset protection lawyers hear such questions as "What documents should be included or created when forming a new LLC?" or "Why is it necessary to do anything more than file a bare minimum certificate of formation?"

Clients asking such questions are usually motivated by a desire to keep things both simple and inexpensive. They suspect that lawyers want to over-complicate projects with lengthy documents in order to collect higher fees. After all, in merry old England (from whence much of our law is derived), lawyers were actually paid by the word—this is true—and solicitors of the day were thus rewarded for creating long documents full of obscure verbiage.

Properly documenting an LLC has nothing to do with this dubious history. First, there are organizational, management, and accounting issues to be dealt with. Secondly, when involved in litigation relating to an LLC, one of the first things a plaintiff's attorney will demand in discovery is the company book with all relevant documentation. If this documentation does not exist, or is inadequate, the plaintiff may in a fraud case seek to pierce the company's liability barrier. This occurs with exasperating regularity in spite of Texas' actual fraud rule. See chapter 28, *Piercing the Veil of an LLC.*

LLC Documents Generally

It is not just the quantity of LLC documentation that matters but its quality and sophistication. *LLC documents should contain asset protection clauses and provisions from the very beginning of the formation process.* Formation documents can be several pages long and include reference to such matters as series specifications, notice of restrictions on sale or transfer or membership interests, and division of membership interests into Class A and Class B. Since the certificate of formation is a filed document and public record, creditors are put on notice from the outset that this particular company is the real thing. LLC documents should include, at minimum:

(1) the certificate of formation ("COF");
(2) a comprehensive company agreement (also called an operating agreement);
(3) the minutes of the first meeting of members (organizational meeting);
(4) signed and issued membership certificate(s);
(5) signed consent by the registered agent; and
(6) warranty deeds and bills of sale conveying assets into the LLC or its individual series.

All of the foregoing documents should be organized and kept in a company book with labeled tabs. The company seal should also be kept with the company book. Although the seal has no true legal effect in Texas, it adds ceremonial and decorative value to official company documents and be should be applied to membership certificates in the space provided.

The Certificate of Formation (COF)

The COF supplies the essential information required by the Business Organizations Code and Secretary of State in order to establish a traditional or series LLC. It may also contain such additional information concerning the business and operations of the company as the initial members may wish to make public. For confidentiality and anonymity reasons, however, the COF should include no more information about its members than is prudent or advisable.

Every company must have a registered agent to receive service of process. This person's name and physical address (not a post office box) must be specified in the COF. The COF must also disclose the name and address of the company's initial manager. Note that the manager's address *may* be a post office box. In fact, we recommend a post office box or office address rather than disclosing one's home address. The third name is that of the organizer, often an attorney who must be an authorized representative of the company.

If the company is to be a series LLC then the Business Organizations Code requires that the COF contain a "notice of limitation on series liability." It is recommended that the COF go into considerable detail on this, clearly stating that each series is independent and not responsible for the debts and liabilities of other series or the company at large.

The Company Agreement

The company agreement governs internal operations. It should be designed to maximize asset protection and will be one of the first documents demanded in discovery if the company is sued, since it is not recorded with the Secretary of State or anywhere else. The plaintiff will want to see, first, if one exists and second, if it contains any provisions that may be an impediment to a monetary recovery.

The company agreement should not be confused with the organizational meeting of members. Although the content of these two documents may occasionally overlap, they are conceptually different and are designed to address separate items and issues.

Company agreements are fairly lengthy and should be customized to fit the circumstances. However, all company agreements contain certain key provisions including but not limited to:

Series LLC provisions. Designation of the company as a series LLC (if applicable) and a description of series characteristics, operations, membership, and management.

Voting of percentage interests. A quorum should be defined. Most decisions should made by majority vote, but major decisions may require either a supermajority or unanimous vote.

Two classes of membership. These are Class A ("regular" members) and Class B members who are defined to be any persons who gain membership or influence by means of a court judgment, execution upon a judgment, assignment of a membership interest in satisfaction of a debt, charging order, or contested divorce. Class B members have very few rights in the company—basically the right to receive notices and be present at meetings. They cannot vote. This structure assures that members do not wind up in a disastrous partnership with other members' creditors or ex-spouses, since these persons are usually seeking to dissolve the company or sell off its assets for cash.

Restrictions on sale or transfer of membership interests. Language to the following effect should be included: "No Member may assign, convey, sell, encumber or in any way alienate all or any part of that Member's Membership Interest without the prior written unanimous consent of all the other Members, which consent may be given or withheld, conditioned or delayed, as the remaining Members may determine in their sole discretion, without any requirement that such consent not be unreasonably withheld." Including a provision of this kind is critical to the successful operation of a small company. Basically, each member should have a right of first refusal to purchase the interest of every other member. If there are multiple members, then the membership interest to be sold will be divided *pro rata* among members choosing to exercise this right.

Dispute resolution. The members should agree to mediate unresolved disputes prior to resorting to litigation or the filing of a complaint with any government agency.

The First Meeting of Members

The organizational meeting should address a whole array of items pertaining to the company's start-up. Important elements include:

Persons present. The initial paragraphs of the minutes recite the date and location of the meeting as well as persons present. The attorney who drafted the company's formation documents is often listed as present and being the one who prepares the minutes.

COF. The members approve and ratify the details of the COF and the various expenses incurred in forming the company.

Company purpose. A general-purpose statement is prefer-red, e.g., "any and all lawful purposes for which a limited liability company may be organized under the Texas Business Organizations Code." The minutes may go on to state that the company will focus its attention upon a particular business such as investing in real property.

Initial members and percentages. The initial members, their respective initial contributions (whether in the form of capital or services rendered), and their respective percentage interests in the company should be specified.

Approval of company agreement. The company agreement should be reviewed and approved.

Election of managers. One or more managers are designated with the operational authority to manage day-to-day operations. Officers may also be elected if the company agreement so provides. See Tex. Bus. Org. Code Sec. 101.251.

Official seal. The company seal should be affixed and approved.

Membership certificates. The form and issuance of membership certificates should be approved.

Organizational expenses. Expenses incurred incident to forming and establishing the LLC should be approved and ratified. Reimbursement for company organizational expenses should be approved.

Appointment of registered agent. The registered agent and registered address should be recited and approved.

Assumed names. These are often recited and approved.

Series LLC provisions. Provisions establishing the company as a series LLC are included, along with approval of conveyance of assets into individual series.

Banking and bookkeeping. This section should approve obtaining an EIN, opening an operating account, and check-writing authority.

Conclusion. The concluding paragraphs of the minutes should resolve that the company may commence business, state that members waive notice of the meeting, and approve the minutes. All members sign.

Annual and Special Meetings

For company maintenance purposes, the company should have at least one formal meeting per year—"formal" in the sense that it is reduced to writing and included in the company record book. The basic elements of the annual meeting are review and ratification of the preceding year's actions by the company, its managers, and officers; specific approval of any major decisions; recognition of any unusual events or circumstances not in the company's ordinary course of business; and election of new managers and officers who will serve in the forthcoming year.

It is also advisable to hold special meetings to approve any major decision, approve the purchase or sale of real property, approve a loan to the company, or accept new members. Special meetings addressing such issues may be held anytime.

LLC documents contain common elements that should be addressed in the case of every new company. However, enterprises vary. Their purposes and members are different. The formation and organizational documents should be carefully drafted to reflect these differences. They should also provide tough protection from creditors and plaintiffs who may seek to pierce the veil and hold individual members personally liable for debts and actions of the company. Ongoing annual and special meetings should be held to preserve and maintain records and the independent legal character of the company. All relevant documents should be organized and contained in the company record book.

Chapter 26

THE SERIES LLC

A Preferred Vehicle for Real Estate Investors

The traditional Texas LLC has long been a favorite of real estate investors and others, especially after limited partnerships were made subject to the Texas franchise tax in 2007. Investors who formerly created investment structures based on limited partnerships (with a corporation as general partner) then shifted their focus to LLCs, which are cheaper to file and less complicated to manage and maintain. New filings at the Secretary of State reflect that formation of other types of entities is down significantly, while LLCs compose the majority of new filings. It is not an exaggeration to say that for most smaller-scale real estate investors the limited partnership and the corporation appear to be languishing. The LLC has largely taken their place.

A newer type of LLC—the series LLC—has been available in Texas since 2009 (see Chapter 101, Subchapter M of the Texas Business Organizations Code). The series LLC is an excellent way for real estate investors to own multiple assets since it allows for the sorting of individual properties into separate compartments that are isolated and insulated from one another.

Series LLCs (which were born in 1990 with the Delaware Business Trust act) were initially designed to cater to the mutual fund and asset securitization industries. Series entities have since shown their worth in real estate investing and are now available in at least thirteen jurisdictions (Delaware, Texas, Nevada, Alabama, the District of Columbia, Illinois, Iowa, Kansas, Missouri, Montana, Tennessee, Utah, and Puerto Rico). Our preference is for Texas and Nevada, which have similar statutes. The series LLC is an idea whose time has come, particularly for real estate investors who wish to acquire multiple properties while avoiding complex structures with numerous entities.

This chapter discusses structural and operational details of a series LLC as they relate to an asset management and protection program. Note that it is not necessary to implement the series aspect of a series company unless and until one is ready to do so; until then the company operates exactly the same as a traditional LLC. Accordingly, there is no downside to electing to form a series LLC rather than a traditional LLC, even if there is no immediate intention to implement the series feature of the company.

What is a series company?

A series LLC allows an investor to hold assets and liabilities within separate cells or series which effectively operate as sub-companies. However, the series are *not* stand-alone legal entities in their own right—at least not technically according to Section 101.633 of the Texas Business Organizations Code (the "BOC")—but in many respects they act as if they are. An individual series is statutorily empowered to file and defend lawsuits; enter into contracts; buy, sell and hold title to property; grant liens and security interests; and "exercise any power or privilege as necessary or appropriate to the conduct, promotion, or attainment of the business, purposes, or activities of the series." BOC Sec. 101.605(5). A series can obtain its own EIN if it chooses and be treated separately for federal tax purposes. A series may (but is not required) to have its own bank account. A series can (and should) operate under its own assumed name. Additionally, BOC Section 1.201(b)(27) has now been amended to include a series within the definition of a legal "person." Given all of these characteristics, declaring that a series is not technically a stand-alone legal entity may be a distinction without a difference, at least most of the time.

Note that the Texas Comptroller, for its purposes, states that a "series LLC is treated as a single legal entity. It pays one filing fee and registers as one entity with the Texas Secretary of State. It files one franchise tax report as a single entity, not as a combined group, under its Texas taxpayer identification number."

The series LLC shares characteristics with the traditional LLC, including the benefit of informal management, an effective liability shield, and pass-through taxation; but a series LLC also has the ability to segregate and compartmentalize assets and liabilities within individual series. This offers significant protection and operational flexibility.

How does a series LLC differ from a traditional LLC? The answer is found in one word: *exposure*. In the case of a judgment against a traditional company, *all* assets of the LLC are available for purposes of satisfying that judgment. Not so with a series LLC. If a series is sued, liability is contained within that series and does not spill over to other series or the company at large.

Legal Authority

The Texas series LLC (like traditional Texas LLCs, corporations, and limited partnerships) is governed by Chapter 101 of the BOC. Changes to the BOC made in 2009 (including authorization of the series LLC) along with subsequent improvements have made it a model of progressive legislation and improved Texas' already deserved reputation as an excellent place to do business *and* engage in asset protection. There is no longer any good reason to go to another state to form an LLC unless one is specifically looking for an extra layer of protection by virtue of physical and jurisdictional distance.

BOC Sections 101.601 and 101.602 read:

§ **101.601. Series of Members, Managers, Membership Interests, or Assets**

(a) A company agreement may establish or provide for the establishment of one or more designated series of members, managers, membership interests, or assets that:

(1) has separate rights, powers, or duties with respect to specified property or obligations of the limited liability company or profits and losses associated with specified property or obligations; or

(2) has a separate business purpose or investment objective.

(b) A series established in accordance with Subsection (a) may carry on any business, purpose, or activity, whether or not for profit, that is not prohibited by Section 2.003.

§ **101.602. Enforceability of Obligations and Expenses of Series Against Assets**

(a) Notwithstanding any other provision of this chapter or any other law, but subject to Subsection (b) and any other provision of this subchapter:

(1) the debts, liabilities, obligations, and expenses incurred, contracted for, or otherwise existing with respect to a particular series shall be enforceable against the assets of that series

only, and shall not be enforceable against the assets of the limited liability company generally or any other series; and

(2) none of the debts, liabilities, obligations, and expenses incurred, contracted for, or otherwise existing with respect to the limited liability company generally or any other series shall be enforceable against the assets of a particular series.

(a) Subsection (a) applies only if:

    (1) **the records maintained for that particular series account for the assets associated with that series separately from the other assets of the company or any other series;**

    (2) **the company agreement contains a statement to the effect of the limitations provided in Subsection (a); and**

    (3) **the company's certificate of formation contains a notice of the limitations provided in Subsection (a).**

Benefits of Simplicity and Economy

Lawyers are frequently asked "How many LLCs do I need, and how many properties can I safely hold in one LLC?" The series LLC eliminates these issues, at least up to a point. Our answer to the first question is most often "One LLC or perhaps two if you choose a two-company structure in order to separate assets from activities." Our response to the second question is "No more than 20 or so properties should be held in a single LLC, even a series LLC." This is our arbitrary, but informed, opinion. The statute permits an infinite number of series, but prudence suggests that even a series company should have some limit on the number of properties it owns. When an investor has filled Series A through Series Z—that's 26 properties—it is past time to consider forming another holding entity. Asset protection is a cautious enterprise.

What if an investor has only one property or business to put into the company? Should he or she still consider a series LLC? Perhaps the question should be "Why not?" since there are no significant additional up-front costs and one can delay implementation or activation of series until an appropriate time. *Until series are created or made operational, the company behaves exactly the same as a traditional LLC.*

It is not necessary that one already have multiple properties or businesses in order to form a series LLC. If real estate investment or multiple businesses are in one's future, it may be wise to go ahead and establish a series LLC at the outset, so that leases, contracts, accounts, and so forth can all be established in a way that is consistent with a series structure. Otherwise, it will be necessary later to use assignments or bills of sale to move these items into individual series.

Those averse to the idea of multiple series may elect to form a traditional LLC, which continues to be useful for a single investment or business purpose. A traditional LLC is also suitable to act as a management company.

Series LLC Formation and Conversion of Traditional LLCs

In order to establish a series LLC, BOC Section 101.604 requires that specific wording be included in the certificate of formation. The filing of the COF is an excellent opportunity to put the public on notice that the company has a serious asset protection firewall in place. Accordingly, minimalist filings, in particular Internet forms, should be avoided. These are seldom adequate for any serious asset protection purpose, and they certainly fall short in the context of a series LLC.

It is possible to convert an existing traditional LLC to a series LLC by means of a certificate of amendment. Unfortunately, nearly all of the company documentation of the traditional company (organizational minutes, company agreement, etc.) will need to be replaced so there is little in the way of cost savings, except for a lower filing fee. Note that this approach is not recommended unless the existing traditional company is free of baggage such as debts, tax liabilities, contractual obligations, pending or threatened litigation, and the like. Otherwise, it is advisable to start a new entity that is unencumbered by such burdens.

Insulation of Each Series

A series LLC contains individual series in which properties or businesses can be held separately and apart from the assets held by other series and by the company at large. In other words, each series may contain a separate rental property (a common arrangement); or, alternatively, by way of example, Series A could contain a rental fourplex; Series B could contain a strip center; Series C could contain a business that buys and sells real estate notes; and so on. The important point is that each series is insulated from the other as well as from assets and liabilities held by the company at large.

A point of clarification here: a series LLC can still own property without a series designation, as an asset of the company at large. For example, property transferred into "ABC LLC" would become a general company asset, even if the company is a series LLC, because no specific series is named in the transfer.

Let's return to the main distinction between a traditional LLC and a series LLC. Suppose there is a foreclosure on a property contained in Series A, and there is a deficiency at the foreclosure sale (i.e., the property sold for less than the amount owed the lender). The lender then sues and obtains a deficiency judgment. Assuming that the series company and its transactions were properly structured, the judgment would be enforceable *only* against Series A assets, *not* against the assets of Series B, Series C, or the assets of the company at large. This is not true of a traditional LLC which holds its properties in a collectively vulnerable pool. All by itself, this is a compelling reason to establish a series LLC rather than a traditional LLC.

Record Keeping

Good record keeping is both important and required. In fact, series insulation is preserved only so long as "records maintained for that particular series account for the assets associated with that series separated from the other assets of the company or any other series." Tex. Bus. Orgs. Code Sec. 101.601(b)(1). In other words, records must be maintained "in a manner so that the assets of the series can be reasonably identified by specific listing, category, type, quantity, or computational or allocational formula or procedure." Tex. Bus. Orgs. Code Sec. 101.603(b). Implicit in the statute is the idea that assets and liabilities of a series can and should be separate both from the assets and liabilities of other series *and* those of the company at large. Commingling among these categories should be avoided.

Series record keeping is not as daunting as it may sound. A simple coding system for company assets and expenditures (all within a single checking account) would satisfy the statutory requirement of reasonableness. It is *not* necessary to establish a bank account for each series in order to comply with Section 101.603(b)—although a real estate investor may decide to take this step if the properties held by each series are significantly and substantively different, either operationally or in terms of tax treatment. One account for the entire company is more common.

As always, records should be kept in anticipation of litigation, particularly litigation that includes piercing allegations, since such allegations (abusive though they may be in non-fraud situations) are common. Internal documents that reasonably identify the activities of each series are therefore important from the standpoint of preparing for litigation.

Series Assets

An investor should think carefully before mixing and matching entirely different businesses within the same company. Generally speaking, one should not place an asset or enterprise in one series that:

(1) creates a much higher level of liability or potential for legal action than businesses in other series;

(2) has a significantly different debt structure (involving development loans, personal guarantees, and the like) than that in other series;

(3) receives significantly different tax treatment from other series or is involved in a payment plan with the IRS;

(4) serves as a management entity with exposure to the public (tenants, vendors, contractors, and the like) since this function is better placed in a separate LLC altogether.

Entities with any of the foregoing characteristics should be placed in separate, stand-alone LLCs (either traditional or series), referred to among asset protection advisors as "single purpose entities" or "SPEs." Examples are restaurants, retail stores, and apartment complexes. Merely because the BOC permits entirely different enterprises to be contained within the same entity does not mean that it is prudent to do so.

Title Insurance and Assumed Names

Some title companies and lenders are new to transactions involving specific series, so this is an evolving area at the level of practice. For instance, title companies typically require a certificate of good standing for an LLC, whether traditional or series. Title companies can be obsessive about this. We have even encountered title companies that demand a certificate of good standing for specific series. This reflects a misunderstanding of the law and the series concept. Since series are created privately, without necessity for public notice or state filing, no official method exists for establishing that a series (as opposed to the company at large) is in good standing. Some lawyers argue that the statute should be amended to provide for registration of series and therefore the ability of the state to determine if a particular series is in good standing or not. We oppose this idea on anonymity and asset protection grounds. As much company activity as possible, including the creation of series, should be kept out of the public records. Amending the statute to require series registration and good standing would only serve to make Texas a less attractive asset protection destination.

One should also expect that a title company will require that an assumed name certificate be filed indicating that the company is doing business by and through one of its series—e.g., "ABC LLC DBA Series A." See chapter 33, *Assumed Names.*

Anticipate that a title company will also require a company resolution evidencing both the creation of a series and its authority to enter into the subject transaction—not a problem since these are simple documents to prepare. It may also be necessary to educate the title company (and possibly its attorney) as to the fact that series are empowered by statute to hold title to real property and grant liens (see Tex. Bus. Orgs. Code Sec. 101.605(3), (4)), although this has become less common as use of series entities has spread and title companies have become more comfortable insuring title held by individual series.

Title companies often demand a copy of the company agreement, a demand we resist whenever feasible. Company agreements are private, proprietary documents that are not usually the business of anyone but members of the company.

Separating Assets from Activities: The Two-Company Structure

Our recommended asset protection structure for long-term real estate investors involves two LLCs, a shell management company (which can be a traditional LLC) and a holding company (a series LLC). The fact that the holding company (formed in either Texas or Nevada) does not enter into contracts or business dealings makes its assets beyond reach in most cases. Few investors or business persons need anything more complex than a two-company structure, although there may be good reasons to vary or customize this model as circumstances require.

Chapter 27

LLCs: TAX AND BANKING ISSUES

Every Investor Should Have a Good CPA

Obtaining an EIN

The quickest way to secure an EIN is from the IRS website (www.irs
.gov). Alternatively, one may complete the IRS hard-copy SS-4 form and
mail or fax it to Internal Revenue Service, Attn: EIN Operations,
Cincinnati, OH 45999 (fax number 859-669-5760). An EIN may be also be
obtained by calling (800) 829-4933 between 7:00 a.m. and 10:00 p.m.
Monday through Friday. Note that the EIN application requests that the
applicant list a "responsible party" along with that party's social security
number. The reason that many lawyers decline to obtain an EIN for a
client is that they (understandably) do not want to list themselves as the
responsible party.

The EIN process with respect to series LLCs is not complicated. Each
series of a Texas series LLC is permitted (but not required) to have its
own EIN, assumed name, and bank account. Some Texas banks (local or
regional ones, for the most part) remain unfamiliar with series entities
and an investor may have to explain to the bank officer applicable law
found in the Business Organizations Code.

Federal Tax Returns

An LLC is required to file its own annual federal income tax return
unless the company (and its series, if the LLC is a series company) is
treated for federal income tax purposes as a "disregarded entity." A
"disregarded entity" is disregarded as an entity that is separate from its
owner for federal income tax purposes. Under the IRS default rules for
entity classification, IRS Regulations Section 301.7701-3(b), a single-
member LLC is automatically disregarded and a multi-member LLC is
automatically taxed as a partnership. In a case where a natural person
(Form 1040 filer) is the only LLC member, the activities of the
disregarded entity are reported on the taxpayer's Form 1040—Schedule
C. In a community property state like Texas, a husband and wife who

wholly own an LLC as community property have the option of either receiving disregarded or partnership treatment. IRS Rev. Proc. 2002-69.

Alternatively, your CPA may assist you in filing the entity classification election to receive tax treatment other than that provided by the default rules (accomplished by means of Form 8832). The other option for a single-member LLC is being classified as an association taxable as a "C" corporation (in which case the entity would file Form 1120—a "U.S. Corporation Income Tax Return"); or an "S" corporation (in which case the entity would file Form 1120S—a "U.S. Corporation Income Tax Return for an S Corporation"). A multimember LLC may also elect to be classified as an association taxable as a "C" or an "S" Corporation. Unless there is a compelling business reason to elect "C" corporation status, this status should not be elected for most real estate investors. In general, according to IRS regulations, once an entity has made its tax election, an election may not be changed for 60 months.

So should your entity make an S Corporation election rather than stick with the default position of a disregarded entity? It depends. If the IRS considers the client as a dealer (doing this business for their livelihood), then their business income is subject to self-employment tax. The S Corporation election can be used to minimize that. If classified as a dealer, none of the gains are considered capital gains. It's all considered ordinary income, subject to the tax rate the individual is in, plus self-employment tax.

Series IRS Returns

Should a series file its own tax return? Not usually, but it may. If a series has its own EIN, activities that are different from other series, and/or a different membership structure, a separate annual federal income tax return may be best. Let your CPA know that the U.S. Treasury Department has proposed regulations, 26 C.F.R. pt. 301 (Sept. 14, 2010), which state that the IRS will treat individual series as separate entities— each of which may elect "pass through" tax treatment if the established criteria are met. The *Journal of Accountancy* states that "the tax treatment of the series will then be governed by the check-the-box regulations (Treas. Reg. §§ 301.7701-1 through 301.7701-3). . . . The IRS decided that the factors supporting separate entity status for series outweigh the factors in favor of disregarding series as entities. . . . They specifically looked at the fact that the rights, duties, and powers of members associated with a series are direct and specifically identified. They also noted that individual series may have separate business purposes and investment objectives. The IRS concluded that these factors are sufficient to treat domestic series as entities formed under local law." Among other things, this means that individual series will have their own K-1 (www.journalofaccountancy.com/Web/20103328.html).

The IRS offers a helpful online tax workshop for new businesses designed to help small business owners learn their tax rights and responsibilities.

Texas Franchise Tax

As for Texas taxes, the Comptroller of Public Accounts sends a notice to new filers of the date on which the first state franchise tax report is due (May 15th). It will also show the LLC's state taxpayer number (which is different from the file number at the Secretary of State's office). The letter will also ask that you complete an online Tax Accountability Questionnaire within 30 days.

A Texas Franchise tax return must be filed with the Comptroller even if the company has no income. It is due by May 15th of the year following formation. Many new companies are eligible to file the No Tax Due Information Report (Form 05-163) if the LLC is a passive entity as defined in Tax Code Section 171.0003; if it has annualized income less than the statutory threshold ($600,000); if the company has zero Texas gross receipts; or if the company is a real estate investment trust ("REIT") as defined by Tax Code Section 171.0001(c)(4). If your company does not fall into one of these categories, one will likely be filing the EZ Computation Report (Form 05-169).

The Franchise Tax Reduction Act of 2015 (Tax Code Sec. 171.002 and Sec. 171.1016) reduced the franchise tax rate for most businesses to .75% of the taxable margin. The rate for entities engaged in retail or wholesale businesses was reduced to .375%. All subject to change, of course.

For owners of more than one Texas registered entity, it will likely be necessary to include an Affiliate Schedule (Form 05-166). This is an unsettled area. The Comptroller is inclined to take the self-serving view that all real estate ventures with common ownership are "affiliated" for purposes of assessing tax. Investors with multiple, varied interests know this may not reflect their true situation.

The Comptroller's Public Information Report (PIR)

The annual filing of a Public Information Report (the "PIR", Form 05-102) is required by the Comptroller. It is due by May 15th of the year following formation. It is a simple form. The PIR requires disclosure of the names of each current "officer, director, or member" of the LLC. This is different from the Certificate of Formation which called for the names of the initial managers, not members. Since LLCs do not have directors, that is not an issue; however, one needs to supply the name of any person or entity who is a member, a managing member, or a non-member manager. This of course has implications for any anonymity strategy an investor may have.

Visit the Comptroller's website at www.window.state.tx.us. to view resources available. Their phone number is (800) 252-1381.

Failure to Pay Franchise Tax

Failure to pay Texas taxes will result in the company's right to transact business, as well as the right to sue and defend itself in Texas courts, being forfeited. If the company's right to transact business is lost, then the company's officers, directors, partners, members or owners may become liable for debts of the entity, including taxes, penalties and interest, which are incurred after the due date of the report and/or payment. See Tex. Tax Code §§ 171.251, 171.2515, 171.252, 171.256. For future reference, to determine if the company is in good standing with the Texas Comptroller, call (800) 252-1281 or go to www.ecpa.cpa.state .tx.us/ coa/ index.html. An LLC that is not in good standing cannot buy or sell property.

There is no annual filing required at the Secretary of State's office.

Not paying franchise taxes also has liability consequences for officers, shareholders, and members. Section 171.255(a) of the Texas Tax Code provides that such persons are not personally liable for the debt of an entity that has been forfeited because of non-payment of franchise taxes, but only so long as the debt was incurred prior to the forfeiture. If the debt was incurred afterwards, that is another matter.

Banking with a Series LLC

Banks have differing policies levels of familiarity with respect to series LLCs. These entities were adopted in Texas in 2009 and have been around in other states long before that, so there is really no excuse for a "business banker" at any major bank not to have knowledge of them— and yet lawyers hear about this occasionally. Local and regional banks present more difficulties than major banks.

There is no difference, operationally or legally, between a bank account that is opened for a traditional LLC and a bank account that is opened in the name of a series LLC for the company at large. Even so, an investor may have to point the bank officer to Section 101.601(20)(b) of the Texas Business Organizations Code: "A series established in accordance with Subsection (a) may carry on any business, purpose, or activity, whether or not for profit, that is not prohibited by Sec. 2.003." Having said that, whether a bank will open an account for an individual series of an investor's company is not a matter of legality. It is definitely allowed by law. Banks, however—for their own individual (and occasionally inscrutable) underwriting reasons—choose what kind of accounts to open, what loans to make, and so forth. These are private business decisions on the part of the bank. No bank is obligated to open any sort of account if it does not want to. Your remedy is to choose another bank.

Tax Versus Legal Considerations in Asset Protection

One should distinguish between asset protection (generally) and asset protection structures (specifically) that are approached from a legal versus a tax point of view.

An asset protection lawyer is primarily focused on likely courtroom outcomes—specifically avoiding adverse ones involving large monetary judgments, since a large judgment can be an extinction event for a small business—unlike a slightly higher tax bill. Focusing on avoiding liability and lawsuits, and the protection of non-exempt assets in the event of a judgment . . . that is what an asset protection lawyer does.

Approaching entity formation and deal structuring from a purely tax-driven perspective is a different avenue entirely, often employed by CPAs who may have no experience in a courtroom and lack knowledge concerning the vulnerability of assets. A narrow tax-driven approach may not always be entirely consistent with the legal approach.

In some cases, the legal and tax perspectives coincide. In others, an investor may have to decide where his or her emphasis is going to be: saving on taxes versus maximizing protections on the legal side. It may not always be feasible to maximize both sets of considerations. One can build a cruise liner or a battleship, but probably not both in the same vessel. My money is on the battleship, which is far more useful in the event pirates show up.

This chapter has been intentionally brief. Even though basic tax information has been presented, it is not a substitute for ongoing advice and guidance from a good CPA who is a regular member of the investor's team. All new LLC owners should consult a CPA concerning the best way to handle their new company for federal and state tax purposes. Certain tax benefits may be available but are not automatic.

Chapter 28

PIERCING THE VEIL IN TEXAS

An Avoidable Catastrophe

This chapter addresses "piercing the veil," which refers to the limited circumstances under which the liability shield of a registered legal entity (an LLC or corporation) may be pierced and the individuals behind that entity held personally accountable. Knowing when this might or might not occur is an important factor in asset protection since a piercing event defeats the central purpose of forming an entity in the first place.

Piercing the veil is an equitable remedy which is available only in exceptional circumstances. *Wilson v. Davis*, 305 S.W.3d 57, 59, 69 (Tex.App.—Houston [1st Dist.] 2009, no pet.). Section 101.114 of the Business Organizations Code ("BOC") states: "Except as and to the extent the company agreement specifically provides otherwise, a member or manager is not liable for a debt, obligation, or liability of a limited liability company, including a debt, obligation, or liability under a judgment, decree, or order of a court."

Nationally, most states allow some sort of veil piercing. Texas is an exception with its "actual fraud rule."

The Actual Fraud Rule

Historically, Texas law permitted piercing the corporate veil when "(1) the corporation is the alter ego of its owners and/or shareholders; (2) the corporation is used for illegal purposes; [or] (3) the corporation is used as a sham to perpetrate a fraud." *Rimade Ltd. v. Hubbard Enterprises*, 388 F.3d 138 (5th Cir. 2004). However, these traditional piercing standards were cast aside in 2006 when the legislature enacted BOC Section 101.114 (quoted above) which significantly narrowed legitimate avenues for piercing. Section 21.223 further defines and limits the exposure of shareholders and members:

§ 21.223. Limitation of Liability for Obligations

(a) A holder of shares, an owner of any beneficial interest in shares, or a subscriber for shares whose subscription has been accepted, or any affiliate of such a holder, owner, or subscriber of the corporation, may not be held liable to the corporation or its obligees with respect to:

(1) the shares, other than the obligation to pay to the corporation the full amount of consideration, fixed in compliance with Sections 21.157-21.162, for which the shares were or are to be issued;

(2) any contractual obligation of the corporation or any matter relating to or arising from the obligation on the basis that the holder, beneficial owner, subscriber, or affiliate is or was the alter ego of the corporation or on the basis of actual or constructive fraud, a sham to perpetrate a fraud, or other similar theory; or

(3) any obligation of the corporation on the basis of the failure of the corporation to observe any corporate formality, including the failure to:

(A) comply with this code or the articles of incorporation or bylaws of the corporation; or

(B) observe any requirement prescribed by this code or the articles of incorporation or bylaws of the corporation for acts to be taken by the corporation or its directors or shareholders.

(b) Subsection (a)(2) does not prevent or limit the liability of a holder, beneficial owner, subscriber, or affiliate if the obligee demonstrates that the holder, beneficial owner, subscriber, or affiliate caused the corporation to be used for the purpose of perpetrating and did perpetrate an actual fraud on the obligee primarily for the direct personal benefit of the holder, beneficial owner, subscriber, or affiliate.

Actual fraud committed primarily for the direct personal benefit of the corporate shareholder or LLC member is thus required, at least for contract-type claims. Further, to "determine if the [members of an LLC] are liable under the asserted veil-piercing theories, the Court must analyze both the question of whether the facts satisfy any of the asserted veil-piercing strands and the question of whether any of the [members] caused [the LLC] to be used for the purpose of perpetrating and did perpetrate an actual fraud on [the plaintiff] primarily for the direct personal benefit of the considered defendant." *In re JNC Aviation, LLC*, 376 B.R. 500, 527 (Bankr. N.D. Tex. 2007), *aff'd*, 418 B.R. 898 (Bankr. N.D. Tex. 2009). "[The] veil of an LLC may be pierced with respect to the entity's contractual liability only upon proof that [a member or manager] used the LLC to perpetrate actual fraud for the defendant's direct personal benefit. *Shook v. Walden*, 368 S.W.3d 604, 607 (Tex.App.—Austin 2012, pet. denied). Mere allegations of "alter ego" or "sham company" are insufficient. *Metroplex Mailing Servs. v. RR Donnelley & Sons Co.*, 410 S.W.3d 889 (Tex.App.—Dallas 2013, no pet.).

Accordingly, allegations by the plaintiff that the defendant company is a sham without substance or is operated as the alter ego of its owners—both of which appear regularly in Texas pleadings—are insufficient *as a matter of law* to achieve a piercing. Actual fraud is required. Texas courts recognize the "strict restrictions on a contract claimant's ability to pierce the corporate veil." *Ocram, Inc. v. Bartosh*, No. 01-11-00793-CV2012, WL 4740859, at *2-3 (Tex.App.—Houston [1st Dist.] 2012, no pet.).

As an example of what the actual fraud rule allows one to get away with, look at the case of *AvenueOne Props. v. KP5 Ltd. P'ship.*, 540 S.W.3d 643 (Tex.App.—Amarillo 2018, no pet.). The real estate broker defendant created a new company and openly moved substantial assets into it and out of the old company which was the object of the suit, effectively depleting the old company and rendering it judgment proof. The court denied the plaintiff's attempt to pierce the veil of the new company, finding insufficient evidence of actual fraud.

In a case reminiscent of Texas' cattle baron days, the alter-ego doctrine was found relevant to a judgment for *reverse piercing* (meaning accessing the LLCs assets as a result of an individual member's fraudulent actions) where a member used the LLC as a mere "shadow of his personality." The existence of actual fraud remained, however, an essential element of the ruling. *Clement v. Blackwood*, No. 11-16-00087-CV, 2018 WL 826856 (Tex.App.—Eastland 2018, pet. denied).

There is also a procedural barrier against veil piercing. BOC Section 101.113 prohibits suing an LLC and a member in the same suit, which is problematic for a plaintiff since this is the typical way piercing cases are pursued. Since veil piercing is not itself a cause of action, but only a means of imposing liability on an individual in the event a true cause of action (such as fraud) is proven, then piercing allegations cannot stand alone. They are subject to being dismissed for failure to state a proper cause of action.

Alter Ego Allegations

What does "alter ego" mean? "Under the [now-discarded] alter ego theory, courts disregard the corporate entity when there exists such unity between the corporation and individual that the corporation ceases to be separate and when holding only the corporation liable would promote injustice." *Mancorp, Inc. v. Culpepper*, 802 S.W.2d 226, 228 (Tex. 1990). In other words, the company had failed in its mission to maintain itself as a legal entity independent of its owner. While Business Organizations Code Section 21.223(a)(2) eliminates the alter-ego theory *as a basis* for veil piercing, it cannot be eliminated *as a factor* in a case where actual fraud is present, particularly since piercing in Texas has always been linked to values of fairness and justice.

During the discovery phase of a lawsuit involving a corporation or LLC, the plaintiff's attorney will likely request production of the company book and all relevant company documentation. Purpose? If the company has no documentation other than a certificate of formation and a certificate of filing, the plaintiff's attorney may then amend his pleadings to include alter ego allegations that are linked to allegations of fraud. In such instances, the defending attorney will *always* prefer that his client has a well-kept company book that can be produced in discovery.

In *SSP Partners v. Gladstrong Investment (USA) Corp.*, 275 S.W.3d 444, 451-52 (Tex. 2008), the Texas Supreme Court stated that the limitation on entity liability may be ignored only when the corporate form has been used as part of an unfair device to achieve an inequitable result. Continuing this line of thought, the Houston Court of Appeals in *Tryco Enterprises, Inc. v. Robinson*, 390 S.W.3d 497 (Tex.App.—Houston [1st Dist.] 2012, pet. dism'd), stated that in order "[t]o pierce the corporate veil and impose liability under an alter ego theory of liability pursuant to *SSP Partners*, a plaintiff must show: (1) that the persons or entities on whom he seeks to impose liability are alter egos of the debtor, and (2) that the corporate fiction was used for an illegitimate purpose," meaning "actual or constructive fraud, a sham to perpetrate a fraud, or other similar theory." What factors are important in assessing whether or not such a fraud has occurred? The Court of Appeals in *Tryco* listed the following:

(1) whether the entities shared a common business name, common offices, common employees, or centralized accounting;

(2) whether one entity paid the wages of the other entity's employees;

(3) whether one entity's employees rendered services on behalf of the other entity;

(4) whether one entity made undocumented transfers of funds to the other entity; and

(5) whether the allocation of profits and losses between the entities is unclear.

Any and all of the above should be considered red flags in a piercing case. From an asset protection perspective, all can be avoided by sound planning and documentation. Looking at the broad picture, keeping good records remains a prudent thing to do, in spite of BOC Section 21.223(a)(3) which denies veil piercing merely on the basis of failure by an LLC to observe traditional formalities. Why get into a potentially disastrous court fight about whether a certain measure is a mere "formality" or something more substantive, particularly given the inherent powers of a Texas court to enforce equity? Is failing to have an annual or special meeting approving borrowing money to acquire property for the company a mere formality or a serious lapse? If you do not think lawyers could engage in a serious battle on this point, then you do not know lawyers.

Piercing lawsuits remain relatively common even though the alter ego theory *by itself* has been essentially dead in Texas for quite some time. As a result, business lawyers defending LLCs and corporations are regularly called upon to expend resources responding to such cases. From an investor's point of view, it is far better to take simple steps to document and regularly maintain the company (having annual meetings and so forth) so that these sorts of allegations will have no basis in the first place.

Liability of Company Officers and Managers

The signature by a corporate officer or LLC manager does not, by itself, make that individual personally liable for company obligations,

Corporate Rules Applied to Limited Liability Companies

The reader may note that the foregoing statute refers specifically to corporations. What about LLCs? Business Organizations Section 101.002 provides the answer by importing the piercing provisions of Section 21.223 into the realm of LLCs. In other words, the same standards apply to both corporations and LLCs even though provisions of the statute may refer to a corporation rather than an LLC and to shareholders rather than members. Accordingly, LLC members can expect to receive the same treatment as shareholders of a corporation, no more, no less. *Penhollow Custom Homes, LLC v. Kim,* 320 S.W.3d 366 (Tex.App.—El Paso 2010, no pet.).

Liability of Company Officers and Managers

The signature by a corporate officer or LLC manager does not, by itself, make that individual personally liable for company obligations, even if the signature line fails to specify that the signer is acting solely in his or her capacity as an officer or authorized representative. *Neel v. Tenet HealthSys. Hosps. Dallas, Inc.,* 378 S.W.3d 597, 604-04 (Tex.App.—Dallas 2012, pet. denied). This rule tracks a central tenet of agency law: an agent is not liable on contracts made on behalf of a principal whose identity has been disclosed. Nonetheless, it is always the better practice to make sure that the signer on a contract fully discloses the capacity and authority to act on behalf of the entity for which he or she signs.

Directors and officers face full personal exposure, however, if the entity fails to pay its taxes. Tex. Tax Code Sec. 171.255. If a registered entity's status is forfeited for non-payment of taxes, then each director, officer, or manager may be held liable for debts of the entity from the date on which the tax was due up to the time the entity is reinstated. *In re Trammel,* 246 S.W.3d 821 (Tex.App.—Dallas 2008, no pet.).

Single-Member LLCs

Clients often worry whether or not the LLC liability shield will hold up if there is only one member. This is not a concern in Texas. Since Business Organizations Code Section 101.002 makes it clear that rules in this area relating to corporations also apply to LLCs, then (subject to the piercing rules outlined above) an LLC's liability shield remains intact even though there is only one member.

Implications for Series LLCs

A series LLC (as opposed to a traditional LLC) allows for different compartments or series that are insulated from the assets and liabilities of other series within the company. While not technically separate legal entities, these individual series nonetheless behave as subcompanies capable of doing business independently of the company at large, entering into contracts, and holding title to property. There is not yet published Texas case law on this subject, although extensive precedent exists from other jurisdictions to which a Texas court may look for guidance in the series context. It is our view that even if a particular series is pierced, the other series within the company have the potential to remain intact.

Company Documentation

Many business persons utilize online services or otherwise engage in no-frill LLC filings involving a one-page COF and the payment of a filing fee—and then believe they are safe from lawsuits. This may not be so if the company fails to follow up with a company agreement, issuance of membership certificates, minutes of meetings, and the like. While Section 21.223(a)(3) expressly eliminates the failure to observe corporate formalities as a basis for piercing, such failure may well be subtly considered *as a factor* by a real-world court in determining whether or not an actual fraud was perpetrated. Add an inflamed jury, one that is outraged at a perceived injustice, and the risk that a court will pierce the veil grows more likely. The law is not yet ruled by artificial intelligence. One cannot underestimate the human factor. It is more prudent to be safe than sorry when it comes to company documentation and other formalities.

What if documentation for an LLC or other entity has not been attended to for years? Fortunately, it is legal to go back in time and document a company's activities, so long as this is not linked to actual fraud. Such documents are signed by the members as of a retroactive effective date, regardless of the date of actual signature. For more detail on the content of principal LLC documents, read chapter 25 on *LLC Governing Documents*.

Paying Franchise Taxes

Failing to pay Texas franchise tax and subsequent loss of the company's charter can be disastrous for asset protection. Note the following from the Tax Code:

§ 171.255. Liability of Directors and Officers

(a) **If the corporate privileges of a corporation are forfeited for the failure to file a report or pay a tax or penalty, each director or officer of the corporation is liable for each debt of the corporation that is created or incurred in this state after the date on which the report, tax, or penalty is due and before the corporate privileges are revived. The liability includes liability for any tax or penalty imposed by this chapter on the corporation that becomes due and payable after the date of the forfeiture.**

(b) The liability of a director or officer is in the same manner and to the same extent as if the director or officer were a partner and the corporation were a partnership.

(c) A director or officer is not liable for a debt of the corporation if the director or officer shows that the debt was created or incurred:

> **(1)** over the director's objection; or
>
> **(2)** without the director's knowledge and that the exercise of reason-able diligence to become acquainted with the affairs of the corporation would not have revealed the intention to create the debt.

(d) If a corporation's charter or certificate of authority and its corporate privileges are forfeited and revived under this chapter, the liability under this section of a director or officer of the corporation is not affected by the revival of the charter or certificate and the corporate privileges.

Trusts and Piercing Rules

Trusts—whether created for the purpose of anonymity, facilitating land transactions, or for probate avoidance—can be an important element in an overall asset protection structure. However, trusts are not legal entities in the same sense as a corporation or an LLC, although they often act like it in the real world. Trust agreements are not officially filed anywhere and have no state registration or approval requirements. Accordingly, there is no liability barrier and piercing rules do not apply. The participants in a trust—the trustor-grantor, the trustee, and the beneficiaries—are *automatically* exposed to lawsuits in their personal and individual capacities, which can be a dangerous position in which to find oneself. For this reason, investment trusts are most effectively used in conjunction with an LLC. The exception is a stand-alone living trust for the homestead since the homestead and related assets are already protected by Texas Constitution Article XVI, Section 50 and Property Code Chapters 41 and 42.

A related point worth making is that a judgment lien will not attach to trust property for which the judgment debtor is serving as trustee. *Davis v. Gayer*, 2004 WL 638140 (Tex.App.—Houston [1st Dist.]. Expect a hassle, however, from the plaintiff's attorney if your "trust" has no written trust agreement to back it up, no deeds of property into it, no EIN or bank account, and no records.

Conclusion

The law applicable to piercing continues to evolve. The safest practice is to establish and maintain an LLC with thorough and ongoing documentation that is contained in a company book. Certificates for membership interests should also be issued. It is sound business practice to periodically document significant activities and events affecting one's company using resolutions, special meetings, and the like, thereby pre-empting alter-ego type piercing allegations before they arise.

Chapter 29

PARTNERSHIPS AND JOINT VENTURES

Collaborating with other Investors

Applicable Law

Texas partnership law is found in Business Organizations Code ("BOC") Title 4. A joint venture differs from a general partnership in its narrower scope, but is otherwise governed by the law of general partnerships. *Smith v. Deneve*, 285 S.W.3d 904, 913 (Tex.App.—Dallas 2009, no pet.). For real estate investors, it is also important to have a working knowledge of the Texas Property Code. Professional investors should keep a paperback copy of the Property Code on their desks.

A partnership or joint venture is a form of contract. Texas courts have historically supported the concept of freedom of contract, allowing the parties to make agreements and allocate risks as they see fit, so long as some express statutory or common law principles are not violated in the process. *El Paso Field Servs., L.P. v. MasTec N. Am., Inc.*, 389 S.W.3d 802 (Tex. 2012).

Written Verses Oral Agreements

A partnership agreement may be oral or written, but it is certainly more prudent for real estate investors to reduce their agreement to writing. There's an old saying about marriage that is equally applicable to partnerships: "Going in, it's all about love. Coming out, it's all about money." So it's best to have the exits clearly marked.

BOC Section 152.052 sets forth rules for determining if a partnership has been created (the so-called "five factors" to which reference is frequently made in partnership cases):

(1) receipt or right to receive a share of profits of the business;

(2) expression of an intent to be partnership in the business;

(3) participation or right to participate in control of the business;

(4) agreement to share or sharing;
    (A) losses of the business; or
    (B) liability for claims by third parties against the business; and
(5) agreement to contribute money or contributing money or property to the business.

No one of the above factors is dispositive. They are also non-exclusive, meaning that not all factors need be demonstrated in any particular case. Just "one factor standing on its own can be strong enough to support the existence of a partnership"—even an oral partnership. *Black v. Redmond*, 709 Fed. App. 766 (5th Cir. 2017). The existence or non-existence of a partnership thus depends on the totality of the circumstances.

BOC Section 152.051(b) provides that a partnership exists when two or more persons associate together for the purpose of carrying on a business for profit, regardless of whether or not they actually intended to create a partnership or use the term "partners." All sorts of circumstantial information can be used to make this determination, even the bankruptcy schedules later filed by the parties after the business has failed. *Palasota v. Doron*, No. 10-16-00326-CV, 2018 WL 2054511 (Tex.App.—Waco May 2, 2018, no pet. h.).

A true legal partnership, however, must rise to a higher level than mere casual collaboration. A Houston appeals court decision describes a situation where a partnership was *not* found to exist: "The parties did not associate for the purpose of carrying on a single business in which they each held an ownership interest; instead, the four separate businesses agreed to work together for their mutual, but individually realized, benefit. Such coordinated business efforts do not, alone, create a partnership under Texas law. The parties did not share profits, losses, or liabilities." Further, the court failed to find any evidence that the businesses in question ever actually *intended* to be partners in the legal sense—an important and essential element. *Westside Wrecker Serv. v. Skafi*, 361 S.W.3d 153, 173 (Tex.App.—Houston [1st Dist.] 2011, pet. denied).

Whether or not a partnership exists is unfortunately the subject of much litigation. A plaintiff typically alleges the existence of a partnership in order to invoke the fiduciary duty responsibilities of a partner—or, more specifically, how the defendant "partner" in question may have violated that duty by misappropriating funds or assets.

The moral here is that one does not want to casually slide into an inadvertent partnership that could have unfortunate consequences in terms of liability. A partnership should be established deliberately and correctly with a comprehensive written partnership or joint venture agreement.

One should not, for instance, casually refer to one's business associates as "partners" (a much-overused term) unless they are in fact partners in the legal sense. You may be creating an unintended partnership. Also, if an associate of yours falsely represents to others that a partnership exists, and those others reasonably rely on that representation to their detriment, then a partnership (known as a "partnership by estoppel") may be created. *Fleishman-Hillard, Inc. v. Oman*, No. SA-11-CA-921-H, 2012 WL 13028770 (W.D. Tex. Nov. 21, 2012).

General Partnerships

General partnerships are the focus of BOC Title 4, Chapter 152. A general partnership is an association of two or more persons or entities (all of which assume unrestricted personal liability for partnership debts and activities) who intend to carry on a business for profit. Each partner has equal rights in the management and conduct of the business of a general partnership. In contrast with the common law, the BOC does not specifically require an intention to share profits or losses, although this is an important evidentiary factor in determining whether or not a partnership exists. *Ingram v. Deere*, 288 S.W.3d 886, 895-96 (Tex. 2009).

A "joint venture is governed by the same rules as a partnership." *Enterprise Prods. Partners, L.P. v. Energy Transfer Partners*, L.P., 529 S.W.3d 531 (Tex.App.—Dallas 2017, pet. filed).

Texas subscribes to the entity theory when it comes to partnerships and joint ventures. Both are considered to be legal entities which may be sued and held liable for damages. A partnership is an entity distinct from its partners, and partnership property is not considered to be the individual property of the partners (BOC Sec. 152.056 and 152.101). A partner may use or possess partnership property only on behalf of the partnership. This ties in with the fiduciary duty of partners both to the partnership and to one another, specifically including a partner's duty of loyalty (BOC Sec. 152.205) and duty of care (BOC Sec. 152.206). More on the partners' fiduciary duty below.

Even though a partnership is a distinct entity, each partner nonetheless remains jointly and severally liable for all debts and obligations of the partnership. Personal liability is not automatic, however, at least not if the partnership alone is the object of a lawsuit. A judgment against a partnership as an entity must be accompanied by a judgment against the individual partners (named separately as defendants) in order to be enforceable against the partners' individual non-partnership assets. *American Star Energy and Minerals Corporation v. Stowers*, 457 S.W.3d 427 (Tex. 2015). See also BOC Section 152.306, which requires that a judgment against a partnership must go unsatisfied for 90 days before a creditor may proceed against an individual partner and his assets.

The most important contrast with an LLC is that neither a general partnership nor a joint venture has a liability barrier—no firewall, which is a distinct disadvantage in a business as litigation-prone as real estate investing. When it comes to potential liability and protection of personal assets, there is little difference between a partnership format and simply owning assets in one's individual name. For this reason, general partnerships and joint ventures should almost always be structured so that the partners themselves are LLCs or corporations. Anytime an investor is considering a transactional structure, one of the first questions should be "Where is the firewall? Where is the liability barrier that is going to protect my personal assets?"

Fiduciary Duty of the Partners

BOC Section 152.205 describes the general partners' duty of loyalty to one another. Partners in a general partnership are, to use the legal term, fiduciaries, which requires honest and honorable conduct. "As a fiduciary, a partner is under an obligation not to usurp opportunities for personal gain, and equity will hold a partner accountable to the partnership if he does so. . . . Thus, the [general] partnership relation imposes upon all partners an obligation of the utmost good faith, fairness and honesty in the dealings with each other with respect to matters pertaining to the partnership business." *In re. Leal*, 360 B.R. 231, 235-6 (Bankr.S.D.Tex. 2007).

If the totality of circumstances supports it, courts will go to considerable lengths, first to find that a partnership exists where none was expressly stated, and then to find that one partner breached his fiduciary duty to the other, all resulting in an award of actual and exemplary damages plus attorney's fees. *Harun. v. Rachid*, No. 05-16-00584-CV, 2018 WL 329292 (Tex.App.—Dallas Jan. 9, 2018, no pet. h.).

Different rules apply to partners in limited partnerships so long as the limited partner in question does not change hats and exercise operating control over the LP business, since that crosses a legal boundary that has multiple implications. No fiduciary duty exists in the case of a limited partner simply because he is a limited partner. *Strebel v. Wimberly*, 371 S.W.3d 267, 281 (Tex.App.—Houston [1st Dist.] 2012, pet. denied).

There is a four-year statute of limitations for breach of fiduciary duty actions contained in Chapter 16 of the Texas Civil Practice & Remedies Code.

Liability for the Actions of other Partners

Pick your partners well. Supposedly, a general partnership (and the individual partners) are liable only for actions of a partner when those actions fall within the ordinary course of business of the partnership or are authorized by the partnership (BOC Sec. 152.303). So two things need to be considered here: first, the fact that real estate investing involves a truly broad range of activities, which means that almost anything done on or about an investment property, or even indirectly affecting the property, can conceivably be considered as within the partnership's ordinary course of business; and second, trial courts (in their capacity as finders of fact) have significant flexibility in interpreting any given set of circumstances before them, a level of flexibility to which appeals courts tend to defer.

Take an admittedly extreme example: suppose your managing partner, unbeknownst to you and the other partners, opens a shady massage parlor on the premises. Are you liable for the consequences (at least the civil ones)? The answer is almost certainly *yes*, given that the actual use of the property is something that is definitely the business of the entity that owns it. This is another good reason to enter into partnerships, if at all, *in the capacity of an entity that possesses a liability barrier, and not in your personal name.*

In Texas, a plaintiff must first secure a judgment against the partnership before pursuing actions against the individual partners. *American Star Energy and Minerals Corp. v. Stowers,* 457 S.W. 3d 427 (Tex. 2015) referencing Bus. Orgs. Code Sec. 152.306.

Piercing the Veil of a Partnership or Joint Venture

How difficult is it to pierce the veil of a general partnership? The question is based on a misunderstanding of the law, since a general partnership or joint venture has no veil to pierce. *Shoop v. Devon Energy Prod. Co., L.P.,* No. 3:10-cv-00650-P, 2013 WL 12251353 (N.D. Tex. Mar. 29, 2013). Piercing and alter-ego-type allegations are "inapplicable with regard to a partnership because there is no veil that needs piercing. . . . *Pinebrook Props., Ltd. v. Brookhaven Lake Property Owners Ass'n,* 77 S.W.3d 487, 500 (Tex.App.—Texarkana 2002, pet. denied). The partners in a general partnership or joint venture are potentially jointly and severally liable for all of it, which reiterates the importance of engaging in a partnership only in the capacity of an LLC or corporation.

Veil-piercing in the case of limited partners is a slightly different case, but is generally rejected in Texas because a "person doing business with [a limited partnership] always has recourse against any general partner. . . ." *Peterson Grp. v. PLTQ Lotus Grp.*, 417 S.W.3d 46, 56-57 (Tex.App.— Houston [1st Dist.] 2013, pet. denied).

The presence of fraud or misrepresentation can affect the outcome of any court case, but especially ones involving piercing. As is true with LLCs, do not rely on a limited partnership to limit your liability if you utilize the entity to commit actual fraud. "As a general matter, a limited partnership is an entity separate and distinct from its partners, with separate, distinct liabilities and obligations. Nevertheless, Texas law allows the separateness of the entity to be ignored if the limited partnership is used as a straw man for the purposes of obtaining an impermissible result [such as actual fraud] under Texas law. . . ." *In re Sewell*, 413 B.R. 562, 571-72 (Bankr.E.D.Tex. 2009).That being said, "limited partners are generally not responsible for the limited partnership's obligations unless they take some action to accept or subject themselves to such liability"—such as interfering with management or control of the business. *Peterson Grp. V. PLTQ Lotus Grp.*, 417 S.W.3d 46, 56-57 (Tex.App.—Houston [1st Dist.] 2013, pet. denied).

The Partnership Agreement

A partnership agreement consists of "any agreement, written or oral, of the partners concerning a partnership" (BOC Sec. 151.001(5)). To the extent that a partnership agreement does not otherwise provide, the BOC governs. *Deere v. Ingram*, 198 S.W.3d 96,101 (Tex.App.—Dallas 2006). Fundamentally, partnership agreements are contracts between the partners, and the law applicable to the construction of contracts applies unless the BOC provides to the contrary. Sensible investors will insist on having a clear and comprehensive written partnership agreement that does not require the intervention of a court to interpret and apply it. *Exxon Corp v. Breezevale Ltd.*, 82 S.W.3d 429, 443 (Tex.App.—Dallas 2002, pet. denied).

Joint Ventures

Joint ventures are a subset of partnerships. The practical difference is this: general partnerships are usually created for the long term for a broad range of business purposes. They may contemplate engaging in various enterprises with the intention that the partnership will endure from one transaction to the next into the indefinite future. Joint ventures, by contrast, generally have a specific task or time frame. They perform that task, net profits are distributed, and they are done. One example would be investors pooling resources and efforts in order to buy, rehab, and re-sell either a specific residential house or a commercial project—a flip, in other words. Another example would be investors acquiring raw land to hold for a couple of years and then sell.

"A joint venture is a distinct legal entity. This relationship is similar to a partnership, but the principal distinction is that a joint venture is usually limited to one particular enterprise. A joint venture must be based on an agreement, either express or implied." *Varosa Energy, Ltd. v. Tripplehorn*, No. 01-12-00287-CV (Tex.App.—Houston [1st Dist.] 2014, no pet.). The agreement must provide for the sharing of both gains and losses. *Arthur v. Grimmett*, 319 S.W.3d 711 (Tex.App.—El Paso 2009, pet. denied). "A joint venture has four elements: (1) a community of interest in the venture; (2) an agreement to share profits; (3) an agreement to share losses; and (4) a mutual right of control or management of the enterprise. Generally, a joint venture is governed by the [same] rules applicable to partnerships." *Smith v. Deneve*, 285 S.W.3d 904, 913 (Tex.App.—Dallas 2009, no pet.).

The first step in creating a sound joint venture is to draft a clear written agreement. Avoid junk forms from the Internet. The second step is usually to convey the subject property into it. A joint venture agreement dealing with real estate does not, by itself, represent an interest in property or act as a transfer of that property. For that, a deed is required as a necessary second step. *Sewing v. Bowman*, 371 S.W.3d 321 (Tex.App.—Houston [1st Dist.] 2012, pet. dism'd].

Limited Partnerships

In a limited partnership, the general partner is the only member to assume unrestricted liability. The limited partners have liability only to the extent of their contributions to the partnership. For this reason, the general partner is usually a corporation or limited liability company established specifically for the purpose of managing the LP and nothing else. The limited partners may be any sort of entity, including another limited partnership.

LPs are governed by BOC Title 4, Chapter 153, but also Chapters 151, 153 and 154 and Title 1, to the extent applicable. At least in the context of real estate investment, all of the partners usually are (or should be) LLCs or corporations. It is important to note that the limited partners are prohibited from engaging in the conduct or management of the business. This job is the sole province of the general partner. Accordingly, LP agreements tend to be heavy in their emphasis upon the powers and duties of the general partner.

Example of an LLC-Based
Limited Partnership

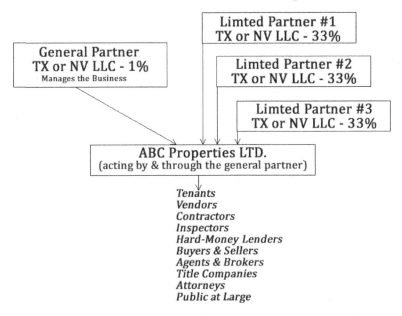

LPs are more common in commercial transactions, but their usefulness in other investment arenas should not be overlooked. A basic LP (illustrated in the accompanying diagram) includes a general partner that owns a 1% interest and a limited partner that owns a 99% interest. There may of course be more partners. If there is more than one GP, then one of them should be designated the managing partner.

An LP is an excellent way to bring in a passive "money partner" who is cautious about incurring liability beyond the amount invested.

Tenant-in-Common Arrangements

What about TICs? How are these different from other partnerships? Our explanation will reveal our bias against these arrangements, at least insofar as they involve individual rather than corporate participants.

TICs are written up as general partnerships but are nonetheless focused on a specific deal, often a larger project such as an apartment complex or a strip center. Promoters seek out investors, usually affluent novices, who are packaged together in their personal capacities. In other words, these newbie investors do not form an LLC or corporation to act on their behalf in the deal; they sign the TIC agreement individually and then go on to personally guarantee a seven or eight-figure note to a bank.

If the value of the investment (often inflated to begin with in order to provide up-front fees for the promoters) declines, the results are usually unfortunate for the investors. The promoters—who have since taken their profits and moved on to other schemes—are the winners.

Real estate lawyers are accustomed to counseling TIC investors who have awakened to find that a lender suddenly seeks to hold them individually liable for a very large sum. Few consulted an attorney before signing up with the TIC. Many are otherwise smart and successful professionals who should have known better.

Minimal Contents of a Partnership Agreement

When it comes to drafting contracts and agreements, partnership agreements included, we prefer that the effective date, the name and contact information of the parties, and the subject property all be plainly visible on the first page. The agreement should go on to address the following:

> What are the respective percentage interests of the partners?

> How will the partnership be managed? By majority vote? Will some issues require unanimous vote? Will there be a managing partner? What are the limits of his authority? What are the specific actions and duties required of each partner?

> What about the investment property or project itself? Are there parameters for its rehabilitation and resale that need to be stated?

> What will be the term (length) of the agreement? Presumably it will end when the project is finished and net proceeds are distributed, but this needs to be spelled out.

> How will funds be handled? Who will sign checks? What about additional, future contributions if necessary?

> Will there be loans as well as capital contributions by the partners? What about loans made by banks or hard money lenders? Promissory notes will need to be authorized and executed.

What about meetings of the partners? What constitutes a quorum? Who controls the agenda?

Suppose a partner wants to sell his interest or cash in? Suppose a partner dies? Will remaining partners have a right of first refusal to buy the decedent's interest? On what terms?

What happens if a partner's spouse files for divorce? Will remaining partners unwillingly wind up in business with the ex?

Every contract or agreement should have a default paragraph. What constitutes a default by a partner? If default occurs, what is the procedure for expelling a defaulting partner?

A good partnership agreement should address the issue of dispute resolution. Will mediation be required before one partner may sue another? That is usually good policy.

Finally, never underestimate the "miscellaneous" paragraph at the end of a contract. It deals with such issues as amending the agreement, which law applies and where venue will be located if a suit is filed, and so forth.

A complete partnership agreement will address all of these items and more, which is not to say that partnership agreements need to be unduly complex, long, or intimidating. Consult an attorney knowledgeable in the field in order to draft a partnership agreement and before signing one. Never use forms off the Internet for this purpose.

Good partnership agreements also include provisions by which they can be amended. Partnerships, like marriages, evolve over time and there should be an express mechanism in the partnership agreement that allows for amendments.

Intelligent Structuring

No contract or transaction should ever be entered into without a consideration of asset protection ramifications if the deal fails. It is often the attorney who must counsel a starry-eyed, in-a-rush client that a proposed transaction could fail as well as succeed. In the event of failure, what is the exit strategy? Which of the client's assets will be exposed and how can that exposure be limited?

Lawyers can often see disaster looming, not because they are prescient but because they have seen this film before. In certain cases, when a happily oblivious client is determined to self-destruct, a lawyer may find it necessary to decline the representation.

Intelligent structuring implies an awareness not only of the mechanics of a proposed transaction but also of potential outcomes and their consequences. A willingness to look down the road, so to speak, where it may fork one way or another. Clients are sometimes astonishingly reluctant to this, accusing the attorney of trying to "kill the deal"—an unjust charge in most cases. An attorney's job is to make the deal work, ideally in the client's best interest, which brings us back to structuring issues.

Knowledgeable investors will have an entity, a management company, that (acting through an assumed name) is utilized for business with tenants, vendors, contractors, brokers, and other persons who might one day file a lawsuit. The management company is substantially a shell that contains employees, rental furniture, leased vehicles, and minimal cash. It is an equity-free dead-end for creditors. Hard assets reside in a separate holding company that does business with no one. The public should not even know that the holding company exists. In any case, prudent investors avoid signing contracts, leases, and the like in their personal name. All decisions that may have liability implications are made with an eye toward asset protection.

In the context of a partnership, it is therefore preferable for the investor to choose an existing entity (or perhaps form a new entity) in order to participate in the deal, *making the enterprise a partnership of entities.* This provides the best protection. And when it comes to personal signatures and guarantees, the solution is often to *just say no.*

The Menace of Family and Friends

Why not collaborate with friends and family members? They know you best, after all. Caution, however, is advised. All lawyers can tell stories of clients who propose doing a transaction with a brother-in-law, or perhaps borrowing money from parents, and declare that no partnership agreement is necessary because the other party is family or a close friend. In fact, the reverse is true. *In transactions involving family and friends it is more important to reduce the agreement to a signed writing, not less so.* Anyone who has witnessed the agony of intra-family litigation knows this to be true.

Chapter 30

BUYING OR SELLING YOUR BUSINESS

Query: Convey the Company or its Assets?

This chapter discusses the elements of buying or selling a small business LLC in Texas, whether the business is focused on real estate investment or otherwise. The heart of the transaction is the purchase and sale agreement (entered into in anticipation of a closing to be held later) which resembles an earnest money contract to sell real estate. In fact, if the business owns real property, then the agreement may also serve as a contract to convey that property.

There is a consistent rule of thumb relating to the sale of a business: *The transaction is never as simple or inexpensive as the seller and buyer would like it to be.* The complexity, due diligence burden, and professional expense (lawyer, CPA, business broker, appraiser, etc.) incurred by both sides in such transactions often substantially exceeds that which would accompany a comparably-sized sale of real estate alone.

The Purchase and Sale Agreement

The purchase and sale agreement will, at the very least, identify parties and the business to be sold; state whether the sale is a transfer of a company as an entity or of assets only, and then list those assets; specify the sales price and how it will be paid; provide for earnest money; include an inspection period for the buyer's due diligence; contain representations and warranties by both seller and buyer; provide protections for confidential information; specify conditions precedent that must be met for the transaction to close; and provide remedies in the event either party defaults. Various exhibits and attachments (deeds, an inventory of personal property, a list of liabilities, a copy of the office lease, copies of employee agreements, etc.) should accompany the purchase and sale agreement.

If realty is involved then brokers will likely use the Texas Association of Realtors Commercial Contract - Improved Property (Form 1801) with appropriate addenda in order to make an offer on the property. Why not simply add the Non-Realty Items Addendum and use this contract to buy both business and realty? This is generally an inadequate approach unless the business is dormant and consists of nothing more than a few tables and chairs. Reason? A going business has many more variables and factors that need to be considered. Buying a business is similar in many ways to buying real estate, but nonetheless materially different in critical respects. More often than not, a standard real estate contract is just not up to the task.

At closing, documents in addition to the purchase and sale agreement will be required, for example: a deed of real property to the new owner; if an asset sale, a bill of sale for inventory as well as furniture, fixtures, and equipment; a promissory note and security agreement if there is seller financing; a deed of trust if a loan against realty is involved; approval by the landlord for the buyer to assume an existing lease; a customer or client list; various assignments; notice letters to customers and vendors; UCC forms; and other documents necessary to create a smooth and secure transition to new ownership.

The Parties

The first step is to ascertain the identity of seller and buyer. Is the seller a sole proprietorship? A corporation? An LLC? A determination needs to be made as to who actually owns the enterprise that is being transferred, who has authority to speak for and convey the business, and whose consent must be obtained (this may include spouses). If the selling entity is a corporation or an LLC, then that entity will need to be in good standing with the Secretary of State and Comptroller and have proper, up-to-date records that the buyer should carefully examine as part of the due diligence process.

Similarly, will the buyer be an LLC? An individual or a partnership of individuals? A joint venture of LLCs? If the buying entity is as yet unformed or unknown, the buyer should be listed by name in the contract or agreement followed by the phrase "and/or his assigns (Buyer may assign without notice to or consent from Seller)" thereby providing an opportunity to get an entity formed and membership issued prior to closing of the sale.

It is often advisable to establish a single purpose entity (SPE) to take title to and operate a newly-acquired business. Most businesses of substance merit their own, stand-alone LLC. This is done for obvious reasons of liability protection as well as convenient allocation of percentage interests among the investors participating.

Sale of Assets or Entity?

In buying a business, the buyer can acquire either the assets of the enterprise or the entity that owns those assets. In an asset sale, the assets transferred are specifically listed, as are the assets that are excluded. Ownership of the entity remains with the seller, as do the entity's debts and liabilities, unless specific exceptions are made. In the sale of a corporation or LLC, the seller's stock or membership interest is assigned and transferred to the buyer. Since ownership of assets remains with the entity, a warranty deed and bill of sale are not usually required.

Buyers' counsel generally prefer an asset purchase because it comes without the potential for hidden or undisclosed liabilities. On the other hand, acquiring the seller's entity may be accompanied by advantages such as an existing credit rating, established vendor accounts, or lines of credit. However, buying an entity may significantly increase the amount of due diligence that must be performed by the buyer.

The Sales Price

As with any transaction, the sales price can be paid in cash, partly in cash and partly by bank or SBA financing, or by means of cash plus seller financing. Existing indebtedness may also be wrapped or taken "subject to." In the case of third-party financing, the buyer will want closing to be contingent upon obtaining financing approval. If the deal is seller-financed, the seller will want to evaluate and qualify the buyer before giving final approval for closing. If either contingency fails, then all or part of the earnest money is usually refunded, less any independent consideration paid for the inspection period.

How the sales price is divided up—between inventory, furniture, fixtures, and equipment, goodwill, and the like—is less a matter of legal principle than old-fashioned common sense. Caution to buyers: *Do not overpay for goodwill.* Often the single most valuable assets of a business (a service business in particular) are its employees and its lease, or what remains of it.

It is generally in the seller's best interest to provide that if the business is subsequently transferred, any outstanding seller financing must be paid in full (a due-on-sale clause). The seller should also reserve the right to inspect the business and its records to assure continued compliance with the purchase and sale agreement.

Due Diligence and the Inspection Period

Nothing is more critical for the buyer than effective use of the inspection period to perform prudent due diligence. What kind? The following is a basic list excerpted from a purchase and sale contract:

(a) physical inspections, including inspections of the business premises, inventory, furniture, fixtures, and equipment; (b) economic and financial evaluations including but not limited to a detailed examination of the books and records of the business; annual and quarterly tax returns as well as ad valorem tax records; records of utilities usage; any agreements with contractors and/or employees; financial statement of the business; (c) current credit report; (d) marketing evaluation, including examination of the customer/client list, receivables history, and related files; and (e) any appropriate environmental assessment or engineering study including performance of tests such as soil tests, phase I or II environmentals, materials tests, equipment tests, and air sampling.

Depending on the nature and circumstances of the business to be sold, one could easily come up with additional items for scrutiny.

The important point for the buyer is to be able to terminate the contract prior to expiration of the inspection period, if the business is unsuitable for the buyer's intended purpose, is not in satisfactory physical or financial condition, or is otherwise unacceptable for any reason. Timely termination allows the buyer to receive the return of the earnest money less the inspection consideration. If the results of the buyer's inspections are satisfactory, it is common for additional earnest money to be due at that point. In fact, investors should generally want to structure payment of earnest money in two parts, even in purchases of rental houses: a modest initial amount followed by payment of additional earnest money after due diligence is completed.

Paradoxically, or so it would seem, the seller *wants* the buyer to have a right to terminate. Why would the seller of a business want a reluctant buyer, particularly if the seller is going to finance him?

Attempting to cut corners in the area of due diligence can have calamitous consequences. Buyers and sellers seeking to avoid legal fees may use some sort of contract off the Internet, not even knowing if it is valid in Texas, and when one party defaults, make the unpleasant discovery that litigation costs far exceed the expense of having properly documented the transaction in the first place.

Representations and Warranties

Both seller and buyer usually make representations and warranties ("reps and warranties"), breach of which is a default or at least a basis for terminating the agreement. Reps and warranties can be made to survive closing, survive closing for a limited time, or not survive closing at all. Buyers want the seller's reps and warranties to be broad and extensive in time and scope; sellers naturally want to limit their ongoing liability, preferring that reps and warranties expire at closing and merge into the closing documents, thereby putting a period on liability.

Examples of typical seller's reps and warranties include an assurance of authority to enter into the transaction; good and marketable title to the assets; full disclosure of liens and liabilities; no litigation pending or threatened; and the like. A buyer's focus is on full disclosure. A seller often wants to eliminate reps and warranties entirely and convey the business "as is"—something only foolish buyers go for. The result is usually a compromise.

For their part, buyers need to assure the seller of sufficient expertise and financial soundness to fund operations and pay liabilities as they arise. No seller wants to have to take a business back and sell it a second time.

Confidential Information

Confidential information about the business will likely be revealed during the course of the buyer's due diligence, and the seller has a right to demand that this remain permanently confidential. In addition to proprietary information about products, services, marketing strategies, and so forth, the seller is also in possession of sensitive information about employees and co-owners. As a result, the purchase and sale agreement should include a strict covenant on the part of the buyer, enforceable by injunction if necessary, not to reveal confidential information at any time to third parties. This covenant should apply whether or not the deal eventually closes. It should also prohibit the buyer from utilizing the information in order to compete with the seller in the future.

Seller's Covenant Not to Compete

If the transaction closes, a legitimate concern of the buyer is that the seller may set up shop nearby and continue in the same line of work. Accordingly, the purchase and sale agreement should usually contain a covenant by the seller not to compete with the buyer. Courts have upheld non-compete agreements so long as they are reasonable in duration and in geographical scope. What is reasonable? Like so much in the law, it depends. In the Houston area, for example, there are three large counties (Harris, Fort Bend, and Montgomery) that vie for the metropolitan area's business. Therefore, any meaningful covenant not to compete would include these three counties.

The seller should also be prohibited from soliciting the buyer's customers and employees. This can happen in subtle ways so the agreement needs to be carefully drafted to encompass both direct and indirect action of this sort.

The Closing

At some point the deal must close or the sale fails, so there should be a date certain for closing. Certain items (ad valorem taxes, receivables, and current rent, for instance) may need to be prorated. If real property is involved, the buyer should weigh the need for title insurance versus obtaining a title report or abstract of title. If title insurance is not required, closing at an attorney's office is just as effective as closing at a title company and it may be a lot faster.

When closing at a title company, it is not advisable to allow the title company attorneys to prepare documents for the sale of a business. There are two reasons for this: first, they represent the title company, not the buyer or seller, and have no incentive to draft documents in anyone's best interest other than that of the title company; second, sales of businesses are not usually their expertise; and third, they will likely draft minimalist documents that may not address all concerns of buyer and seller.

Default

Every contract should specify what happens in the event one party fails to perform. Typically, the seller will want to provide for minimal liability if he defaults—the buyer gets to keep the earnest money as liquidated damages and the agreement terminates. Similarly, if the buyer defaults, the seller should be content with keeping the earnest money and moving on to the next buyer. The remedy of specific performance is not usually a practical or effective remedy against buyers, so it is of no great importance if the seller waives it.

A buyer wants more. After all, a buyer is expending more than just earnest money. The cost of effective due diligence can be many thousands of dollars and if the seller changes his mind about selling then the buyer may be substantially out-of-pocket. The agreement should therefore provide that the buyer can recover these expenses from a defaulting seller. The buyer will also want to reserve the right to sue for specific performance, a meaningful remedy for a buyer.

If a buyer defaults post-closing (usually for not paying a seller-financed note), the seller's remedies are contained in the note and security agreement and, if real estate is involved, in a deed of trust (or a combined deed of trust and security agreement). Essentially, the seller's remedy is to take the business and property back. This is usually a disaster since inventory is depleted, equipment missing, the lease is in arrears, and customer goodwill is down the drain. It is therefore critical that a seller choose the right buyer to begin with and get a solid down payment.

Get a Good Business Attorney

Both buyer and seller should get an experienced business transactions lawyer and listen to his or her advice. Clients are often driven by emotions—the desperate desire to get rid of a business or an irrational determination to acquire one. Since the lawyer does not usually receive a commission, he or she has no stake in the transaction and may be the only person providing factual and objective advice.

PART VI

ASSET PROTECTION
STRATEGIES

Chapter 31

ASSET PROTECTION IN TEXAS

Strategy, Planning, and Execution

Keys to Asset Protection

Strategies

- advance, preemptive planning before lawsuits and creditor action
- creating a legal barrier to personal liability with the appropriate entity
- separating assets (properties) from activities (contracts, leases, etc.)
- maximizing anonymity in the public records
- utilizing homestead and income protections afforded by the Texas Constitution and Property Code
- asset spreading and compartmentalization (series LLC)
- equity stripping by maximizing one's (apparent) debt in the public records
- generally exhausting an opponent's resolve and resources

Tools

- shell management LLC to do business with the public, tenants, vendors, etc.
- holding company for assets (TX or NV series LLC) that stays in the background
- anonymity LLC formation
- anonymous land trusts
- assumed name certificates (DBAs)—state and county
- attorney-client privilege (use of attorney as registered agent)
- living trust for the homestead to achieve probate avoidance

The History

Texas has an established history of being a haven for debtors. For over a hundred years there has been a saying "So-and-so has gone to Texas." Sometimes this meant the person had physically relocated to Texas; just as often it implied that he had left town to beat his creditors. This grand, if ethically sketchy, tradition continues. The Texas Constitution, the Business Organizations Code, and the Property Code make it possible for individuals and businesses to establish fortress-like operating structures *and* shield substantial income and assets from execution upon a judgment. Together, these laws make the Lone Star State an advantageous venue for asset protection.

Homestead Protections for Individuals in Texas

Texas offers unique protections for residents that should be integrated into any asset protection plan. These "homestead protections" are contained principally in the Texas Constitution Article XVI, Section 50 and in Texas Property Code Chapters 41 and 42. They apply to both income and assets. In other states, execution on a judgment can strip you of your possessions and put you on the street, but that is usually not true in Texas. If a lawsuit is anticipated, or if a judgment creditor is expected to attempt collection, then it is wise to review and maximize these protections well in advance of litigation. It is even wiser to formulate an asset protection strategy long before adverse events occur.

The homestead is the crown jewel of exemptions. It is protected from forced sale for purposes of paying debts and judgments *except* in cases of purchase money, taxes (both ad valorem and federal tax liens against both spouses), owelty of partition (divorce), home improvement loans, home equity loans, reverse mortgages, liens pre-dating the establishment of homestead, refinance loans, or the conversion or refinance of a lien on a mobile home that is attached to the homestead. Other liens are void. No matter how much the home is worth, an ordinary judgment creditor cannot force its sale in the absence of fraud. *In re McCombs*, 659 F.3d 503, 507 (5th Cir. 2011). Texas homestead laws are liberally construed by the courts. *London v. London*, 342 S.W.3d 768, 776 (Tex.App.—Houston [14th Dist.] 2011, no pet.). Other than the types of encumbrances listed in [Property Code Section] 41.001(b), "judgment liens that have been properly abstracted nevertheless cannot attach to a homestead while that property remains homestead." *Fairfield Fin. Grp. v. Synnott*, 300 S.W.3d 316, 320 (Tex.App.—Austin, 2009, no pet.). Furthermore, an attempt by a creditor to place or enforce a lien against the homestead can be defeated using the procedure in Property Code Section 53.160. See chapter 35, *Lien Removal*.

It is also possible to move safely from one homestead to another. Property Code Section 41.001(c) states: "The homestead claimant's proceeds of a sale of a homestead are not subject to seizure for a creditor's claim for six months after the date of sale." This expressly permits homestead equity to be rolled over. *Taylor v. Mosty Bros. Nursery, Inc.*, 777 S.W.2d 568, 570 (Tex.App.—San Antonio 1989, no writ). However, beware of the propensity of title companies to collect for the payment of judgments upon sale of the homestead in disregard of Section 41.001(c). Some title companies have a self-serving reflex requiring that all judgments on Schedule C of the title commitment be paid or released. If that occurs, and if the property is homestead, then the seller should aggressively assert Section 41.001(c). If the title company continues to insist that the judgment be paid, then the remedy may be to change title companies.

The homestead must be rooted in real estate. As much as one might enjoy living on the water, a yacht is not homestead but moveable chattel, i.e., not realty but personal property. *Norris v. Thompson*, 215 S.W.3d 851 (Tex. 2007).

Article 1, Section 28 of the Texas Constitution prohibits garnishment of wages, which protects the income of a person who receives a salary or wages. A creditor cannot touch either one, at least not while they are on their way to the debtor.

Considerable personal property is also exempt from execution. Property Code Sections 42.001 et seq. specifically list the amount and types of exempt personal property, including a vehicle for each licensed driver in the household; home furnishings; and the debtor's IRA or 401(k). In keeping with Texas' frontier spirit, you can even keep two horses if you wish.

Also exempted are certain savings plans "to the extent that the plan, contract, annuity, or account is exempt from federal income tax, or to the extent federal income on the person's interest deferred until actual payment of benefits to the person" under the Internal Revenue Code (Prop. Code Sec. 42.0021); college tuition funds (including IRS Section 529 funds and accounts established under Subchapter F (Education Code Ch. 54,) which are exempted under Section 42.0022; and the cash value of annuities and life insurance policies exempted under Section 1108.001 of the Insurance Code—at least to the extent those items are exempt from garnishment, attachment, execution, or other seizure under Chapter 42 generally. See chapter 34, *Homestead Protections in Texas*.

The Cash Problem

Cash not associated with a retirement plan is the most vulnerable of all assets, even in Texas. What should a debtor do with it when pursued by creditors? Options are to (carefully and incrementally) convert it to homestead-exempt assets such as the home or vehicles; use it for reasonable expenses (e.g., retaining an attorney, paying the IRS, paying a child's tuition, etc.); and progressively withdraw it from the bank over time for legitimate purposes. The conversion process can be tricky, particularly if a lawsuit is already pending. It should not be rushed. If challenged, a debtor must be able to credibly assert the "ordinary course of business" defense of Property Code Section 42.004. *In other words, conversion of cash into exempt assets should be accomplished in the orderly course of business or personal life for purposes that can be reasonably justified independent of any threatened or pending litigation.*

Homestead Exemptions and Registered Entities

Only individuals (not corporations, LLCs, or partnerships) may take advantage of homestead protections. This is one reason it is suggested that when it comes to entity structuring investors draw a red line between investments assets and the homestead.

In Texas, stock in a corporation is non-exempt personal property (Tex. Bus. Orgs. Code Sec. 21.801) that can be subject to levy (Tex. R. Civ. P. 641; Tex. Bus. & Com. Code Sec. 8.112), garnishment (Tex. R. Civ. P. 669), or turnover (Tex. Civ. Prac. & Rem. Code Sec. 31.002). However, partnership and LLC interests are subject only to a charging order, which means that *if* distributions occur, and *only* if they occur, then the creditor may attach them. Tex. Bus. Orgs. Code Sec. 101.112 (LLCs), Sec. 152.308 (partnerships).

Going Beyond Statutory Homestead Protections: Forming an LLC

If in addition to the homestead one has investment properties and significant cash, then clearly the statutory homestead regime is insufficient for asset protection. The next level of protection is achieved by forming an LLC which accomplishes two critical goals: it creates a liability shield for protection of member-owners and, in the case of a series LLC, it creates individual compartments or series which insulate each series from the liabilities associated with other series and the company at large. Visualize a firewall between Series A, Series B, etc. The benefits? Simplicity and economy. An investor with multiple similar assets may no longer need a multiplicity of entities to safely do business. Note that this is not the correct approach when it comes to assets or enterprises that merit their own stand-alone entity. Examples are restaurants, retail outlets, construction companies, mobile home parks, apartment complexes, and so forth, previously described in this book as meriting their own single-purpose entities.

The Two-Company Structure

A sound asset protection structure involves two LLCs, one to hold title to assets (a holding company) and the other to manage them and engage in business generally (a management company). The holding company should be a series LLC while the management company may be either a traditional or series LLC. We prefer Texas and Nevada as states of formation.

A series holding company will have multiple compartments or series that are insulated from one another. For example, if there is a lawsuit affecting an asset in series A, then series B, C, and so on are not affected. The holding company stays quietly in the background, avoiding contractual or transactional privity with anyone. Few people, especially tenants, should even know that it exists. The holding company's name should not even be similar to the name of the management company— and, of course, neither name should provide a clue to the identity of the investor-owner.

In contrast to the holding company, the management company is visible and active. It collects rents, signs leases, deals with contractors and vendors, employs personnel, leases office furniture and vehicles, and otherwise engages with the public. It is a separate, stand-alone entity with no real assets, an *intentional* target for litigation. If sued, one remedy is to walk away, form a new management company, and continue business as usual. If the result is a judgment against the old management company (which should have been maintained as nearly an empty shell) the loss to the investor is minimized. Additionally, using the two-company structure does your attorney a favor, since if the holding company is also sued, he or she may successfully argue that it should not be a defendant at all. Why? Because the holding company did no business with anyone, had no privity with anyone, and therefore there is no legitimate basis for a cause of action against it.

The investor should instruct tenants, creditors, vendors, and the public generally that they are doing business with the LLC's chosen DBA. That's right, *the DBA*. Is there any reason to even tell them the proper legal name of the LLC? Not usually. If an investor is utilizing a two-company strategy, then the DBA used should be that of the management company. It is the public face of the investor's business. Invoices, payments, and the like should all be sent to the management company DBA and never addressed to the investor individually. When a W-9 is required, it should contain the LLC's tax identification number. The investor's personal name should not appear except perhaps in the capacity of an authorized representative who signs on behalf of the entity. Why? *Because when a personal name appears, a plaintiffs' attorney sees a potential additional defendant.*

Two-Company Structure

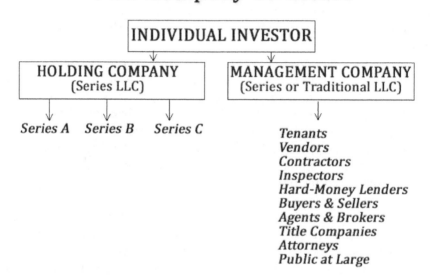

Hub-Sub Structure

Another advanced approach is available for clients with diverse interests—investors who own rental properties but also own a construction company or a restaurant or an apartment complex. The goal is to integrate these various enterprises into a single, layered two-company structure with multiple firewalls. We call this double series LLC structure a "hub-sub."

The heart of the structure is the hub company—a series LLC formed either in Texas or Nevada, which is in turn owned by an anonymity trust with a post office box (we discuss anonymity trusts later in this book). The attorney acts as organizer and, for Texas LLCs, as registered agent.

Series A of the hub company owns another series company (usually a Texas series LLC). Series A of the hub company is the sole member and manager of this subsidiary, listing either a Texas postal box or an address in Nevada as the registered address. This second series entity is thus a wholly-owned subsidiary of (and managed by) series A of the hub company. Again, the attorney acts as organizer to maintain anonymity.

The subsidiary series LLC is where individual rental properties are held. For example, series A of the sub may own 123 Oak Street; series B 458 Elm Street; and so on.

There is nothing new in arranging LLCs or corporations in a parent-subsidiary relationship. The innovation of the hub-sub is that this accomplished (1) using two series LLCs that are (2) structured so as to maximize anonymity.

Now back to the hub company and its potential for accommodating diverse investments. Recall that it is a series entity, and that series A is now occupied by a subsidiary (another series LLC) that owns rental properties. What about the other series of the hub company? The answer is that these are open and available for the investor's other business interests. Series B of the hub company might own a retail store. Series C might be sole member and manager of a traditional Texas LLC that owns a construction company. Why use a traditional LLC for these subsidiary businesses? Because such businesses are usually sufficiently substantial to warrant their own single-purpose entity (SPE). Additional variations on the foregoing are limited only by the investor's imagination. The result is a compact, efficient, and largely anonymous structure which provides the diversified investor with everything he needs and nothing he doesn't.

Hub-Sub Structure

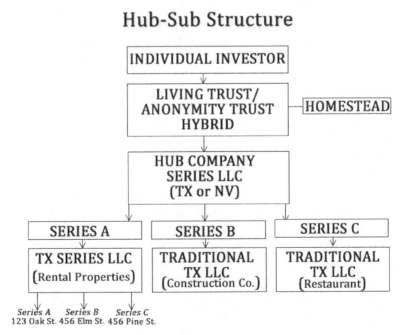

Drafting LLC Documents

This book includes a chapter on LLC governing documents (chapter 25) and we will not repeat it here. To sum up its premise: all LLC documents—beginning with the certificate of formation (Texas) or articles of organization (Nevada) and continuing with the company agreement, the first meeting of members, and the rest—should be drafted with an eye toward asset protection. *Every company document should be prepared with the expectation that it will be intensely scrutinized by both an opposing attorney and a judge.*

Part of asset protection is deterrence. Filed documents should include provisions that discourage creditors from suing the company in the first place. For instance, the COF should contain more than the statutory minimum wording; it should go into detail concerning matters such as series separation and insulation. It should also declare two classes of membership interest—Class A for "regular" members and Class B for creditors who acquire an interest or influence (one way or another) in the company. Owners of Class B are second-class citizens. Class B is unable to vote, may not serve as manager, may not direct that assets be encumbered or sold, and may not alter or impair the company's ability to do business. What sensible plaintiffs' attorney would want to spend time and money suing a company when a victory would consist of acquiring ownership or influence over Class B? He or she certainly might be reluctant do so on a contingent fee arrangement. A substantial retainer would likely be required of the plaintiff. And that brings us back to one of the core strategies of asset protection, to wit, *exhausting an opponent's resolve and resources.*

Transferring Assets to an LLC

An essential asset protection measure is to transfer investment property out of one's personal name and into an LLC—or, if a two-company structure is used, into individual series of the holding company. For real estate, this is done by means of a general or special warranty deed. If the asset is a business or other non-realty, then a bill of sale is generally used. Other assets may call for an assignment of interest. Executed originals should be kept in the LLC's company book.

The due-on-sale clause contained in nearly all deeds of trust is seldom a factor in the transfer of investment properties to a borrower's personal LLC for purposes of asset protection. Historically speaking, it is unlikely that a lender will accelerate a performing loan when the purpose of the transfer was made clear . . . which is not to say that acceleration cannot occur as a result of transferring property into an LLC (lawyers are always hesitant to predict the actions of any particular lender), only that it is highly unlikely in the case of a performing loan.

Company Maintenance

There are minimum actions and formalities that should be prudently observed in order to not only preserve business records but enhance preservation of the LLC's liability barrier—which, after all, is the principal reason one forms an LLC in the first place. These include well-drafted organizational minutes and a company agreement; issuance of membership certificates; minutes of annual meetings; obtaining an EIN and filing tax returns; having a company bank account; and other actions to validate the independent nature of the entity. Failure to do this sort of routine maintenance when accompanied by allegations of actual fraud can make a company vulnerable to "piercing the veil" allegations. Such allegations are so common as to be virtually automatic nowdays. Even if they ultimately fail (as they should in most Texas cases), it is time-consuming and expensive to dispose of them. So why offer the opposition an opening on these issues in the first place? We know in advance that a creditor-plaintiff will ask to see the contents of the company book during the discovery process. It is a given. When produced, the documentation should be flawless.

Pre-Suit Asset Protection Strategies

Asset protection strategies fall into two groups: strategies implemented in advance of collection action or suit by a creditor-plaintiff; and strategies that are feasible afterward. It is preferable to plan ahead and be prepared, since the range of pre-suit alternatives is far greater. After suit is filed, depending on the circumstances, options are reduced by laws relating to fraudulent transfers—moving assets around to defeat legitimate claims of creditors (see chapter 37). Creditors and courts are on the lookout for these. For details, look at Chapter 24 of the Business Organizations Code, entitled the "Uniform Fraudulent Transfer Act." The purpose of UFTA is to prevent debtors from placing assets beyond the reach of creditors. See also *Mladenka v. Mladenka*, 130 S.W.3d 397 (Tex.App.—Houston [14th Dist.] 2004, no pet.).

After suit is filed, the actions of a defendant may be challenged under Property Code Section 42.004, which states that an exemption is lost if non-exempt assets are used to buy or pay down indebtedness on exempt assets "with the intent to defraud, delay, or hinder" a creditor. The defense? The transfer was made in the ordinary course of business as permitted by Property Code Section 42.004(c). In practical terms, this translates as "in the ordinary course of business and daily life."

Competent planning should make effective use of this defense relatively easy.

Post-Suit Strategies

Once litigation is commenced, obvious attempts to maneuver and manipulate assets will likely be detected and scrutinized, at least if the creditor-plaintiff is on the ball. The court may be asked to set aside or unwind an allegedly preferential or fraudulent transaction. Such transfers are generally indicated by "badges of fraud" including the following stand-out items: transfers to a family member; whether or not suit was threatened before it was filed; whether the transfer was of substantially all of the person's assets; whether assets have been removed, undisclosed, or concealed; whether there was equivalent consideration for the transfer (as opposed to a gift or a transfer for $10 and OVC); and whether or not, after the transfer, the transferor became essentially insolvent as a result (i.e., made his cash or other non-exempt assets disappear all at once).

Fraudulent transfer rules usually allow courts to reach back up to two years. Waiting until one has no recourse remaining other than to engage in an obviously fraudulent transfer is simply poor asset protection.

In post-suit strategy, it is important to move assets so as to be able to convincingly claim that a certain action would have been taken anyway, for good reasons that have nothing to do with avoiding a creditor's claims. After all, life does not end merely because a lawsuit has been threatened or filed. People continue to engage in commerce, buy and sell houses and vehicles, make new investments, and otherwise go about the business of living and supporting themselves and their dependents.

The Discovery Process

How do creditor-plaintiffs find out when you move your assets around? Principally, by using the discovery process (interrogatories, requests for production of documents, and depositions—all required to be answered under oath) in order to inquire into a debtor-defendant's transactions. The scope of this process can be wide indeed, reaching back years. Failure to fully respond is grounds for contempt, although "fully respond" should never be interpreted as supplying more information than is absolutely necessary. Creditor-plaintiffs may do research on a defendant, particularly if the debt is substantial, but most have only the information that a debtor voluntarily gives them in pre- and post-judgment discovery. Contrary to popular fiction (where the computer whiz hits a few keys and then summarizes a person's entire life and finances), the Internet has yet to reach the point where it easily reveals everything about everyone to anyone who asks.

For defendants, the most pernicious discovery occurs post-judgment, since creditor-plaintiffs can then go beyond the facts of the case and compel disclosure of sources of income as well as the location and value of assets—*even assets that are legally exempt and which (supposedly) cannot be touched.* This can be a headache because the creditor-plaintiff may nonetheless attempt to go after such exempt assets, forcing a debtor-defendant to seek court protection. One can see why it is important that the defending attorney make a creditor-plaintiff fight vigorously for every bit of information provided in responses to discovery.

AP Level 1: Basic Asset Protection for Investors (the Texas Series LLC)

(1) form a series LLC to own and manage investment properties and businesses in separate series, establishing insulation and multiple liability barriers;

(2) file an assumed name certificate (DBA) for this company and utilize the DBA in business dealings, contracts, leases, etc.;

(3) establish a checking account for the company under its DBA and have checks, letterhead, cards, etc. printed that way and phone numbers listed that way;

(4) transfer properties held in personal names into individual series of the holding company (Series A, Series B, etc.) using deeds that cite series protections;

(5) separate homestead and other creditor-exempt items from investments and businesses, then reduce debt on these items in order to maximize protections afforded by the Property Code and Texas Constitution; and

(6) form a living trust for the homestead to avoid probate, transfer the home into it, and then execute a pour-over will to transfer other assets to the trust upon death.

AP Level 2: Two-Company Structure (the "Texas Two Step")

(1) establish a Texas series LLC or Nevada series LLC to own and hold—but not manage—investment properties and businesses (a holding company, which has no privity with anyone);

(2) form a separate, stand-alone Texas LLC (no cross-ownership) to act as a shell management company to acquire properties

and then after closing transfer them to the holding company; meanwhile the management company signs leases and contracts and deals with tenants, vendors, contractors, and the public; income passes through to the holding company as consulting fees and returns to the management company, if needed, as management fees;

(3) file assumed name certificates (DBAs) for both the holding company and for the management company and utilize these names in all dealings;

(4) establish checking accounts for each company under their respective DBAs and have checks, letterhead, cards, etc. printed that way, and phone numbers listed that way;

(5) transfer properties held in personal names into individual series of the holding company (Series A, Series B, etc.) using deeds that cite series protections;

(6) separate homestead and other creditor-exempt items from investments and businesses, then reduce debt on these items in order to maximize protections afforded by the Property Code and Texas Constitution;

(7) form a living trust for the homestead to avoid probate, transfer the home into it, and then execute a pour-over will to transfer other assets to the trust upon death.

AP Level 3: Texas-Nevada Combination (the "Two-State Solution")

(1) establish a Nevada series LLC to own and hold, but not manage, investment properties and businesses (a holding company) achieving a measure of physical and legal distance plus relative anonymity from Texas plaintiffs;

(2) form a separate stand-alone Texas LLC (no cross-ownership) to act as a shell management company (no significant assets) to acquire properties and then after closing transfer them to the holding company; meanwhile the management company signs leases and contracts and deals with tenants, vendors, contractors, and the public; income passes through to the holding company as consulting fees and returns to the management company, if needed, as management fees;

(3) file assumed name certificates (DBAs) for both the holding company and for the management company and utilize these names in all dealings;

(4) establish checking accounts for each company under their respective DBAs and have checks, letterhead, cards, etc. printed that way, and phone numbers listed that way;

(5) transfer properties held in personal names into individual series of the Nevada holding company (Series A, Series B, etc.) using deeds that cite series protections;

(6) separate homestead and other creditor-exempt items from investments and businesses, then reduce debt on these items in order to maximize protections afforded by the Property Code and Texas Constitution;

(7) form a living trust for the homestead to avoid probate, transfer the home into it, and then execute a pour-over will to transfer other assets to the trust upon death.

AP Level 4: Texas-Nevada Combination ("Hub-Sub") for Multiple Enterprises

(1) Establish a Nevada or Texas series LLC (the hub company);

(2) form a Texas LLC (series or traditional) for one enterprise, designating Series A of the Nevada company as sole member and manager;

(3) form another Texas LLC (series or traditional) for a second enterprise, designating Series B of the hub company as sole member and manager; and so on,

(4) all of which results in separate businesses that are insulated from one another horizontally while protecting the investor vertically with a double-liability firewall.

Role of Trusts in Asset Protection

Trusts come in all shapes and sizes so do not be fooled—there is no standard form of a living trust, land trust, or anonymity trust that is good for all purposes in all states. Texas has its own trust laws and practices and any trust agreement used must be compliant to be effective. So long as it is drafted properly, a trust can be useful in providing:

(1) probate avoidance, since beneficiaries acquire their interests automatically without probate or court intervention;

(2) ease and privacy of transferability, since beneficial interests can be assigned without recording a deed or other instrument; and

(3) anonymity, (although as noted previously this may generate issues with title companies and require clean-up prior to sale).

Caution: a trust does not have a liability barrier as does an LLC, so trusts standing alone are generally insufficient for asset protection. Trusts are merely one tool in the investor's toolbox.

Since both title companies and courts want to see a trust agreement before conceding that a trust actually exists, a written trust agreement must always be prepared and executed.

Apart from investment land trusts, there are also living trusts for the homestead (see chapter 22 on this subject) which are valuable probate-avoidance devices. Anyone who has probated an estate may be familiar with the procedural nightmare that can occasionally occur when dealing with attorneys and judges who will happily reduce the deceased's castle to rubble.

Anonymity and an LLC

An investor's goal should be to achieve maximum anonymity combined with the liability barrier created by one or more LLCs. Such a strategy creates legal, practical, and psychological obstacles to a potential creditor-plaintiff.

Anonymity is a legitimate goal that is more important to some investors than others. Those for whom there is pending or threatened litigation would certainly fall into this category. An investor's goal should be to achieve maximum anonymity combined with the liability barrier created by one or more LLCs.

An LLC provides a measure of anonymity depending on the amount of information that is disclosed in the certificate of formation (or articles of organization in the case of Nevada). The COF requires three names and addresses: the registered agent (physical address only), the initial manager (a post office box is acceptable), and the organizer (often the attorney) who must be an authorized person.

Anonymity begins at LLC formation. Avoid using the home as the registered address. Disclosing it hardly enhances anonymity, nor does it prevent a constable from banging on your door at 5:30 a.m. to serve a lawsuit. The world is both a legally and physically dangerous place. We have even had a client whose home was bombed by an angry tenant. Tenants, vendors, contractors, and the public at large should *never* have an investor's homestead address.

The COF requires a physical address, not a box, since the constable cannot serve a mailbox with a lawsuit. Recently, the Secretary of State has become more aggressive in checking whether or not registered addresses are really mailbox stores. They occasionally even google the address. If they think it is a box, the COF will be rejected.

It is recommended that an investor should either use his or her office address or use an attorney as registered agent of the company (which also has the benefit of invoking the attorney-client privilege under certain circumstances). Otherwise, arrangements must be made for a registered agent at a real street address, which cannot contain PMB, POB, Box, a double suite number, or any other indication of a box.

Back to the COF, which requires the designation of an initial manager. This is usually where the owner's name goes. A creative approach is to name an anonymity trust in this capacity, but this is an advanced technique to be used only with guidance from a specialized attorney. An additional benefit: one now has an anonymity trust, backed by a trust agreement, that is able to be utilized for other purposes beyond its role as member and manager of the LLC—including buying more property anonymously. This is an example of how the component parts of an asset protection structure can work together synergistically.

The Role of Insurance

Is liability insurance alone sufficient for asset protection? The answer is a resounding *no*. Insurance is a passive measure that has its place in the mix. True asset protection requires one to be proactive. Asset protection experts unanimously recommend a sensible blend of insurance *and* active asset protection measures. The principal reason is that insurance can never be truly relied upon, since *insurers are in the business of collecting premiums and denying claims.* That is what they do, that is their business plan, which is why they are among the wealthiest corporations in America. Expect that every effort will be made by an insurer to exclude or avoid coverage in case of loss—which will make your "good neighbor" your attorney, not the insurance company. There may also be special issues if a creditor-plaintiff alleges fraud, which is never covered. It may then become necessary to sue the insurance company.

Even if an insurer concedes coverage, extravagant claims made in lawsuits may (and often do) exceed available limits. Moreover, the existence of a sizable policy and umbrella may actually encourage a lawsuit because it will be perceived as a tempting target. Nonetheless, having adequate insurance is a necessary evil.

Bankruptcy

Bankruptcy is the nuclear option in asset protection, being broadly effective. Even so, rules against fraudulent transfers ("preferences" in the

Bankruptcy Code) apply in this area as well, and more strictly. The bankruptcy court can reach back a year or more. Also, false information in a bankruptcy petition may be investigated by the FBI. And of course bankruptcy does not discharge income taxes (although the IRS may be more likely to work with you on a payment plan), child support obligations, student loans, and any items that a debtor fails to list on the petition.

The Bankruptcy Code allows a debtor to choose between the federal exemptions (i.e., list of exempt assets) or the state ones. In Texas it is more common to choose the state exemptions since they are so favorable.

By and large, filing bankruptcy is an admission that previous asset protection strategies have failed. The bankruptcy trustee and the court assume control of your life. It is a last resort.

Lifestyle Considerations

One's lifestyle should be consistent with maintaining an effective asset protection strategy. In addition to all the other suggestions relating to anonymity, creating a liability shield, maximizing protections under the homestead laws, and the like, one should:

(1) avoid conspicuous consumption—live a notch below your means (at least outwardly) so as to make a less appealing target for plaintiffs and their attorneys;

(2) avoid personally guaranteeing any business debt or cosigning on others' notes;

(3) carry health and term life insurance on yourself as well as key-man term life insurance on your business partners;

(4) avoid all forms of debt that do not result in an income stream, including nearly all consumer debt which, after the thrill of possessing a new item dissipates merely serves to keep you up at night;

(5) reduce all business arrangements—including those with family and friends (*especially* those with family and friends)—to a written agreement that contains an exit strategy, including buy-sell and dispute resolution provisions;

(6) diversify assets and investments, preferably within one or two LLCs, at least one of which should be a series company; and

(7) put 5 to 10% of your assets into gold, cash, and other doomsday assets. The worst-case scenario could actually happen. Some think it is happening already.

Other Asset Protection Devices

There are many other asset protection devices and entities that are beyond the scope of this discussion. Included among them are:

Family Limited Partnerships. Texas FLPs (like LLCs) must be filed with the state and pertinent ownership information is revealed; also an in-state registered agent must be designated to receive service of process if the partnership is sued. So why not just form an LLC (especially a series LLC if assets are in real estate) and then move title to assets into a land trust? The result is arguably superior liability protection and anonymity. Another drawback of the FLP is its concept of a friendly lien on the homestead, not very workable in Texas.

Limited Partnerships with an LLC or Corporate General Partner. These vehicles are more complex and expensive and are usually employed in larger commercial transactions, which are beyond the scope of this book.

Asset Protection in the Real World

Total asset protection is probably not achievable, even in Texas, in spite of claims made by Internet and seminar gurus (and even some lawyers) who have never spent time in a real court of law in front of a real judge who has contempt power. Do you recall Einstein's theory that a traveling spaceship may approach the speed of light but never actually reach it? Asset protection is like that. The goal is to get as close to an ideal AP situation as possible, by using the correct structure and by layering asset protection devices.

To summarize, asset protection is ultimately about preparation and advance planning that have the effect of *establishing* a sound structure, *deterring* lawsuits, and *exhausting* your opponent's determination and resources. If you can make it difficult to find your assets and make it unacceptably expensive and time-consuming for a plaintiff's attorney to reach them, then your asset protection plan has done its job.

Chapter 32

ANONYMITY IN TEXAS REAL ESTATE

A Relatively Achievable Goal

This chapter addresses legitimate privacy alternatives for the Texas investor or business person when engaging in real estate transactions. Why is privacy important? First, because information is power, and it is preferable that your opponents have as little power as possible over you; and second, because we live in a combative and litigious world—and offering gratuitous, vital information about yourself in the public domain provides others with a roadmap to your identity, business strategy, and assets.

Every day there is a John Smith who files to form an LLC under the name "John Smith Investments LLC" and then lists himself (and often his unsuspecting wife) as initial managers at his homestead address, placing his core personal information in the public domain. Of course this investor does the filing work himself, without assistance from an asset protection attorney, because he is smarter than any lawyer—even though he may have been educated as a software engineer or a medical doctor. After all, the law is easy, right? Just a matter of filling out a few forms?

Guiding rule: every member of the public, every single business partner, every single contract party, every single buyer, every single seller, every single title company, every single attorney, every single vendor, and every single agent or broker should be viewed as a potential adversary in a lawsuit. As long as you have what they want—cash or property—it may be only a matter of time before they come for you. Recognition of this reality should lead sensible investors to proactively limit exposure by implementing an asset protection plan.

Litigation Nation

Why is there so much litigation? Two reasons: first, because of contingent-fee arrangements by which some attorneys take dubious cases and then utilize the legal system to harass legitimate businesspersons into settlement; and second, because the American justice system for the most part imposes no significant penalty upon those who have filed failed or frivolous lawsuits.

Common Questions Pertaining to Anonymity

Three anonymity-related questions frequently present themselves: (1) how can I hold title to property without revealing that I am the true party in interest (this question has to do with status of title—where does true ownership reside)? (2) How can I transfer property held in my personal name to my LLC without showing that it came from me (this pertains to chain of title—what is the recorded link between seller and buyer)? (3) How can I blend anonymity features with the liability shield of an LLC?

When discussing anonymity, two important groups in the real estate world must be considered: county clerks, who maintain the real property records and whose job includes filing documents to reflect chain of title; and title companies, which examine and insure both the status of title and the chain of title.

Status of Title

Title to property can be held in a surprising variety of capacities—as an individual, a corporation, a limited liability company, a general or limited partnership, in a trust, and so forth—or as a combination of any of the foregoing. Property law is flexible in this respect. What if an investor wants to hold 50% of title in his or her personal name, 25% in an LLC, and the remaining 25% in a family living trust? Not a problem. Whether or not it is wise to structure ownership in such a way is another matter.

Looking past who nominally holds title (determining who is really in control) can be a challenging exercise, but in most cases it is possible to trace this information through local real property records, DBA filings at the county or state level, or through the Secretary of State and Texas Comptroller—not to mention miscellaneous data accessible on the Internet. The exception occurs when a cautious individual or entity has made a deliberate and diligent effort *from the beginning* to remain as anonymous as possible.

So in considering issues of anonymity, one should distinguish between *absolute anonymity*, which is difficult to achieve in an informed and interconnected world, and *relative anonymity*, which is a more attainable goal. Think of it as a sliding scale. An effective asset protection strategy seeks to maximize relative anonymity, moving the dial as far as possible in that direction. How far can that be? It depends on the circumstances and an investor's willingness to be creative.

Note that it is possible to purchase, own, and convey property without recording transfer documents. There is no law or requirement that all deeds must be recorded. It is likewise possible to purchase, own, and convey property without ever buying a policy of title insurance or entering the offices of a title company. But the reality is that unrecorded interests are difficult to sell. How would a prospective buyer verify the seller's ownership? Also, buyers in the real world often want title insurance, and their lenders will (by law) require it.

Chain of Title

There is no effective method of defeating, ignoring, or bypassing the chain of title. Each link in the chain of title is represented by a deed or other conveyance recorded in the county clerk's office—and one cannot break the chain and still preserve one's status as record owner. A broken link equals questionable title. Questionable title equals unsellable property.

So what is the response to the question posed above, "How can I transfer property held in my personal name to my LLC (or other entity or person) without showing that it came from me?" The answer is that *you cannot*, at least not if you are going to be deeding the property to the LLC outright—as opposed, for instance, to using a more creative approach.

One alternative is to arrange for the property to pass through one or more intermediate transfers so that its origin is progressively more remote in the chain. The more these intermediate transfers have the appearance of bona fide sales for monetary consideration, the more likely the original transferor is to remain in the background, beyond immediate scrutiny. Again, it is a question of relative rather than absolute anonymity.

Another alternative would be to deed the property into a trust which then privately transfers the beneficial interest in the trust to the LLC. This method has a drawback, however: there is now a trustee (an individual) who is exposed without a liability barrier.

Pre-Closing Anonymity

Acquisition of real property begins with negotiation of the earnest money contract, which calls for the name and address of the buyer. Although earnest money contracts are not recorded, they can be the start of anonymity issues, since dealing with realtors, appraisers, inspectors, surveyors, title company personnel, and neighbors is often quite public and leaves an extensive paper trail. Also, people involved in the process inevitably gossip about pending transactions.

There are two advisable choices at the contract phase: either purchase property in the name of an LLC or trust; or, alternatively, list a personal name for the buyer but follow it with the phrase "and/or his or her assigns." The latter provides a means of switching into the preferred method for holding title at the last minute, before closing. This option may be unavailable if the property is financed, since lenders require that the principal obligor on the note and the name of the grantee on the deed be one and the same. In that event, the investor should promptly transfer the newly-acquired property into an asset-holding LLC after closing.

Does this raise due-on-sale issues? Unlikely. It is seldom that a lender accelerates a performing loan because it has been transferred into an investor's personal company, but technically it could happen. In actual practice, the potential consequences of leaving investment property in a personal name substantially outweigh any risk involved in moving it promptly into the investor's LLC. See chapter 20 on this subject.

Returning to the subject of earnest money contracts: it is important to realize that contracts can either convey a lot of information or just a small amount of it. Be attuned to this. For instance, is there any reason to list one's home address as opposed to a postal box? A home phone versus your office or cell phone? Do not provide any more personal information than is essential to make the deal. Do not say *anything* to a realtor that you do not *expect* to be conveyed to the other side, the realtor's duty of confidentiality notwithstanding. Again, people talk.

Use of LLCs, Corporations, and Limited Partnerships as Transfer Vehicles

Another method of achieving relative anonymity in the chain of title involves establishing a registered entity (an LLC, for example) that is filed with the Secretary of State. The first step, of course, is to establish the LLC; the second is to transfer the property to the entity; the third step involves transferring an interest in the entity to some third person or entity, accomplished by means of an unrecorded "Sale and Assignment of LLC Membership Interest." The LLC continues to own the asset, but the person owning the LLC will have changed. There would be nothing in the real property records (chain of title) or in appraisal district records that reflects the principals who are now behind the LLC.

Note, however, that registered entities must file an annual Public Information Report with the Texas Comptroller listing the "name, title, and mailing address of each officer, director, member, general partner, or manager" (see Comptroller form 05-102). Eventually, therefore, someone truly determined to discover the real nature of the transfer may do so by accessing the Comptroller's records after the next annual PIR is filed, although this vulnerability may be mitigated by using a trust and certain anonymity layering techniques. Without employing such advanced techniques, the longer-term use of an LLC as a transfer vehicle qualifies only as "anonymity lite."

Limited partnerships are also common anonymity structures, particularly in larger commercial transactions. LPs are often set up as a group of corporations or LLCs with a shell entity as the general partner. These may be owned by other entities. LPs are relatively expensive structures more typically used to buy office buildings and shopping malls. Accordingly, they are beyond the scope of this book and we will not discuss them in detail.

Anonymity Trusts

In an anonymity trust, title is taken in the name of, for instance, the "Series A Trust" with no mention of a trustee. While county clerks generally have no problem accepting such deeds for filing, the technical problem is that a trust is not a legal entity that can hold title. Even though trusts often act like legal entities in the real world, *a trust is not an entity but a relationship*, specifically a relationship between trustor, trustee, and beneficiary, each with rights and duties as a consequence of that relationship.

Accordingly, problems occur when a title company is later asked to insure title as part of a proposed sale of the property. The title company will correctly assert that a deed into an anonymity trust fails as a matter of law, and this is true—even though there has been a deed of record in the trust's name that has successfully preserved anonymity for the investor during his or her entire period of ownership (so the investor's anonymity goals have been substantially achieved). The issue is what the title company will require *now* in order to move forward, which will usually be two things from the seller: a copy of an acceptable trust agreement or, alternatively, a "certification of trust" pursuant to Property Code Section 114.086; and a re-deeding of the property with specific mention of the trustee's name.

How to plan for this? The seller should execute two deeds when conveying property into an anonymity trust: one that omits the name of the trustee along with a second one that does—but record only the first one. The second should be held in reserve (a "deed in the drawer" technique) in anticipation of a future title company's objections, ready to be produced and recorded at that time.

We neither encourage nor discourage the use of anonymity trusts of this type. They can certainly be effective. Just note that they are for

aggressive investors who do not mind being lectured by a title company and doing re-deeding work before sale of the property.

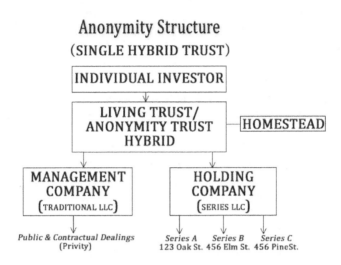

Assumed Name Certificates (DBAs)
====

Anonymity Structure

(SINGLE HYBRID TRUST)

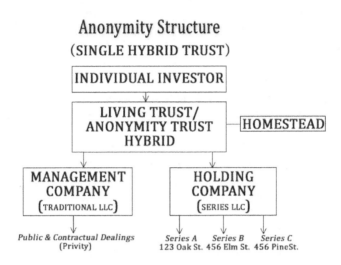

Assumed Name Certificates (DBAs)

Can property be deeded into a DBA as grantee? Does a DBA exist as an entity that can hold property? The answer is *no*. An assumed name filing is, after all, merely *a public notice* that a person or entity will be using a different front-name in business transactions. It does not in and of itself establish a new entity, nor is there the equivalent of a trust agreement behind it. The result is that use of a DBA alone to hold title to property likely means there has been no transfer at all. Title insurance would be unavailable for conveyances out of the DBA. Result? This practice is fatally flawed and should be avoided.

Having said the foregoing, it is nonetheless true that assumed names are highly useful devices in anonymity layering. As a rule, each LLC an investor owns should do as much business as possible through its DBA. A bank account should be opened in the DBA name and checks should be printed that way. Leases and contracts should be signed using the DBA. Even though research at the county clerk's office may uncover underlying ownership behind the DBA, an assumed name is nonetheless an important part of the process.

Anonymity Using a Two-Company Structure

It is best to separate activities from assets. Assets should be held in an LLC (preferably a series company that stays out of sight and does little or no public business) while dealings with tenants, contractors, vendors, and the like should be conducted by a separate near-shell management company. This two-company structure can be effectively used for anonymity purposes without any add-ons other than the usual assumed names for each company. For instance, the management company can purchase properties (and, in so doing, do business with a seller, one or more brokers, rehab contractors, etc.) and then, after closing and fix-up, transfer the property to the investor's holding company, which is largely immune from a successful lawsuit. Why? Because it has no legal connection (privity) with anyone, meaning it has not conducted business directly with anyone.

As a result of this strategy, the owner of the holding company is relatively remote and anonymous by a couple of steps—not a perfect strategy (none is) but a very good one. In certain cases, it may be useful to split the two LLCs between two states, what we call the "two-state solution."

The Hub-Sub Structure AKA the Chinese Puzzle Box

Another alternative is to establish an entity within an entity—an LLC that is owned by another LLC, for instance. If this is your choice, one of our favorite recommendations is to establish a primary operating LLC in Texas (either a traditional or series LLC) which is in turn owned by Series A of a Nevada series LLC. We favor the series format in most cases because of the additional firewall protection between individual series, a significant benefit if an investor has multiple and diverse assets or enterprises.

Mixing Trusts and LLCs: LLC as Beneficiary of a Trust

Benefits can be achieved by mixing a trust and an LLC. There are a couple of possibilities. Before discussing those, it would be useful to answer two common questions: yes, an LLC (or a series of an LLC) *can* be the beneficiary of a trust; and no, an LLC generally *cannot* be the trustee. The trustee must be a natural person unless an entity is approved as a trustee by the state (a marathon process involving massive disclosure).

One option is to utilize an LLC as a beneficiary of a land trust. This method consists of three steps: first, creating an anonymity trust, of which the LLC is the 100% beneficiary; second, conveying property into the trust by recorded warranty deed; and third, designating a series of the LLC (Series A, for example) to own and hold a 100% beneficial interest in the trust.

But what about a liability shield? The trustee is personally exposed—and this is the principal drawback of any trust, since persons acting as trustees are very often named individually in suits against the trust. This is one reason no sensible lawyer will agree to act as trustee for investment trusts established by his or her clients.

The reader is cautioned against non-lawyer seminar gurus who make overblown claims concerning trusts and asset protection systems they are marketing. Trust agreements available on the Internet should also be avoided. These are almost always of questionable legality and effectiveness. Such schemes are seldom suitable for Texas which has a unique Property Code and Business Organizations Code.

Chapter 33

ASSUMED NAMES

Don't Leave Home without One

The use of one or more assumed names or "DBAs" is an important part of an overall asset protection plan. Why? Because asset protection is, at least in part, about layering of incremental obstacles to a potential plaintiff. The more hurdles a plaintiff and his attorney have to get over in order to get to you and your assets, the better. The objective is to *deter*, *discourage*, and *deplete* a potential plaintiff's resources. Although assumed name records are publicly available for inspection, sometimes online, this is an additional level of research that—believe or not—some plaintiffs will be too lazy to undertake.

Public Interest in Disclosure

What is the intent of the statute requiring the filing of a DBA? Both simple and practical: public disclosure of the true party in interest and the location at which that party may be served with process if suit is filed. The premise behind the law is that it is in the public interest to be able to ascertain whom to sue and where service of process may be physically achieved.

From a disclosure perspective, DBA filing requirements operate in favor of potential plaintiffs. There is, however, a sense in which they favor defendants. Suits are filed everyday against assumed-name defendants, particularly at the justice court level. Consider a hypothetical auto dealership, "Northside Chevrolet." If a suit is filed against Northside Chevrolet, it is subject to immediate dismissal upon motion by Northside's attorney. Why? *Because Northside Chevrolet is not a legal entity*. It is merely the assumed name of someone else, almost certainly a corporation or LLC with a liability barrier that is doing business under the name Northside. The result is that the plaintiff must now go home, do research, and re-file the case (paying additional fees and costs in the process) against the true principal behind the DBA. The legal entity may not even have its business headquarters in that county, requiring a request for out-of-county service of process, another delay and expense. A certain percentage of plaintiffs will instead give up at this point.

An assumed name is merely a trade name and has no legal existence of its own. *Steer Wealth Mgmt., LLC v. Denson*, 537 S.W.3d 558 (Tex.App.—Houston [1st Dist.] 2017, no pet. h.).

Law Applicable to Assumed Names

There is no statutory limit on the number of DBAs an individual or company may have, either at the state or county level. A filing is good for 10 years and fees are nominal. A DBA may also be terminated or abandoned by filing a form. Go to the county clerk's website in the county in which you are headquartered or in which you propose to operate. For state-level filings, go to www.sos.state.tx.us/corp/forms and complete Form 503. This form requires an applicant to state the counties in which an assumed name will be used. If the entity will potentially use its assumed name in all counties in Texas, check the box for "All."

Texas Business & Commerce Code, Title 5, Chapter 71—the "Assumed Business and Professional Name Act"—requires a notarized DBA filing for individuals, companies, and others under the following circumstances:

§ 71.002. Definitions

(2) "Assumed name" means:

(A) for an individual, [if the enterprise proposes to operate under] a name that does not include the surname of the individual;

(B) for a partnership, [if the enterprise proposes to operate under] a name that does not include the surname or other legal name of each joint venturer or general partner;

(C) for an individual or a partnership, [if the enterprise proposes to operate under] a name, including a surname, that suggests the existence of additional owners by including words such as "Company," "& Company," "& Son," "& Sons," "& Associates," "Brothers," and similar words, but not words that merely describe the business being conducted or the professional service being rendered;

(D) for a limited partnership, [if the enterprise proposes to operate under] a name other than the name stated in its certificate of formation;

(E) for a company, [if the enterprise proposes to operate under] a name used by the company;

(F) for a corporation, [if the enterprise proposes to operate under] a name other than the name stated in its certificate of formation or a comparable document;

(G) for a limited liability partnership, [if the enterprise proposes to operate under] a name other than the name stated in its application filed with the office of the secretary of state or a comparable document; and

(H) for a limited liability company, [if the enterprise proposes to operate under] a name other than the name stated in its certificate of formation or a comparable document including the name of any series of the limited liability company established by its company agreement.

The filer must include the physical address of its place of business. If the proposed county of business is different from the county where the enterprise is headquartered, then a DBA must be filed in both counties.

Suppose you have a Nevada LLC and want to operate under an assumed name in Dallas or Houston, may you file an assumed name certificate in either county (or both) and do so? Absolutely. The statute expressly includes both domestic and foreign entities within its scope.

State Versus County Filing of DBAs

Obtaining a DBA is a logical next step after forming an LLC. But where should the filing occur—at the county clerk's office or with the secretary of state? Under Business and Commercial Code Section 71.103, the DBA must be filed at both levels: "The corporation, limited partnership, limited liability partnership, limited liability company, or foreign filing entity shall file the certificate in the office of the secretary of state and in the office or offices of each county clerk as specified by Subsection (b) or (c)." Notice that the statute says *and* when referring to state and county filings, although filing with the Secretary of State is frequently overlooked by smaller companies who often file only in their local county.

At the county level, the county clerk will want to determine if a proposed DBA is available. The customary standard is that your proposed name must not be the same as or deceptively similar to another entity's filed assumed name within that county. At the state level, however, the DBA filing is purely a notice filing, meaning that it is not necessary to first ascertain if a certain name is available. Just create a name and file Form 503.

Texas has 254 counties. If you are obtaining a county-level assumed name for banking purposes and everyday usage, does it matter in which county you file? Surprisingly, not much. Even if you are doing business in Houston, a bank will usually accept a DBA from El Paso County for purposes of opening an account and ordering checks in the assumed name. Another noteworthy point: there is currently *no central database* linking the assumed name records of Texas counties.

Trusts and DBAs

Interestingly, the statute does not mention trusts, which are a common asset protection device. Are these covered by the law? Must a trust file a DBA if the trust is doing business under anything other than its complete formal name? Our view is in the affirmative, even though trusts are technically not stand-alone legal entities, though they often act as such in the real world. A trust likely falls under the term "company," at least for purposes of this law; and "company" is defined as "a real estate investment trust, a joint-stock company, or any other business, professional, or other association or legal entity that is not incorporated, other than a partnership, limited partnership, limited liability company, limited liability partnership, or foreign filing entity." But this is actually good news. If one has a land trust and is doing business with it then one *should* acquire an assumed name and use it.

A Series LLC Doing Business through One of Its Series

What about individual series of a series limited liability company? Series are, in many respects, sub-companies and are largely empowered to behave that way. Business Organizations Code Section 101.605 provides that an individual series has the power (1) to sue and be sued; (2) to contract; and (3) to hold title to real and personal property. In order to fulfill these functions at the series level (rather than at the level of the company at large), the series must operate or hold title under its own name (for example, as "ABC LLC—Series A") which in turn requires that the series obtain an assumed name certificate. Why is this so? *Because the series is not, as a technical matter, an independent legal entity; and since it is operating under a name other than the name stated in the company's COF, it must have a DBA on file.* Moreover, to be fully compliant, the DBA filing must take place both at the county and state levels.

The basic assumed name filing for a series LLC would be in the name of the company doing business as an individual series. For example: "ABC LLC doing business as ABC LLC—Series A." Section 71.103 would require such an assumed name filing both in the county where Series A does business and also at the office of the Secretary of State.

An Individual Series Doing Business on Its Own

What about filing an assumed name certificate for a specific series—for instance "ABC LLC—Series A DBA Ace Investments?" County clerks have no problem with this formulation and are more than willing to accept your DBA filing fee. However, the Secretary of State would currently reject it with the following notation: "Our records do not show an entity by the name shown on the document which was submitted for filing." In other words, the Secretary of State is taking a strict stance here, i.e., that the individual series of a series LLC are not in and of themselves separate legal entities. Therefore, in the State's view, they cannot have assumed names. Since, for asset protection purposes, we would nonetheless prefer to throw a cloak of anonymity over individual series, we must for now be content with series DBA filing at the county level only—unless the Secretary of State revises its interpretation of the statute. As it turns out, this works sufficiently well for asset protection purposes.

Banks and Series DBAs

As to banking, the importance of having a DBA for Series A, Series B, Series C, and so forth is relevant if one chooses to open a bank account solely and specifically for the use of an individual series. A bank will require an assumed name certificate if "ABC LLC—Series A" wants to open an account in the name of "Ace Investments" and have checks printed that way. Having such a DBA also entitles the series to lawfully print business cards and stationery that read "Ace Investments" with no disclosure that the principal behind the scenes is in fact an individual series of a series LLC.

Title Companies and DBA Requirements

Title companies are also sensitive to DBA issues. Expect that if a company (whether traditional or series) has not filed a required assumed name certificate it will be asked to do so before closing on either the purchase or sale of real property.

As a practical matter, neither banks nor title companies appear to care whether one's assumed name certificate is issued by the Secretary of State or by the local county clerk, just so long as a filed certificate exists.

Statutory Penalties

Will one go to the penitentiary for failing to file an assumed name? No. Penalties for failing to fully comply with the Assumed Business and Professional Name Act are generally mild:

§ 71.201. Civil Action; Sanction

A person's failure to comply with this chapter does not impair the validity of any contract or act by the person or prevent the person from defending any action or proceeding in any court of this state, but the person may not maintain in a court of this state an action or proceeding arising out of a contract or act in which an assumed name was used until an original, new, or renewed certificate has been filed as required by this chapter.

In an action or proceeding brought against a person who has not complied with this chapter, the court may award the plaintiff or other party bringing the action or proceeding expenses incurred, including attorney's fees, in locating and effecting service of process on the defendant.

In a civil suit, then, a violator may need to immediately file an assumed name certificate in order to proceed with the prosecution or defense of a suit. It may also be ordered to pay the costs and fees associated with inconveniencing the other party. These are not heavy sanctions. Note that "failure to register an assumed name does not 'impair the validity of any contract or act by the person.' Accordingly, when evidence shows an entity is doing business under another name, it may be held liable under that name without regard to whether it filed an assumed name certificate." *Broemer v. Houston Lawyer Referral Serv.* 407 S.W.3d 477, 482 (Tex.App.—Houston [14th Dist.] 2013, no pet.).

There is a criminal penalty for an intentional violation (whatever that may be):

§ 71.202. Criminal Penalty: General Violation

(a) A person commits an offense if the person:

(1) conducts business or renders a professional service in this state under an assumed name; and
(2) intentionally violates this chapter.

(b) An offense under this section is a Class A misdemeanor.

We are unaware of an abundance of prosecutions in this area. Why? As with most criminal offenses, the district attorney must prove *criminal intent*. It is far more likely that a person or company failing to fully comply inadvertently overlooked the details of the statute. Forged or fraudulent filings, however, are a more serious matter—a third-degree felony. Bus. & Com. Code Sec. 71.203.

Entitlement to Exclusive Use of an Assumed Name

The filing of an assumed name certificate does *not* assure exclusive use of a DBA and is *not* the equivalent of obtaining a trademark or copyright:

§ 71.157. Effect of Filing

> **This chapter does not give a registrant a right to use the assumed name in violation of the common or statutory law of unfair competition or unfair trade practices, common law copyright, or similar law.**
>
> **(a) The filing of a certificate under this chapter does not in itself constitute actual use of the assumed name stated in the certificate for purposes of determining priority of rights.**

Even if one obtains a DBA in the local county, there are still 253 other Texas counties (not to mention the Secretary of State's office) where someone else may lawfully file to use the same or a similar assumed name.

Having said that, the filing of an assumed name will likely, over time, build and increase one's entitlement to the assumed name as a matter of common law. The name acquires public acceptance and recognition in the area in which it is used. County clerks, of course, aid in this process by declining to issue identical assumed names to rival enterprises within their borders. A DBA is nonetheless no substitute for obtaining a proper trademark or copyright, which is a highly technical field. Consult an expert.

It should also be noted that an assumed name certificate is not a business license, which is not required in Texas except for specific industries. Nevada, on the other hand, currently charges $200 annually for its required LLC business license.

LLC Bank Accounts and DBAs

Forming an LLC, whether traditional or series, and then failing to get a DBA and do business under it reflects an incomplete process from an asset protection perspective. Get the required DBA and one or more optional DBAs. As many activities as possible should be conducted under a DBA name. There is simply no good reason to make it easy for a potential plaintiff to know the identity or location of the true party in interest behind either an entity or a transaction.

Use of DBAs with a Two-Company Structure

Our recommended asset protection structure involves two LLCs—a management company and a holding company. Both should obtain and utilize assumed names. This is particularly important for the management company in its dealing with residential tenants. The Property Code states:

> **Section 92.201. DISCLOSURE OF OWNERSHIP AND MAN-AGEMENT. (a) A landlord shall disclose to a tenant . . . the name and either a street or post office box address of the holder of record title, according to the deed records in the county clerk's office, of the dwelling rented by the tenant. . . . (f) For the purposes of this section, an owner or property manager may disclose either an actual name or names or an assumed name if an assumed name certificate has been recorded with the county clerk.**

Accordingly, the preferred practice from an asset protection point of view is to keep the proper name of the management company as private as possible and whenever possible use that company's assumed name on leases, checks, and other dealings with tenants and the public.

The choice of name for an LLC is far less important than the DBA. Most of our clients unnecessarily spend considerable time and energy choosing an LLC name that unwisely includes or reveals their personal names or other sensitive information. Something generic for the LLC is always better, accompanied by a catchy assumed name.

Chapter 34

HOMESTEAD PROTECTIONS IN TEXAS

Power to the People (and to Their Homes, Cars, Horses, etc.)

This chapter outlines unique protections available to an individual's residence and personal property by what are commonly referred to as "Texas homestead laws," found in Texas Constitution Article XVI, Section 50 and Property Code Chapters 41 and 42. Our focus is on Texas law, not rules or exemptions under federal or bankruptcy law. It is worth observing, however, that bankruptcy rules are tougher on debtors than Texas law. Generally speaking, if a debtor can stay out of bankruptcy, hunker down, and maximize Texas state protections, that is the preferable course.

The term "homestead" is often used in the context of the homestead exemption from property taxes, which excludes a specified amount of the appraised value from the taxable value of the home. Most school districts across Texas provide that $25,000 of the homestead's appraised value is exempted. Homeowners over 65 qualify for an additional exemption of $10,000. However, the purpose of this chapter is not to discuss the tax aspect of the homestead, and we will leave that subject behind at this point. Rather, when discussing homestead, we will specifically refer to the protections the homestead receives from creditors and execution upon judgments.

The homestead has always been sacred in Texas, reaching back to the Republic of Texas and even before. See Stephen F. Austin, Code of Civil Regulations (1824). The Texas Constitution (Art. 1, Sec. 28) and Property Code Section 41.001 provide that the homestead of a family or single adult is protected from forced sale except in cases of purchase money, taxes (both ad valorem and federal tax liens against both spouses), owelty of partition (divorce), home improvement loans, home equity loans, reverse mortgages, liens predating the establishment of homestead, refinance loans, or the conversion or refinance of a lien on a mobile home that is attached to the homestead. Other liens are void. Further, even a permitted lien must be in writing and signed by both spouses to be valid. The protection of the homestead combined with the prohibition against garnishment of wages has long made Texas a favorable destination for debtors.

It is quite possible to make a good salary (no monetary limit), own a paid-for million-dollar home, drive a paid-for car, have numerous judgments against you (from Texas or other states), and be reasonably secure from creditors—although dealings in current cash accounts may be severely restricted. As to the home itself, there is no dollar limitation on its exempt value. *In re. McCombs*, 659 F.3d at 507.

Asset protection planning in Texas relies on constitutional and statutory homestead protections plus formation of an LLC (or a two-LLC or hub-sub structure) for investments, with the goal of utilizing anonymity techniques whenever feasible. Add a living trust to the mix, and asset protection and basic estate planning can be effectively integrated.

Homestead laws are liberally construed by the courts. *London v. London*, 342 S.W.3d 768, 776 (Tex.App.—Houston [14th Dist.] 2011, no pet.). "Indeed, a court must uphold and enforce the Texas homestead laws even though in so doing the court might unwittingly assist a dishonest debtor in wrongfully defeating his creditor." *PaineWebber, Inc. v. Murray*, 260 B.R. 815, 822 (E.D. Tex. 2001). Unless a judgment debtor owns investment real estate, cash or cash-equivalent on deposit, or a business with attachable inventory—or engages in detectable fraud in concealment of assets—a Texas judgment against an individual may be uncollectable.

Homestead protections are available only to individuals—not corporations, partnerships, or LLCs—and they do not encompass investment or business assets (which should be held in an LLC); nor is a debtor's ownership in corporations, partnerships, or LLCs protected from the consequences of a judgment. Such business interests are non-exempt personal property.

What is a homestead?

The answer is not as obvious as one might think. Although a person's homestead is primarily a question of intent, and the claimant need not actually reside on the property, there must be some overt act in preparation for physical occupancy. Mere intent standing alone may not be enough. *Gilmore v. Dennison*, 115 S.W.2d 902 (Tex. 1938). A person claiming homestead has the burden of proving that fact; however, once that is accomplished, the designation tends to stick.

A homestead claim must also be based on a real property interest. For instance, neither a mobile home unaffixed to the realty nor a boat qualify. But a vacant lot can be homestead if the owner has reasonable expectations of building a home on it; a leasehold estate (rental property) can be homestead; a life estate may also qualify; and even a beneficial interest in a trust that holds real estate can be homestead.

What about minerals? Homestead protections extend to and include mineral interests that are located under the homestead. For this reason, both spouses must join in signing oil and gas leases. *Gulf Production Co. v. Continental Oil Co.*, 132 S.W.2d 553 (Tex. 1939). Royalties from a mineral lease of the homestead are exempt from a turnover order since they are derived from the underlying exempt homestead. *Fitzgerald v. Cadle Company*, No. 12-16-00338-CV (Tex.App.—Tyler 2017, no pet.). Severed crops, however, are subject to execution on a judgment. *Aetna finance Company v. First Federal Savings & Loan Ass'n*, 607 S.W.2d 312 (Tex.Civ.App.—Austin 1980, writ ref'd n.r.e.).

The homestead cannot be of unlimited size. Property Code Section 41.002 supplies the following limitations on urban and rural homesteads:

(a) **If used for the purposes of an urban home or as both an urban home and a place to exercise a calling or business, the homestead of a family or a single adult person not otherwise entitled to a homestead shall consist of not more than 10 acres of land which may be in one or more continuous lots, together with any improvements thereon.**

(b) **If used for the purposes of a rural home the homestead shall consist of:**

   (1) **for a family, not more than 200 acres, which may be in one or more parcels, with the improvements thereon; or**

   (2) **for a single, adult person, not otherwise entitled to a homestead, not more than 100 acres, which may be in one or more parcels, with the improvements thereon.**

The statutory definition applies to realty and fixtures, not movable personal property. Movable, non-affixed items are not considered part of the homestead and are not exempt from execution unless included in the list of exempt personal property under Property Code Section 42.002 (details below).

Urban Verses Rural Homesteads

A person may claim an urban homestead or a rural homestead but not both. What constitutes "urban" versus "rural" has been the subject of litigation. It is a fact issue that differs from case to case. Once established, however, the initial characterization of the property as urban or rural continues even if the nature of the surrounding area changes. *United States v. Blakeman*, 997 F. 2d 1084 (5th Cir. 1992).

Also, one may not have both an urban residential homestead and an urban business homestead (a place to exercise a calling or business). To qualify, the homestead must be used either for residential homestead or as both residential homestead and business homestead. Tex. Const. Art. XVI, Sec. 51; Tex. Property Code Sec. 41.002(a); *Majeski v. Estate of Majeski*, 163 S.W.3d 102 (Tex.App.—Austin 2005, no pet.). Neither the constitution nor the Property Code provides for the overlapping use of a rural homestead as a business, but this may be compensated for by the larger acreage allowance for rural properties (200 acres versus 10 acres). Tex. Const. Ann. Art. XVI, Sec. 51; Tex. Prop. Code Sec. 41.002(b); *Riley v. Riley*, 972 S.W.2d 149 (Tex.App.—Texarkana 1998, no pet.).

Unlike the urban homestead, the rural homestead may consist of one or more parcels that are not required to be contiguous. Tex. Prop. Code Sec. 41.002(b). Whether or not all of the parcels in question will actually be legally considered part of the homestead will depend on if they are used for purposes of a home. *Painwebber, Inc. v. Murray*, 260 B.R. 697 (Bankr. W.D. Tex. 2011).

What is a family?

A family may have only one homestead—which raises the question, what is a family? That is a flexible definition in Texas so long as the head of household is legally or morally required to support a least one other family member. The Texas Constitution was amended in 1973 to extend homestead protections to single adults who may now be a family unto themselves. Note that individual family members may not claim separate homesteads.

Moving to Texas

Can persons from other states declare their intent to reside in Texas and designate a protected homestead within the state? *Yes.* If the issue is raised in court, it will be a fact issue to determine whether or not such a declaration was made in good faith (or with the obvious intention of defrauding creditors) and if there is some evidence to support the debtor's intent—e.g., actual occupancy of the property as well as perhaps a Texas driver's license, voter registration card, etc. This is not a difficult test since there is no minimum number of days a person must physically reside in Texas in order to claim a homestead. If someone has multiple lawsuits and judgments, then moving to Texas to establish a homestead may be an excellent asset protection strategy, particularly if it can plausibly be done in the ordinary course of life and business. After all, people move to Texas every day for many good reasons.

Conveyance of the Homestead

Texas Family Code Section 5.001 requires the signature of both spouses in order to convey the homestead except under unusual circumstances. This is true whether the homestead is considered to be community property or the separate property of either spouse. If there is any question as to whether or not the property is homestead, a title company will require the joinder of the spouse on the deed, if only in a pro forma capacity.

Moving from One Homestead to the Next

Property Code Section 41.001(5)(c) states that "[t]he homestead claimant's proceeds of a sale of a homestead are not subject to seizure for a creditor's claim for six months after the date of sale," permitting homestead protections to be rolled over from one homestead to the next—notwithstanding the perverse inclination of title companies to insist on clearing judgments upon sale of the homestead. See *also Taylor vs. Mosty Brothers Nursery, Inc.,* 777 S.W.2d at 570 (Tex.App.—San Antonio 1989, no pet.).

Designating a Homestead

It is useful, both for ad valorem tax purposes and for protection from creditors, to file an affidavit designating the homestead in the real property records of the county in which the property is located. See Property Code Section 41.005 for the required contents of this affidavit. However, the "mere filing of a homestead designation is insufficient by itself to establish a homestead as a matter of law." *Lares v. Garza,* No. 04-03-00546CV (Tex.App.—San Antonio 2004, no pet.). Still, the homestead arises automatically when the required legal conditions occur, with or without a filed designation. *Graham v. Kleb,* Civ. Act. Nos. H-07-2279, H-07-2878, 2008 WL 243669, at *4 (S.D. Tex. Jan. 29, 2008) (not selected for publication). Also, if a person receives a homestead tax exemption from the appraisal district, then creditor protection is automatic.

A debtor (or his assignees) must carry the burden, at least initially, of establishing that a certain property is homestead and therefore exempt from execution upon a judgment. *Dominguez,* 163 S.W.3d at 330. However, a creditor is on notice that homestead protections will likely apply if the debtor occupies a homestead. "When a homestead claimant is in actual occupancy of his homestead, it will be deemed that a lender or encumbrancer acted with knowledge of the occupant's right to invoke the rule of homestead." *Sanchez v. Telles*, 960 S.W.2d 769, 772 (Tex.App.—El Paso 1997, pet. denied). Moreover, the homestead is presumed to endure. "Once property has been dedicated as homestead, it can only lose such designation by abandonment, alienation, or death. After the party has established the homestead character of the property, the burden shifts to the creditor . . . to disprove the continued existence of the homestead. In other words, a homestead is presumed to exist until its termination is proved." *Wilcox*, 103 S.W.3d at 472. Once obtained, homestead rights are not easily lost. "Abandonment" may not be presumed merely from a change in the owner's residence. A homestead claimant may even temporarily rent the property so long as another homestead is not acquired. Tex. Prop. Code Sec. 41.003; *Thomas v. Graham Mortgage Corporation*, 408 S.W.3d 581 (Tex.App.—Austin 2013, no pet.). Accordingly, the existence or non-existence of a homestead is a fact issue that is highly specific to the circumstances.

The act of living upon and utilizing real property essentially settles the issue of whether or not it is homestead. The possession and use of land by one who owns it and who resides upon it makes it homestead in both fact and law. However, it is not necessary that a homestead claimant actually reside on the property at the time homestead is claimed. "A homestead exemption may be established upon unoccupied land if the owner presently intends to occupy and use the premises in a reasonable and definite time in the future, and has made such preparations toward actual occupancy and use that are of such character and have proceeded to such an extent as to manifest beyond doubt the intention to complete the improvements and reside upon the place as a home." *Farrington v. First Nat'l Bank*, 753 S.W.2d 248, 250-51 (Tex.App.—Houston [1st Dist.] 1988, writ denied). The key issues are *intent* and *preparation*. Generally, however, in order to make a conclusive and indisputable homestead claim, a person must have a present and exclusive possessory interest in the property.

A person may also execute an affidavit disclaiming particular property (and, optionally, designating other property) as homestead, and a lender is entitled to rely on such an affidavit in making a loan that will be secured by non-homestead property. This is typically referred to as a "non-homestead affidavit."

Although there is a conceptual overlap, the homestead protection laws should not be confused with the homestead tax exemption as reflected on the rolls of an appraisal district, which is designed to lower ad valorem taxes on homeowner-occupied property.

Abandoning the Homestead

As noted above, a property owner does not abandon the homestead for exemption purposes merely by moving to another residence. "Rather, evidence establishing abandonment of a homestead 'must be undeniably clear' and show 'beyond almost the shadow, at least of all reasonable ground of dispute, that there has been a total abandonment with an intention not to return and claim the exemption. . . .' That is, it must be clear that there has been a discontinuance of the use of the property coupled with an intention not to use it as a homestead again." *Thomas v. Graham Mortgage Corporation*, 408 S.W.3d 581 (Tex.App.—Austin 2013, no pet.). It is all a question of the facts and evidence that exist in a specific case. To prove abandonment, and thus make the homestead vulnerable to execution upon a judgment, a creditor must show that the debtor claiming homestead protections clearly, conclusively, and undeniably moved away from the homestead with no intention to return. *Marincasiu*, 441 S.W.3d at 551. Since this, at least to some extent, requires reaching into the debtor's head to establish his subjective intentions, more than a mere conclusory assertion by the creditor is required.

Division of community property (by divorce or otherwise) is not abandonment when it comes to the homestead exemption. When a couple divorces and one spouse moves out and conveys his or her interest to the other, the homestead endures so long as the resident spouse remains. A judgment lien against the departing spouse does not attach to the property because the resident spouse's homestead interest is undivided and unaffected. *Hankins v. Harris*, 500 S.W.3d 140 (Tex.App.—Houston [1st Dist.] 2016, no pet.).

Judgments against the Homestead

"Texas law is well settled that [a properly abstracted, unsecured judgment lien] cannot attach to a homestead as long as the property remains homestead." *Wilcox v. Marriott*, 103 S.W.3d 469, 473 (Tex.App.—San Antonio 2013, pet. denied). Any liens against a homestead that are not specifically listed in the Texas Constitution are void. *Dominguez v. Castaneda*, 163 S.W.3d 318, 330 (Tex.App.—El Paso 2005, pet. denied).

Judgments against the homestead are nonetheless a headache. Texas courts have ruled that although a judgment lien may be unenforceable against a homestead, it may nonetheless constitute a cloud on title, even if it is invalid. *Tarrant Bank v. Miller*, 833 S.W.2d 666 (Tex.App.—Eastland 1992, writ denied). This may result in a title company refusing to issue insurance unless a seller-debtor's judgments are paid, notwithstanding the six-month rollover protection. The homeowner's remedy is Property Code Section 52.0012 which provides a statutory method for securing a release of a judgment lien against homestead property—but only for judgments abstracted after 2007. See chapter 35, *Lien Removal.*

Homestead protections extend to purchasers of a judgment debtor's homestead, who receive the property free and clear of any judgment lien. *Gill v. Quinn,* 613 S.W.2d 324, 325 (Tex.Civ.App.—Eastland 1981, no writ). ("[T]he exemption has been interpreted as allowing a judgment debtor to sell and dispose of the homestead without restraint."). "A subsequent purchaser of homestead property may assert the prior person[']s homestead protection against a prior lienholder so long as there is no gap between the time of homestead alienation and recordation of his title." *Dominguez,* 163 S.W.3d at 330. "However, where a judgment debtor's homestead protection elapses prior to sale, the judgment creditor's abstracted lien may attach to the property by operation of law and be enforced against future owners of the property." *Marincasiu v. Drilling,* 441 S.W.3d 551 (Tex.App.—El Paso 2014, pet. denied) citing *Wilcox,* 103 S.W.3d at 473.

Community Property

In Texas, property in the possession of either spouse is presumed to be community property (Tex. Fam. Code Sec. 3.003(a)) and therefore available to be executed upon to satisfy a judgment. The Family Code goes into detail with regard to separate property, sole management community property, and joint management community property, most of which is beyond the scope of this chapter. Suffice it to say that a judgment creditor of either spouse will be looking for the debtor spouse's separate property, community property which is under the sole management of the debtor spouse, and all joint management community property—which in most cases is likely to be nearly everything in the way of marital assets.

Protection of Personal Property

It is not just realty that is protected. Chapter 42 of the Property Code states that personal property valued at $60,000 for a family or $30,000 for a single adult (exclusive of liens) is exempt from garnishment, attachment, execution or other seizure so long as it is on the following list:

§ 42.002(a). Personal Property

(1) home furnishings, including family heirlooms;
(2) provisions for consumption;
(3) farming or ranching vehicles and implements;

(4) tools, equipment, books, and apparatus, including boats and motor vehicles used in a trade or profession;

(5) wearing apparel;

(6) jewelry not to exceed 25 percent of the aggregate limitations prescribed by Section 42.001(a);

(7) two firearms;

(8) athletic and sporting equipment, including bicycles;

(9) a two-wheeled, three-wheeled, or four-wheeled, motor vehicle for each member of a family or single adult who holds a driver's license or who does not hold a driver's license but who relies on another person to operate the vehicle for the benefit of the non-licensed person;

(10) the following animals and forage on hand for their consumption:

    (A) two horses, mules, or donkeys and a saddle, blanket, and bridle for each;

    (B) 12 head of cattle;

    (C) 60 head of other types of livestock; and

    (D) 120 fowl; and

(11) household pets.

If the value of the personal property exceeds the specified dollar amounts, then the excess property is subject to levy pursuant to Property Code Section 42.003, although this seldom occurs as a practical matter.

Income and Wages

Pursuant to Property Code Section 42.001(b)(1), "current wages for personal services, except for the enforcement of court-ordered child support payments" are exempt "from garnishment, attachment, execution, and other seizure." This includes severance pay. Note that wages are expressly exempted from the $60,000 family limit and the $30,000 single adult limit. Additionally, "unpaid commissions for personal services not to exceed 25 percent" of these limits are also protected.

Can you create a corporation, LLC, or partnership that will pay you wages so that you can declare them exempt? Quite possibly, so long as it can be shown that the corporation, LLC, or partnership is truly a distinct entity that independently conducts business and declares income. Justifying such measures almost always comes down to the "ordinary course of business" defense (see below).

Case law imposes some caveats, however, on the protection of wages. "Once wages are received by the debtor, they cease to be current wages and are not exempt from attachment, execution or seizure for the satisfaction of liabilities"—although this is not true of Social Security payments. 42 U.S.C. Sec. 407. In other words, cash in hand from whatever source is usually vulnerable. It can be attached, and very easily so if it resides in a bank or investment account. Also, the term "current wages" is interpreted to mean a regular salary or hourly pay, not compensation paid to an independent contractor. Payments to independent contractors are not protected. See *Brink v. Ayre*, 855 S.W.2d 44 (Tex.App.—Houston [14th Dist.] 1993, no writ). This is surely an unjust gap in the overall regime.

Additional Exemptions

Retirement plans (IRAs and 401(k)s) are exempted under Section 42.0021 so long as contributions do not exceed the amount that is deductible under current law. Rollover proceeds are exempt for 60 days.

Also exempted under Section 42.0021 are certain savings plans "to the extent that the plan, contract, annuity, or account is exempt from federal income tax, or to the extent federal income on the person's interest is deferred until actual payment of benefits to the person" under the Internal Revenue Code. This includes health savings accounts.

College tuition funds (including IRS Section 529 funds and accounts established under Subchapter F, Chapter 54 of the Education Code) are exempted under Section 42.0022.

Exemption for Life Insurance and Annuities under the Insurance Code

The Insurance Code adds to the exempt list the cash value of annuities and life insurance policies which are declared to be "exempt from garnishment, attachment, execution, or other seizure." Tex. Ins. Code Sec. 1108.051. This "applies to any benefits, including the cash value and proceeds of an insurance policy, to be provided to an insured or beneficiary under . . . an insurance policy or annuity contract issued by a life, health, or accident insurance company." There is no dollar limit. There is, however, an exception in Section 1108.053 for premiums paid "in fraud of a creditor."

No Exemption for Fraudulent Intent

Property Code Section 42.004 provides that an exemption is lost if non-exempt assets are used to buy or pay down indebtedness on exempt assets "with the intent to defraud, delay, or hinder" a creditor. This reaches back two years for liquidated claims, one year for unliquidated or contingent claims. However, proving such intent (and thereby getting a transfer set aside) can be challenging for a creditor. Additionally, Property Code Section 42.004(c) offers the debtor a defense if the transaction occurred in the ordinary course of business. As a practical matter, this definition may be expanded to include "the ordinary course of business and life."

It remains the burden of the creditor to both discover such transfers and prove that they were impermissible. Judgment creditors vary widely in the energy and determination they expend on post-judgment collection efforts. For instance, most judgment creditors will send post-judgment discovery demanding disclosure of assets; but many creditors do not even bother to do this, perhaps electing to wait until the debtor attempts to sell non-exempt real property and a future title company requires that the judgment be paid. Creditor aggressiveness in any particular case is unpredictable.

Here is an interesting example of fraudulent intent: a failed builder, owing millions on notes that he signed or guaranteed, conspired with his wife to file for divorce and then transfer substantially all of their community assets to the wife in the settlement. After the divorce was final, the husband filed bankruptcy showing few or no assets and sought to discharge the debts. The bankruptcy trustee noticed that the husband never moved out of the couple's very expensive home, and he rightfully became suspicious. Not a surprise.

In a recent novel, a fellow who absconded with 50 million dollars was told by the man chasing him: "You took too much money. If you had just taken 5 million, we would have written it off. Now we will chase you to the ends of the earth." So the size of the debt is also a factor.

Role of a Living Trust

The Texas Constitution and the Property Code already provide the homestead with substantial asset protection. However, placing the homestead into a living trust can add some anonymity and, when joined with a pour-over will, accomplish a measure of estate planning as well, since the delay and expense of probate (although modest in Texas) are reduced or eliminated. Why? Because the living trust does not die, and title therefore remains in the trust regardless of the death of one of the beneficiaries. Also, Property Code Section 41.0021, entitled "Homestead in a Qualifying Trust," specifically allows a homestead to be transferred into a living trust without losing its exempt character.

Investment Properties and Business Assets

Homestead law has been heavily litigated, and any steps taken by either a creditor or debtor are subject to review of the specific facts of a case. The result may occasionally be difficult to predict. Nonetheless, maximizing statutory and constitutional homestead protections is an important part of asset protection. However, investment properties and business assets do not receive the same treatment, so investors should plan accordingly. As a rule, investment properties should be kept separate from the homestead and placed in an LLC, preferably a series LLC which has the ability to compartmentalize assets and insulate them from liabilities associated with other company assets. There is no good reason, from an asset protection perspective, to have the homestead in the same entity as investments assets.

Chapter 35

LIEN RELEASE AND REMOVAL

Different Types of Liens and Procedures for Removing Them

This chapter addresses procedures available to secure the release of the following types of liens:

(1) invalid mechanic's and materialman's liens ("M&M liens");

(2) judgment liens against the homestead;

(3) child support liens; and

(4) fraudulent liens.

The first relevant event in the overall process is the filing by a judgment creditor of an abstract of judgment in the real property records of the county where the property is located (or in any county where the judgment creditor believes that the debtor may have assets). This is true because a judgment by itself does not act as a lien on anything. "The judgment creditor's first step in creating a judicial lien is to obtain an abstract of judgment. When properly recorded and indexed [in the county clerk's real property records], an abstract of judgment creates a judgment lien on non-exempt real property that is superior to the rights of subsequent purchasers and lienholders. The purpose of the abstract of judgment is to create a lien against the judgment debtor's real property and to provide notice to subsequent purchasers and encumbrancers of the existence of the judgment lien." *Rogers v. Peeler*, 271 S.W.3d 372, 375 (Tex.App.—Texarkana 2008, pet. denied). The key distinction is between exempt and non-exempt property, a critical difference when one is discussing the homestead.

Note on tax liens: liens for ad valorem taxes as well as federal income tax liens resulting from the tax debt of both spouses are expressly permitted by Texas Constitution Article 16, Section 50(a). There is no removal procedure for such liens other than entering into a payment arrangement with the taxing authority.

Liens Revealed by the Title Commitment

The existence of a judgment lien or other type of lien is usually discovered when a title company checks the property records and produces a title commitment in anticipation of a sale or refinance. The appearance of one or more liens on the commitment (schedule C) will adversely affect a property's marketability. This is so because a title company may demand that the lien be paid and released as a condition of issuing a title policy—regardless of whether the lien is valid or not. The title company is being asked to insure title and is going to look after its own interests first and foremost by avoiding unnecessary liability.

The First Step in Lien Release or Removal

The first step in lien release or removal is to contact the judgment creditor or its attorneys, inform them that the lien is invalid (see Part One below) or is currently showing against the homestead (see Parts Two and Three below) and then make formal demand that the creditor execute a partial release—or legal action will be taken without further notice. Creditor attorneys are knowledgeable concerning potential liability for their clients, so they will often advise the creditor to sign a partial release when the homestead is involved. Sometimes, however, this does not happen and it will be necessary to proceed with additional action.

The best way to commence the process is to ask your real estate lawyer to send an explanatory demand letter with an already-prepared partial release enclosed, ready to be signed by the creditor. This approach has credibility. Note that any old release will not do. *The statutory release must be carefully and correctly drafted or (1) the creditor may not sign it, or (2) a title company may not accept it.*

PART ONE: MECHANIC'S AND MATERIALMAN' LIENS

What is an M&M lien?

"Chapter 53 of the Property Code governs mechanic's and materialman's liens. . . . A person who provides labor or materials to construct a building or improvement under a contract with the property owner, the owner's agent, or an original contractor is entitled to a lien against that property. . . . A subcontractor is considered a derivative claimant and must rely on his statutory lien remedies. . . . A subcontractor may seek recovery from 'trapped' funds held by the property owner or funds 'retained' by the owner. . . . 'Trapped' funds are funds not yet paid to the original contractor at the time the property owner receives notice that a subcontractor has not been paid; on receiving such notice, the owner may withhold those funds from the original contractor until the claim is paid or settled or until the time during which a subcontractor may file a lien affidavit has passed." *Pham v. Harris County Rentals, L.L.C.*, 455 S.W.3d 702 (Tex.App.—[1ˢᵗ Dist] 2014, no pet.). A subcontractor or supplier "is a derivative claimant and, unlike a general contractor, has no constitutional, common law, or contractual lien on the owner's property.

As a result, a subcontractor's lien rights are totally dependent on compliance with the statutes authorizing the lien." *Moore v. Brenham Ready Mix, Inc.*, 463 S.W.3d 109 (Tex.App.—Houston [1ˢᵗ Dist.] 2015, no pet.).

The Bias of Texas Law

It is no secret that Texas law is biased in favor of the worker who supplies labor and materials in new construction, whether residential or commercial. The M&M lien is enshrined in Texas Constitution Article XVI, Section 37, which states:

> **Mechanics, artisans and materialmen, of every class, shall have a lien upon the buildings and articles made or repaired by them for the value of their labor done thereon, or material furnished therefor; and the Legislature shall provide by law for the speedy and efficient enforcement of said liens.**

This constitutional lien is in addition to the statutory mechanic's lien available pursuant to Property Code Sections 53.001 et seq. Case law states that "the mechanic's and materialmen's lien statutes of Texas are to be liberally construed for the purpose of protecting laborers, materialmen, and owners." *Trinity Drywall Systems, LLC v. TOKA General Contractors, Ltd.*, 416 S.W.3d 201 (Tex.App.—El Paso 2013, no pet.). All of this legal protection assumes that contractors and subcontractors will act in good faith, timely comply with notice requirements, and file only liens that reflect money legitimately owed them. But this is not always the case. It has been said that the majority of liens filed in Texas are defective in some way, and that is probably true. In addition, there are always nefarious characters who file wrongful or invalid liens in an effort to shake down an owner or stop a closing until they are paid.

Enforcement of M&M Liens

M&M liens may cloud title but they are not self-enforcing (i.e., they do not collect themselves without further action). Property Code Section 53.154 provides that a "mechanic's lien may be foreclosed only on judgment of a court of competent jurisdiction foreclosing the lien and ordering the sale of the property subject to the lien." In other words, a lawsuit by the lienholder and a judicial foreclosure is required. "To prevail on its claim, the lienholder must prove it performed the labor or furnished the materials and the debt is valid. . . . In addition, the statutory lienholder must establish it substantially complied with the statutory requirements for perfecting a lien. . . ." *Crawford Services, Inc. v. Skillman International Firm, L.L.C.*, 444 S.W.3d 265 (Tex.App.—Dallas 2014, pet. dism'd).

General Rule Applicable to Release of M&M Liens

Property Code Section 53.157 lists six ways that a mechanic's lien may be discharged of record. The best method is of course to file a release (or partial release, as the case may be) in the real property records. Four other methods listed in the statute require the filing of a bond. The sixth means of discharge is failure by the lienholder to foreclose within the statute of limitations, which is two years.

Expedited Procedure for Removal of Invalid or Defective Liens

What if the mechanic's lien is alleged to be invalid or defective? Property Code Section 53.160 provides an expedited procedure for removal of an "invalid or unenforceable" lien from any real property, whether homestead or not. Grounds must be among those specified in the statute, specifically:

(1) notice of claim was not furnished to the owner or original contractor as required by Section 53.056, 53.057, 53.058, 53.252, or 53.253;

(2) an affidavit claiming a lien failed to comply with Section 53.054 or was not filed as required by Section 53.052;

(3) notice of the filed affidavit was not furnished to the owner or original contractor as required by Section 53.055;

(4) the owner complied with the requirements of Section 53.101 and paid the retainage and all other funds owed to the original contractor before:

(A) the claimant perfected the lien claim; and
(B) the owner received a notice of the claim as required by this chapter;

(5) all funds subject to the notice of a claim to the owner and the perfection of a claim against the statutory

retainage have been deposited in the registry of the court and the owner has no additional liability to the claimant;

(6) when the lien affidavit was filed on homestead property:

(A) no contract was executed or filed as required by Section 53.254;

(B) the affidavit claiming a lien failed to contain the notice as required by Section 53.254; or

(C) the notice of the claim failed to include the statement required by Section 53.254; and

(7) the claimant executed a valid and enforceable waiver or release of the claim or lien claimed in the affidavit.

Filing Suit to Remove an M&M Lien

The least expensive means of contesting a wrongful or invalid M&M lien would be to file a countervailing affidavit in the real property records, but this would merely state one's sworn opinion that the lien is invalid, perhaps for some title company to evaluate with regard to a future transaction. It would not remove or release the lien.

Section 53.160 prescribes the approved procedure for filing a "motion to remove a claim or lien." This may occur as a motion filing (standing alone) or in the context of either a suit to foreclose the lien or a suit to declare the lien invalid. Either way, an actual lawsuit is probably required in order to effectively pursue the Section 53.160 avenue, since most attorneys would normally prefer to have the option of going forward and getting a judgment if need be.

Procedural Requirements under Section 53.160

The motion procedure requires that the defendant (i.e., the person who filed the lien) be given at least 21 days' notice of the hearing. The motion should be supported by relevant documents and at least one sworn affidavit. The hearing is an evidentiary hearing, a "mini-trial," and testimony will be taken for the record. The judge then rules and the effect is immediate. There is no requirement that 30 days elapse before the ruling is final, as is the case with ordinary judgments. A certified copy of the order should be filed in the real property records and forwarded to any title company that may be involved. Sale of the property can then proceed without further delay.

Section 53.156 provides that "the court shall award costs and reasonable attorney's fees as are equitable and just." An affidavit of attorney's fees and costs should be attached to the motion.

It is at the discretion of the plaintiff as to whether or not, following a ruling on the motion, any underlying suit should continue or be dismissed. It is likely that this decision will turn on whether or not the ruling itself provides the plaintiff with sufficient compensation.

PART TWO: RELEASE OF JUDGMENT LIENS
AGAINST THE HOMESTEAD

What is a judgment lien?

The opportunity to acquire an investment property at a bargain price may often be accompanied by one or more judgments against the owner. Note, however, that a court judgment against a person does not become a lien against real property merely by virtue of its existence as a final judgment. Several steps must first occur. Pursuant to Chapter 52 of the Property Code, the judgment creditor must obtain an abstract of judgment from the court and then file it in the real property records of the county where the property is located. "Without the abstract of judgment filed in the real property records, the rendition of a judgment does not create a judgment lien against the property." *Austin v. Coface Seguro de Credito Mexico. S.A. de C.V.*, 506S.W.3d 707, 712 (Tex.App.—Houston [1st Dist.] 2016, pet. filed). In other words, there may be a judgment, but *there is no lien against specific real estate* until the judgment is abstracted and filed and indexed by the county clerk. Abstracts filed in multiple counties create separate, independent liens.

A judgment lien attaches to the property only and not to any rents that or other profits that might arise from the property. *Donley v. Youngstown Sheet & Tube Co.*, 328 S.W.2d 192 (Tex.Civ.App.—Eastland 1959, writ ref'd n.r.e.).

A judgment lien properly placed against real property may be executed upon even though the underlying judgment is being appealed, and even if an appeal bond has been posted. *In re. Dawkins*, 11 B.R. 213 (Bankr. N.D. Tex. 1981).

Legal Background Relating to Judgments and the Homestead

Texas Property Code Section 52.0012(c) states that a judgment lien does not attach to, and does not constitute a lien on, a judgment debtor's exempt real property, including the debtor's homestead. This is simply a fact. Assertion of a bona fide homestead is therefore an absolute defense in the event a creditor seeks to execute on a judgment by forcing the sale of the homestead. The creditor may seek to discover other non-exempt assets of the debtor and attempt execution on those, but not on the homestead. Moreover, if the homestead is sold, Property Code Section 41.001(5)(c) provides that the proceeds are not subject to seizure for a creditor's claim for six months after the date of sale. Having said all of that, it is not uncommon to encounter a title company that demands that liens be released prior to closing—even if it is the homestead which is being sold—so lien release (or at least a partial release as to the homestead) can become an issue.

Some interesting caveats relating to timing: if a judgment lien attaches to property which subsequently becomes the debtor's homestead, the validity of the lien is not affected. The debtor's newly-acquired homestead interest is taken subject to the already-attached judgment lien. Similarly, if a debtor occupies a protected homestead but then abandons it, the judgment lien will attach. *Barrera v. State*, 2005 WL 1691037 (Tex.App.—Houston [14th Dist.] 2005). If a judgment debtor acquires a homestead after a judgment lien is abstracted, filed, and indexed in the county records, the property is nonetheless protected as long as it continues to be the debtor's homestead. *Hughes v. Groshart*, 150 S.W.2d 827, 830 (Tex.Civ.App.—Galveston 1941, no writ).

Issues are also raised by the death of the owner of a homestead. If the owner of a protected homestead dies (either testate or intestate), and there exists an abstracted judgment against the decedent, then so long as the lien never actually attached to the property, the homestead descends to the heirs free of the judgment lien. *National Union Fire Ins. Co. v. Olson*, 920 S.W.2d 458, 461 (Tex.App.—Austin 1996, no pet.). However, if an heir is the subject of a judgment lien, then the lien attaches to the heir's share of the former homestead the moment the heir acquires an interest—i.e., immediately upon death of the decedent. *Woodward v. Jaster*, 933 S.W.2d 777, 781-82 (Tex.App.—Austin, 1996, no pet.). Presumably this rule would not apply if the property were also the existing homestead of the heir at the time of death.

Returning to the issue of which rules apply to release and removal of a particular judgment, one needs to first determine if the judgment in question was abstracted before or after September 1, 2007.

Judgment Liens Abstracted Prior to September 1, 2007 (Old Law Applies)

In the case of judgment liens abstracted prior to September 1, 2007, the old law as set out in the 1992 case of *Tarrant Bank v. Miller*, 833 S.W.2d 666 (Tex.App.—Eastland 1992, writ denied), applies. *Tarrant Bank* decided that a judgment creditor may be liable in damages if it fails after demand to give a partial release of a judgment as to the debtor's homestead. The best approach to removing an older lien would therefore be to send the creditor's attorney a demand for a partial release accompanied by a credible threat of litigation if the release is not signed. In other words, this is a demand-negotiation scenario rather than a statutory procedure. Since the creditor cannot be compelled to accept anything less than full payment, eventual recourse to litigation cannot be ruled out.

Judgment Liens Abstracted after September 1, 2007 (New Law Applies)

Property Code Section 52.0012(c), in contrast to the old law, is a statutory notice and affidavit process available as to liens against the homestead which are abstracted after September 1, 2007. Note the use of the word "abstracted." If the judgment was rendered before this key date but it was not abstracted until afterward, then the new law would apply. The abstract date is the key date, not the judgment date.

A judgment lien does not attach to a judgment debtor's exempt real property, including the debtor's homestead. It can be difficult, however, to persuade a title company that they should ignore a judgment. Even though a judgment lien does not attach to a judgment debtor's exempt real property, including the debtor's homestead, it can be difficult to persuade a title company that they should ignore *any* judgment. A title company's automatic, self-serving reaction is usually to require that all liens be cleared. The homeowner should resist this pressure and insist on his or her homestead rights.

As is true with other liens, the first step in the process under the new law is a demand letter—in this case, a 30-day letter to the judgment creditor and its attorney. If there is no response, Property Code Section 52.0012 provides that a judgment debtor may file a "Homestead Affidavit as Release of Judgment Lien" which "serves as a release of record of a judgment lien established under this chapter." The affidavit must be in proper form, meeting all requirements of the statute. However, if the judgment creditor files a contradicting affidavit, and if after filing such a contradicting affidavit a purchaser or mortgagee of real property acquires the purchaser's or mortgagee's interest from the judgment debtor, then the debtor's affidavit does *not* act as a release of the judgment lien with respect to the purchaser or mortgagee. If the process is followed step-by-step, then the affidavit which the debtor files *may* be accepted by title companies as release of the judgment lien against the homestead. Nothing in the applicable law forces a title company to do anything.

Statutory Process under the New Law

The following is a checklist for evaluating whether or not the Section 52.0012(c) procedure applies in a particular case. Generally speaking, a title company will not insure over a homestead lien using the new law unless:

1. the abstract of judgment is abstracted after September 1, 2007;

2. a 30-day demand letter has been sent by CM/RRR to the creditor and its attorney enclosing a copy of the affidavit that is intended to be filed, with evidence of homestead status included;

3. proof exists (e.g., a signed USPS green card) that the creditor and its attorney received the letter and affidavit at least 30 days prior to the date that the affidavit was recorded;

4. the title company's plant is certified to the 31st day following the mailing of the letter and affidavit;

5. no contradicting affidavit is recorded by the creditor;

6. the size of the property does not exceed 10 acres, if urban, or 200 acres, if rural (100 acres if the debtor is single); and

7. the proposed purchaser or lender is a bona fide third party, paying money for or lending money against the property.

Judgment Creditor Response

The judgment creditor has a couple of options. There is nothing in the statute that *requires* the judgment creditor to do anything. The creditor can choose to take no action at all and usually suffer no consequences. However, potential liability could arise if the abstract actually obstructs or delays the sale of the debtor's exempt homestead. Property Code Section 52.0012(c) states that a judgment lien does not attach to, and does not constitute a lien on, a judgment debtor's exempt real property, including the debtor's homestead. If the property is clearly indicated to be residential homestead in the records of the county where it is located, the path of least resistance for a judgment creditor may be to execute a partial release of that property from the judgment lien—and then live to fight another day as to property that is non-exempt.

Alternatively, the creditor can (if grounds exist) choose to be pro-active and file an affidavit contradicting the one filed by the judgment debtor. Section 52.0012(d)(2)(e) provides that the debtor's affidavit "does not serve as a release of record of a judgment lien . . . with respect to a purchaser or mortgagee of real property that acquires the purchaser's or mortgagee's interest from the judgment debtor after the judgment creditor files a contradicting affidavit." What happens if the creditor files such a contradicting affidavit? The judgment debtor's affidavit is stopped in its tracks, and the whole matter—you guessed it— heads to the courthouse.

In order to avoid possible liability for filing a false affidavit, however, a judgment creditor would need to have some plausible grounds for the contradicting affidavit, something more than mere unsubstantiated belief.

The Flaw in the Process

From the point of view of the judgment debtor, there is a flaw in the process since there is nothing in the statute that *requires* a title company to accept the statutory affidavit and then go forward with closing and issuing one or more title policies. In other words, the law is not self-enforcing. Title companies, being conservative institutions, may hesitate or refuse to go along, which can be a disappointment to a seller (and his or her attorney) who have diligently followed the provisions of the lien removal statute. A title company determined to avoid potential liability may simply claim that one's affidavit is unacceptable to them—and not even explain why, which has happened to this author more than once. What the title company is really saying is that even if the statutory affidavit were inscribed on a tablet of gold by the best lawyers in Texas, they would not accept it, for reasons of their own. As in other situations, it may be necessary to shop title companies until one is found that is amenable to this process.

Expectations of Judgment Debtor Clients

The usual question from a debtor client is "Can you get this lien against my homestead released?" The expectation is that the attorney will obtain a release of lien that when recorded will conclusively, as a matter of fact and law, permanently remove the lien. Attorneys must be careful to manage the client's expectations in this regard. The statute does *not* provide for a traditional release of lien. It provides for a "Homestead Affidavit as Release of Judgment Lien," which only serves as a release if the title company says it does. That is a critical difference. Accordingly, the attorney must be careful not to guarantee any particular outcome— only that the statutory notice and affidavit process will be followed. In turn, the client must accept the potential limitations on the process.

When asking that an attorney initiate the process of removing a lien from the homestead, the client should be prepared with a number of items: (1) a copy the abstract of judgment (if a copy of the judgment itself is available, supply that as well); (2) a copy of the warranty deed to the homestead; (3) a print-out from the local appraisal district indicating that the property is classified as homestead (sometimes there is a notation that it is "HS"); (4) the name and address of each judgment creditor and/or its attorneys; and (5) correspondence between the judgment creditor and the client.

Note item (4). Clients often expect a lawyer to be able to locate their creditors as part of the lien removal process. This may not be a reasonable assumption, since lawyers are not usually also private investigators. Demand letters may be returned labeled "no such address" or the like. If an investigator is needed, the client should be prepared to bear that additional expense.

By now it should be clear that a lawyer cannot offer any guarantees relating to the removal of liens from the homestead—either guarantees that negotiations with a creditor will be successful (in the case of pre-9/2007 liens) or that a title company will accept a statutory affidavit as a release of lien (in the case of post-9/2007 liens).

PART THREE: RELEASE OF CHILD SUPPORT LIENS

Texas Family Code Section 157.3171 establishes a process by which an obligor may obtain the release of a child support lien against the obligor's homestead. The procedure involves the filing of an affidavit and is identical to that contained in Section 52.0012 (discussed above). The law states that "the obligor is considered to be a judgment debtor under that section and the claimant under the child support lien is considered to be a judgment creditor under that section." The person claiming the lien may file a contradicting affidavit: "If the claimant files a contradicting affidavit as described by Subsection (d), the issue of whether the real property is subject to the lien must be resolved in an action brought for that purpose in the district court of the county in which the real property is located and the lien was filed." If the property is in the same county in which a divorce or action for child support was had, then the court that heard the case would likely have jurisdiction over the lien issue as well.

PART FOUR: REMOVAL OF FRAUDULENT LIENS

Removal of a Fraudulent Lien

There are instances where a purported lien or claim against real property is outright fraudulent. Subchapter J of the Government Code provides three avenues of relief in the event a fraudulent instrument is filed. The first is based on action to be taken at the clerk level. If a court clerk or county clerk has a "reasonable basis" for believing that a filed document is fraudulent, Section 51.901 provides that the clerk shall, after giving notice, "(1) request the assistance of the county or district attorney to determine whether the document is fraudulent before filing or recording the document; (2) request that the prospective filer provide to the county clerk additional documentation supporting the existence of the lien, such as a contract or other document that contains the alleged debtor or obligor's signature; and (3) forward any additional documentation received to the county or district attorney."

What would provide a reasonable basis for a clerk to take action? Someone would likely have to point out the issue or supply the clerk with an appropriate affidavit.

The second avenue of relief is provided by Government Code Section 51.902 and is based on action by the person aggrieved by filing of a fraudulent judgment lien:

§ 51.902. Action on Fraudulent Judgment Lien

(a) **A person against whom a purported judgment was rendered who has reason to believe that a document previously filed or recorded or submitted for filing or for filing and recording is fraudulent may complete and file with the district clerk a motion, verified by affidavit . . . requesting a judicial determination of the status of a court, judicial entity, or judicial officer purporting to have taken an action that is the basis of a judgment lien filed in the office of said clerk[.]**

If the motion is successful, a district judge will rule that the instrument in question not be accorded "lien status."

A third type of action is contained in Government Code Section 51.903 and again requires the action and initiative of the person who was harmed by the fraudulent instrument:

§ 51.903. Action On Fraudulent Lien On Property

(a) A person who is the purported debtor or obligor or who owns real or personal property or an interest in real or personal property and who has reason to believe that the document purporting to create a lien or a claim against the real or personal property or an interest in the real or personal property previously filed or submitted for filing and recording is fraudulent may complete and file with the district clerk a [Motion for Judicial Review of Documentation or Instrument Purporting to Create a Lien or Claim] verified by affidavit . . . requesting a judicial determination of the status of documentation or an instrument purporting to create an interest in real or personal property or a lien or claim on real or personal property or an interest in real or personal property[.]

Since instruments "purporting to create an interest in real or personal property" are expressly mentioned, this statute includes fraudulent deeds filed in the county clerk's real property records.

Section 51.903 supplies a statutory form of "Motion for Judicial Review of Documentation or Instrument Purporting to Create a Lien or Claim." The motion asks the district court to find that the document or instrument:

(1) IS NOT provided for by specific state or federal statutes or constitutional provisions;

(2) IS NOT created by implied or express consent or agreement of the obligor, debtor, or the owner of the real or personal property or an interest in the real or personal property, if required under the law of this state or by implied or express consent or agreement of an agent, fiduciary, or other representative of that person;

(3) IS NOT an equitable, constructive, or other lien imposed by a court of competent jurisdiction created by or established under the constitution or laws of this state or the United States; or

(4) IS NOT asserted against real or personal property or an interest in real or personal property. There is no valid lien or claim created by this documentation or instrument.

Under this statute, "the court first must affirmatively find that the document purports to create a lien or claim against real or personal property. Additionally, to find the subject document fraudulent, the court must determine that it is not one of the following three types of legitimate liens or claims: (1) a document or instrument provided for by state or federal law or constitutional provision; (2) a document or instrument created by implied or express consent or agreement of the obligor, debtor, or the owner of the real or personal property; or (3) a document or instrument imposed by a court as an equitable, constructive, or other lien." *In re Nguyen*, 456 S.W.3d 673 (Tex.App.—Houston [14th Dist.] 2015, no pet.).

Note that if the court so finds, it nonetheless makes no finding as to the underlying claim—only as to the filing of the document or instrument in question. The underlying claim may still be litigated.

Penalties for Fraudulent Liens

Chapter 12 of the Civil Practice & Remedies Code addresses "Liability related to . . . a fraudulent lien or claim filed against real or personal property." A person who knowingly and intentionally files a fraudulent lien may be held liable in civil district court for the greater of $10,000 or actual damages, exemplary damages, and recovery of attorney's fees and costs. It is also a criminal offense. Tex. Penal Code Sec. 37.01. If applicable, a cause of action under Civil Practice & Remedies Code Section 12.002 should be included in any suit against the lien claimant.

Filing of a fraudulent lien may under certain circumstances also form part of a cause of action under the Deceptive Trade Practices Act. Tex. Bus. & Com. Code Sec. 17.44 et seq.

Chapter 36

EQUITY STRIPPING FOR ASSET PROTECTION

The Importance of Perception in the Public Records

Equity stripping is the art and science of making a business appear to be worth less than it really is. It has been said that perception is everything, an aphorism that is definitely true in asset protection. If a review of public records indicates that a potential target company is in debt and its assets are encumbered by liens, why would a plaintiff file and pursue an expensive lawsuit in order to wind up with an uncollectable judgment? A target company that is apparently judgment-proof may make it less likely that a contingency-fee attorney will accept a case against it.

Core Documents

The core documents of an equity stripping system are:

(1) a secured promissory note in a substantial amount (usually authorizing funding of up to $1 million or more);
(2) a line-of-credit agreement supplementing the terms and conditions of the note;
(3) a deed of trust and security agreement listing real and personal property collateral subject to a lien to secure payment of the note;
(4) a company resolution authorizing the loan; and
(5) a pre-signed release of note and lien held for later filing.

Only the deed of trust and security agreement is filed of record, but that is enough. This document states clearly that both a company's real estate, the improvements, and its FF&E (furniture, fixtures, and equipment) are subject to a lien to secure repayment of a very sizeable amount of money. The other equity-stripping documents are kept with the company record book as documentary support.

The note is payable on demand. The borrower should be the investor's limited liability company. If the borrower is a series LLC, the note should state that all series are jointly and severally liable for payment, not just the company at large.

What about the lender in an equity-stripping scenario?

The identity of the lender may vary. Ideally, however, the lender should have all the appearances of a disinterested, unaffiliated third party. An anonymity company that is not traceable back to the "borrower" would be preferred. Nevada is a good choice of venue for the formation of this entity, since the Nevada component may make it marginally more difficult for a plaintiff to obtain information or subject the lender to compulsory document production in a Texas court.

How is the lien released?

The easiest method is to hold a pre-signed and notarized release in reserve until it is necessary or advantageous to file it and undo the equity stripping. Alternatively, the equity stripping lender can conduct a friendly foreclosure with the goal of eliminating any subordinate liens that may have arisen against the property.

The Role of Deterrence

Recall that a key principle of asset protection is deterrence. Deterrence in the form of equity stripping affects the process at two possible points: first, when the plaintiff and his lawyer perform due diligence (as they likely will) on the available assets of their target before launching a lawsuit; and second, during document production, when the defendant produces copies of the note and the deed of trust and security agreement—documents which, at least on paper, vastly reduce net worth. Given the soaring expense of litigation, most plaintiffs would then pause and carefully evaluate the prospects for a tangible recovery. After all, a lawsuit is just another form of investment, and a rational plaintiff is looking for a return on that investment. Similarly, a plaintiffs' attorney who has accepted the case on a contingency basis may be wary. The attorney may even go to the client and demand a substantial retainer if the case is to proceed. Result? The lawsuit may end there.

Equity Stripping and the Two-Company Structure

As mentioned elsewhere in this book, we recommend a two-company structure for most real estate investors: one LLC as a management company and another a stand-alone holding company. Activities are thereby separated from assets, greatly minimizing risk. Since in this system the management company is already a shell (or nearly so), it is the holding company that should be considered as a candidate for equity stripping.

Is equity stripping a form of fraud against creditors?

The answer is *no*, so long as the process is handled correctly. The note is a line-of-credit note which *authorizes* advances of up to $1,000,000; but the public filing does not indicate how much money (if any) has *actually* been advanced. No representation is being made to anyone on that score. The deed of trust and security agreement (the only recorded document) merely states the maximum possible loan amount and reveals nothing about advancements or other details of the loan agreement.

It would be a different matter if one is queried during the discovery process as to how much of the loan had been advanced. One should never be untruthful in discovery; however, it is a corollary to this rule that one should provide only the minimum information necessary to be adequately responsive. If the plaintiff does not ask, then the defendant is under no obligation to provide gratuitous information.

The Issue of Existing Lienholders

Unless one's company is fortunate enough to own its properties outright, then there will be existing lienholders to consider when it comes to equity stripping. First-lien deeds of trust recite that the priority status of their lien must be preserved or the borrower will be in default. Is this a problem? It should not be. The reason is that the deed of trust and security agreement used for equity stripping expressly states that its lien is inferior to earlier liens of record.

A County-by-County Process

Equity stripping can be a useful asset protection technique if a one has a substantial investment in a single property and legal action involving that property is a possibility. It is paradoxical that it may be in your best interest to appear less wealthy than you are, but by reducing the apparent worth of a company in the public records, a lawsuit may be deterred. Procedural note: equity stripping occurs county-by-county and Texas has 254 counties, so an equity stripping deed of trust and security agreement is usually filed only in the county or counties where the property is located. The usual procedure is to strip the equity of each individual property separately. However, when there are a large number of properties, an alternative approach is to group the properties by county and file a blanket deed of trust against all in-county properties at once, avoiding the need for excessive documentation.

Chapter 37

FRAUDULENT TRANSFERS

The Eyes of Texas Creditors Are Upon You

In Texas, execution on a valid judgment may not be thwarted by a fraudulent transfer or conveyance ("fraudulent transfer" being a term of art further discussed below) that is designed to hinder, delay, or defraud a judgment creditor, regardless of when the transfer is made—either before entry of judgment or after filing an abstract. *Texas Sand Co. v. Shield*, 381S.W.2d 48 (Tex. 1964). Any such transfer is voidable, meaning that if a court examines the transaction and finds it to be shady, it may be set aside. This is old law in Texas, dating back to an 1840 Act of the Republic of Texas. The key has always been how to discern and define a transfer that is fraudulent.

According to current law (the Texas Uniform Fraudulent Transfer Act or "TUFTA," contained in Chapter 24 of the Business and Commerce Code), a "transfer" is defined to mean "every mode, direct or indirect, absolute or conditional, voluntary or involuntary, of disposing of or parting with an asset or an interest in an asset [tangible or intangible], and includes payment of money, release, lease, and creation of a lien or other encumbrance." This is an extremely broad definition that is likely to encompass any attempt by a judgment debtor to move assets out of reach of creditors.

Primary Applicable Law

TUFTA is located in Chapter 24 of the Business and Commerce Code. Also relevant is Tax Code Section 111.024 dealing with tax liability on the part of recipients of fraudulent transfers, as well as Penal Code Section 32.33 (Hindering Secured Creditors). Federal bankruptcy law relating to this topic is found at 11 U.S.C. Sec. 548 but will not be discussed, since this book addresses Texas law exclusively.

An action by a creditor under TUFTA must be brought within one to four years, depending on which section of TUFTA is cited as a cause of action by the creditor. Tex. Bus. & Com. Code Sec. 24.010.

Of particular interest is TUFTA Section 24.005(b)(1)-(11) which includes a *non-exclusive* list of eleven factors that may be used in determining actual fraud:

(1) the transfer or obligation was to an insider;

(2) the debtor retained possession or control of the property transferred after the transfer;

(3) the transfer or obligation was concealed;

(4) before the transfer was made or obligation was incurred, the debtor had been sued or threatened with suit;

(5) the transfer was of substantially all the debtor's assets;

(6) the debtor absconded;

(7) the debtor removed or concealed assets;

(8) the value of the consideration received by the debtor was not reasonably equivalent to the value of the asset transferred or the amount of the obligation incurred;

(9) the debtor was insolvent or became insolvent shortly after the transfer was made or the obligation was incurred;

(10) the transfer occurred shortly before or shortly after a substantial debt was incurred; and

(11) the debtor transferred the essential assets of the business to a lienor who transferred the assets to an insider of the debtor.

No one of the foregoing factors will determine a court's decision, but if several of these factors are present then a finding of fraud is legally supportable. Also, "[a]ctual intent to defraud creditors ordinarily is a fact question. Circumstantial proof may be used to prove fraudulent intent because direct proof is often unavailable. Facts and circumstances that may be considered in determining fraudulent intent include a non-exclusive list of 'badges of fraud' prescribed by the legislature in §24.005(b))." *Ho v. MacArthur Ranch, LLC*, 395 S.W.3d 325, 328-29 (Tex.App.—Dallas 2013, no pet.).

Under TUFTA, the creditor must carry the burden of proving the elements as to each alleged fraudulent transfer by a preponderance of the evidence. *Walker v. Anderson*, 232 S.W.3d 899, 913 (Tex.App.—Dallas 2007, no pet.). The statute explicitly states the standard a plaintiff must meet:

§ 24.006. Transfers Fraudulent as to Present Creditors

(a) **A transfer made or obligation incurred by a debtor is fraudulent as to a creditor whose claim arose before the transfer was made or the obligation was incurred if the debtor made the transfer or incurred the obligation without receiving a reasonably equivalent value in exchange for the transfer or obligation and the debtor was insolvent at that time or the debtor because insolvent as a result of the transfer or obligation.**

The same standard applies to transfers to insiders. Bus. & Com. Code Sec. 24.006(b).

TUFTA is an unusually cooperative statute when it comes to state courts working together with other states to implement its provisions. TUFTA "shall be applied and construed to effectuate its general purpose to make uniform the law with respect to the subject of this chapter among states enacting it." Tex. Bus. & Com. Code Sec. 24.012.

Limitations apply. An action by a judgment creditor seeking to void a fraudulent transfer is subject to a four-year statute of limitations, but if discovered later, then the applicable period is within one year after the transfer should have reasonably been detected (TUFTA Sec. 24.010). "Whether a plaintiff filed his claim within one year of the time when the fraudulent transfer was or could reasonably have been discovered is a question of fact for the [trial judge or jury]." *Walker v. Anderson*, 232 S.W.3d 899, 909 (Tex.App.—Dallas 2007, no pet.).

Is fraudulent intent required under TUFTA?

No. Proof of intentional fraud is not required for a creditor to prevail on a claim of fraudulent transfer by a debtor—which makes this a rather peculiar form of fraud, an offense which in other areas of the law almost always requires proof of intent. The action or transfer may have been undertaken by a debtor in the belief that is was lawful and even fair, but such a belief may not change the action's potential voidability. The reason can be found in Bus. & Com. Code Section 24.006(a), which states that "A transfer made or obligation incurred by a debtor is fraudulent as to a creditor whose claim arose before the transfer was made or the obligation was incurred if the debtor made the transfer or incurred the obligation without receiving a reasonably equivalent value in exchange for the transfer or obligation and the debtor was insolvent at that time or the debtor became insolvent as a result of the transfer or obligation." So if the action or transfer had this effect, then the requirement of intent can be dispensed with. *Esse v. Empire Energy III, Ltd.*, 333 S.W.3d 166 609 (Tex.App.—Houston [1st Dist.] 2010, no pet). Looked at in this way, the term "fraud" probably could (and should) be dropped in favor of the phrase "voidable if certain statutory conditions are met." The term one sees in the cases where clear intent is absent is "constructive fraud" which is another way of saying that the debtor's state of mind does not always matter. Accordingly, one sees actual fraud cases where intent is present versus constructive fraud cases where intent may be less susceptible to proof.

The largest percentage of fraudulent transfers are transactions conducted with an insider or affiliated person without payment of reasonably equivalent value in return (two of the badges of fraud listed above). An insider is "an entity whose close relationship with the debtor subjects any transactions made between the debtor and the insider to heavy scrutiny." *Tel. Equip. Network, Inc. v. TA/Westchase Place, Ltd.*, 80 S.W.3d 601, 609 (Tex.App.—Houston [1st Dist.] 2002, no pet.). According to Bus. & Com. Code Section 24.004(d), the term "'[r]easonably equivalent value' includes, without limitation, a transfer or obligation that is within the range of values for which the transferor would have sold the assets in an arm's length transaction." Combine these definitions and it is clear that intentionally moving assets out of reach of creditors can indeed be a challenge in the face of this law.

The rights of creditors when it comes to transfers to spouses are governed by Tex. Fam. Code Section 4.106, which states that" a provision of a partition or exchange agreement made under this subchapter is void with respect to the rights of a pre-existing creditor whose rights are intended to be defrauded by it." Note the requirement of intent.

Creditor Remedies

Creditor relief usually begins with an injunction. Under TUFTA, "injunctive relief is an available remedy to a fraudulent transfer for which the claimant asserts an equitable interest" in order to preserve the status quo until trial. *Sargeant v. Al Saleh*, 2016 WL 362772 (Tex.App.—Corpus Christi Jan. 28, 2016, no pet.). Business & Commerce Code Section 24.008 (a)(3)(A) provides:

(a) **In an action for relief against a transfer or obligation under this chapter, a creditor, subject to the limitations in Section 24.009 of this code, may obtain:**

(1) **avoidance of the transfer or obligation to the extent necessary to satisfy the creditor's claim;**

(2) **an attachment or other provisional remedy against the asset transferred or other property of the transferee in accordance with the applicable Texas Rules of Civil Procedure and the Civil Practice and Remedies Code relating to ancillary proceedings; or**

(3) **subject to applicable principles of equity and in accordance with applicable rules of civil procedure:**

(A) **an injunction against further disposition by the debtor or a transferee, or both, of the asset transferred or of other property;**

(B) **appointment of a receiver to take charge of the asset transferred or of other property of the transferee; or**

(C) **any other relief the circumstances may require.**

If a transfer cannot be practicably voided, the creditor's goal will be a money judgment for the value of the asset transferred. Business & Commerce Code Section 24.009(b) provides that "the creditor may recover judgment for the value of the asset transferred . . . against: (1) the first transferee of the asset or the person for whose benefit the transfer was made; or (2) any subsequent transferee other than a good faith transfer who took for value or from any subsequent transferee." The person for whose benefit the transfer was made "may include the actual debtor or someone attempting to avoid a debt. *Citizens Nat'l Bank v. NXS Constr., Inc.,* 387 S.W.3d 74 (Tex.App.—Houston [14th Dist.] 2012, no pet.).

For rules relating to restraining orders on financial institutions which hold funds on behalf of customer debtors, see Texas Finance Code Section 59.008.

Nothing in the foregoing is intended to diminish the rights of lenders holding a security interest in the property of the debtor. The creditor can always foreclose. "A secured party is entitled to foreclose on its security interest in the event of default. [Doing so] does not constitute a voidable transfer. Nor is the subsequent transfer of the assets from the foreclosure sale actionable under [TUFTA]." *Yokogawa Corp. v. Skye Int'l Holdings,* 159 S.W.3d 266, 269 (Tex.App.—Dallas 2005, no pet.).

Exception: Ordinary Course of Business or Financial Affairs

24.009(f) A transfer is not voidable under Section 24.006(b) of this code:

    (1) to the extent the insider gave new value to or for the benefit of the debtor after the transfer was made unless the new value was secured by a valid lien;

    (2) if made in the ordinary course of business or financial affairs of the debtor and the insider; or

    (3) if made pursuant to a good-faith effort to rehabilitate the debtor and the transfer secured present value given for that purpose. . . .

Readers may recognize the above "ordinary course of business exception" as being similar in theme and effect to Property Code Section 42.004(c) which protects exempt property in the event of execution on a judgment. Life and business continue after a judgment. Transactions continue. Business and personal items may be bought and sold. It is just that now, the debtor is under scrutiny and either the debtor or his transferee may have to bear the burden of asserting this affirmative defense.

The Relevance of Recording and BFPs

Whether or not a conveyance of real property was recorded at the county clerk's office can be important in determining whether or not a judgment creditor can reach the property. The Texas recording statute (Prop. Code Sec. 13001(a)) states that a "conveyance of real property or an interest in real property or a mortgage or deed of trust is void as to a creditor or to a subsequent purchaser for valuable consideration without notice unless the instrument has been acknowledged, sworn to, or proved and filed for record as required by law."

What is an asset?

One can start with determining what does *not* constitute an asset. Under TUFTA Section 24.002(2) the term "asset" does not include property to the extent it is encumbered by a valid lien. However, "the value of property in excess of a valid lien [i.e., the equity] . . . is an 'asset' as defined by UFTA. *Citizens Nat'l Bank v. NXS Constr., Inc.* 387 S.W.3d 74, 82-83 (Tex.App.—Houston [14th Dist.] 2012, no pet.). Nor does "asset" include property to the extent it is generally exempt under non-bankruptcy law (details below) or an interest in property held in tenancy by the entireties to the extent it is not subject to process by a creditor holding a claim against only one tenant, under the law of another jurisdiction.

The common law bona fide purchaser doctrine operates side-by-side with the recording statute and protects bona fide purchasers who pay reasonably equivalent value for the property. A person is a BFP (and therefore protected) if he or she is a good-faith purchaser of legal title to real property; pays valuable consideration; and does so without actual or constructive notice of the judgment lien—meaning the buyer cannot have any awareness (from whatever source) of the existence of a judgment against the seller. So a last-minute transfer by the judgment debtor to his brother-in-law for ten dollars and other valuable consideration will fool no one and is voidable. "A person who invokes [the bona fide purchaser] affirmative defense carries the burden of establishing good faith and the reasonable equivalence of the consideration obtained." *Hahn v. Love*, 321 S.W.3d 517, 526 (Tex.App.—Houston [1st Dist.] 2009, pet. denied).

Assets Exempt under State Law

The TUFTA definition of "asset" does not include exempt assets under non-bankruptcy law including the Texas homestead laws contained in Article XVI, Section 50 of the Texas Constitution and Property Code Chapters 41 and 42. However, Property Code Section 42.004 provides that a transaction may be set aside if non-exempt assets are used to buy or pay down indebtedness on exempt assets "with the intent to defraud, delay, or hinder" a creditor. This reaches back two years. However, proving such intent (and therefore getting the transfer set aside) can be difficult, particularly if the debtor asserts that the transaction occurred in the ordinary course of business, which is a solid defense in Texas under Property Code Section 42.004(c).

Post-Judgment Discovery

Judgments are final after thirty days, after which post-judgment discovery (interrogatories, requests for production, and depositions directed at the defendant by a judgment creditor) are commonly used not only to determine the location and value of the defendant's assets but also whether or not there is a trail suggesting fraudulent transfers. The scope of this process can be wide indeed, reaching back several years. A debtor can be held in contempt (resulting in a fine or jail) for failing to provide timely responses, so one should never ignore post-judgment discovery.

Fraudulent Transfers and the IRS

In re Wren Alexander Investments LLC, No. 08-52914-RBK, 2011 WL 671961 (Bankr. W.D. Tex. Feb. 17, 2011), illustrates the difficulty in moving assets beyond the reach of the IRS. In this case, the IRS successfully argued that the taxpayer's transfer was fraudulent (1) under BOC Section 24.006(a) since the taxpayer did not receive reasonably equivalent value in exchange and was insolvent at the time of or became insolvent as a result of the transfer, and (2) under Section 24.005(a) since the transfer was made with "actual intent to hinder, delay, or defraud" a creditor.

Implications for Asset Protection Planning

As noted elsewhere in this book, asset protection strategies fall into two groups: strategies implemented in advance of collection action and suit by a creditor-plaintiff; and strategies that can reasonably be put into effect afterward. After suit is filed, creditors are on the lookout for the movement of assets intended to defeat their legitimate claims. A Texas defendant may be limited to attempting to convert non-exempt assets into homestead-exempt items (one's primary residence, cars, etc.) in an "ordinary business" type of way, holding cash at home, and prepaying certain key items (taxes, attorney's fees, and the like which are unlikely to be questioned as fraudulent). The debtor's attorney needs to be able to plausibly argue to a court that the steps taken by the debtor could reasonably have been taken in the ordinary course of life or business, regardless of whether or not the debtor was subject to collection on a judgment.

PART VII

EVICTIONS, FORECLOSURE, & LITIGATION

Chapter 38

EVICTIONS

Forcible Entry and Detainer

Eviction is a judicial process by which an owner recovers possession of real property and, if appropriate, a judgment for unpaid rent, attorney's fees, and court costs against a defaulting tenant or occupant. A note on technical legal terms: "forcible detainer" applies when an owner seeks to evict a person lawfully in possession (e.g., a tenant); by contrast, "forcible entry and detainer" (or FED for short) occurs when a person without legal authority to be on the premises (e.g., a trespasser) refuses to surrender possession. In practice, the terms are commonly used interchangeably.

"An action for forcible detainer is a 'summary, speedy, and inexpensive remedy for the determination of who is entitled to the possession of premises'. . . . The only issue to be resolved in a forcible detainer action is the right to immediate possession of the property; the merits of title are not adjudicated." *Yarbrough v. Household Finance Corporation III*, 455 S.W.3d 277 (Tex.App.—Houston [14th Dist.] 2015, no pet.).

Superior Right to Immediate Possession

The legal key is *superior right to immediate possession*. "To establish a superior right to immediate possession, [landlord] had the burden to prove (1) [landlord] owns the property, (2) [tenant] is either a tenant at will, tenant at sufferance, or a tenant or subtenant willfully holding over after the termination of the tenant's right of possession, (3) [landlord] gave proper notice to [tenant] to vacate the premises, and (4) [tenant] refused to vacate the premises . . . . The only dispute is whether the record conclusively establishes that [tenant's] right of possession terminated." *Shields L.P. v. Bradberry*, __ S.W.3d __ (Tex. 2017) (No. 15—0803; 5-12-17).

The landlord's objective is usually to gain a judgment and a writ of possession. The judgment can be for both possession and damages or for possession only. Because collecting judgments against residential tenants can be difficult in Texas (there is an extensive list of assets that are exempt from execution) a residential landlord may occasionally choose to be content with a judgment for possession only.

Justice Courts

Justice courts have original jurisdiction in eviction cases. (Tex. R. Civ. P. 510.3(b) and Tex. Prop. Code Sec. 24.004) and may award damages up to $10,000. Note, however, that the "forcible entry and detainer action is not exclusive, but cumulative, of any other remedy that a party may have in the courts of this state. If all matters between the parties cannot be adjudicated in the justice court in which the forcible entry and detainer proceedings are pending due to the justice court's limited subject matter jurisdiction, then either party may maintain an action in a court of competent jurisdiction for proper relief." *McGlothlin v. Kliebert*, 672 S.W.2d 231, 233 (Tex. 1984).

Evictions are conducted in justice courts located in various neighborhood precincts spread around Texas' 254 counties. When an investor arrives ready to do his first eviction, he may be told that the "forcible docket" begins at a certain time and that there are perhaps twenty or more cases ahead of him.

Basic Law and Procedure

Evictions are governed by Property Code Chapter 24 and Civil Procedure Rule 500 et seq. The process begins with proper notice, governed by Section 24.005, which requires that "the landlord give at least three days' written notice to vacate the premises before the landlord files a forcible detainer suit." A written lease may provide for either a shorter or longer period. However, as with all legal notice requirements, it is best not to cut the prescribed time period too close. Doing so may unwittingly provide the tenant with a defense. Also, if a landlord wishes to attempt to recover attorney's fees pursuant to Section 24.006, the notice to vacate "must state that if the tenant does not vacate the premises before the 11th day after the date of the receipt of the notice and if the landlord files suit, the landlord may recover attorney's fees." As always, the best practice is to send the notice by both certified and first-class mail. It may also be posted on the door of the dwelling.

The eviction should be filed with the justice of the peace in whose precinct the property is located. At the hearing, the judge will determine which party has the superior right to immediate possession and what damages (e.g., back rent, attorney's fees, and court costs), if any, will be awarded to the landlord. These are the only issues to be considered by the court. A counterclaim by the tenant, regardless of subject matter or merit, is *not* permitted in an FED. Such tenant suits must be brought by separate action in any court (including that same justice court) where venue and jurisdiction are allowed (Tex. Rule Civ. P. 510.3(e)). It is also inappropriate to raise issues of title, since justice courts do not have authority over suits "for trial of title to land. . . ." (Tex. Gov. Code Sec. 37.031). Jurisdiction over title issues generally resides with district courts.

Month-to-Month Tenancies

In the case of a month-to-month tenancy (e.g., after a lease is expired) with no tenant default, the landlord may give a month's written notice that the landlord desires possession. No more than that need be said—no allegation of default is necessary. If the tenant does not leave, then an FED can be filed. In the case of default on an existing lease—failure to pay rent, for example—then a written 3-day notice to vacate should be given, after which the landlord may file an FED (Tex. Prop. Code Sec. 24.005).

If the property is abandoned, is an eviction necessary?

If a tenant has truly abandoned and vacated a property, then the owner may peaceably re-enter without judicial process, take possession, and change the locks. However, problems can occur when some of the tenant's possessions remain on the premises, raising the question of whether the property has actually been abandoned or not. Abandonment has occurred when a property is "empty, that is, without contents of substantial value . . . the term 'substantial value' does not mean merely substantial monetary value, but the term includes value attributable to the utility of the furniture. It is well known that furniture, because of age and condition, may have little monetary value, but to the owner or user has substantial utility, and retention in the house would evidence the absence of complete abandonment. From the evidence recited we are of the view that the reasonable mind could conclude there was furniture of substantial value in the house and therefore it was not vacant." *Knoff v. U.S. Fidelity*, 447 S.W.2d 497 (Tex.App.—Houston, 1969, no writ). If a substantial amount of personal property remains, the safer legal course is to pursue a formal eviction. It is a fact issue and a judgment call to be decided by the investor and his attorney.

Eviction Pursuant to an Executory Contract

Eviction of a buyer-tenant under an executory contract (e.g., a contract for deed) is a special case. Texas law views buyers under contracts for deed as more than mere tenants, and so more care must be taken (and more requirements met) in the eviction process. Property Code Section 5.063 outlines requirements which must followed exactly if the notice letter and eviction are to be valid in these cases. Note that the delinquent amount under the executory contract must be broken down into principal and interest. If the buyer-tenant has paid less than 40% of the amount due or made less than 48 monthly payments, the seller-landlord must provide a 30-day notice and opportunity to cure before seeking to regain possession of the property. If the default is not cured, then a 3-day notice to vacate may be given and an eviction may proceed normally from that point forward.

If the buyer-tenant under an executory contract has paid more than 40% of the amount due or made 48 or more monthly payments, then eviction is not available as a primary remedy. Pursuant to equity protection provisions of Property Code Section 5.066, the seller-landlord must afford a 60-day notice and cure period, which is then followed by appointment of a trustee and a non-judicial foreclosure. Depending on the circumstances, an eviction may thereafter be required to regain possession.

What about mobile homes?

A forcible detainer action applies in the case of real property, not personal property. Mobile homes are personal property unless the owner has filed a statement of ownership in the local real property records pursuant to Occupations Code Sec. 1201.207. *Segoviano v. Guerra*, 557 S.W.3d 610 (Tex.App.—El Paso 2017, pet. denied).

Possession Verses Title Issues

As noted previously, there is a distinction between disputes concerning *possession* and disputes concerning *title*—although both issues may arise within the same case. Generally, justice courts have original jurisdiction over possession (Tex. Prop. Code Sec. 24.004) and district courts have original jurisdiction over title (Tex. Const. Art. V, Sec. 8; Tex. Gov't Code Sec. 26.043). Procedure Rule 510.3(e) also provides that the justice court must adjudicate the right to actual possession and not title. "Justice courts do not have jurisdiction to determine or adjudicate title to land, and neither does a county court exercising appellate jurisdiction in a forcible detainer action." *Yarbrough v. Household Finance Corporation III*, 455 S.W.3d 277 (Tex.App.—Houston [14th Dist.] 2015, no pet.). In *Yarbrough*, the plaintiff claimed that the eviction arose from a wrongful foreclosure that was based on a fraudulent deed of trust—a title issue, so the case belonged in neither justice court nor county court but in district court.

Gibson v. Dynegy Midstream Services, L.P. 138 S.W.3d 518, 522 (Tex.App.—Fort Worth 2004, no pet.) puts this way: "Justice courts may adjudicate possession when issues related to the title of real property are [only] tangentially or collaterally related to possession. If, however, the question of title is so integrally linked to the issue of possession that the right to possession cannot be determined without first determining title, then the justice courts and, on appeal, the county courts, lack jurisdiction over the matter." A Houston appeals court elaborates: "Although a justice court has subject-matter jurisdiction over a forcible detainer action, the justice court, and a county court on appeal, lack jurisdiction to resolve any questions of title beyond the immediate right to possession . . . . On the other hand, a justice court is not deprived of jurisdiction merely by the existence of a title dispute; rather, it is only deprived of jurisdiction if the right to immediate possession necessarily requires the resolution of a title dispute." *Black v. Washington Mutual Bank*, 318 S.W.3d 414 (Tex.App.—Houston [1st Dist.] 2010, pet. dism'd w.o.j.). A justice court is deprived of jurisdiction *only* if resolution of a title dispute must occur *before* a determination of the right to immediate possession can be made. *Jelinis, LLC v. Hiran*, 557 S.W.3d 159 (Tex.App.—Houston [14th Dist.] 2018, pet. denied).

A question as to whether or not there are defects in the chain of title (and therefore the landlord's ownership) does not deprive a justice court of jurisdiction, since the only issue for adjudication at the justice court level is the superior right to possession. This does not require that the plaintiff landlord prove title, only the existence of a landlord-tenant relationship. *Isaac v. CitiMortgage, Inc.*, 563 S.W.3d 305 (Tex.App.—Houston [1st Dist.] 2018, pet. denied).

This places a burden on a tenant who believes for whatever reason that the he or she has a title claim, since a different remedy in a different court must now be pursued. Burdensome as this might be, it has been ruled that this is not a denial of due process. *Reynoso v. Dibs US, Inc.*, 541 S.W. 3d 331 (Tex.App.—Houston [14th Dist.] 2017, no pet.).

The practical result? Cases with title and possession issues that are "integrally linked" usually wind up in district court. A district court may pre-empt a justice court (or a county court that is hearing a FED appeal) on issues of possession when questions of title and possession are so intertwined that possession may not be determined without first determining title. In such cases, and only in such cases, may the justice court be deprived of jurisdiction. *Bynum v. Lewis*, 393 S.W.3d 916 (Tex.App—Tyler 2013, no pet.). But there is a caveat: the justice court (or county court on appeal) loses jurisdiction only if the right to immediate possession of the property *first* requires that title be adjudicated. *In re. American Homes for Rent Properties Eight, LLC*, 498 S.W.3d 153 (Tex.App.—Dallas 2016, no pet.).

Tenants and their attorneys should know that "merely raising the issue of title is not enough to defeat the justice court's original jurisdiction. The Property Code provides for parallel, separate title and possession suits in the justice court and the county courts at law unless resolution of possession necessarily requires the resolution of a title dispute." *Gonzalez v. Wells Fargo Bank*, 441 S.W.3d 709, 713 (Tex.App.—El Paso 2014, no pet.).

Another caveat: although justice courts have exclusive jurisdiction over forcible detainer (eviction) cases, there is an assumption involved that a landlord-tenant relationship exists between the parties. In the absence of such a relationship, the justice court may not be able to ascertain who has the right to immediate possession with first addressing title issues—something it lacks the authority to do. *Goodman-Delaney v. Granthan*, 484 S.W.3d 171 (Tex.App.—Houston [14th Dist.] 2015, no pet.).

Note that in Harris County, the county courts at law (but not the justice courts) have the benefit of an exception under the Government Code and may hear title issues.

If the concepts of possession and title are legally distinct, is it then possible to pursue a judgment for possession in justice court while independently seeking the declaratory judgment of a district court regarding title? Yes. Moreover, the judgment rendered in the justice court as to possession is not determinative of the outcome of the district court proceeding. *AAA Free Move Ministorage, LLC v. OIS Investments, Inc.*, 419 S.W.3d 522 (Tex.App.—San Antonio 2013, pet. denied). The justice court remedy of forcible detainer is designed to be a fast and efficient means of establishing which party has the superior right to immediate possession of the property—so the *res judicata* effect of such a judgment is limited to this single narrow issue. The parties are free to sue one another under a different cause number (either in justice court or in a different forum) on other, related issues. *Federal Home Loan Mortgage Corporation v. Pham*, 449 S.W.3d 230 (Tex.App.—Houston [14th Dist.] 2014, no pet.).

Appeals: Cash Bonds Versus Pauper's Affidavit

Motions for new trial are not allowed in justice court eviction cases. However, within five calendar days of judgment, the losing party may (with or without good reason) appeal the justice court's judgment to the local county court at law. Tex. R. Civ. P. 510.9. The appeal results in the file being sent to the county courthouse where it will be heard de novo (as a new case). Why is this so? It results from an interesting historical quirk: the justice court is not a court of record. No transcript is kept of the proceedings or testimony, so the appeal to county court automatically vacates and annuls the judgment of the justice court. Everything starts over.

The justice of the peace will set a cash appeal bond which may be three times the monthly rent. Property Code Sections 24.00511 and 24.00512 require that the JP's judgment set the amount of the bond, a long overdue change. Either party may then contest the amount of the bond within five days. However, the cash bond may be waived if the tenant files an affidavit stating that he or she cannot afford it. The content of the "pauper's bond" or "pauper's affidavit" is prescribed by statute (Tex. Prop. Code Sec. 24.0052) and is considerably more complex than it used to be.

Once a pauper's affidavit is filed, the landlord has the right to request a hearing and contest the affidavit, alleging that the tenant does in fact have sufficient resources for the bond. The tenant can be questioned on the subject of his or her assets and income. It is generally pointless to go through this exercise, however, since pauper's bonds are almost always approved by justices of the peace, and the file is then turned over to county court (Tex. R. Civ. P. 510.9(c)).

What happens if there is no appeal?

If the tenant does not appeal within five days, the judgment of the justice court becomes final and the landlord may proceed to the enforcement phase by obtaining and serving a writ of possession. This requires going to the county clerk's office and paying a nominal fee. The constable then serves the writ, but first usually posts a notice on the tenant's door allowing 48 hours to move out. After that, the constable may show up with a truck, forcibly evict the tenant, and put the tenant's possessions in storage where charges accrue at the tenant's expense.

Pauper's Bond Appellants

Important: a tenant who files a pauper's affidavit must, after notice, pay a month's rent to the justice court pursuant to Property Code Section 24.0053—and do so *before* the file is shipped to county court. If the tenant fails to do so, Section 24.0054 provides:

> (a) **During an appeal of an eviction case for non-payment of rent, the justice court on request shall immediately issue a writ of possession, without hearing if:**
>
> (1) **A tenant fails to pay the initial rent deposit into the justice court registry within five days of the date the tenant filed a pauper's affidavit as required by**

> Rule 749b(1), Texas Rules of Civil Procedure, and Section 24.0053;
>
> (2) The justice court has provided the written notice required by Section 24.0053(a-1); and
>
> (3) The justice court has not yet forwarded the transcript and original papers to the county court as provided by Subsection (a-2).

This provision gives landlords who prevail an effective remedy at the justice court level, without having to wait until the entire eviction file is transferred to the county clerk's office and set up as a new case.

Rule 510.9 Motion in County Court: Obtaining a Writ of Possession

The use of pauper's affidavits in appeals may in some respects appear unfair, but it can be turned to the landlord's advantage: if the pauper's bond is approved, and the county court takes over the case, the tenant is then obliged to begin making monthly rental payments to the court and continue to do so during the pendency of the appeal. If the tenant fails to do this (and most do) the landlord may seek *immediate* possession from the county court based on motion pursuant to Texas Rule of Civil Procedure 510.9(c)(5)(B), which permits a tenant to remain in possession only so long as the following requirements are met:

> (i) Within 5 days of the date that the defendant files a sworn statement of inability to pay [the appeal bond], it must pay into the justice court registry the amount set forth in the notice provided at the time the defendant filed the statement. If the defendant was provided with notice and fails to pay the designated amount into the justice court registry within 5 days, and the transcript has not been transmitted to the county clerk, the plaintiff is entitled, upon request and payment of the applicable fee, to a writ of possession, which the justice court must issue immediately and without hearing.
>
> (ii) During the appeal process as rent becomes due under the rental agreement, the defendant must pay the designated amount into the county court registry within 5 days of the rental due date under the terms of the rental agreement.

Cash or Surety Bond Appeals

If an appeal bond (cash or surety) is posted, there is no *requirement* that the tenant pay rent while the appeal is pending. Even so, it is good practice for the landlord's attorney to file a motion requesting payment of rent into the court registry based on the theory that no one should live for free, an argument to which judges are generally receptive. A preferential setting should also be requested if the county court in question does not already automatically provide such a setting in eviction cases.

The bad news for landlords? If the tenant is a professional deadbeat who has played this game before, the property may be tied up for months.

Post-Foreclosure Eviction

The remedy of foreclosure is available to lenders if the borrower defaults on a real estate lien note. Specified notice and other requirements must be followed if the foreclosure is to be valid. Tex. Property Code Sec. 51.002 et seq. Foreclosure sales are held in Texas on the first Tuesday of each month between 10 a.m. and 4 p.m. This process gives the new owner *title*; the next step is to obtain *possession*.

The successful bidder at the foreclosure sale (likely the lender) gets a trustee's deed which cuts off all junior liens including purchase-money liens and mechanics liens. A valid foreclosure usually terminates existing leases as well. *Coinmach Corp. v. Aspenwood Apartment Corp.* 417 S.W.3d 909 (Tex. 2013). Even so, the new owner may not simply lock out a residential tenant. Tex. Prop. Code Sec. 92.0081.

A brief review of leasehold terminology may be useful at this point. A tenant who remains in possession after expiration of a lease is a "holdover tenant." If the tenant holds over without consent from the landlord, he is a "tenant at sufferance;" if holding over occurs with landlord consent, the tenant is a "tenant at will."

If the occupant of residential property is a tenant at will or by sufferance then the new owner under the trustee's deed must give the usual three-day notice to vacate, file an FED petition in justice court, get it served, have it heard by the justice of the peace, and then wait five days for a final judgment and a writ of possession. The new owner must then wait until the constable posts a 48-hour notice on the door and then forcibly removes a former borrower who is otherwise unwilling to leave. Elapsed time? Often three to four weeks, and even then, the former borrower may appeal, possibly gaining additional free-rent time in the property.

Section 24.005(b) provides that new owners who have purchased foreclosed property must give a residential tenant in good standing "at least 30 days' written notice if the purchaser [at foreclosure] chooses not to continue the lease."

What if there is a wrongful foreclosure case pending in district court? Can the district court enjoin the eviction?

District courts have no jurisdiction to issue an injunction stopping an eviction. *McGlothin v. Kliebert*, 672 S.W.2d 231, 232 (Tex. 1984); *TMC Medical, Ltd. v. The Lasaters French Quarter Partnership*, 880 S.W.2d 789 (Tex.App.—Tyler 1994, writ dism'd, w.o.j.).

Collecting Judgments from Tenants

The key objective for the owner is to gain a writ of possession. Obtaining a judgment for monetary damages against a residential tenant is usually an empty formality since such judgments are seldom collected. Texas has long been a safe haven for debtors, and both the Texas Constitution and the Property Code exempt a long list of real and personal property from execution upon a judgment. The average residential tenant has very little that a landlord will be allowed to take and, since garnishment of wages is unconstitutional, collection may be problematic. Often the best strategy is to record an abstract of the judgment against the tenant in the real property records in the hopes that some day in the next ten years the tenant will become affluent enough to own and sell property. If this transaction occurs through a title company, the title company can be expected to collect funds to pay the judgement.

What does the attorney need from the client?

When asking that an attorney initiate the eviction process, the client should be prepared to supply (1) a copy of the lease agreement; (2) copies of any correspondence or demand letters; and (3) a brief summary of the specific items of monetary and technical default.

Chapter 39

FORECLOSURES

Both an Investment Opportunity and an Expedited Remedy

The remedy of foreclosure is available in the event of a borrower's monetary default (non-payment) or technical default (e.g., failure to pay taxes or keep the property insured). In order to determine if there has been a default, the loan documents—the note, the deed of trust, the loan agreement, and so forth—should be carefully examined. Notice and opportunity to cure requirements contained in these documents and applicable statutes must be strictly followed if a foreclosure is to be valid.

Foreclosures may be judicial (ordered by a court following a judgment in a lawsuit) or non-judicial ("on the courthouse steps"). These two remedies cannot be pursued simultaneously. *Kaspar v. Keller*, 466 S.W.2d 326, 328 (Tex.App.—Waco 1971, writ ref'd n.r.e.). Most foreclosures in Texas are non-judicial. These are governed by Chapter 51 of the Property Code and are held on the first Tuesday of each month between 10 a.m. and 4 p.m. at a designated spot (usually at or near the county courthouse). The effect of foreclosure is to cut off and eliminate junior liens, including mechanic's liens, but not tax obligations.

Notices of foreclosure sales of a residential homestead must be filed with the county clerk and posted (usually on a bulletin board in the lobby of the courthouse) at least 21 calendar days prior to the intended foreclosure date. Notices are entitled "Notice of Trustee's Sale" or "Notice of Substitute Trustee's Sale." They provide information about the debt, the legal description of the property, and designate a three-hour period during which the sale will be held. In larger metropolitan areas there are foreclosure listing services which publish a monthly list of properties posted for foreclosure.

Commencement of the Non-Judicial Foreclosure Process

One of the first steps in assessing a loan default and contemplating a foreclosure is to make sure that the lender is acting within the statute of limitations. Section 16.035(d) of the Civil Practice & Remedies Code states that a foreclosure is void if not commenced within four years of the date the cause of action accrues. A second step is to evaluate all loan documentation to make sure that the loan is legal and the lien is valid.

Notices are the next step. Foreclosure notices must be given to the borrower in accordance with Property Code Sections 51.002 et seq. and the deed of trust. The content of foreclosure notices is technical and must be correct in order to insure a valid foreclosure that cannot later be attacked by a wrongful foreclosure suit. Clients often protest when their lawyer advises re-noticing the debtor—"But I've already sent them an email telling them they are in default." Not good enough. "To lawfully exercise an option to accelerate upon default provided by a note or deed of trust, the lender must give the borrower both notice of intent to accelerate and notice of acceleration, and in the proper sequence." Further, "both notices must be clear and unequivocal." *Karam v. Brown*, 407 S.W.3d 464 (Tex.App.—El Paso 2013, no. pet.).

Required Notices to a Residential Homestead Borrower

Accordingly, two certified-mail notices to the borrower are required, the first being a "Notice of Default and Intent to Accelerate" which gives formal notice of the default and affords an opportunity for the borrower to cure (at least 20 days for a homestead, although if the deed of trust is on the FNMA form, 30 days must be given). Note that S.B. 766 and S.B. 472, which did not make it out of committee in the 81st Legislature, would have extended the 20-day period. This legislation may be revived in the future. Many lawyers consider it best to routinely give a 30-day notice, in order to be safe, even if the deed of trust or applicable statute calls for a lesser minimum period of time.

After the cure period has passed, a "Notice of Acceleration and Posting for Foreclosure" must be sent to a residential homestead borrower at least 21 days prior to the foreclosure date. This second letter must also specify the location of the sale and a three-hour period during which the sale will take place. A separate "notice of foreclosure sale" should be enclosed. This notice is also filed with the county clerk and physically posted at the courthouse. If there is going to be a change in the trustee who was named in the deed of trust, it will also be necessary to file a written appointment of substitute trustee signed by the lender.

Foreclosure on non-homestead or commercial property is less regulated, but must still comply with the requirements and timelines set forth in the deed of trust.

Notices are addressed to the last known address of the borrower contained in the lender's records (this is the legal requirement), but it is wise for the lender to double-check this to avoid later claims by the borrower that notice was defective. Attention should also be paid to electronic communications. In *Bauder v. Alegria*, 480 S.W.3d 92 (Tex.App.—Houston [14th Dist.] 2015, no pet.), the court found that text messages from the borrower were reasonable notice of the borrower's change of address. In spite of this ruling, it would be reckless for any attorney or prudent investor to rely on text messaging for any such legally important purpose.

It is prudent to send legal notices by both first-class and certified mail—and not just in the area of foreclosure. Why? The reason has to do with Texas' mailbox rule, i.e., that a notice properly deposited in the U.S. mail is presumed to be delivered. "Common sense . . . dictates that regular mail is presumed delivered and certified mail enjoys no [such] presumption unless the receipt is returned bearing an appropriate notation." *McCray v. Hoag*, 372 S.W.3d 237, 243 (Tex.App.—Dallas 2012, no pet. h.). The best practice is not to scrimp on the notices or the plausible addresses to which they are sent. A careful lender will send notices to *all* likely addresses where the borrower may be found. Potentially duplicate notices do no legal harm (they consume only paper and postage) and may be useful if the foreclosure is challenged.

Other lienholders (whether junior or senior) are not entitled to notice. Depending on the first lienholder's strategy, however, it may be useful to discuss the issue with them.

If the borrower is able to cure, a reinstatement agreement should be executed unless the terms of the debt have been changed (e.g., payments have been lowered or the term extended) in which case a hybrid reinstatement/modification agreement or even a new note (a "replacement note") may be appropriate.

Fair Debt Collection Practices

Foreclosure notice and demand letters are attempts to collect a consumer debt. Accordingly, the federal Fair Debt Collection Practices Act (15 USC 1962, et seq., the "FDCPA") and its companion Texas statute, the Texas Debt Collection Act contained in Finance Code Chapter 392, both apply. The term "debt" is defined by the FDCPA as "any obligation or alleged obligation of a consumer to pay money arising out of a transaction in which the money, property, insurance, or services which are the subject of the transaction are primarily for personal, family, or household purposes, whether or not such obligation has been reduced to judgment." 15 U.S.C. Sec. 1692a(5). Failure to disclose and provide verification of the debt when the borrower has requested it in writing has serious penalties under both laws, as do threats, coercion, or similar heavy-handed practices.

Requirements for collection letters—including foreclosure notice and demand letters—are found in 15 U.S.C. Sec. 1692g. In the world of collection attorneys, such letters are referred to as "G notices." A proper G notice (such as a notice of default on a real estate loan) must advise the debtor of the amount of the debt; the name of the current creditor; the debtor's right to dispute the debt, both verbally and in writing; and the debtor's right to know the address of the original creditor. These requirements pertain to the specifics of the debt itself. The collector must also disclose that it is a debt collector, that it is attempting to collect a debt, and that any information obtained will be used for that purpose.

Real estate attorneys (or anyone else) sending foreclosure notices and conducting a foreclosure are, whether they are fully aware of it or not, debt collectors when it comes to communicating with a debtor for purposes of attempting to collect or reinstate a defaulted real estate note. As such, the court-applied standard is to require compliance with the FDCPA when viewed from the point of view of an unsophisticated consumer. *Youngblood v. GC Servs., Ltd. P'ship,* 186 F. Supp. 2d. 695 (W.D. Tex. 2002). The conceptual overlap with the definition of a consumer under the Deceptive Trade Practices Act is unavoidable here. Having said the foregoing, it is unlikely that mere technical or procedural violations of the FDCPA will get a collector in trouble; some materiality including real injury to the debtor will likely be required to establish liability under the statute. *Spokeo, Inc. v. Robins,* 136 S. Ct. 1540 (2016).

As noted, the FDCPA requires that a borrower be given 30 days to make a written request to obtain verification of the debt. The lender or its attorney may nonetheless give notice of default, accelerate the debt, and even post for foreclosure in less time, but the foreclosure sale itself should not be conducted until the 30-day debt verification period has expired.

Notwithstanding the foregoing, a trustee exercising the power of sale contained in a deed of trust is not a debt collector (Tex. Prop. Code Sec. 51.0075(b)).

Home Equity Loans are a Different Case

Article 16, Section 50(a)(6) contains the requirements for home equity lending, i.e., the extension of credit secured by a lien on a borrower's homestead evidenced by a "Texas Home Equity Security Instrument" rather than the usual deed of trust. Although an expedited foreclosure process is available in the event of default, a home equity lien may be foreclosed only by means of a court order which provides a specific date for the sale to take place. *Wells Fargo Bank, N.A. v. Robinson,* 391 S.W.3d 590 (Tex.App.—Dallas 2012, no pet.).

Rules 735 and 736 of the Texas Rules of Civil Procedure govern the process by which a lender may file a verified application in the local district court seeking foreclosure of a home equity loan. The proceeding is limited in scope. "The only issue to be determined in a Rule 736 proceeding is the right of the applicant [the lender] to obtain an order to proceed with foreclosure under the applicable law and the terms of the loan agreement, contract or lien sought to be foreclosed. A respondent [the borrower] may file a response to the application, but the response may not raise any independent claims for relief, and no discovery is permitted." *In re One West Bank, FSB*, 430 S.W.3d 573 (Tex.App.—Corpus Christi 2014, pet. denied).

Foreclosure Pursuant to an Executory Contract

In the days before the 2005 reforms to the Property Code concerning executory contracts, a buyer-tenant was truly at a disadvantage when it came to a contract for deed. Buyer-tenants could forfeit all sums paid if they defaulted and be evicted as ordinary tenants. No longer. If the buyer-tenant has paid more than 40% of the amount due or made 48 or more monthly payments, then pursuant to the equity protection provisions of Property Code Section 5.066, the seller-landlord must provide a 60-day notice of default and opportunity to cure the default. If the default is not cured, then a trustee may be appointed who can proceed with a non-judicial foreclosure.

Multiple Liens

Properties may (and often do) have multiple liens against them. "A valid foreclosure on a senior lien (sometimes referred to as a 'superior' lien) extinguishes a junior lien (sometimes referred to as 'inferior' or 'subordinate') if there are not sufficient excess proceeds from the foreclosure sale to satisfy the junior lien . . . In general, mechanic's liens whose inception is subsequent to the date of a deed-of-trust lien will be subordinate to the deed-of-trust lien." *Trinity Drywall Systems, LLC v. TOKA General Contractors, Ltd.*, 416 S.W.3d 201 (Tex.App.—El Paso, 2013, no pet.). As to competing M&M liens, a perfected M&M lien is deemed to relate back in time to the date of its inception.

Leases, including ground leases, are generally terminated by a foreclosure sale as well. *Kimzey Wash, LLC v. LG Auto Laundry, LP*, 418 S.W.3d 291 (Tex.App.—Dallas 2013, no pet.).

Notice to the IRS

The best practice is to do a title search prior to foreclosure to determine if there is an IRS tax lien or other federal lien. If so, notice must be given to the IRS and/or the U.S. Attorney at least 25 days prior to the sale, not including the sale date. 26 U.S.C. Sec. 7425(c)(1). If this is not done, any IRS tax lien on the property will not be extinguished by the sale. Note that the IRS also has 120 days following the sale to redeem the property, although this seldom happens. The successful bidder on an IRS-liened property is therefore not entitled to breathe a sigh of relief until the 121st day.

Due Diligence by an Investor Prior to Purchasing Property at a Foreclosure Sale

Buying property at foreclosure sales is a popular form of investment but it contains traps for the unwary. The investor's goal is to acquire instant equity in the property by paying a relatively modest sum at the foreclosure sale. However, apparent equity can evaporate if the property is loaded down with liens and unpaid taxes. It is advisable, therefore, to check the title of the property that will be sold. Is the lien being foreclosed a second or third lien? If so, then the first lien (usually a purchase-money lien held by a mortgage company) will continue in force. First liens are king. They are not extinguished by foreclosure of an inferior lien. What about IRS liens? Improvement liens? Liens imposed by homeowners associations? Any or all of these could consume whatever equity might otherwise have existed in the property. If an investor is unsure as to which liens will be wiped out in a foreclosure sale, then copies of each lien document should be pulled and taken to the investor's real estate attorney for review.

As far as researching title is concerned, obtaining a title report is a good idea. One should also obtain copies of the warranty deed and any deeds of trust or other lien instruments.

If more information is needed about the property itself, one can contact the trustee named in the Notice of Trustee's Sale. Trustees vary in their level of cooperation but are often willing to provide additional information if they have it. They may have a copy of an inspection report on the property which they may be willing to share. It might even be possible to arrange to view the property if it is unoccupied.

The investor should also check the military status of the borrower, since Property Code Section 51.015 prohibits non-judicial foreclosure of a dwelling owned by active duty military personnel or within 9 months after active duty ends. Knowingly violating this law is a Class A misdemeanor.

Property Condition

It goes without saying that the investor should physically inspect the property if at all possible, although one should not trespass on occupied property to do this. It is legal, however, to stand in the street (public property) and take photos.

When one buys at a foreclosure sale, it is "as is." Property condition is therefore important. When buying residential properties in particular, an investor should be especially curious about condition of the foundation (learn to recognize signs of settlement), whether the property is flood-prone, and whether or not there may be environmental contamination (generally not a problem if the house is in a restricted subdivision). It is usually best to avoid any property that suffers from one or more of these deficiencies. Other items that involve significant expense are the roof and the HVAC system.

The past or continuing presence of hazardous substances can impose huge potential liability (particularly on commercial properties) since both Texas and federal law provide that any owner of property (including the investor) is jointly and severally liable with any prior owner for cleanup costs. The Texas Commission on Environmental Quality ("TCEQ") maintains a web site at www.tceq.state.tx.us where the environmental history of a property can be researched.

Valuation

It is, of course, important not to bid more than the equity in the property (fair market value less the total dollar amount of the liens, if any, that will survive the foreclosure sale). So how does one discover fair market value? Again, it is a question of getting the right information. One of the best ways to do this is to obtain a comparative market analysis or broker price opinion (BPO) from a realtor.

Last-Minute Bankruptcies

Foreclosures can be rendered void by last-minute bankruptcy filings. Some professional investors will check with the bankruptcy clerk's office the morning of the sale to make sure that the borrower has not filed under any chapter of the U.S. Bankruptcy Code *before* they bid on the property. A prudent practice. Note that the bankruptcy clerk's office opens at 9 a.m. and bidding commences at 10 a.m. Checking bankruptcy filings is a wise precaution if the borrower has previously filed or threatened bankruptcy. It can be cumbersome and inconvenient to get money back from a trustee on a void sale; plus, there are lost time and opportunity costs to consider.

Conduct of the Sale

Foreclosure sales in the larger counties can seem chaotic, with many sales going on at once. There are two general types: sales by trustees (usually attorneys) for individual and institutional lenders and sales by the county sheriff for unpaid taxes. Sales are held at the location designated by the commissioners of the county where the property is located—often the courthouse steps or close by.

The sale is conducted by the named trustee unless a substitute trustee has been duly appointed and notice of the appointment has been filed of record. Tex. Prop. Code Sec. 51.0074(a). As a practical matter, the foreclosing trustee is usually the attorney for the lender. However, the trustee "must act with absolute impartiality and with fairness to all concerned." *First Fed. Sav. & Loan Assoc. of Dallas v. Sharp*, 359 S.W.2d 902, 904 (Tex. 1962). Before the day of sale, a trustee should obtain written instructions from the lender clearly directing that the sale be conducted and addressing any special circumstances that may arise (e.g., in the event of a credit bid).

There is no standard or required statutory script for a trustee to follow in auctioning property, although it is a good idea for a trustee to have one prepared. Before the bidding begins, a trustee may set "reasonable conditions" for the sale and the bidding (Tex. Prop. Code Sec. 51.0075(a))—for example, terms of payment requiring either cash or cashier's check. Trustees then usually go on to recite the details of the note and lien, the fact that the note went into default, proper notice was given, the note was subsequently accelerated, the property was duly posted for foreclosure, and the property is now for sale to the highest bidder. As noted above, the trustee has a duty to conduct the sale fairly and impartially and not discourage bidding in any way (this can result in "chilled bidding," which is a defect).

Bidding at the Sale

The lender often bids the amount of the debt plus accrued fees and costs, so this bid can be anticipated. If the sale generates proceeds in excess of the debt, the trustee must distribute the excess funds to other lienholders in order of seniority and the remaining balance, if any, to the borrower.

Chapter 22 of the Business & Commerce Code requires a winning bidder (other than the foreclosing mortgagee or mortgage servicer) to supply the trustee with certain information pertaining to the buyer's identity, including name, address, taxpayer number, and photo ID. Failure to supply such information may result in the trustee may canceling the sale. Clearly this statute has implications for a purchaser whose goal is to remain anonymous. If anonymity is important, an investor should anticipate these requirements and establish an entity such as an LLC for these purposes.

If the investor is the successful bidder, he or she should be prepared to make payment "without delay" or within a mutually agreed-upon time. In order to be prepared, seasoned bidders carry with them some cash plus an assortment of cashier's checks in different amounts made payable to "Trustee." If the high bidder is for any reason unable to complete the purchase, then the trustee will reopen the bidding and auction the property again. The successful bidder will, within a reasonable time, receive a trustee's deed or substitute trustee's deed which conveys the interest that was held by the borrower in the property—no more, no less.

Property Code Section 51.009 states that a buyer at a foreclosure sale "acquires the foreclosed property 'as is' without any expressed or implied warranties, except as to warranties of title, and at the purchaser's own risk; and is not a consumer." The "consumer" part of that statement is meant to prevent any DTPA claims.

Elapsed Time

Compared to other states, Texas has a streamlined non-judicial foreclosure process that is nearly as quick as an eviction. The minimum amount of time from the first notice to the day of foreclosure is 41 days, unless the deed of trust is a FNMA form, in which case the time is 51 days, although it is never wise to cut *any* legal deadline that close. Why risk a void sale or give the borrower a possible wrongful foreclosure claim?

The advantage of a foreclosure over an eviction is that there are no effective defenses to the foreclosure process except for the borrower to block it with a temporary restraining order or file bankruptcy. For either option, the buyer needs money and probably an attorney.

Rescission of a Non-Judicial Foreclosure Sale

Property Code Section 51.016 permits a non-judicial foreclosure sale to be rescinded by a mortgagee, a trustee, or a substitute trustee within 15 days under certain specific circumstances: if the legal requirements of the sale were not met; if the borrower cured the default before the sale was conducted; if it turns out that a receivership or dependent probate administration was in effect; if a condition of sale set by the trustee was not complied with; or if the borrower filed bankruptcy and there was an automatic stay in effect when the sale took place. Written notice of the rescission must be given to the buyer (who gets his or her money back) and each debtor (who must return any excess profits). Anyone interested in challenging the rescission has 30 days to do so.

Deficiency Suits

In the event that proceeds of the foreclosure sale exceed the amount due on the note (including attorney's fees and expenses), then surplus funds must be distributed to the borrower. More often, however, the price at which the property is sold at foreclosure is less than the unpaid balance on the loan, resulting in a deficiency. A suit may be brought by the lender to recover this deficiency any time within two years of the date of foreclosure. Tex. Prop. Code Sec. 51.003. Federally-insured lenders have four years.

As part of a defense to a deficiency suit, the borrower may challenge the foreclosure sales price if it is below fair market value, and receive appropriate credit if it is not. Tex. Prop. Code Sec. 51.003(b). Note that "fair market value" is, according to the statute, determined by reference to the foreclosure sales price—at least if the borrower does not exercise its right to have a court determine this number. The argument by one lender that fair market value should be computed according to the amount for which the bank later sold the property has been rejected. *PlainsCapital Bank v. Martin*, No. 13-0337 (Tex. 2015).

Any money received by a lender from private mortgage insurance is credited to the account of the borrower. One case states that the purpose of this "is to prevent mortgagees from recovering more than their due."

What happens when multiple sources of collateral secure the same loan? Should a deficiency amount be determined after each individual property sale or after all sales are completed? The answer, of course, could have serious consequences for the borrower's aggregate personal liability. The 14th Court of Appeals in Houston affirmed that it was necessary to look at the big picture and consider whether or not a deficiency exists after all properties have been foreclosed upon. *Marhaba Partners Limited Partnership v. Kindron Holdings, LLC*, 457 S.W.3d 208 (Tex.App.—Houston [14th Dist.] 2015, pet. denied).

For borrowers on non-homestead properties, deficiencies can be as significant a loss as the foreclosure itself since the IRS deems the deficiency amount to be taxable ordinary income.

Servicemembers Civil Relief Act

The Servicemembers Civil Relief Act (or SCRA found at 50 U.S.C. App. Sec. 501 et seq.) provides protections for those serving in the armed forces. For example, except by court order, a landlord may not evict a servicemember or dependents from the homestead during military service. The SCRA provides criminal sanctions for persons who knowingly violate its provisions.

Right of Redemption

There is no general right of redemption by a borrower after a Texas foreclosure. The right of redemption is limited to:

(1) *Sale for unpaid taxes.* After foreclosure for unpaid taxes, the former owner of homestead or agricultural property has a two-year right of redemption (Tax Code Sec. 34.21a). The investor is entitled to a redemption premium of 25% in the first year and 50% in the second year of the redemption period, plus recovery of certain costs that include property insurance and repairs or improvements required by code, ordinance, or a lease in effect on the date of sale. For other types of property (i.e., non-homestead), the redemption period is 180 days and the redemption premium is limited to 25%.

(2) *HOA foreclosure of an assessment lien.* Property Code Section 209.011 provides that a homeowner may redeem the property until no "later than the 180th day after the date the association mails written notice of the sale to the owner and the lienholder under Section 209.101." A lienholder also has a right of redemption in these circumstances "before 90 days after the date the association mails written notice . . . and only if the lot owner has not previously redeemed." These provisions are part of the Texas Residential Property Owners Protection Act designed to reign in the once arbitrary power of HOAs (Chapter 209 of the Code). Note that an HOA is not permitted to foreclose on a homeowner if its lien is solely for fines assessed by the association or attorney fees.

"It has long been the practice of in Texas to liberally construe redemption statutes in favor of redemption. [However, for] redemption under Section. 209.011 the owners . . . bear the burden at trial of proving a right to redemption." The burden is carried when the homeowner demonstrates substantial compliance with the statute. *Laguan v. Lloyd*, 493 S.W.3d 720, 723-24 (Tex.App.—Houston [1st Dist.] 2016, no pet.).

A prudent investor should be prepared to hold the property and avoid either making substantial improvements to it or reselling it until after any applicable rights of redemption have expired, even though redemption is statistically unlikely. Read chapter 45, *Redemption Issues for Investors*.

Post-Foreclosure Eviction

Foreclosure gives the new owner *title*; the next step is to obtain *possession*, and the procedure for doing this is outlined in the previous chapter. It is generally necessary to give the usual 3-day notice to vacate and file a forcible detainer petition in justice court. After judgment, the new owner must wait until the constable posts a 48-hour notice on the door and then forcibly removes a former borrower if that person is otherwise unwilling to leave.

An investor should build eviction costs into the budget from the beginning. It is advisable to hire an attorney for the first couple of evictions, after which an investor will likely be prepared to handle them solo. Never, however, attempt to conduct an eviction appeal to county court without an attorney.

Stopping a Foreclosure Sale

It is a myth that lawyers can wave a wand and, with a phone call or nasty letter, stop foreclosure. Attorneys have no such power. It is a fact that foreclosure *can* be stopped, but the only sure way to do so is to file a lawsuit *and* successfully persuade a judge to issue a temporary restraining order *prior* to the foreclosure sale. After the sale occurs, the remedy that remains—a suit for wrongful foreclosure—is slightly different. Relief may be limited to a money judgment if the property was sold at foreclosure to a third party for cash (a bona fide purchaser or "BFP"). If a BFP is in the mix, the possibility that the property itself can be recovered by the borrower is near zero.

Clients will often report that they have been engaged in reinstatement negotiations with the lender, usually consisting of phone calls and messages, and ask if that is sufficient to avoid a scheduled foreclosure. The answer is a resounding *no*. Unless there is payment of the arrearage *and* a signed reinstatement agreement, the foreclosure will almost certainly go forward, even if the client was talking settlement with the lender just the day before. Note that reinstatement agreements must be in writing and signed by both parties. *Phone calls mean nothing in this business.*

Borrowers occasionally assert that since a note has been sold multiple times, and the chain of transfers may be unclear, the foreclosing entity is not the lawful owner or holder of the debt. Unfortunately for this argument, the Property Code does not require the foreclosing party to first prove that it is either the owner or the holder of the note. *EverBank, N.A. v. Seedergy Ventures, Inc.*, 499 S.W.3d 534 (Tex.App.—Houston [14th Dist.] 2016, no pet.). Nor does it do any good to claim that the deed of trust lien was not properly assigned; in Texas, the rule is that the mortgage follows the note. Texas courts liberally construe alleged clerical defects in favor of the noteholder.

Clients will sometimes state that they don't want to sue the lender; they just want to get a restraining order to stop the foreclosure. The lawyer must reply "Sorry, it doesn't work that way, you can't split the two." A restraining order is an ancillary form of relief, meaning that it arises from an underlying suit. In other words, there must be an actual lawsuit in place to provide a basis for requesting a TRO. Fortunately, the suit and application for the TRO can be filed simultaneously and a hearing obtained usually within a day or two.

There is an additional issue: a borrower must have grounds for legal action or possibly face penalties for filing a frivolous suit. Some clients have difficulty understanding this. "Why," they ask, "can't you just go and get a TRO for me?" The answer is that the lawyer must first file a lawsuit that contains some credible basis for relief and then make an argument with a straight face before a judge in order to get a TRO. Having said that, if such a credible basis exists, then obtaining a TRO should not be difficult although it will be only short-term in its effect—up to 14 days. It is much more of a challenge to convert the TRO into a temporary injunction after the TRO expires. The posting of a bond is also required. See chapter 40, *Texas Litigation*.

A Pre-Foreclosure TRO is a Better Remedy

As a general rule, it is far better for a borrower to obtain a restraining order to stop a foreclosure than it is to bring suit after the fact. Texas law favors the finality of foreclosures, making wrongful foreclosure suits an uphill battle. If the property was sold to a third party who has no knowledge of any claims or alleged defects there is little chance that the borrower will get the property back. The third party is a protected BFP, and any remedy for the borrower will therefore likely be limited to monetary damages. Bottom line? If in doubt about whether or not a foreclosure is going to occur, file suit and attempt to get a temporary restraining order to stop it. "Wait and see" is the worst possible strategy in this case, since it is always more difficult to correct the situation after the foreclosure sale has occurred. The judge will likely ask without much sympathy, "Why, since you knew about these various alleged defects, did you not take action to stop the foreclosure?"

The key to a pre-foreclosure remedy is a temporary restraining order. A TRO is considered an emergency short-term measure necessary to avoid irreparable harm. Its purpose is to preserve the status quo (up to 14 days) until the court can hold a hearing to determine whether a temporary injunction (TI) should be granted. *In re Newton*, 146 S.W.3d

648, 651 (Tex. 2004). The TI—the second step in the process—goes further and freezes the current state of affairs until a trial on the merits can be held. See Civil Practice & Remedies Code Chapter 65 for the rules on injunctions.

So why don't more people sue to stop a foreclosure? Money. A person in financial distress will have difficulty coming up with both cash for legal fees and money for the TRO bond. Here is the blunt truth: if a borrower or investor cannot readily write a substantial retainer check to an attorney for purposes of suing a lender, then that person probably has no business in the expensive world of litigation.

Wrongful Foreclosure Suits

"Wrongful foreclosure" is not technically a proper cause of action under Texas law, at least not standing alone, so the plaintiff-borrower must specifically allege certain facts or defects in order to state a cause of action in state court. A suit for wrongful foreclosure may be maintained if there are grounds for alleging that the loan documents (e.g., the note and deed of trust) were defective in some way (e.g., if the notices leading up to the foreclosure were done or timed incorrectly or if there was some alleged impropriety in the sale itself); the property was sold for a grossly inadequate sales price; <u>and</u> (3) a causal connection can be shown between the defect and the grossly inadequate sales price. *Martins v. BAC Home Loans Servicing, L.P.*, 722 F.3d 249, 253 (5th Cir. 2013), *Sauceda v. GMAC Mortg. Corp.*, 268 S.W.3d 135, 139 (Tex.App.—Corpus Christi 2008, no pet.). "For a party to recover damages for wrongful foreclosure and breach of the deed of trust, he must show that he has suffered a loss or material injury as the result of an irregularity in the foreclosure sale. In general, this is shown where the actions of the lender or note holder have caused the property to be sold for a grossly inadequate price." *Wells Fargo Bank v. Robinson*, 391 S.W.3d 590, 594 (Tex.App.—Dallas 2012, no pet.).

As a matter of practicality, wrongful foreclosure suits based on defective notice nearly always go nowhere. Most large lenders are represented by law firms who know quite well how to write proper foreclosure notice and demand letters. What about the argument that the notices were sent to the wrong address? Remember, in Texas the lender's obligation is to send these notices to the borrower's last address as shown in the lender's files. The burden is on the borrower to "show that the mortgage servicer held in its records the most recent address of the debtor and failed to mail a notice by certified mail to that address," which is a challenging burden to carry. *Saravia v. Benson*, 433 S.W.3d 658 (Tex.App.—Houston [14th Dist.] 2014, no pet.).

Another common borrower tactic is to demand that the plaintiff lender in a deficiency action produce the original note as a prerequisite to getting a judgment. In spite of the popularity of the "show-me-the-note" theory on the Internet, it is entirely ineffective in Texas, since under Texas law "the note and deed of trust are severable . . . . Although a mortgagee must give notice and follow other specified procedures, there is no requirement that the mortgagee possess or produce the note that the deed of trust secures in order to conduct a non-judicial foreclosure." *Morlock, L.L.C. v. Bank of New York*, 448 S.W.3d 514 (Tex.App.—Houston [1st Dist.] 2014, pet. denied); also *Martins*, 722 f.3d at 255. In a digital world, there is diminishing sanctity and value to be found in a hard-copy document with an original wet-ink signature.

If any doubt remained that clerical defects and discrepancies do not void a foreclosure in Texas, then the door to that argument was nailed shut by *Edwards v. Fannie Mae*, 545, S.W.3d 169 (Tex.App.—El Paso 2017, pet. denied). In that case, the foreclosure documentation did not even reference the correct note and deed of trust. The court nonetheless dismissed such concerns because the property and the parties were the same and sufficient links existed to establish that the foreclosure should pass master. After all, the court reasoned, certain "inaccuracies in mass-produced loan documents and foreclosure paperwork" are inevitable.

If a wrongful foreclosure suit is being considered, it should be filed quickly so that notice of the suit (a notice of lis pendens—see chapter 6) can be filed in the real property records. If the lender was the successful bidder, this notice may effectively prevent the lender from transferring the property to a BFP.

The action available under Property Code Section 51.004 (discussed above) is different from a wrongful foreclosure remedy per se. Relief is granted if the court finds that the fair market value is greater than the sale price, but only in the context of a deficiency claimed by the lender.

The cruel fact for borrowers is that wrongful foreclosure suits face challenges from the beginning. A plaintiff can realistically expect the following in a wrongful foreclosure lawsuit: (1) the lender will *not* rush to settle, since lenders pay high fees to large litigation firms to fight tooth and nail to avoid doing the right thing; (2) written discovery (interrogatories, requests for production, and requests for admission) from the plaintiff will be nearly entirely objected to by lender's counsel, so extensively as to make the responses essentially useless (a deposition will therefore be required); and (3) lender's counsel will remove the case from state court to federal court where judges are more conservative and lenders can use Federal Rule 12(b)(6) to dismiss the case.

Note that other grounds for suit may be available to a plaintiff borrower, including breach of contract, common-law fraud, statutory fraud, negligent misrepresentation, and violations of either the federal or state debt collection practices acts. The typical "wrongful foreclosure suit" may recite such causes of action in addition to allegations of procedural defect and inadequate sales price. These sometimes work if the lender's misbehavior is egregious. By contrast, allegations of deceptive trade practices under the DTPA will likely fail, since a "person cannot qualify as a consumer if the underlying transaction is a pure loan because money is considered neither a good nor a service." *Fix v. Flagstar Bank*, FSB, 242 S.W.3d 147, 159 (Tex.App.—Fort Worth 2007, pet. denied).

Removal of a Wrongful Foreclosure Case to Federal Court

Removal of the case by the defendant-lender to federal court is allowed if there is a federal question (which there nearly always is) or if diversity exists (if the amount in controversy exceeds $75,000 and the parties are from different states), which is also common. The reality is that much if not most Texas home mortgage litigation of any significance now takes place in federal court. As noted above, removal facilitates the use of federal Rule 12(b)(6), which has been effectively weaponized by lenders as a means of getting rid of plaintiffs who allege lender misconduct. The standard applied is whether or not borrower's complaint fails "to state a claim upon which relief can be granted." Since such dismissals happen often, federal district court has effectively become a graveyard of wrongful foreclosure cases that were initially filed in state court.

Removal to federal court can also create complications for the attorney representing the borrower, who may be accustomed to practicing in state rather than federal court. Even if licensed in federal court (not all lawyers are), an attorney may be reluctant to switch venues since federal practice has become more of a specialty in recent years. Often, therefore, the plaintiff must go through a change of lawyers as a result of the removal.

The deadline for lender's counsel to remove a case to federal court is 30 days after the lender is served.

Prolonged Negotiations for a Modification

Clients often report that they were engaged in prolonged negotiations to modify their existing loan prior to the foreclosure sale. Of course, these communications were usually conducted by phone and there is no signed written agreement binding the lender to stop the sale, so there is likely no basis for a wrongful foreclosure suit. Do lenders pursue this strategy intentionally, so as to make it appear that they are willing to be reasonable, when in fact it is in their interest to foreclose instead? Opinions vary. In 2018, Wells Fargo—already in the midst of scandal as result of creating millions of fake accounts, assessing unfair mortgage fees, and charging customers for car insurance they did not request or need—admitted that it had wrongfully foreclosed upon hundreds of borrowers, citing a software error.

If the parties make an agreement to hold off on a scheduled foreclosure, then that should be evidenced by a signed forbearance or standstill agreement. Without such a signed agreement, there is very little to keep the lender from proceeding to a foreclosure sale while still negotiating with the borrower or the borrower's attorney. An email exchange is not sufficient for this purpose. In any case, modifying a loan that exceeds $50,000 is subject to the statute of frauds and requires a signed writing.

What a Lawyer Needs from a Client Wanting to Foreclose

First and foremost, the lawyer needs to see the foreclosing client's deed, note, and deed of trust. Most foreclosures that arrive in law offices involve documents that the attorney did not personally write. *Anyone* could have written them, including the client himself (there are lots of DIY real estate investors out there who, by and large, are their own worst enemies when it comes to legal documentation). So the documents must be evaluated first. Are they legally valid? Were the deed and deed of trust recorded? Who is the current owner and holder of the note, and does the holder have possession of the original? Is there a guarantor? Have there been any modifications, express or implied, since the original note was executed? What are the timeline requirements for notice of default and opportunity to cure? Who is the trustee named in the deed of trust, and will a substitute trustee have to be appointed? Has the borrower filed bankruptcy? What is the exact nature of the default (monetary or technical)? Does the property itself have any legal issues (e.g., environmental)? Are there other liens against the property, and how does the client's lien rank among these? Is there the possibility of an IRS lien? If so, a title report should be ordered. Has the client already given some sort of notice? Notices given by clients who have not yet consulted an attorney can be problematic at best (and have to be re-done with correct notices) or, at worst, may contain offers of settlement that might (or might not) have been accepted by means of the parties' course of conduct. All of these factors must be scrutinized before an attorney should even consider accepting a foreclosure case. Accordingly, every foreclosure case should begin with a consultation that includes a thorough document review.

Obtaining a title report (or "down date" as it is sometimes called) may also be prudent under the circumstances. Who knows what has been recorded against the property since the last title policy was issued? Such filings could potentially affect the course of the foreclosure process as well as notices that may be required.

Chapter 40

TEXAS LITIGATION – A PROCESS OVERVIEW

A Nuts and Bolts Tour for Investors

This chapter discusses basic rules and procedures involved in Texas litigation. For our purposes, "litigation" refers to the filing and prosecuting of a real estate-related lawsuit, or defense against one, in the Texas county civil courts at law or the civil district courts. We will not discuss divorce cases, criminal defense, or litigation in federal court.

The cost and complexity of litigation has doubled in the last 10 years, in no small measure due to the impact of computers and technology. What is *capable* of being done with all our electronic gadgets is now *expected* to be done. Ironically, the result is more, not less, paper. A prime culprit is the "docket control order" or DCO, also called a "scheduling order," generated by the clerk's computer shortly after the lawsuit is filed. In times past these orders contained only a few dates, including the discovery completion date, the date by which experts were to be designated, and a trial date. DCOs have now expanded to include many more dates and deadlines. Meeting dates and deadlines not only costs money but is the attorney's professional obligation, to the client and to the court. Attorneys must therefore be prudent when signing on as attorney of record. The attorney must not only be confident that the case has merit but that the client has the commitment and financial means to pursue litigation at today's level of complexity and expense.

In contemplating filing or defending against a lawsuit, one should keep in mind three cardinal rules, which shock clients when they learn them: (1) *There is no such thing as a perfect case and yes, that includes yours*; (2) *no one ever gets exactly what they want in court and yes, that includes you*; and (3) *litigation always costs more than you think it will.*

References to rules in this chapter are to the Texas Rules of Civil Procedure.

Why worry about legal fees? Aren't all lawsuits handled by contingency fee?

No. Contingency fee arrangements are usually unavailable in real estate and business cases (since there is generally no insurance pot of gold at the end of the rainbow) so the client will be required to post a substantial initial retainer and then pay hourly. Many real estate and business attorneys require an initial retainer of around $10,000 (plus costs such as filing fees) with supplementary retainer installments to follow. Larger or more specialized firms may require up to $25,000 up front. There is a reason for these retainers. For attorneys, there are few situations more frustrating than being in a lawsuit governed by a complicated DCO while stuck with a client who cannot or will not pay the bills for the work that order requires.

Evaluating the Case

A good case consists of (1) facts that clearly show liability, and (2) monetary damages in an amount that makes the process worthwhile. *Both factors must be present.* Good liability facts are not helpful if there is no real monetary loss; and large damages will not help a plaintiff who cannot show a clear path to holding the defendant legally liable. One or more established causes of action (fraud or breach of contract, for example) must apply. Note that *legal* liability is not the same as *moral* liability. The justice system, like every human institution, is imperfect. It is not only unable but unwilling to right every wrong

As a rule of thumb, there should be at least $25,000 in actual damages to make it worthwhile to file a suit in county or district court. Plaintiffs with $5,000 and $10,000 cases should consider filing a small claims action in justice court where an attorney is not required. Otherwise, such cases are not cost-effective. The days when it was reasonable to hire an attorney for a low-damage claim are gone. A breach-of-contract claim in a real estate transaction of, say, $2,500 is *not* the basis for a lawsuit. It is more appropriately considered a collection item or a business write-off.

If an investor is contemplating litigation, the first step is to consult with a real estate litigator to go over the facts, review and analyze documents, and evaluate the potential for success. At the initial meeting, the client should be prepared with copies of all relevant documents and correspondence as well as a written summary and a timeline of events. The prospective litigant should also be ready to demonstrate that he or she can afford the litigation. If the client arrives prepared, most attorneys can evaluate a case in an hour. As is the case with major medical decisions, obtaining a second opinion may be a good idea.

Representing Oneself as a Pro Se Litigant

Because of mushrooming complexity, representing oneself as a pro se litigant is no longer practical for non-attorneys except in small claims cases in justice courts, which hear controversies involving up to $10,000. These courts are also handy because they are located in various neighborhood precincts. For many, justice court may be the best option, but even there one sees more and more attorneys at the bench, and few things are more foolish than a pro se litigant attempting to match wits or knowledge of the rules with a trial lawyer. It goes without saying that representing oneself at higher court levels—county court or district court—is inviting trouble. The Rules of Civil Procedure, the Civil Practice & Remedies Code, and the Rules of Evidence govern trial work. These are complicated even for lawyers who appear in court frequently. They can appear illogical, incomprehensible, and Byzantine to others.

Note that corporations and limited liability companies are required to have an attorney in Texas. They are not permitted to represent themselves, either in filing or answering a lawsuit.

Obligations of the Client

A client cannot expect to meet with an attorney, pay a retainer, and then walk away and forget about the lawsuit. The client must be an active and essential participant, since a case in litigation will involve considerable time, effort, and expense. Patience and persistence are also required since it can take nine months or so to move a case to trial, and there are invariably bumps in the road.

The attorney-client relationship is based on trust, candor, participation, and communication. A client should tell the attorney everything pertinent to the case and provide all relevant documents.

A plaintiff who does not know the location of the person or entity to be sued should be prepared to incur the expense of a private investigator.

Clients should resist the temptation to micro-manage a lawsuit. Reach an agreement with the attorney on general goals and strategy and then let him or her do the job. Even so, no attorney can ever make a guarantee concerning the outcome of a case. Attorneys are merely the agents of their clients within the system.

Jurisdiction

The term "jurisdiction" has three aspects: first, whether a particular court is enabled by law to handle certain subjects ("subject-matter jurisdiction"); second, whether damages fall within certain monetary limits ("monetary jurisdiction"); and third, whether the court has jurisdiction over the parties and property involved ("personal jurisdiction" and "*in rem* jurisdiction," respectively). All of these requirements must be satisfied.

County courts and district courts have subject-matter jurisdiction over the full range of real estate and business matters. However, in certain counties other than Harris County, matters pertaining to title to real estate must be brought in district court. Justice courts have original jurisdiction over possession of real property, so evictions must be brought there.

County courts have monetary jurisdiction up to $100,000. District courts can hear cases that exceed $500 in value, and there is no upper limit. Often, but not always, litigation in county court is cheaper and faster than in district courts.

Venue

Venue refers to the county in which a lawsuit is brought. Pursuant to Civ. Prac. & Rem. Code Sec. 15.002, one cannot file suit just anywhere. Venue is proper in a particular county if (1) all or a substantial part of the events or omissions giving rise to the claim occurred in that county; or (2) the defendant resides in that county or, if a corporation or other registered entity, does business there; or (3) the real property the subject of the suit lies in that county. If suit is filed in the wrong county, the opposing party will likely make a special appearance in order to ask for a change of venue. Failing to pay attention to proper venue results in wasted time and money.

Causes of Action

In order to be an effective lawsuit, a case must meet all the required elements of one or more causes of action. Causes of action derive from common law (legal history and tradition) and from specific statutes. Examples:

>
> breach of contract and specific performance
> breach of express or implied warranty
> common law fraud
> statutory fraud
> conversion
> negligence
> deceptive trade practices
> conspiracy
> wrongful foreclosure
> slander of title
> suit to quiet title
> trespass to try title
> suit for specific performance

suit for declaratory judgment

violation of real estate license act

These causes of action are common in real estate litigation. There are, of course, many more.

Specific Performance of Contracts

Specific performance of real estate contracts is an issue that arises with sufficient frequency as to merit special attention. What do you do when an opposite party fails to perform a valid contract? The answer may be a suit alleging breach of contract and seeking an order compelling the other party to do what that party agreed to do. "Specific performance is an equitable remedy that may be awarded, at the trial court's discretion, for a breach of contract . . . and is an alternative remedy to damages. When the recovery of monetary damages is inadequate to compensate the complainant, the transgressor is compelled to perform the promise of its contract . . . Specific performance is not a separate cause of action, but rather it is an equitable remedy used as a substitute for monetary damages when such damages would not be adequate." *Marx v. FDP, LP,* 474 S.W.3d 368 (Tex.App—San Antonio 2015, no pet.).

The remedy of specific performance, as a practical matter, is more effective against a breaching seller than a breaching buyer. In the case of a seller breach, one is demanding the acknowledged signature of the seller on a deed and other documents, which is not a major burden in practical terms. It is a different situation in the case of a buyer. In the real world, it is difficult to force a buyer to apply for a loan, sign a note and deed of trust, and so forth. Disappointed sellers are most often in the position of keeping the buyer's earnest money and moving on.

Injunctions

Injunctive relief (a temporary restraining order or temporary injunction) may also be requested after suit is filed. Injunctions are useful in preventing another party from taking certain action, such as foreclosure, that will cause irreparable harm to the applicant (Rule 680) for which there is no adequate remedy at law (i.e., an award of damages will not cure the prospective harm). A temporary restraining order (TRO) is a form of emergency, equitable relief that is good up to 14 days. A TRO is granted, if at all, after notice to both sides and a hearing. A temporary injunction (TI)—which is the next step in the process after the TRO expires—requires a more thorough hearing, usually a mini-trial, at which the applicant must show a likelihood of prevailing upon the merits at trial of the case. A TI usually remains in effect for the duration of the litigation.

Finally, a permanent injunction may be granted as part of a judgment and is usually for an indefinite period. Civ. Prac. & Rem. Code Chap. 65.

Note that a bond is always required if a TRO or TI is granted. The amount can be nominal (say, $100) or it can be more significant. Bonds in the amount of $5,000, $10,000, or $20,000 are common, although the amount can be set much higher depending on the circumstances of the case and the inclinations of the judge. The amount of the bond is discretionary with the judge and is designed to protect the interests of the party against whom injunctive relief is awarded—in case, for instance, the plaintiff's case is ultimately shown to have no merit.

An applicant for a TRO or TI needs to be prepared to post the cash (which is refundable if the applicant prevails in the case) within 24 hours of the hearing or utilize the services of a bondsman to do so. Bondsmen will require 10-20% of the bond amount as a non-refundable premium as well as collateral (e.g., a lien on real estate). *Do not ask your attorney to seek a TRO or TI unless you have sufficient resources with which to post a bond.*

No one has a right to a TRO or TI. Whether either can be obtained depends on several factors including the attitude and charitable disposition of the judge. Generally, the plaintiff must be prepared to show that her or she has a legitimate cause of action against the defendant; there is a probability that the relief requested will be granted upon trial of the case; and, if injunctive relief is not granted immediately, there will be imminent and irreparable harm to the plaintiff that will not be adequately addressed by a subsequent damages remedy. *Kennedy v. Gulf Coast Cancer & Diagnostic Ctr. At Se., Inc.*, 326 S.W.3d 352, 359 (Tex.App.—Houston [1st Dist.] 2010, no pet.). The outcome of an application for a TRO or TI is never automatic or guaranteed. For the attorney, an application for injunctive relief adds a significant layer of complexity and expense to a lawsuit and can therefore be expected to substantially increase the client's legal fees.

Discovery

"Discovery" refers to mechanisms for obtaining information, documents, and tangible things about an opponent's case. Tex. R. Civ. P. 190 et seq. Discovery can be divided generally into written discovery (requests for disclosure, interrogatories, requests for admission, and requests for production) and depositions of parties, witnesses, and experts. Discovery is necessary and it is expensive. No modern case can be effectively litigated without doing thorough discovery, which is at least partially responsible for soaring costs. The period for discovery can go on for quite a while (months), although the docket control order usually contains a date by which discovery must be completed.

Generally, lawyers prefer to do written discovery first and then, as needed, take oral depositions. It should be noted that this system is broken. Many lawyers who bill by the hour can be intentionally obstructionist by objecting to a broad swath of even routine interrogatories and production requests. This is at best contrary to the spirit of the rules, at worst unethical. The net effect of objecting to everything is to make oral depositions inevitable, since the inquiring party needs the information, one way or another, in order to prepare for trial. Depositions are time-consuming and expensive for the client, but for those lawyers who bill by the hour that is just fine. Chances are you will be doing at least two depositions in your case—yours and your opponent's. Average cost? Between the court reporter and legal fees, around $3,000 each.

Clients occasionally question the need to do discovery, hoping to avoid the expense, but attorneys know that it is always better to go to trial with thorough foreknowledge of the opponent's case. Their own clients will be the first to blame them if they do not. A lawyer will usually prefer to fire a client who insists on cutting discovery costs rather than risk harm to his or her reputation by going to trial unprepared on the facts.

Motions for Summary Judgment

A motion for summary judgment is an attempt to dispose of all or part of the case without proceeding to a full trial on the merits. Tex. R. Civ. P. 166a. Such a motion may be partial, i.e., limited in scope to certain issues or certain parties, or it may affect the entire case. Disposition by summary judgment is proper only when the movant establishes there are no genuine issues of material fact such that the movant is entitled to judgment as a matter of law. That's a high standard. In evaluating a motion for summary judgment, the reviewing court must "indulge every reasonable inference in favor of the non-movant and resolve any in its favor." *Nixon v. Mr. Property Mgmt.*, 690 S.W.2d 546, 548 (Tex. 1985). Therefore, all evidence favorable to the non-movant will be taken as true and all doubts must be resolved in the non-movant's favor—meaning the non-movant gets the benefit of the doubt across the board as to the merits of its case. The practical result is that summary judgments are difficult to obtain. Judges are reluctant to deprive a party of his or her day in court.

MSJs are useful, however, when one wants to address just part of the dispute—possession of real property, for instance, leaving issues of title for trial. Or an MSJ may be a way to remove a party from a suit if that party was sued improperly in an individual capacity. In any case, MSJ hearings are limited to lawyer argument supported by documentary evidence and affidavits. Live witness testimony is not allowed.

One of the most basic criterion by which an attorney evaluates a case is whether or not it will survive an MSJ by the other side.

Mediation

Parties should expect to mediate, like it or not, since most judge's order it automatically (it is usually one of the deadlines in the DCO). All judges will order mediation if either side requests it. It may be for a half day or a full day. It is voluntary in the sense that neither side is obligated to accept any particular outcome. All aspects of mediation are confidential and (like settlement discussions) cannot later be brought up in court.

The cost of the mediator's services is usually $500 to $700 per side for a half-day. Clients must come to mediation prepared with a cashier's check or money order payable to the mediator. This is collected before mediation begins. Attorney fees are in addition to this amount. While some may consider this expensive, mediation is nonetheless far cheaper than going forward with trial of the case.

Clients should also come to mediation prepared to be reasonable, since it is seldom that anyone in the legal system gets exactly what he or she wants. No attorney wants a client who will not mediate or will not mediate in good faith. Incentives for settlement at mediation include (1) the cost and aggravation of continued litigation, and (2) having certainty and control over the outcome, rather than leaving it to a judge or jury who can return unpredictable and even whimsical results. Any experienced lawyer has stories about times when he or she was shocked and dumbfounded by an unexpected verdict.

See chapter 42 for details on the mediation process.

Jury Trial Versus Trial to the Judge

Jury trials are more suitable in cases where one desires to inflame the passions of jurors in order to get a bigger verdict. This is more likely in personal injury (tort) cases than in real estate or business cases, where issues of blood and malice are usually (but not always) absent. In the latter, technical questions of contract law and the like are often best left for a judge to decide (rather than sending these issues to a jury) since the judge has the training and expertise and hears similar cases often.

Phases of the Case

The litigation process can be broken down into predictable phases:

Initial Pleadings and Discovery

    original petition or original answer
    application for temporary restraining order (TRO)
    hearing to convert TRO to Temporary Injunction (TI)
    ongoing attorney-client conferences
    settlement negotiations with the opposition
    written discovery
        requests for disclosure
        interrogatories
        requests for admission
        requests for production

Continuing Discovery/Motions/Mediation Phase

    responding to written discovery
    amending pleadings, including filing a counter-claim or cross action
    hearings on various motions
    half-day mediation
    continuing settlement negotiations
    oral depositions
    motion for summary judgment
    locate experts and obtain expert reports
    ongoing attorney-client conferences

Pre-Trial Phase

    ascertain compliance with docket control order
    final amendment of pleadings
    additional motions, if appropriate
    supplementation of discovery responses
    designation of experts by the deadline
    business records affidavit
    pre-trial order preparation
    conferences with client to prepare testimony
    conferences with witnesses to prepare testimony
    pre-trial research and preparation
    correspondence and conversations with the opposition

Trial Phase

    trial of the case by judge or jury

entry of judgment

Post-Trial Phase

motion for new trial or defense of motion for new trial
request for findings of fact and conclusions of law
post-judgment discovery
abstraction, execution, and attempt to collect the judgment

The total time to trial is approximately nine to twelve months, varying from court to court and county to county. Cases are usually heard in the order of oldest first. They are set for a certain term of court (often one week in county courts and two weeks in district court). During this time, the attorney, the client, and the witnesses are all on call, which can be inconvenient and expensive (if, for instance, one must pay hourly experts to sit around and wait). There is a lot of sitting around and waiting involved in trial work.

Dismissal for Baseless Causes of Action—Rule 91a
The 82nd Legislature introduced a much-needed reform by creating Rule 91a, which provides that causes of action with no basis in law or fact may be dismissed within 45 days of the filing of an appropriate motion. It provides a dismissal remedy early in the process rather than having to wait for discovery to be completed to file a motion for summary judgment.

Expedited Trial
Another welcome rule change pertains to "expedited actions" for monetary relief not exceeding $100,000. Rules 47 and 169 now apply. Unfortunately—*very* unfortunately for real estate investors—this innovation does not apply to actions brought under the Property Code.

Judgment
Judgment may occur as a result of motion for full or partial summary judgment, a jury or bench trial, or by default if the defendant does not file a written answer. All parties must be notified. "When the final judgment or other appealable order is signed, the clerk of the court shall immediately give notice to the parties or their attorneys of record by first-class mail advising that the judgment or order was signed" (Rule 306(a)(3)). The judgment becomes final thirty days after the judge's signature unless there is a motion for new trial or other action by the defendant to vacate or modify the judgment.

A surprising number of judgments occur by default, but these are relatively easy to set aside if timely action is taken. Typical grounds include allegations of no service or defective service along with other technical defects. "A default judgment should be set aside and a new trial ordered in any case in which the failure of the defendant to answer was not intentional, or the result of conscious indifference . . . but was due to a mistake or accident; provided the motion for new trial sets up a meritorious defense and is filed at a time when the granting thereof will occasion no delay or otherwise work an injury to the plaintiff." *Craddock v. Sunshine Bus Lines, Inc.*, 133 S.W.2d 124 (Tex. 1939). The court goes on to state that this rule "prevents an injustice to the defendant without working an injustice on the plaintiff." Plaintiffs might of course disagree since swift recourse has now been delayed, but courts nonetheless take a forgiving attitude in this regard consistent with Texas' historical partiality in favor of debtors.

Once a judgment is final, the only means of attack is a bill of review. These are generally unsuccessful unless fraud was involved in obtaining the judgment. The complainant must assume "the burden of proving that the judgment was rendered as the result of the fraud, accident or wrongful act of the opposite party or official mistake unmisted with any negligence of his own. . . ." *Baker v. Goldsmith*, 582 S.W.2d 409 (Tex. 1979). Although the word "accident" is mentioned here, subsequent cases make it clear that some sort of fraud (concealment or misrepresentation), not just accident, will be required for a successful bill of review.

Collection on a Judgment

Collecting on a judgment against an individual is difficult in Texas because of homestead laws and the constitutional prohibition against garnishing wages. If the loser has no insurance coverage, collection can be a real problem. Similarly, satisfying a judgment against a corporation or LLC may be challenging if assets have been moved out of the company name or located in other jurisdictions. Attorneys are fond of saying that they could "paper the walls" of their offices with judgments obtained but never collected. That is the reality in Texas, especially when it comes to judgment debtors who are individuals.

Execution on a judgment is most likely to be successful when the defendant has cash in the bank, investment real estate, or a business with substantial inventory or receivables. If none of these is present, the plaintiff's best option may be to file an abstract of judgment in the real property records and hope that the defendant will sell property through a title company during the 10 years that the AJ remains on file. See chapter 43, *Judgments in Texas.*

Post-Judgment Discovery

Post-judgment discovery enables a creditor to determine whether or not he is dealing with a judgment-proof debtor or perhaps a debtor who negligently failed to make an asset protection plan and whose assets are widely exposed. Written discovery requires responses within 30 days unless an extension is granted. An oral deposition is also possible. The format and procedure is the same as for any trial deposition, except the focus is now on assets, their location, and their value.

Post-judgment discovery can be lengthy and brutal. Attempting to represent oneself in this process is the equivalent of swimming through piranha-infested waters.

Conclusion

A lawsuit is a business enterprise, and a tough and demanding one at that. It should never be taken personally. One function of the attorney is to help the client keep a cool head and evaluate the case rationally.

Legal fees and costs expended to pursue a suit represent a form of business investment. Alternatively, for instance, one could put that same money into stocks, real estate, or a gambling trip to Las Vegas. The client needs to estimate the rate of return on the investment in exchange for time, effort, and money expended. Putting dollars to work in a lawsuit represents an opportunity cost in economic terms, meaning those funds are not available for other uses. Clients who say these sorts of businesslike calculations are beside the point, that their suit is all about principle, are the first to tire of the process and quit, leaving their attorneys with unpaid bills and egg on their faces. Attorneys do not like to quit and they do not like to lose. Clients must have both the fortitude and the finances to support their attorney's efforts to thoroughly litigate and win the case.

Chapter 41

WHAT IS A DECEPTIVE TRADE PRACTICE?

Anything the Judge and Jury Say It Is

The Deceptive Trade Practices-Consumer Protection Act ("DTPA," found at Chapter 17 of the Texas Business & Commerce Code) was passed in 1973 to protect Texas consumers against unscrupulous sellers of consumer goods and services. Tex. Bus. & Com. Code Section 17.44(a) states that the DTPA "shall be liberally construed and applied to promote its underlying purposes, which are to protect consumers against false, misleading, and deceptive business practices, unconscionable actions, and breaches of warranty and to provide efficient and economical procedures to secure such protection." All states now have some version of this sort of law.

The enactment of the DTPA also provided a healthy subsidy to the plaintiffs' bar by creating a profitable avenue for collecting contingent fees—not good news for real estate investors. Anytime a plaintiff is relieved of the burden of raising legal fees and costs in order to pursue a lawsuit, then suits become both more numerous and harder to settle.

Originally one of the most progressive consumer protection laws in the U.S., the broad tools and remedies of the DTPA have been curtailed by amendments over the years, most significantly in 1995 when a conservative legislature riding the wave of tort reform (also referred to as "tort deform" if you are not a fan of those changes) amended the Act to include provisions more favorable to the defendant. The DTPA remains, however, a formidable consumer weapon.

The issue of whether or not real estate is a consumer good subject to DTPA remedies was resolved long ago. It is. *Chastain v. Koonce*, 700 S.W.2d 579, 582 (Tex. 1985). In fact, the definition of consumer good includes just about everything except intangibles such as accounts receivable, stock, and money.

Consumers

You must qualify as a consumer to seek relief under the DTPA. A "consumer" in the DTPA context may be an individual, partnership, corporation, LLC, or even a state agency. Excluded are business consumers with assets of 25 million or more. Suits may also be brought in the interest of consumers at large by the Texas attorney general's consumer protection division and, with the AG's consent, by local county and district attorneys.

Amazingly, it is not required that the consumer actually pay for the goods or services in question—only that the consumer must be seeking or in the process of acquiring them by means of either purchase or lease. *Martin v. Lou Poliquin Enterprises, Inc.,* 696 S.W.2d 180 (Tex.App.—Houston [14th Dist.] 1985). There is not even a requirement that the consumer be in privity (in a direct contractual or business relationship) with the defendant—only that the claimed violation occurred in connection with the consumer's transaction. *Amstad v. U.S. Brass Corp.,* 919 S.W.2d 644, 649 (Tex. 1996). The consumer is simply required to be the intended beneficiary of goods or services (a very broad requirement indeed). *Arthur Anderson & Co. v. Perry Equip. Corp.,* 945 S.W.2d 812, 815 (Tex. 1997). "The connection can be demonstrated by a representation that reaches the consumer or by a benefit from the second transaction to the initial seller." *Todd v. Perry Homes,* 156 S.W.3d 919, 922 (Tex.App.—Dallas 2005, no pet.).

A consumer may not sell, assign, or transfer his or her DTPA claim to another. *PPG Indus. v. JMB/Houston Ctrs. Partners,* 146 S.W.3d 79, 82 (Tex. 2004).

Certain Exemptions

Fortunately for attorneys and real estate brokers, their services fall within the professional services exemption of Section 17.49(c). This exemption is lost, however, in cases of fraud or misrepresentation. Since fraud is nearly always alleged in suits involving real estate, professionals in this area should expect to have to fight diligently to protect their status under this exemption.

Certain large transactions are also exempted under Section 17.49, although (significantly for real estate investors) the large transaction exemption does *not* apply in the case of a consumer's residence.

Causes of Action under the DTPA

If a real estate investor is sued, it is a given that allegations of deceptive trade practices will be among the causes of action. Note that DTPA causes of action are cumulative as to other remedies (Tex. Bus. & Com. Code Sec. 17.43), meaning that a plaintiff can throw not only DTPA allegations at a defendant but just about everything else from both statutory and common law except (perhaps) the kitchen sink, so long as the plaintiff can plausibly argue that the defendant's conduct was a "producing cause" of economic damages or damages for mental anguish. Tex. Bus. & Com. Code Sec. 17.50(a).

A related note: the DTPA states that in event the Act conflicts with the Property Code, then the Property Code provisions will prevail. Tex. Bus. & Com. Code Sec. 17.44(b).

The Statute

Business & Commerce Code Section 17.46(a) declares:

> **False, misleading, or deceptive acts or practices in the conduct of any trade or commerce are hereby declared unlawful and are subject to action by the consumer protection division under Sections 17.47, 17.58, 17.60, and 17.61 of this code.**

Section 17.46(b) of the DTPA also declares the following to be unlawful:

(1) passing off goods or services as those of another;

(2) causing confusion or misunderstanding as to the source, sponsorship, approval, or certification of goods or services;

(3) causing confusion or misunderstanding as to affiliation, connection, or association with, or certification by, another;

(4) using deceptive representations or designations of geographic origin in connection with goods or services;

(5) representing that goods or services have sponsorship, approval, characteristics, ingredients, uses, benefits, or quantities which they do not have or that a person has a sponsorship, approval, status, affiliation, or connection which he does not;

(6) representing that goods are original or new if they are deteriorated, reconditioned, reclaimed, used, or secondhand;

(7) representing that goods or services are of a particular standard, quality, or grade, or that goods are of a particular style or model, if they are of another;

(8) disparaging the goods, services, or business of another by false or misleading representation of facts;

(9) advertising goods or services with intent not to sell them as advertised;

(10) advertising goods or services with intent not to supply a reasonable expectable public demand, unless the advertisements disclosed a limitation of quantity;

(11) making false or misleading statements of fact concerning the reasons for, existence of, or amount of price reductions;

(12) representing that an agreement confers or involves rights, remedies, or obligations which it does not have or involve, or which are prohibited by law;

(13) knowingly making false or misleading statements of fact concerning the need for parts, replacement, or repair service;

(14) misrepresenting the authority of a salesman, representative or agent to negotiate the final terms of a consumer transaction;

(15) advertising of any sale by fraudulently representing that a person is going out of business;

(16) using or employing a chain referral sales plan . . . ;

(17) representing that a guarantee or warranty confers or involves rights or remedies which it does not have . . . ;

(18) promoting a pyramid promotional scheme, as defined by Section 17.461;

(19) representing that work or services have been performed on, or parts replaced in, goods when the work or services were not performed or the parts replaced;

(20) failing to disclose information concerning goods or services which was known at the time of the transaction if such failure to disclose such information was intended to induce the consumer into a transaction into which the consumer would not have entered had the information been disclosed.
. . .

Relief for Consumers

Section 17.50 spells out relief available to consumers. Basically, a consumer who claims to have suffered economic damages or damages for mental anguish may seek relief if the other party's action was a "producing cause" of the damages. That is a rather liberal standard, especially considering that most events in life and business have multiple causes—and the defendant's alleged action is required to be *only one of them*. Any offense enumerated in the laundry list of Section 17.46 is a basis for a consumer claim, so long as the defendant's actions were "relied on by a consumer to the consumer's detriment" (Sec. 17.50(B)).

Additionally, a consumer may file suit if the consumer has relied to that consumer's detriment upon:

17.50(a)(2) breach of an express or implied warranty;

17.50(a)(3) any unconscionable action or course of action by any person. . . .

Breach of warranty would seem to be reasonably clear. But what about "unconscionability?" Isn't that rather subjective? What exactly does it mean? It turns out that the key factor in unconscionability is the taking advantage of another who is less sophisticated and less informed—something real estate investors are accused of doing nearly every day in courts across Texas. *Insurance Co. of N. Am. v. Morris*, 981 S.W.2d 667,677 (Tex. 1998). Further, it is likely that a real estate investor will be considered the party with superior knowledge in nearly every encounter with a consumer, making it easier for a plaintiff to paint a picture of exploitation. This is true regardless of whether the investor is a real estate license holder or not.

In terms of seller disclosure requirements: *there is no doubt that failure by a seller of real property to disclose material adverse conditions and defects is a violation of the DTPA.* Refer to chapter 2 for more discussion of the obligation to disclose.

If a trial court determines that the defendant committed a deceptive act, breach of warranty, or unconscionable act *knowingly*, then the availability of treble damages plus attorney's fees is triggered (Sec. 17.50(b)(1)). Otherwise, a DTPA claim does not require that the consumer prove that the defendant acted knowingly or intentionally, at least so long as the plaintiff's objective is merely actual rather than exemplary damages. *Miller v. Keyser*, 90 S.W.3d 712, 716 (Tex. 2002). Note, however, that exemplary damages may be available to the plaintiff by other means—common law or statutory fraud, for instance.

Practice note: alleging and proving intent can be hazardous when it comes to the defendant's insurance. Intentionality generally voids coverage, which can limit the plaintiff's chances for a sizeable settlement or judgment.

"Mere Puffing"

It should be clear by now that a real estate investor may begin to incur potential liability the moment he or she starts advertising. But doesn't the law cut some slack when it comes to the game of luring consumers through the front door? It does. A certain level of factual flexibility in advertising is recognized by courts as the commercial norm—so "mere puffing," as the case law calls it, is not actionable. "Three factors are considered in determining whether a representation is 'mere puffing:' (1) the specificity of the representation; (2) the comparative knowledge of the buyer and seller; and (3) whether the representation relates to a future event or condition." *Bossier Chrysler Dodge II, Inc. v. Rauschenberg*, 201 S.W.3d 787, 800 (Tex.App—Waco, 2006). We again return to the concept that *taking advantage of another who possesses less knowledge or experience seldom turns out well in a court of law.*

"Bait and switch" is not considered mere puffing. See Sec. 17.46(B)(10); *Martin v. Lou Poliquin Enterprises, Inc.,* id.

Notice Requirement

A requirement of 60 days' notice and demand was included in the DTPA to promote settlement and avoid frivolous lawsuits:

§17.505. NOTICE; INSPECTION.

(a) **As a prerequisite to filing a suit seeking damages under Subdivision (1) of Subsection (b) of Section 17.50 of this subchapter against any person, a consumer shall give written notice to the person at least 60 days before filing the suit advising the person in reasonable detail of the consumer's specific complaint and the amount of economic damages, damages for mental anguish, and expenses, including attorneys' fees, if any, reasonably incurred by the consumer in asserting the claim against the defendant. During the 60-day period a written request to inspect, in a reasonable manner and at a reasonable time and place, the goods that are the subject of the consumer's action or claim may be presented to the consumer.**

(b) **If the giving of 60 days' written notice is rendered impracticable by reason of the necessity of filing suit in order to prevent the expiration of the statute of limitations or if the consumer's claim is asserted by way of counterclaim, the notice provided for in Subsection (a) of this section is not required, but the tender provided for by Subsection (d), Section 17.506 of this subchapter may be made within 60 days after service of the suit or counterclaim.**

(c) **A person against whom a suit is pending who does not receive written notice, as required by Subsection (a), may file a plea in abatement not later than the 30th day after the date the person files an original answer in the court in which the suit is pending. This subsection does not apply if Subsection (b) applies.**

Offer of Settlement

As an accommodation to defendants, the DTPA provides a means of minimizing a potential damage award by making a reasonable offer of settlement, but this offer *must* encompass both the consumer's damages and attorney's fees:

§17.5052. OFFERS OF SETTLEMENT.

(a)A person who receives notice under Section 17.505 may tender an offer of settlement at any time during the period beginning on the date the notice is received and ending on the 60th day after that date.

(b)If a mediation under Section 17.5051 is not conducted, the person may tender an offer of settlement at any time during the period beginning on the date an original answer is filed and ending on the 90th day after that date.

(c)If a mediation under Section 17.5051 is conducted, a person against whom a claim under this subchapter is pending may tender an offer of settlement during the period beginning on the day after the date that the mediation ends and ending on the 20th day after that date.

(d)An offer of settlement tendered by a person against whom a claim under this subchapter is pending must include an offer to pay the following amounts of money, separately stated:

(1) an amount of money or other consideration, reduced to its cash value, as settlement of the consumer's claim for damages; and

(2) an amount of money to compensate the consumer for the consumer's reasonable and necessary attorneys' fees incurred as of the date of the offer.

(e)Unless both parts of an offer of settlement required under Subsection (d) are accepted by the consumer not later than the 30th day after the date the offer is made, the offer is rejected.

(f)A settlement offer tendered by a person against whom a claim under this subchapter is pending that complies with this section and that has been rejected by the consumer may be filed with the court with an affidavit certifying its rejection.

(g) If the court finds that the amount tendered in the settlement offer for damages under Subsection (d)(1) is the same as, substantially the same as, or more than the damages found by the trier of fact, the consumer may not recover as damages any amount in excess of the lesser of:

(1) the amount of damages tendered in the settlement offer; or
(2) the amount of damages found by the trier of fact.

(h) If the court makes the finding described by Subsection (g), the court shall determine reasonable and necessary attorneys' fees to compensate the consumer for attorneys' fees incurred before the date and time of the rejected settlement offer. If the court finds that the amount tendered in the settlement offer to compensate the consumer for attorneys' fees under Subsection (d)(2) is the same as, substantially the same as, or more than the amount of reasonable and necessary attorneys' fees incurred by the consumer as of the date of the offer, the consumer may not recover attorneys' fees greater than the amount of fees tendered in the settlement offer.

Subsection (g) is the key provision here, limiting the defendant's potential liability.

A settlement offer is not an admission of guilt or liability and cannot be introduced into evidence at trial. Tex. Bus. & Com. Code Sec. 17.5052(k). Given the foregoing, missing an opportunity to make a reasonable offer of settlement in response to a DTPA claim is simply negligent on the part of a potential defendant.

Notice Letters—Comments for Prospective Plaintiffs

Writing a good notice and demand letter entails both substance and style and should always be handled by an attorney experienced in that particular field of law. There are at least two reasons for this. Firstly, an attorney is not only more likely to comply with the express requirements of the statute (ensuring that a corrected notice will not have to be re-given later), but will also take into account the practical realities and nuances of pre-litigation legal diplomacy. The tone of the letter will be designed to strike the right balance between toughness and conciliation.

Secondly, a letter from a qualified attorney always carries more weight than a letter directly from the aggrieved person. It has credibility. If nothing else, an attorney letter demonstrates that the prospective plaintiff is both serious and willing to spend money on legal fees in order to get the issue solved.

Any good notice and demand letter should do at least three things: (1) explain the basics—list the parties, offer a detailed description of the circumstances (at least from the complainant's point of view), and provide an historical timeline; (2) cite specifically which statutes and remedies may apply; and (3) offer some proposal for moving forward (e.g., settlement, correction of the alleged violation, mediation, etc.) which must be met or agreed to within a specific timeframe (often 10 days unless a statute requires more, as is the case with the DTPA) or suit may be filed without further notice.

Notice Letters—Comments for Prospective Defendants

When receiving such a letter, the first step is to take a breath. Not all such demands result in lawsuits. Not all of them are followed by further action. Occasionally, the complainant will run out of determination or money or both and simply go away. Having said that, it is seldom wise to ignore a legal demand letter. No matter how preposterous the demand, it is almost always better practice to send a response with a plausible rationale for declining same.

First, an investor on the receiving end of a demand letter should investigate the facts and determine what merit the allegations have. Next, evaluate the letter itself. Does it meet the three-prong test outlined above? Does it come from an attorney—and not just any attorney but one well-credentialed and experienced in real estate law or civil litigation? If so, you should most definitely respond within the prescribed time period. A bona fide offer of settlement will take treble damages off the table, an essential part of minimizing damage from this event and thus integral to asset protection.

The Value of a Good "As Is" Clause

The value of an effective "as is" clause cannot be underestimated in Texas, and not just in the context of the DTPA. For DTPA purposes, such a clause—when properly written—negates the requirement of "producing cause," letting the defendant off the hook so long as the consumer knowingly and voluntarily signed a contract containing such a clause. *Prudential Insurance Company of America v. Jefferson Associates, Ltd.*, 896 S.W.2d 156 (Tex. 1995). As a reminder, an "as is" clause should be clear, unequivocal, and conspicuous (bold and capitalized). A sample "as is" clause is provided in chapter 2, although such clauses should always be customized to the circumstances.

Waiver of Consumer Rights

A consumer may also waive his or her DTPA rights in writing pursuant to Section 17.42, but the requirements for a valid waiver are extremely strict (including the requirement that the consumer be represented by a lawyer), so these tend to be uncommon. In fact, Section. 17.42(a) declares that "*Any* [emphasis added] waiver by a consumer of the provisions of this subchapter is contrary to public policy and void. . . ." The statute goes on to describe the very limited circumstances under which such a waiver might be enforceable. Moreover, the defense of waiver is not assertable in an action that is brought by the attorney general on behalf of the public generally (Sec. 17.42(e)); nor will a waiver be effective against anything the DTPA defines as a deceptive act. *Southwestern Bell Tel. Co. v. FDP Corp.*, 811 S.W.2d 572, 576-77 (Tex. 1991).

Attempting to procure an enforceable DTPA waiver from a prospect in a real estate transaction is likely to be not only risky but of questionable value. A court will find the waiver void if it wants to—particularly if the judge or jury dislikes real estate investors, which is true in most cases. And the consumer will most certainly be alarmed at the idea of a blanket waiver of his or her consumer protections and having to get a lawyer to sign off on that (What lawyer will want the liability?). All in all, it may be best to avoid such waivers entirely.

An exception is in connection with the sale of new homes. "[T]he implied warranty of good workmanship [for a new home] may be disclaimed by the parties when their agreement provides for the manner, performance or quality of the desired construction." But the implied warranty of habitability, in the same context, may not be disclaimed. *Centex Homes v. Buecher*, 95 S.W.3d 266, 274-75 (Tex. 2002).

Does an "as is" clause constitute the effective equivalent of a waiver of consumer rights? No, not according to the *Prudential* case. See also *Larsen v. Carlene Langford & Assocs.*, 41 S.W.3d 245, 255 (Tex.App.—Waco 2001, pet. denied).

Statute of Limitations

A suit pursuant to the DTPA must be brought within two years after the false, misleading, or deceptive act took place—or within two years after the consumer should reasonably have discovered such an act. This period may be extended up to 180 days if it can be proven that a late filing resulted from the defendant's wrongful conduct designed to avoid or delay the filing. Tex. Bus. & Com. Code Sec. 17.565. As a practical matter, the two-year rule tends to prevail since courts tend to take the view that the consumer should have discovered the illegal act when it occurred.

Groundless or Bad Faith Lawsuits

The DTPA offers some relief to defendants in Section 17.50(c) which provides that "on a finding by the court than an action under this section was groundless in law or in fact or brought in bad faith, or brought for purpose of harassment, the court shall award to the defendant reasonable and necessary attorneys' fees and court costs." This is, of course, in addition to rejecting the plaintiff's claim. And note the word *shall*. Once a finding of groundlessness or bad faith is made, an award of attorney's fees to the defendant is mandatory.

Receivership after a DTPA Judgment

A court-appointed receiver may be granted broad powers to manage and operate the business of a judgment debtor, including the power to manage its finances. Section 17.59 offers an expedited path to receivership for a judgment creditor, so long as there has been a good-faith but failed attempt to execute on the judgment by the usual means. If such is the case, Section 17.59(a) provides that certain presumptions exist:

(1) that the defendant is insolvent or in danger of becoming insolvent; and

(2) that the defendant's property is in danger of being lost, removed, or otherwise exempted from collection on the judgment; and

(3) that the prevailing party will be materially injured unless a received is appointed over the defendant's business; and

(4) that there is no adequate remedy other than receivership available to the prevailing party.

In other words, all the usual preconditions for receivership are simply presumed, facilitating a relatively smooth appointment process. The consequences of a receiver's intervention, as observed elsewhere in this book, can be devastating and often fatal to the business involved.

The DTPA and Real Estate Investors: Beware of Overly-Clever Schemes

Many real estate investors are engineers, medical doctors, computer people, or others whose education and experience is quantitative rather than legal or linguistic. In their minds, something is either "legal" or it is not.

What non-lawyers typically do not understand is that the law, particularly when it reaches the courtroom, is not black and white, off and on, or yes and no. It is a continuum with shades of gray. And somewhere along that continuum a judge or a jury may feel that the weight of the evidence establishes that something undesirable has occurred—fraud, deception, or the like—and the human urge is to find a remedy and assess a punishment.

In court, once you get past the summary judgment stage (where anything patently frivolous is usually eliminated) then everything, including the plain language of a statute, becomes a subject for interpretation. At that point, it matters that one individual is an unsophisticated ordinary person who has lost his home and the other person is a sharp real estate investor.

Chapter 42

MEDIATION

An Effective Alternative to the Courtroom

Mediation is an opportunity for both sides to exert control over the outcome of their dispute rather than leaving it to an unpredictable and expensive trial. The mediation process itself is a form of settlement conference guided and supervised by a mediator who has either been chosen by the parties or appointed by a judge. The Rules for Mediation (see complete list at the end of this article) put it as follows:

> *Mediation Rule 1: Mediation is a process under which an impartial person, the mediator, facilitates communication between the parties to promote reconciliation, settlement, or understanding among them. The mediator may suggest ways of resolving the dispute, but may not impose his own judgment on the issues for that of the parties.*

> *Mediation Rule 3. The parties consent to the appointment of the individual named as the mediator in their case. The mediator shall act as an advocate for resolution and shall use his best efforts to assist the parties in reaching a mutually acceptable settlement.*

Mediation Required by Contract

Contracts of any type may require that parties mediate before litigating. An example is paragraph 16 of the TREC One to Four Family Residential Contract which states that "Any dispute between Seller and Buyer related to this contract which is not resolved through informal discussion will be submitted to a mutually acceptable mediation service or provider." The intent is to provide a structured opportunity for the parties to air and resolve their grievances before resorting to remedies at the courthouse. This used to be an optional election on the TREC form. No longer.

Mediation During Litigation

The docket control order, generated by the court's computer for scheduling purposes, contains relevant dates and deadlines applicable to a case, and it usually includes a date by which mediation must be completed. It is generally down the road a bit, since most attorneys prefer to do at least preliminary discovery (requests for disclosure, interrogatories, and requests for production), and perhaps consult an expert, *before* mediating, so that all cards will be on the table when the parties meet to talk settlement.

Some judges will name a mediator, others leave it up to the parties to agree upon one. Even though mediation is usually ordered, the outcome (whether or not a settlement is reached) is voluntary. The parties can choose to walk away without settling and go to trial instead, leaving their fate in the hands of a judge or jury. The mediator will report an impasse and all aspects of the mediation, including offers of settlement, remain private and confidential.

Mediation Versus Arbitration

The difference here involves the authority of a mediator versus an arbitrator:

> *Mediation Rule 5. The mediator does not have the authority to decide any issue for the parties, but will attempt to facilitate the voluntary resolution of the dispute by the parties. The mediator is authorized to conduct joint and separate meetings with the parties and to offer suggestions to assist the parties achieve settlement.*

By contrast, in an arbitration, the arbitrator makes a final ruling just as if he or she were a judge. Arbitration is never ordered by a court (unless of course the parties have an arbitration clause in their contract) but may be agreed upon by the parties.

Effectiveness of Mediation

Why is mediation popular? Because statistics show that *it works*. Depending on which numbers you believe, 70-80% of cases settle in mediation. Attorneys know this and encourage their clients to mediate with an open mind. In fact, when a client is recalcitrant and unreasonable about settlement, attorneys can become quite annoyed—and the reason is that lawyers know better than anyone how a trial can consist of rolling the dice. Trial practice is a branch of chaos theory. No outcome is *ever* assured in the legal system, no matter how determined the client or how capable the attorney.

Mediation promotes predictability and certainty, but this requires compromise. *You do not win your case at mediation. In fact, a good mediation is by definition one in which both sides leave unhappy.* Clients find this difficult to accept. Remember, the legal world is not the same as the real world. Clients who rebel against the mediation process and insist on total victory based on principle often lose in the end.

The mediator always asks if all parties are ready and willing to mediate in good faith and work toward a settlement with an open mind. This readiness is the foundation of both mediation and dispute resolution generally, and the mediator will request that the parties make an unconditional commitment to do this. Additionally, it is important to determine that persons present have authority to settle the case. Otherwise, the process can be futile.

It is a rare case when a party is justified in refusing mediation. However, if good grounds exist for doing so, the judge (after motion and hearing) can waive a mediation requirement. Judges do not like to do this for two reasons: first, they are seasoned realists who know that most cases *do* and *should* settle; and second, it assures that another case will be added to an overburdened trial docket. Do you want to alienate the judge? Object to mediation in your case. Many lawyers consider a party's refusal to mediate in good faith to be grounds for attorney withdrawal.

Qualifications and Impartiality of the Mediator

> *Mediation Rule 4. The mediator will only serve in cases in which the parties are represented by attorneys. The mediator shall not serve as a mediator in any dispute in which he has any financial or personal interest in the result of the mediation. Prior to accepting an appointment, the mediator shall disclose any circumstance likely to create a presumption of bias or prevent a prompt meeting with the parties. In the event that the parties disagree as to whether the mediator shall serve on the basis of any of the foregoing conditions, the mediator shall not serve.*

Mediators may or may not be certified. They are usually experienced attorneys or retired judges who act as shuttle diplomats in attempting to resolve the parties' differences. After a joint session in which both sides have the opportunity to vent their grievances, the parties retire to separate rooms, and the mediator goes back and forth in an effort to promote a settlement. In doing so, the mediator points out the strengths and weaknesses of each position without taking sides.

Fees and Expenses of Mediation

> *Mediation Rule 17. The mediator's daily fee shall be agreed upon prior to mediation and shall be paid in advance of each mediation day. The expenses of witnesses for either side shall be paid by the party producing such witnesses. All other expenses of the mediation, including fees and expenses of the mediator, shall be borne equally by the parties unless they agree otherwise.*

Mediators do not have a financial stake in the outcome of the mediation (i.e., mediation fees are not contingent upon a settlement being reached). Mediator fees vary and are paid at the beginning of the session. Half-day mediations are common since all but complex cases can be settled in that amount of time. Half-day mediations typically cost $500 to $700 per side. Mediators often require payment by cashier's check or money order since unhappy parties have been known to go home and stop payment on their checks.

Time and Place of Mediation

> *Mediation Rule 8. The mediator shall fix the time of each mediation session. The mediation shall be held at the office of the mediator or at any other convenient location agreeable to the mediator and the parties, as the mediator shall determine.*

Mediations are scheduled for half a day or for a full day, but may continue longer with consent of the parties. "Midnight mediations" are not uncommon, since the accumulated pressure of time will often force a compromise. One mediation this writer attended reached settlement only after the mediator broke out a bottle of whisky at 10 p.m.

Using the location of the mediation as an opportunity to serve other parties with citations, pleadings, writs, and the like (however tempting that may be) is not allowed.

Rule 14 addresses when mediation may end:

> *Mediation Rule 14. The mediation shall be terminated: (a) by the execution of a settlement agreement by the parties;*

(b) by declaration of the mediator to the effect that further efforts at mediation are no longer worthwhile; or (c) after the completion of one fully mediation session, by a written declaration of a party or parties to the effect that the mediation sessions are terminated.

After the mediation is terminated, the mediator has no further obligations other than to report the result to the court. If mediation was successful, a written summary of the settlement will be prepared and signed by the parties and attorneys before they leave.

Privacy and Confidentiality

Privacy and confidentiality are key elements in mediation. Clients often ask if family members or others may attend, participate, or observe. This is not usually permitted.

Mediation Rule 10. Mediation sessions are private. The parties and their representatives may attend mediation sessions. Other persons may attend only with the permission of the parties and with the consent of the mediator.

Mediation Rule 11. Confidential information disclosed to a mediator by the parties or by witnesses in the course of mediation shall not be divulged by the mediator. . . . The parties shall maintain the confidentiality of the mediation.

Mediators do not testify in court. Nothing said in mediation is admissible into evidence at trial. Recording of the proceedings (either openly or surreptitiously) is forbidden. If mediation fails, it is the evidentiary equivalent of its never having occurred at all.

The Psychology of Mediation

The mediator's job is to promote settlement and be impartial in so doing. In the broadest sense, mediation is about communication—communication that may previously have happened only haphazardly or may never have happened at all. It is also a businesslike endeavor, meaning that it should be stripped of emotion. Each side is encouraged to examine the costs and benefits of the available options and perceive settlement as a cold business decision. Attorneys play an important part in this analysis. They may continue to advocate but in a more muted way.

It is part of a mediator's job to challenge each party's cherished assumptions about the value of their cause of action or defense. Clients often misinterpret this and believe that the mediator is advocating for the other side. Not so. Mediation is designed to push the parties out of their comfort zones and into the zone of compromise. Mediators have the tough but essential job of overcoming the parties' resistance if the case is to settle.

The Rules of Mediation

Mediation Rule 1: Mediation is a process under which an impartial person, the mediator, facilitates communication between the parties to promote reconciliation, settlement, or understanding among them. The mediator may suggest ways of resolving the dispute, but may not impose his own judgment on the issues for that of the parties.

Mediation Rule 2. Whenever the parties have agreed to mediation, they shall be deemed to have made these rules, as amended and in effect as of the date of the submission of the dispute, as part of their agreement to mediate.

Mediation Rule 3. The parties consent to the appointment of the individual named as the mediator in their case. The mediator shall act as an advocate for resolution and shall use his best efforts to assist the parties in reaching a mutually acceptable settlement.

Mediation Rule 4. The mediator will only serve in cases in which the parties are represented by attorneys. The mediator shall not serve as a mediator in any dispute in which he has any financial or personal interest in the result of the mediation. Prior to accepting an appointment, the mediator shall disclose any circumstance likely to create a presumption of bias or prevent a prompt meeting with the parties. In the event that the parties disagree as to whether the mediator shall serve on the basis of any of the foregoing conditions, the mediator shall not serve.

Mediation Rule 5. The mediator does not have the authority to decide any issue for the parties, but will attempt to facilitate the voluntary resolution of the dispute by the parties. The mediator is authorized to conduct joint and separate meetings with the parties and to offer suggestions to assist the parties achieve settlement. If necessary, the mediator may also obtain expert advice concerning technical aspects of the dispute, provided that the parties agree and assume the expenses of obtaining such advice. Arrangements for obtaining such advice shall be made by the mediator or by the parties, as the mediator shall determine.

Mediation Rule 6. The parties understand that the mediator will not and cannot impose a settlement in their case and they agree that a settlement, if any, must be voluntarily agreed to by the parties. The mediator, as an advocate for settlement, will use every effort to facilitate the negotiations. The mediator does not warrant or represent that settlement will result from the mediation process.

Mediation Rule 7. Party representatives must have authority to settle and all persons necessary to the decision to settle shall be present.

Mediation Rule 8. The mediator shall fix the time of each mediation session. The mediation shall be held at the office of the mediator or at any other convenient location agreeable to the mediator and the parties, as the mediator shall determine.

Mediation Rule 9. Prior to the first scheduled mediation session, each party shall provide the mediator and all attorneys of record with an Information Sheet and Request for mediation on the form provided by the mediator, setting forth its position with regard to the issues that need to be resolved.

Mediation Rule 10. Mediation sessions are private. The parties and their representatives may attend mediation sessions. Other persons may attend only with the permission of the parties and with the consent of the mediator.

Mediation Rule 11. Confidential information disclosed to a mediator by the parties or by witnesses in the course of mediation shall not be divulged by the mediator. . . . The parties shall maintain the confidentiality of the mediation.

Mediation Rule 12. There shall be no stenographic record of the mediation process, and no person shall tape record any portion of the mediation session.

Mediation Rule 13. No subpoenas, summons, complaints, citations, writs, or other process may be served upon any person at or near the site of any mediation session upon any person entering, attending, or leaving the session.

Mediation Rule 14. The mediation shall be terminated: (a) by the execution of a settlement agreement by the parties; (b) by declaration of the mediator to the effect that further efforts at mediation are no longer worthwhile; or (c) after the completion of one fully mediation session, by a written declaration of a party or parties to the effect that the mediation sessions are terminated.

Mediation Rule 15. The mediator is not a necessary or proper party in judicial proceedings relating to the mediation. Neither the mediator nor any law firm employing a mediator shall be liable to any party for any act or omission in connection with any mediation conducted under these rules.

Mediation Rule 16. The mediator shall interpret and apply these rules.

Mediation Rule 17. The mediator's daily fee shall be agreed upon prior to mediation and shall be paid in advance of each mediation day. The expenses of witnesses for either side shall be paid by the party producing such witnesses. All other expenses of the mediation, including fees and expenses of the mediator, shall be borne equally by the parties unless they agree otherwise.

Chapter 43

JUDGMENTS IN TEXAS

Collection May Not be as Easy as You Think

A discussion of judgments in Texas needs to be broadly divided into two parts: first, the process of obtaining a judgment (which, after all, is only a non-self-executing piece of paper signed by a judge) and second, actually collecting the money owed, which may be the more challenging task since Texas is notoriously favorable to debtors. It is unconstitutional to garnish wages in Texas, and an individual's home and vehicles are usually beyond reach. Unless a judgment debtor has a going business with valuable inventory or cash flow, rental property, or cash in the bank, collecting on a judgment may be problematic. Often, the creditor's attorney receives word from the constable that he is unable to locate any non-exempt assets and is therefore returning the writ of execution *nulla bona.*

Another method of collecting on a judgment, beside traditional execution and a constable sale, is to file an independent suit to enforce it (which usually takes the form of an *in rem* action against land), but this does not change the reality that many individual borrowers will simply not have sufficient assets that lie outside the protective parameters established by Texas exemption and homestead laws.

To get a more complete picture, the reader may want to review part of chapter 35, where we discussed judgment liens and the homestead.

Finality of Judgments

One can only obtain a judgment after filing a lawsuit and obtaining a judgment, either by means of a trial, summary judgment, or by default. After the judgment is signed, the court clerk will not issue a writ of execution until it is at least 30 days old (21 days in justice court) at which time the judgment is considered final. This post-judgment waiting period exists so that the debtor has ample time to file a motion for new trial as a prerequisite to appeal. If the motion is granted, or if the debtor files an appeal, then execution efforts must cease.

When is a judgment also a lien?

To clarify a common misunderstanding: a judgment standing alone is not a lien. In order to constitute a lien, an abstract of the judgment must be properly recorded and indexed in compliance with Property Code Section 52.001 et seq. Also, the contents of the abstract must strictly comply with the requirements of Property Code Section 52.003.

A judgment lien "comes into existence by the recording an indexing of an abstract of judgment . . . it terminates by the expiration of the ten-year period [and] can never be extended. . . . Clearly, the law contemplates that abstracts of a judgment may be recorded in different counties. If such abstract be recorded in a number of different counties, each is an independent lien. . . . So it is thus seen that one or more liens may exist to secure the same judgment." *Burton Lingo Co. v. Warrant*, 45S.W.2d 750, 752 (Tex.App.—Eastland 1931, writ ref'd). An abstract of judgment must be filed in every county where the debtor owns land in order to fix a judgment lien against land in that county.

Filing an abstract of judgment is often the only realistic way that a judgment creditor has to collect—in some cases years after the judgment was obtained.

Abstracting the Final Judgment

It is normal procedure for the creditor to request an abstract of judgment from the court clerk and then file that abstract in the real property records where it must be indexed by the county clerk (Note that judgment records and real property records are often located in different computers, which explains the occasional disparity). In certain courts and counties, the judgment creditor's attorney may prepare the abstract. Either way, the abstract must substantially comply with the requirements of Property Code Section 52.003 (including providing a list of specific information such as names, addresses, amount of the judgment, and so forth) or no lien attaches. *Texas American Bank v. Southern Union Exploration*, 714 S.W.2d 105 (Tex.App.—Eastland 1986, write ref'd n.r.e.). If a judgment lien is challenged by the debtor, the burden of proof is on the judgment creditor to show that abstract is correct and substantially meets statutory requirements. *Day v. Day*, 610 S.W.2d 195 (Tex.Civ. App.—Tyler 1980, writ ref'd n.r.e.). All of the foregoing apply equally to foreign judgments domesticated in Texas. *Reynolds v. Kessler*, 669 S.W.2d 801 (Tex.App.—El Paso 1984, no writ).

Filing the abstract puts the public on notice that the judgment exists and attaches to non-exempt real property of the debtor. Title companies will search for these AJs to determine if they should collect from sales proceeds to satisfy them. This represents a problem for any judgment debtor who is trying to sell property out of his own name, including homestead property. Even though a judgment lien does not attach to, and does not constitute a lien on, a judgment debtor's homestead, it can be difficult to persuade a title company to ignore a judgment and go forward with closing. A title company's self-serving reaction is to minimize risk to itself and require that all liens be cleared.

The abstract or "AJ" stays on file for 10 years but may be re-filed for successive 10-year periods (Prop. Code Sec. 52.006). Note, however, that a judgment will become dormant if no attempt is made to execute upon it during the 10 years following its effective date. Tex. Civ. Proc. & Rem. Code Sec. 34.001. Dormant judgments may nonetheless be revived if action is taken within 2 years of their dormancy (this is known as a "revival action"). If the judgment creditor fails to get a writ of execution during the ten-year period when the judgment is active, and further fails to instigate a revival action within two years of the judgment becoming dormant, then the judgment is effectively dead.

What about abstracting judgments from other states ("foreign judgments")? These are considered the equivalent of a Texas judgment so long as the judgment is filed in compliance with the Uniform Enforcement of Judgments Act (Civ. Prac. & Rem. Code Sec. 35.001 et seq.). More detail on this below.

Note that filing an abstract of judgment while the debtor is in bankruptcy violates the automatic bankruptcy stay.

The Hunt for Assets

Online resources available to judgment creditors are considerable. A prudent creditor will undertake a search prior to investing in a lawsuit at all, and will then refresh that search after the judgment is final. Possible resources include:

(1) The Secretary of State's website can reveal what Texas companies a judgment debtor has an interest in. Although this database actually indicates managers and officers rather than owners (members or shareholders), it is often the case that a manager of an LLC or the president of a corporation is also at least a part owner of the enterprise. Corporate stock may be attached and LLC membership interests may be placed under a charging order. The Secretary of State also maintains a statewide registry of assumed names (see chapter 33).

(2) The Texas Comptroller's website allows an inquirer to

search sales tax records and ascertain if a company is current with its franchise tax payments and reports. Plenty of information can be gleaned from these.

(3) Appraisal district websites, although not as reliable as the county clerk's real property records, can reveal whether or not a judgment debtor is being taxed on property other than a homestead (which is exempt from execution of course). Let's say that a search of the Secretary of State's website suggests that a debtor may have an interest in an LLC established to invest in real estate; an appraisal district's rolls may give a creditor an idea of exactly which real estate that is.

(4) The county clerk maintains a number of data bases that are useful to a judgment creditor. The first is of course the real property records, which show both current recorded ownership and chain of title as to properties located within the county. The right type of search can show conveyances out of the judgment debtor's name in the recent past—possibly an indication of fraudulent transfers.

The clerk's assumed name records are another useful tool. Assumed names are not legal entities, so if a debtor is operating under a DBA then the assets associated with that DBA could well be subject to execution on the judgment.

The county clerk also maintains a record of UCC filings that can lead a creditor to attachable assets such as inventory and equipment.

(5) The multiple listing service can indicate an attempt by a judgment debtor to move properties out of the debtor's name and also suggest what these properties may be worth.

(6) Judgment creditors frequently use other sites (e.g., TLO, Accurint, and Public Data) to locate other assets such as vehicles.

The Role of Post-Judgment Discovery in Locating Assets

Judgment creditors, often at a disadvantage in Texas, have a particularly important collection tool: post-judgment discovery which includes interrogatories, requests for admission, and requests for production. Tex. R. Civ. P. 621a. This discovery can be incredibly complex since rules pertaining to limits on trial discovery do not apply post-judgment.

The purpose of post-judgment discovery is (1) to ascertain whether or not the debtor possesses non-exempt property sufficient to satisfy the judgment; and (2) to determine if the debtor has fraudulently hidden assets. In addition to written discovery, it is possible to delve into these matters by taking the debtor's oral deposition, although written discovery generally comes first. Note that if a debtor who has been properly served fails to answer post-judgment discovery, he or she may be held in contempt by the judge, resulting in a fine or even jail. Tex. R. Civ. P. 215.

If actionable information is obtained, the judgment creditor can approach the court and request a writ of attachment, Tex. R. Civ. P. 641, Tex. Bus. & Com. Code Sec. 8.112; garnishment, Tex. R. Civ. P. 669; or a turnover order, Tex. Civ. Prac. & Rem. Code Sec. 31.002.

Writ of Execution

The judgment creditor bears the burden of preparing the writ of execution and placing it in the hands of the appropriate officer for execution. *Sintim v. Larson*, 489 S.W.3d 551 (Tex.App—Houston [14th District] 2016, no pet.). The writ of execution is usually sent to the local constable (or sheriff, in some counties) who charges a fee for attempting to collect. The reality is that these officers may not try very hard—no flashing lights, no guns drawn. Often, the constable will knock at the debtor's door early in the morning, present the judgment, and ask if there are any assets available to satisfy it. If the debtor says *no*, then the officer may withdraw and send the unsatisfied writ back to the court. Unless the creditor's attorney can direct the officer to a specific, known, non-exempt asset for attachment or garnishment, then the collection process may come to halt. Other mechanisms available to the judgment creditor include a writ of possession or, for personal property, writs of garnishment and sequestration.

Writs of execution are generally available after the expiration of 30 days, when a judgment becomes final, so long as no supersedeas (appeal) bond has been filed by the debtor. It is, however, possible to get a writ sooner under Tex. R. Civ. P. 628 "upon the filing of an affidavit by the plaintiff in the judgment or his agent or attorney that the defendant is about to remove his personal property subject to execution by law out of the county, or is about to transfer or secrete such personal property for the purpose of defrauding his creditors."

Rule 637 states what happens next: "When an execution is delivered to an officer he shall proceed without delay to levy the same upon the property of the defendant found within his county not exempt from execution, unless otherwise directed by the plaintiff, his agent or attorney. The officer shall first call upon the defendant, if he can be found, or, if absent, upon his agent within the county, if known, to point out property to be levied upon, and the levy shall first be made upon the property designated by the defendant, or his agent. If in the opinion of the officer the property so designated will not sell for enough to satisfy the execution and costs of sale, he shall require an additional designation by the defendant. If no property be thus designated by the defendant, the officer shall levy the execution upon any property of the defendant subject to execution." Once levied upon, real property may then be sold at public auction on foreclosure day.

The Homestead is Exempt from Execution

Many Texas debtors have numerous judgments against them but live in expensive homes. They can do this because the entire homestead equity is exempt from execution. What constitutes a debtor's homestead? Within broad parameters, a homestead is what a person intends it to be, subject to size limitations (10 acres for an urban homestead, 200 acres for a rural one). Tex. Prop. Code Sec. 41.002. A rental property or even a vacant lot can be homestead if the owner has reasonable expectations of building a home on it. Moreover, 41.001(c) states that "proceeds of a sale of a homestead are not subject to seizure for a creditor's claim for six months after the date of sale." This expressly permits homestead protections to be rolled over from one home to the next.

Certain personal property is also exempt under Chapter 42 of the Property Code. Personal property valued at $60,000 for a family or $30,000 for a single adult (exclusive of liens) is exempt from garnishment, attachment, execution or other seizure so long as it is on the statutory list. This includes home furnishings, clothes, jewelry, firearms, and vehicles—even 12 head of cattle—but excludes cash on hand or in checking or savings accounts. Retirement plans (including rollover proceeds) are exempted under Section 42.0021 so long as contributions do not exceed the amount that is deductible under current law. College tuition funds are exempted under Section 42.0022. It is important to note that homestead protections are available only to individuals, not LLCs or corporations.

For more detail on homestead protections, see chapter 34 which is devoted entirely to this subject.

Release of Liens against the Debtor's Homestead

A homestead is exempt from forced sale so long as the property remains the homestead of the debtor. *Exocet Inc. v. Cordes*, 815 S.W.2d 350, 352 (Tex.App.—Austin 1991, no writ). In furtherance of this principle, Property Code Section 52.0012 provides an expedited statutory method for securing a release of any judgment lien against homestead property, available only for judgments abstracted after September 1, 2007.

Section 52.0012 provides for the filing of an Affidavit that must substantially comply with the requirements appearing in this section of the Property Code. Filing of the affidavit must be preceded by a 30-day notice sent by certified mail and addressed to the judgment creditor and its attorney of record. The letter must contain a copy of the affidavit that the homestead owner intends to file in the real property records. The requirements of the letter and the affidavit are highly technical and should be done by an attorney knowledgeable in this procedure. The judgment creditor may contest the homeowner's action by filing a contradicting affidavit if there is reason to believe that the homeowner's affidavit is false. The ultimate result, if this procedure is followed to the letter, is that the homeowner's affidavit when executed and filed serves as a release of the judgment lien as to the homestead property.

A comprehensive discussion this topic can be found in chapter 35, *Lien Release and Removal.*

Turnover Orders and Receivership

A post-judgment turnover order pursuant to Civ. Prac. & Rem. Code Sec. 31.002 et seq. is a "procedural device by which judgment creditors may reach assets of a debtor that are otherwise difficult to attach or levy on by ordinary legal process." *Beaumont Bank, N.A. v. Buller*, 806 S.W.2d 223, 224 (Tex. 1991). The turnover order requires that the judgment debtor bring to the court any non-exempt items available for execution on the judgment, rather than relying solely on the judgment creditor's ability to utilize conventional methods of execution and attachment through the local sheriff or constable. Section 31.002 states that a "judgment creditor is entitled to aid from a court of appropriate jurisdiction through injunction or other means in order to reach [non-exempt] property to obtain satisfaction on the judgment if the judgment debtor owns property, including present or future rights to property that ... cannot readily be attached or levied on by ordinary legal process."

Contempt is serious business. A fine or incarceration (or both) may be employed. "The court may enforce the order by contempt proceedings or by other appropriate means in the event of refusal or disobedience." Civ. Prac. & Rem. Code Sec. 31.002(c).

Included among the tools available is the most powerful weapon in the collection arsenal—the appointment of a receiver—"with the authority to take possession of the non-exempt property, sell it, and pay the proceeds to the judgment creditor to the extent required to satisfy the judgment." Tex. Civ. Prac. & Rem. Code Sec. 31.002(b)(3). Property subject to a receivership order may include limited authority over a defendant's membership interest in a limited liability company. *Bennett v. Broocks Baker & Lange, LLP*, No. 01-13-00674-CV (Tex.App.—Houston [1st Dist.] 2014, no pet.). Even though an LLC membership interest is personal property, the exclusive remedy against it (notwithstanding the presence of a receiver) is still a charging order. *Pajooh v. Royal W. Invs.*, 518 S.W.3d 557, 565-66 (Tex.App.—Houston [1st Dist.] 2017, no pet.). How would this likely play out in practice? The appointed receiver would simply ask the judge for a charging order—but that is as far as the receiver could likely go with respect to the judgment debtor's LLC membership interest. Its sale could not be forced as is the case with other types of non-exempt personal property. More information on charging orders is contained in the next chapter.

Back to the subject of receivers: these individuals are court-appointed czars who have nearly unlimited power to take over not just the business but seemingly the *entire life* of a judgment debtor and wring every available cent from non-exempt assets in order to satisfy the debt—including, of course, the receiver's often crushing fees. Receivership is highly profitable for court-favored attorneys who are appointed to serve in that capacity, but devastating to the debtor. This author has never seen a small business survive a receivership. In the real world, more often than not, receivership of a real estate investment business is the equivalent of a forced liquidation.

Usually, the power of a court to issue or amend orders ends 30 days after the judgment (Tex.R. Civ. P. 329(b)(d)). Not so with receivership. A court's power to enforce a judgment and to enable the judgment creditor to continue to pursue the judgment debtor is essentially indefinite so long as the judgment remains unpaid. See Tex.R. Civ. P. 308; *Matz v. Bennion*, 961 S.W.2d 445, 452 (Tex.App.—Houston [1st Dist.] 1997, pet. denied). Accordingly, a judgment creditor facing an aggressive receiver (particularly one who is motivated to collect a large amount) may find himself on the perpetual defensive.

Judgments against Married Persons: Community Versus Separate Property

This can get complicated because the rules are different for community and separate property. Texas Family Code Sections 3.201-203 govern spousal liability, rules of marital property liability, and the order in which marital property may be subject to execution on a judgment. Generally, a non-debtor spouse's community property interest under the control of both spouses may be levied upon to satisfy a judgment which was rendered against the other spouse alone. A common example is a judgment for credit card debt that is taken against one spouse. Once the judgment becomes final and is properly abstracted, filed, and indexed, the credit card company will then have a lien against all community property that is subject to joint management, control, and disposition by the two spouses—which will be *all* of it in most cases—regardless of whether or not the non-debtor spouse was named in the suit. This is true even if the judgment is against one spouse only for attorneys' fees incurred in the couple's divorce! *Gardner Aldrich, LLP v. Teddler*, 2011 WL 3546589 (Tex.App.—Fort Worth, August 1, 2011).

Separate property is another matter. A judgment lien against one spouse does not generally attach to the separate property of the non-debtor spouse.

Enforcement of Judgments from other States

Unfortunately for Texas debtors, this is not as difficult as it used to be. Enforcement of "foreign judgments" is governed by Civil Practice & Remedies Code Chapter 35, also referred to as the "Uniform Enforcement of Foreign Judgments Act" or "UEFJA." The UEFJA provides that a foreign judgment may be authenticated as follows: (a) at the time the foreign judgment is filed, the judgment creditor or the judgment creditor's attorney must file with the clerk of court an affidavit showing the name and last known address of the judgment debtor and the judgment creditor; (b) the clerk then mails notice of the filing of the foreign judgment to the judgment debtor at the address given; and (c) the notice must include the name and address of the judgment creditor and, if the judgment creditor has an attorney in Texas, the attorney's name and address. If a judgment from another state (a "foreign judgment") is properly domesticated in Texas, it immediately becomes the equivalent of a Texas judgment. *Citicorp Real Estate, Inc. v. Banque Arabe International D'Investissment*, 747 S.W.2d 926 (Tex.App.—Dallas, 1988, writ denied). So long as the judgment is not being appealed in its original jurisdiction, the creditor will have access to post-judgment discovery and other remedies allowed under Texas rules.

The result is that a foreign judgment may be enforced and collected in Texas just as any other judgment, with one limitation: Civil Practice & Remedies Code Section 16.066(b) provides that the foreign judgment may not be enforced in Texas if 10 years have passed since the judgment was rendered in its home state or after the judgment debtor has resided in Texas for 10 years. Good news or bad news, depending on which end of the dispute you are on.

Chapter 44

CHARGING ORDERS

Can a Judgment Creditor Seize Your LLC Membership?

Much is made in asset protection circles about charging orders and the circumstances in which they may occur. What is a charging order? It is a judge's order enabling a creditor to intercept and receive any distributions, payments, or proceeds from a specific entity to the judgment debtor. *The judgment creditor becomes, in effect, a court-ordered lienholder and assignee of any such funds.* It is important to distinguish the applicability and effect of a charging order from the outright attachment or seizure of a judgment debtor's interest in the entity. It is similarly important to identify which entities may be subject to a charging order. In Texas, these are limited liability companies and partnerships (general and limited).

Unlike an LLC membership interest or partnership interest which is only subject to a charging order, corporate stock may be seized and sold at public auction. Stock in a corporation is non-exempt personal property, (Tex. Bus. Orgs. Code Sec. 21.801), that can be subject to levy, Tex. R. Civ. P. 641, Tex. Bus. & Com. Code Sec. 8.112; garnishment, Tex. R. Civ. P. 669; or turnover, Tex. Civ. Prac. & Rem. Code Sec. 31.002.

Law Applicable to Limited Liability Companies
The law relating to charging orders on LLC membership interests is found at Business Organizations Code Section 101.112:

> (a) **On application by a judgment creditor a member of a limited liability company or of any other owner of a member-ship interest in a limited liability company, a court having jurisdiction may charge the membership interest of the judgment debtor to satisfy the judgment.**

> (b) **If a court charges a membership interest with payment of a judgment as provided by Subsection (a), the judgment creditor has only the right to receive any distribution to**

which the judgment debtor would otherwise be entitled in respect of the membership interest.

(c) A charging order constitutes a lien on the judgment debtor's membership interest. The charging order may not be foreclosed on under this code or any other law.

(d) The entry of a charging order is the exclusive remedy by which a judgment creditor of a member or of any other owner of a membership interest may satisfy a judgment out of the judgment debtor's membership interest.

(e) This section may not be construed to deprive a member of a limited liability company or any other owner of a membership interest in a limited liability company of the benefit of any exemption laws applicable to the member-ship interest of the member or owner.

(f) A creditor of a member or of any other owner of a membership interest does not have the right to obtain possession of, or otherwise exercise legal or equitable remedies with respect to, the property of the limited liability company.

The charging order is an exclusive remedy of its type. The judgment creditor gets paid *if and when* distributions from the LLC occur. The charging order is therefore not tantamount to taking over the membership interest of a debtor or seizing control of the company. Moreover, the creditor may not attach the debtor's membership interest; force its sale or transfer; or (absent a judgment piercing the veil) reach any assets of the LLC itself. *In re Prodigy Servs.*, No. 14-14-00248-CV (Tex.App.—Houston [14th Dist.] 2014, orig. proceeding).

What if the LLC pays a member a salary for services? Is this a "distribution" subject to a charging order? Probably not. Such a salary would not be subject to garnishment since it is exempt under Property Code Section 42.001(b)(1) which provides that "current wages for personal services, except for the enforcement of court-ordered child support payments" is exempt "from garnishment, attachment, execution, and other seizure." This includes severance pay.

The exclusive nature of a charging order does not limit a creditor's remedies once a distribution has been carried out. Distributed funds or assets become non-exempt personal property *once they are received by the debtor* and may therefore be reached by attachment, garnishment, or turnover. *Stanley v. Reef Secs., Inc.*, 314 S.W.3d 659 (Tex.App.—Dallas 2010, no pet.).

The rationale behind the exclusivity of the charging order remedy is to avoid undue disruption to the operation of the entity's business; after all, the creditor involved has a judgment against a member, not the entity itself, so the entity should not (at least in theory) be adversely affected. This principle has been eroded somewhat by *Heckert v. Heckert*, No. 02-16-00213-CV, 2017 WL 5184840 (Tex.App.—Fort Worth Nov. 9, 2017, no pet. h.). The Heckert case involved persons who were formerly married and the entity involved merely owned stock and did not operate a business, so the ruling allowing turnover should be viewed within these narrow circumstances.

Law Applicable to Partnerships

The law relating to charging orders on partnership interests mirrors the law applicable to LLCs and is found in Business Organizations Code Section 152.308:

(a) On application by a judgment creditor of a partner or of any other owner of a partnership interest, a court having jurisdiction may charge the partnership interest of the judgment debtor to satisfy the judgment.

(b) To the extent that the partnership interest is charged in the manner provided by Subsection (a), the judgment creditor has only the right to receive any distribution to which the judgment debtor would otherwise be entitled in respect of the partnership interest.

(c) A charging order constitutes a lien on the judgment debtor's partnership interest. The charging order lien may not be foreclosed on under this code or any other law.

(d) The entry of a charging order is the exclusive remedy by which a judgment creditor of a partner or of any other owner of a partnership interest may satisfy a judgment out of the judgment debtor's partnership interest.

(e) This section does not deprive a partner or other owner of a partnership interest of a right under exemption laws with respect to the judgment debtor's partnership interest.

(f) A creditor of a partner or of any other owner of a partnership interest does not have the right to obtain possession of, or otherwise exercise legal or equitable remedies with respect to, the property of the partnership.

It is important to note that a "judgment against a partnership is not by itself a judgment against a partner, so a creditor must obtain a judgment against the partner individually. A creditor may attempt to do so in the suit against the partnership or in a separate suit. It may not, however, seek satisfaction of the judgment against a partner until a judgment is rendered against the partnership." *American Star Energy & Minerals Corp. v. Stowers*, 457 S.W.3d 427, 429-30 (Tex. 2015).

Asset Protection before Suit is Filed

Sound asset protection practice requires that planning and strategy take place well in advance. Once a lawsuit is threatened or filed, it is more challenging to find legitimate ways of reorganizing or redistributing one's assets so as to reduce vulnerability to post-judgment collection efforts. One method of pre-suit planning is to form an LLC with two classes of membership: Class A and Class B. The company agreement should define Class B as any membership interest that has been substantially influenced or made subject to a collection device or court order, including a charging order. The conversion of Class A to Class B occurs automatically if that occurs. The effect? Class B members have no power to vote or serve as managers. Under such circumstances, it is difficult to see how a Class B member could force the liquidation of assets in order to benefit its own interests. Accordingly, Class B membership is of limited value unless the LLC is dissolved. In any case, such measures are generally useful only when taken as part of the set-up of one's asset protection structure, well in advance of threatened or actual litigation.

Asset Protection after Suit is Filed: Fraudulent Transfers

Property Code Section 42.004 seeks to restrain fraudulent transfers, including the pay-down of exempt assets, if undertaken "with the intent to defraud, delay, or hinder" a creditor. This reaches back two years for liquidated claims, one year for unliquidated or contingent claims. However, proving intent may be a difficult task if the judgment debtor goes about his or her business in an orderly, incremental fashion that can plausibly be described as normal, or at least *justifiable* on grounds independent of litigation concerns. Tex. Prop. Code Sec. 42.004(c).

As noted above, charging orders are generally an exclusive remedy, but there are exceptions. In a case where the defendant formed two entities—an LLC and a limited partnership—*after* a divorce suit had been filed against him and for the obvious sole purpose of holding non-exempt assets and avoiding judgment execution, the Fort Worth court of appeals ruled that a turnover order was appropriate. The wife was thus awarded the husband's interest in both entities, defeating his attempt to employ charging order rules as a defensive measure. *Heckert v. Heckert*, No. 02-16-00213-CV, 2017 WL 5184840 (Tex.App.—Fort Worth 2017, no pet.).

PART VIII

OTHER ISSUES OF INTEREST

TO INVESTORS

Chapter 45

REDEMPTION ISSUES FOR INVESTORS

After a Tax Sale or HOA Foreclosure

There is no general right of redemption by a borrower after a Texas foreclosure. The right of redemption is limited to (1) sales for unpaid ad valorem taxes, in which case a former owner of homestead or agricultural property has a two-year right of redemption (for commercial properties, the redemption period is 180 days); and (2) the HOA foreclosure of an assessment lien, in which case a former owner may redeem no later than the 180th day after notice.

The redemption right is the only right retained by the former owner, who is not allowed to occupy, possess, or receive rents from the property during the redemption period. Tex. Tax Code Sec. 34.21(h). The purchaser therefore has the right to proceed with an eviction subject to any limitations that may apply as to eviction of servicemembers or tenants with bona fide leases.

Tax Sales: Homestead and Agricultural Property

Tax Code Section 34.21(a) provides a two-year right of redemption if a property which is foreclosed upon for non-payment of ad valorem taxes is homestead or agricultural in nature:

(a) **The owner of real property sold at a tax sale to a purchaser other than a taxing unit that was used as the residence homestead of the owner or that was land designated for agricultural use ... may redeem the property on or before the second anniversary of the date on which the purchaser's deed is filed for record by paying the purchaser the amount of the purchaser bid for the property, the amount of the deed recording fee, and the amount paid by the purchaser as taxes, penalties, interest, and costs on the property, plus a redemption premium of 25 percent of the aggregate total if the property is redeemed during the first year of the redemption period or 50 percent of the aggregate total if the property is redeemed during the second year of the redemption period.**

Accordingly, the return to the investor on the 366th day is *double* what it was on the 365th. This may provide the investor with an incentive to give the former owner a payment plan that will be completed in the second year of the redemption period. After all, the statute requires that the redeemer pay a certain aggregate amount; it does not require that this amount be paid in one lump sum.

What "costs" are allowed to an investor under this statute? Section 34.21(g)(2) expressly includes sums expended "for maintaining, preserving, and safekeeping the property" which would include insurance, *legally-required* repairs, payment of municipal liens imposed for health or safety reasons, HOA dues, and utility impact or standby fees. Allowable costs do *not* include a general rehab of the property if the repairs and improvements are not required by local ordinance, building code, or lease of the property which was in effect on the date of sale—so over-eager investors who engage in such improvements in anticipation of a quick flip do so at their own risk. Note that a former owner "may request that the purchaser of the property, or the taxing unit to which property was bid off, provide that owner a written itemization of all amounts spent. . . ." It is therefore essential that an investor be conservative and keep a careful record of expenses in order to avoid a dispute.

Tax Sales: Non-Homestead and Non-Agricultural Property
The rules are different for commercial, non-agricultural property. The general commercial right of redemption after a tax sale is 180 days and the redemption premium is more limited. Tex. Tax Code Sec. 34.21(e). The statute provides that:

(1) the owner's right of redemption may be exercised not later than the 180th day following the date on which the purchaser's or taxing unit's deed is filed for record; and

(2) the redemption premium payable by the owner to a purchaser other than a taxing unit may not exceed 25 percent.

Contrary to what one might expect, the commercial rules as to what constitute allowable, recoverable costs are no more liberal than those applicable to homestead and agricultural properties. The same standards apply. Tex. Tax Code Sec. 34.21(g)(2).

Redemption after an HOA Foreclosure

Redemption rights following an HOA foreclosure are part of the Texas Residential Property Owners Protection Act which was designed to reign in the once arbitrary power of HOAs (Tex. Prop. Code Chap. 209). Specifically, Section. 209.011(b) provides that the "owner of property in a residential subdivision or a lienholder of record may redeem the property from any purchaser at a sale foreclosing a property owners' association assessment lien not later than the 180th day after the date the association mails written notice of the sale to the owner and the lienholder. . . ." The notice must be sent by certified mail, not later than the 30th day after the date of sale, to the last known address of the property owner (as reflected in the records of the HOA) and to each lienholder (at the address indicated on the lienholder's most recent deed of trust). Tex. Prop. Code Sec. 209.010.

Note that a lienholder's right to redeem does not commence until 90 days after the statutory notice is given and exists only if the homeowner has not previously redeemed. Tex. Prop. Code Sec. 209.011(b).

So how is redemption (or an investor's response to it) accomplished? The answer is *carefully, by the book, and always in writing.* Section 209.011 is divided into two general parts: the first deals with the situations where the HOA purchases the delinquent property, and the second pertains to purchases by a third party. If the HOA is the purchaser, then it may receive all amounts previously due; interest to the date of redemption (10% if no rate is stated in the association's documentation); costs including attorney's fees; the amount of any subsequent assessment that may have been levied; any sums expended for mortgage payments, repair, and leasing of the property; and any remaining net amount as determined by the purchase price paid by the HOA.

If the property was purchased by a third-party investor, then redemption is essentially accomplished by paying the amounts due the HOA (as outlined above) plus the purchase price paid by the investor; the amount of the deed recording fee; any amounts paid for taxes, penalties, and interest following the sale; and any costs incurred in connection with an eviction relating to the property. *That is all.* There is no premium due the investor. Additionally, if the investor collects rent from the property during the redemption period, this must be credited to the account of the homeowner if he or she redeems. Tex. Prop. Code Sec. 209.011(i).

Finally, to state what should be obvious, the property redeemed remains subject to all liens and encumbrances that existed before the foreclosure sale took place. Tex. Prop. Code Sec. 209.011(k).

If the investor leased the property to a tenant during the redemption period, and the homeowner redeems, then that lease is effectively canceled and the homeowner has the right to immediately re-occupy the premises. Tex. Prop. Code Sec. 209.011(k). Accordingly, any lease entered into by the investor during the redemption period should contain a disclosure and disclaimer to this effect.

An investor who buys property at a tax sale or HOA foreclosure should be prepared to hold the property and avoid either making substantial improvements to it or reselling it until after any applicable rights of redemption have expired. As is the case with all legal deadlines, the redemption period should not be calculated down to the hour and minute. A cushion should be allowed so as to avoid offering the opposition an opportunity to argue that statutorily-required time periods were not fully met.

Chapter 46

SECURITY DEPOSITS IN TEXAS RESIDENTIAL LEASES

The Deck is Stacked against the Investor

Investors who are new to the business of being residential landlords would be best advised to acquaint themselves with the rules concerning security deposits, particularly since the Property Code declares that a landlord is presumed to be acting in bad faith if an accounting is not timely and properly given for these funds. "Bad faith" in this context triggers a $100 statutory penalty and the recovery by the tenant of treble damages plus attorney's fees—and, of course, whenever a law provides for the award of attorney's fees, the door is opened to contingent-fee arrangements. This means that the usual cost-benefit analysis which potential plaintiffs must perform (Is this litigation going to be worth the expense?) does not apply. An aggrieved tenant may pursue an investor at no cost to himself. He is even granted the equivalent of preferred creditor status: "The tenant's claim to the security deposit takes priority over the claim of any creditor of the landlord, including a trustee in bankruptcy." Tex. Prop. Code Sec. 92.103(c).

Applicable Law

Chapter 92, Subchapter C of the Property Code contains requirements pertaining to landlord accounting for and refunding of residential security deposits. It states in part:

§ 92.103. OBLIGATION TO REFUND

(a) Except as provided by Section 92.107 [failure by tenant to give a written statement of forwarding address], the landlord shall refund a security deposit to the tenant on or before the 30th day after the date the tenant surrenders the premises.

§ 92.104. RETENTION OF SECURITY DEPOSIT; ACCOUNTING

(a) Before returning a security deposit, the landlord may deduct from the deposit damages and charges for

which tenant is legally liable under the lease or as a result of breaching the lease.

(b) The landlord may not retain any portion of a security deposit to cover normal wear and tear.

(c) If the landlord retains all or part of a security deposit under this section, the landlord shall give to the tenant the balance of the security deposit, if any, together with a written description and itemized list of all deductions. The landlord is not required to give the tenant a description and itemized list of deductions if:

> (1) the tenant owes rent when he surrenders possession of the premises; and
> (2) there is no controversy concerning the amount of rent owed.

§ 92.106. RECORDS

The landlord shall keep accurate records of all security deposits.

§ 92.109. LIABILITY OF LANDLORD

(a) A landlord who in bad faith retains a security deposit in violation of this subchapter is liable for an amount equal to the sum of $100, three times the portion of the deposit wrongfully withheld, and the tenant's reasonable attorney's fees in a suit to recover the deposit.

(b) A landlord who in bad faith does not provide a written description and itemized list of damages and charges in violation of this subchapter:

> (1) forfeits the right to withhold any portion of the security deposit or to bring suit against the tenant for damages to the premises; and
> (2) is liable for the tenant's reasonable attorney's fees in a suit to recover the deposit.

(c) In an action brought by a tenant under this subchapter, the landlord has the burden of proving that the retention of any portion of the security deposit was reasonable.

(d) A landlord who fails either to return a security deposit or to provide a written description and itemization of deductions on or before the 30th day after the date the tenant surrenders possession *is presumed to have acted in bad faith* [italics added].

Accounting for Security Deposits

The statutory requirement, as stated above, is only that the landlord keep an accurate record when it comes to security deposits. Does this require the ability to produce an Excel spreadsheet? Is a segregated bank account required? The answer is no to both questions, at least as to legally-required minimums, but both ideas are nonetheless good ones and are recommended for the professional investor.

Reasonableness and Bad Faith

The burden is on the landlord to demonstrate the reasonableness and necessity of any deductions. Unreasonable deductions or withholding return of the security deposit entirely raise the prospect of a finding of bad faith. "A landlord acts in bad faith when he retains the security deposit in dishonest disregard of the tenant's rights. Bad faith implies an intention to deprive the tenant of a lawfully due refund. Absent rebutting evidence, the presumption that the landlord acted in bad faith compels a finding of bad faith." *Pulley v. Milberger*, 198 A.Q.3d 418, 428-29 (Tex.App.—Dallas 2006, pet. denied). As it turns out, rebutting evidence may not be that difficult to establish. If the landlord reasonably believed he had the right to retain a security deposit, then that can be rebutting evidence; so can the fact that the landlord was inexperienced and not fully informed on the law. *Johnson v. Waters at Elm Creek L.L.C.* 416 S.W.3d 42, 47-48 (Tex.App.—San Antonio 2013, pet. denied). In this circumstance, it would appear that ignorance of the law can indeed be a defense.

Notwithstanding the foregoing, bad faith on the part of the landlord is *presumed* according to Section 92.109(d) if the required accounting is not sent within 30 days. "A landlord shall have 30 days from the tenant's furnishing of a forwarding address to refund the deposit or provide an itemization of damages before the presumption of bad faith will arise." *Ackerman v. Little*, 679 S.W.2d 799, 75 (Tex.App.—Dallas 1984, no writ).

Although the usual mailbox rule applies (the letter is considered sent when deposited in the U.S. mail per Section 92.1041) it is imprudent for a landlord to wait until the last minute to send a security deposit accounting and risk being (even arguably) late and in presumptive bad faith. In most cases, unless there are extensive repairs to be made, there is no good reason for a competent landlord to delay sending out an accounting past ten days or so after surrender of the premises.

The Requirement of a Tenant Forwarding Address under Section 92.107(a)

The tenant is obligated to provide a forwarding address in writing (Tex. Prop. Code Sec. 92.107(a)). Note that even if the tenant fails to provide such an address, the right to an accounting and refund is not forfeited; it is merely delayed. This same section makes it clear that the landlord's obligation to supply a written description of damages does not arise until a forwarding address is provided. So should the landlord passively wait until a departed tenant gets in touch? We suggest not. Our recommendation to a landlord who has no forwarding address is to timely send the accounting (together with any refund check) to the tenant at the address of the rental property, by certified mail with return receipt requested. The letter will come back if the tenant has left. An investor should always be prepared to demonstrate good-faith compliance with a statute, even if that occasionally means walking the extra mile.

Tenant's Notice of Surrender

Can a lease provide that a tenant must give advance notice of surrender as a condition for refunding the security deposit? Yes, so long as the lease provision is underlined or is printed in conspicuous bold print. Tex. Prop. Code Sec. 92.103(b). If utilizing such a clause, we recommend that it be both underlined and set in bold, 14 point type.

Tenant Substitution of Security Deposit for Final Month's Rent

This is expressly prohibited by Section 92.108(a): "The tenant may not withhold payment of any portion of the last month's rent on grounds that the security deposit is security for unpaid rent." Doing so makes the tenant vulnerable to a finding of bad faith—and yes, that means treble damages plus attorney's fees for the landlord. The reality, however, is that this is seldom granted. The vast majority of residential tenants are judgment-proof, and it is usually a waste of time and money to pursue them. Which does not mean that the investor should not look at each circumstance, case by case, before writing it off.

Landlord's Sale of the Rental Property

What if the investor sells the property to another investor? Who is liable for a deposit under the Code? Unless proper notice is given to the tenant, both seller and buyer may be liable. Section 92.105(a) states flatly that "the new owner is liable for the return of security deposits . . . from the date title to the premises is acquired. . . ." So how does the seller get off the hook? Section 92.105(b) addresses this, providing that the seller "remains liable for a security deposit received while the person was the owner until the new owner delivers to the tenant a signed statement acknowledging that the new owner has received and is responsible for the tenant's security deposit and specifying the exact dollar amount of the deposit." Such a signed statement—with language precisely tracking the statute—should therefore be prepared along with the warranty deed and any other transfer paperwork, and the seller should ensure that it is delivered to the tenant. Otherwise, the seller may remain liable for both the accounting for and return of the security deposit, with all the attendant risks of a potential finding of bad faith.

By now, it should be apparent that security deposit disputes are generally to be avoided by landlords. Although Texas is a business-friendly state, parts of the Property Code are stacked against the investor (the section on executory contracts comes to mind) and this includes provisions relating to security deposits. If an argument over a deposit can be settled reasonably by a landlord, it should be, and quickly. Write off the loss and live to fight another day. And, as in any situation where a monetary dispute is resolved, the landlord should get a release in exchange for the settlement check.

Chapter 47

HARD-MONEY LENDING

Swimming with Sharks

Banks and other conventional lenders evaluate and underwrite loans based on a borrower's ability to repay, the sufficiency of the collateral, and a project's prospect for success. These and other considerations are mandated by federal and state regulations as well as policies of the Federal Reserve. However, no such constraints hamper the operations of hard-money lenders who, more often than not, are individuals with substantial cash looking for an aggressive return on investment. It is a largely unregulated, wild-west kind of market that may work to the benefit of the careful investor—or result in disaster. A central point to keep in mind is that hard-money lenders are not in business to be charities, or seminar promoters, or mentors. Their goal is to make a no-risk, high ROI loan to the investor-borrower and frankly—in spite of pious claims to the contrary—could not care less if the investor-borrower makes a dime or even survives in the real estate business. So *caveat emptor*.

What is a hard-money loan?

This term has come to refer to short-term non-standard financing that is available based on the deal itself. The borrower's credit is not a factor. It is simply a question of numbers, including a loan-to-value ratio that effectively makes the transaction a sure bet for the lender whether or not the investor-borrower is successful in his objectives. Hard-money lending is an important part of the universe of potential financing sources, but it should be utilized only when appropriate safeguards are built into the loan documentation. Otherwise, it can swiftly turn into a "heads I win, tails you lose" scenario in favor of the lender. A pernicious example of this can be found among hard-money lenders who masquerade as gurus or mentors for newbie investors, offering seminars and "training" to those aspiring to financial independence in the world of real estate. Wealth is all but inevitable if the participants will only use the promoter's "system." Some of these seminars are really fantasy-based marketing tools designed to discover good borrower prospects for the gurus and link them to deals upon which hard-money financing can be offered.

There's an old saying in the car business: "Sell the financing, not the car." Why? Because that's where most of the profit is, at least in the long term, which is not so different in the world of real estate. Hard-money financing, particularly when accompanied by up-front points plus an equity participation interest (the lender keeps a percentage of the action in addition to collecting interest on the note), can often be *far* more profitable than directly investing in the underlying "dirt." Do you see how this would be an attractive proposition for someone with available cash? *Let those newbie investors take the deal risk.* A hard-money lender is all but assured of a positive return either way, with very little exposure.

"Just sign these standard forms—and don't show them to your lawyer!"

Firstly, there are no "standard forms" in real estate investing, even though seminar gurus and hard-money lenders often claim otherwise. Even forms promulgated by TREC or published by TAR contain multiple opportunities for slanting the transaction in favor of buyer or seller. Every good broker and real estate lawyer knows this. For example, a lawyer's documentary templates have multiple selections that need to be made throughout the text depending on whether the client is a seller or buyer, lender or borrower. The original template may be 30 pages long; however, once narrowed down to suit the client and focused to the client's advantage, the result may be less than 10 pages. That's how lawyers produce precision documents in favor of their clients. Conclusion? If a document is fill-in-the-blank, it is almost certainly over-simplified junk. Buy your supplies at Office Depot, not your legal documents.

Secondly, many seminar forms are derived from other states and have since undergone all sorts of evolution and amateur modification. They may be less than fully enforceable in Texas and may in fact get an investor in legal trouble. Many real estate lawyers (including this author) refuse to even attempt to make such guru packages Texas-compliant. What sensible lawyer would want the liability for trying to do that?

Thirdly, anytime you are told you do not need to consult your attorney, *run*—don't walk—to the door. If the door is locked, jump out of the nearest window and flee for refuge. It is a monumental failure of due diligence to sign *any* loan documents, particularly hard-money docs, without talking to your real estate lawyer. He or she will have all sorts of constructive comments and suggested improvements designed to avoid disaster. Some lenders will respond that the golden rule applies (*he who has the gold rules*) and no changes to their documents are permitted. Nonsense. Everything is negotiable. And if the documents cannot be written so they fairly balance the interests of lender and borrower, then your lawyer will likely advise you to walk away from that loan. We have said elsewhere that not every deal can or should be made. The same is true for loans.

The Mechanics of Hard-Money Loans

Loans of this type typically come with higher interest rates—often up to 20% or so. Borrowers are also often called upon to pay several up-front points in order to get the loan (a "point" is equal to 1% of the loan). For example, on a $100,000 loan, the lender might require three points at funding ($3,000) which is netted out of the amount advanced, so the borrower in this case actually receives only $97,000.

Hard-money loan documents generally consist of a short-term promissory note (often with a term of 6, 9, or 12 months), a commercial-style deed of trust and security agreement that includes a statement that the property is not the borrower's homestead; and a loan agreement to cover miscellaneous details such as representations and warranties and a provision for alternative dispute resolution (something that should always be included if you are the lender). Occasionally, there may be a participation agreement (sometimes called an equity participation agreement, a profit-sharing agreement, or joint venture agreement), which provides for payment of part of the net profits to the lender when the property is sold. In such cases, the lender is not only collecting fees and interest but also a piece of the action. This is common in the case of "fix and flip loans," which are usually just another example of hard-money lending.

Protections for the Investor-Borrower

What specific documentary measures can an investor-borrower take when negotiating a hard-money scenario? Specific circumstances must always be considered in answering this question but here are some examples:

1. *Never sign a personal guaranty of a hard-money loan.* Hard-money loans are made based on the fundamentals of the deal itself and have very little to do with the borrower (who should, by the way, be an investor's LLC or, in the case of series LLC, one of the LLC's individual series). Signing a personal guaranty pointlessly adds to the potential damage if the purchase/rehab/resale does not work out as planned or within budget. If the deal is not strong enough in the lender's eyes to stand on its

own—that is actually useful information, incidentally—then walk away.

2. *Always include a non-recourse provision in the note.* Here's an example: *Notwithstanding any other provision of this Note or any instrument securing same, Lender may satisfy the debt evidenced by this Note only by the enforcement of Lender's rights in, to, and against the Property and no other property, real or personal, of Borrower.* Since the deal is supposed to stand on its own, it should do just that and extend only to the subject property. An investor-borrower should not allow a hard-money lender to con him or her into putting an entire investment portfolio at risk.

3. *Cap any potential equity participation.* If there is an equity participation agreement, it should be reasonable and not unlimited in dollar amount. It should be effective up to but not exceeding a figure. Sample wording: *Borrower hereby irrevocably grants and conveys to Lender a 5% participatory interest in the net sales proceeds of the Property, not to exceed a maximum of $25,000."* Your lawyer will then want to carefully define the term "net sales proceeds" to account for all the investor-borrower's out-of-pocket costs, including commissions and unforeseen expenses.

Certain participation agreements are worded in absolute dollar amounts rather than as a percentage of net sales proceeds. For example, if closing occurs by a certain date, then the amount due the lender is $15,000; if it closes a month later, the amount increases to $25,000. *Beware of these.* In the view of this author, they are unreasonable on their face and should be avoided. To the extent possible, the hard-money lender should be compelled to share in at least some of the risk that profit may not be as much as anticipated in the original pro forma.

4. *Provide for an extension.* Unfortunate timing, along with under-capitalization, are the causes of most financial loss in real estate investment. If pressed for time, it can be useful for a borrower have the option of falling back on an extension provision allowing payment of a predetermined fee (perhaps another point) in order to get an extra 30 or 60 days to complete the fix and flip.

5. *Scrutinize default provisions.* Remember, hard-money lending is an essentially unregulated market. Many hard-money documents are cobbled together from various sources and contain a maze of vague default provisions that fail to include a specifically-stated notice period and opportunity to cure without penalty. These are dangerous. Others are

designed by very smart lenders' lawyers to put the investor-borrower at every possible disadvantage. These are dangerous as well—particularly if the investor-borrower has bought the line that the loan documents are "standard" and cannot be changed, so he has not consulted a lawyer. General rule: *A lender should never be permitted to have the ability to declare a borrower in default on a whim.* Default parameters should be ascertainable and transparent, as should notice periods and the time in which any alleged default must be cured. Reinstatement procedures (i.e., after a default) should be addressed as well.

6. *Scrutinize due-on-sale or transfer provisions.* Not all due-on-sale clauses track the familiar language of the FNMA deed of trust. They can be custom-written to prohibit a borrower from even leasing a property prior to maturity of the loan. This is unacceptable in a hard-money case. *Read the deed of trust carefully.* Know when the lender can call a loan due and when it cannot.

7. *Beware of Fee Factories.* It should come as no surprise that fraudsters exist in the unregulated world of hard-money lending. We live in a fee-based economy now, so fees happen, but there is a point at which they become not only excessive but fraudulent. We are aware of at least one case currently being prosecuted under Chapter 31 of the Penal Code (theft) in which the "lender" charged over $100,000 in up-front fees with no apparent intention of making a promised $1.5 million dollar loan.

Preserve Profit

Lastly, make sure that the hard-money lender does not crowd out the possibility of a reasonable profit. Returning to the automobile example: car dealers routinely make (at least) $5,000 to $10,000 when flipping a luxury car. Shouldn't an investor make more than that when locating, buying, rehabing, and selling a house—particularly if he or she must incur a loan risk in order to do it? The *minimum goal* should be a net profit of $10,000 to $20,000. Investors who make only $1,500 here and $2,500 there are generally on a high-speed exit ramp out of the real estate investment business.

Chapter 48

PARTITON IN TEXAS

Remedies When Joint Owners Disagree

A principal subject of this book has been structuring the ownership of investment property for purposes of asset protection, including the use of LLCs, trusts, and partnerships. By now the reader will know that this author is inclined to favor LLCs, since they offer an effective liability barrier, while trusts and partnerships do not. There is, however, another important group of issues: transactional efficiency and avoidance of conflict among the interested parties.

Transactional Efficiency and Conflict Avoidance

For purposes of this book, "transactional efficiency" refers to ease of transfer. In the case of an LLC, only one individual—the manager—is usually required to sign documents at the title company. If the LLC has officers, the signing person might instead be the president or vice president. But it is not necessary to obtain the signature of all members of the company and their spouses, even if these other parties disagree with a proposed transaction. This is also true if one of the members of the LLC is now deceased and that member's heirs oppose the transaction.

Trusts can be a bit iffier. Usually it is necessary only to procure the signature of the trustee who is duly named in a proper trust agreement; but if a title company is wary of the trust for some reason (and they are often wary of trusts), the closer may demand signatures of others involved.

Partnerships usually require the signature of all persons who are named in the partnership agreement as general partners, whether that is two or twenty people. Spouses will likely be called upon to sign as well, since Texas is a community property state. If the partnership is a limited partnership, then the signature of the general partner is usually all that is required, but the title company may choose to require the joinder of others if there is obvious conflict among the interested parties with respect to the transaction.

If the property is owned by individual joint owners without a written partnership agreement, you can anticipate that everyone interested will be required to sign.

Based on the foregoing summary, which structure do you think is most efficient in consummating a transaction and avoiding the consequences of conflict among the interested parties? The answer is obviously an LLC. And yet real estate attorneys commonly encounter situations where assets are titled in a general partnership or in the names of several individuals—the worst possible way to own investment real estate. The parties who were once so friendly about their common business goals now vehemently disagree about a proposed transaction. Or how to distribute the proceeds. One or more refuses to sign off. One might become a "hold out" and effectively blackmail the others into receiving more than his rightful share. What then?

What is partition?

"Partition" is the legal term referring to division of real property among joint owners. It may be voluntary, by agreement or partition deed, but that is easy to accomplish and does not concern us here. Our focus in this chapter is on what happens when no agreement can be reached. The disagreement may be relatively amicable, with one or more partners politely refusing to go along, or the partners may literally be at each other's throats. A spouse of a partner may have decided that he or she will oppose the sale of an asset, perhaps preferring to save it for the children rather than liquidate it now. There are countless reasons for opposition, including sheer spite.

The remedy in such a situation is for one or more of the joint owners to seek a court-ordered division by means of a partition suit. It is also possible to file a "friendly" partition action if the parties desire a court decree that ratifies their agreement. Note that partition is not the appropriate remedy when there is no common title or title is in dispute.

There are two kinds of judicially-ordered partition: partition in kind, which refers to the actual physical division of land by metes and bounds; and a judicially-ordered sale of the property, when partition in kind is not feasible or cannot be achieved fairly and equitably.

The Right to Partition

The right to a partition is absolute so long as the petitioning party is a joint owner of the land to be partitioned and has an equal right to possess it with the other joint owners, subject to any leases. There is no effective defense to such an action that is properly brought by someone who qualifies. *Spires v. Hoover*, 466 S.W. 2d 344, 346 (Tex.App.—El Paso 1971, writ ref'd n.r.e.). However, the right to partition may be waived or contracted away in the partnership agreement. *Dimock v. Kadane*, 100 S.W.3d 622, 625 (Tex.App.—Eastland 2003, pet. denied). Barring a valid waiver of the right to partition, Property Code Section 23.001 et seq. applies:

> **A joint owner or claimant of real property or an interest in real property or a joint owner of personal property may compel a partition of the interest or the property among the joint owners or claimants under this chapter and the Texas Rules of Civil Procedure.**

Since personal as well real property is mentioned in this statute, the right to partition extends not just to the realty but also the FF&E (furniture, fixtures, and equipment) that may be located on the premises.

No statute of limitations applies to the right of partition. *Hipp v. Fall*, 213 S.W.2d 732,737 (Tex.App.—Galveston 1948, writ ref'd n.r.e.).

Venue is normally in the district court of the county where the property is located. Tex. Prop. Code Sec. 23.002(a). However, in counties where district and county courts have concurrent jurisdiction in title matters (as in Harris County), county courts may also hear such cases so long as the amount in controversy is within their monetary jurisdiction. *Eris v. Giannakopoulos*, 369 S.W.3d 618, 620-21 (Tex.App.—Houston [1st Dist.] 2012, pet. dism'd).

The real fight in many partition cases is about the *pro rata* shares of the parties and whether or not the property should be partitioned in kind or sold. Generally speaking, the law favors partition in kind over a forced sale. "If the property can be divided in kind without materially impairing its value, a sale will not be ordered, but when dividing the land into parcels causes its value to be substantially less than its value when whole, the rights of the owners are substantially prejudiced." *Cecola v. Ruley*, 12 S.W.3d 848, 855 (Tex.App.—Texarkana 2000, no pet.). Clearly, a 100-acre farm may lend itself favorably to partition in kind while a single-family residence on a lot and block may not.

"The threshold question in a partition suit is whether the property is 'susceptible of partition' or 'incapable of partition' because a 'fair and equitable division' cannot be made. . . . The determination of whether an in-kind partition is fair and equitable includes whether the property can be divided in-kind without materially impairing its value. . . . The party seeking partition by sale bears the burden of proving a partition in-kind would not be fair and equitable. . . . A party is not required to show that partition in kind is physically impossible, but that partition by sale would best serve the parties' interest and restore or preserve the maximum value of the property." *Carter v. Harvey*, 525 S.W.3d 420 (Tex.App.—Fort

Worth [2nd Dist.] 2017, no pet.).

Rule 756 *et seq.* of the Texas Rules of Civil Procedure

The other statutory law applicable to partition can be found in Rule 756 *et seq.* of the Texas Rules of Civil Procedure. Rule 756 and the rules that follow set forth the procedure necessary to accomplish a fair and equitable partition. Other than the specific requirements contained in Sec. 23.001 *et seq.* and Rule 756 *et seq.*, partition cases are governed by the same rules and procedures as other civil cases, including entitlement to a jury trial. All parties with an interest in the property must be joined in the litigation.

Rule 761 provides that if the property can be fairly and equitably divided into separate tracts, then the court shall appoint three or more "competent and disinterested persons" to act as commissioners in designing a plan to divide the land, arrive at an estimated value of each share, and allot the shares among the various owners. The commissioners are appointed by means of a "writ of partition" that is issued by the clerk of court and accompanied by the court's order directing that the property be partitioned. They are often local lawyers or realtors. The writ of partition may also appoint a surveyor to assist the commissioners. A commissioners' report is then prepared and submitted for the court's approval. The parties to the suit have 30 days to file objections to the report. If objections are filed, the court must hold a trial on the objections. The court then enters a judgment that may be appealed as in other civil cases, but the appellate court is directed by Rule 781 to give preference on its docket to an appeal of a partition judgment.

The Outcome

If the partition is "in kind," the final judgment results in the parties obtaining exclusive use and possession of their respective tracts along with the power to dispose of same as they see fit, without consent or involvement by the previous joint owners. The judgment, however, does not create any warranties of title that did not exist before.

Sales of partitioned property are conducted by the sheriff or the constable as in other executions upon judgments. If the property is sold at public auction, the sheriff is required to notify the parties of the date and time of sale. *Gibson v. Smith*, 511 S.W.2d 327, 328 (Tex.App.—Tyler 1974, no writ). Alternatively, the court may direct that a receiver be appointed to sell the property at private or public sale. Any party to the suit may bid on the property along with other members of the public. The proceeds of the sale are returned to the court for distribution.

Damages and Costs

Although a partition action does not generally contemplate monetary damages (except in the event of waste to the property), auxiliary relief such as an accounting for rents and profits may be requested. Contribution and reimbursement issues may also arise as to taxes paid, improvements made, and expenses incurred in connection with the property.

Costs in a partition action are paid by each party *pro rata* according to the value of that party's partitioned share. However, the considerable expense and delay involved in meeting the procedural and substantive requirements of a partition suit are a powerful incentive for the parties to settle. If a receiver is appointed, the cost (paid for by the sales proceeds) can be substantial, even disastrous. A surveyor and appraisers are often employed as well. Additionally, since sheriff sales do not as a rule obtain the best possible price for real property, the parties should carefully consider the advisability of reaching a settlement that avoids court involvement and provides for private sale of the property at the best available price.

Caveat for Partition of Heirship Property

In 2017 Texas adopted the Uniform Partition of Heirs' Property Act which makes partition among heirs a special case not subject to the ordinary rules. If at least 20% of the aggregate interest in property is held by persons related to one another, then Property Code Section 23A.003 et seq. will govern any attempt to force a sale. The law was designed to avoid loss of family property and homestead wealth among poor and minority communities who have been historically less likely to execute wills or do estate planning. The result could be numerous heirs holding ownership in widely varying percentages, only some of whom might live on the property. Others might be difficult or impossible to locate. Investors would take advantage of this situation by acquiring a small ownership stake and then asking a court to force a partition, resulting in a sheriff sale at a price that was usually well below market.

The UPHPA provides an opportunity for heirs to be able to buy out the interest of the cotenant who is attempting to force the sale. If this approach fails, a court may evaluate the circumstances surrounding the property and who resides there in light of relevant sentimental, cultural, and historical factors—and then determine whether partition in kind or partition by sale is the appropriate remedy. If a sale is eventually ordered, the property must be listed with a real estate broker for its fair value, rather than going to a sheriff's sale which usually results in a fire-sale price. As a result, investors pursuing forced partition of heirship property as an investment strategy now have more hoops through which to jump and are more likely to wind up paying a sum that is closer to the property's true market value.

Chapter 49

BUYING AND SELLING REAL ESTATE NOTES

Not as Simple as One Might Think

Real estate investors often buy and sell real estate lien notes, either singly or in a package, a transaction that is customarily effected by a "Sale & Assignment of Note(s) and Lien(s)," which is akin to a bill of sale for personal goods. We will refer to this document simply as an assignment.

The notion of buying or selling a note seems simple until you delve into it. Is the assignment made "as is?" Are there representations and warranties made by either party and, if so, how extensive? Are there recourse provisions and, if so, what is the recourse mechanism? Will an indemnity provision be included? This chapter will deal with these considerations.

For purposes of this discussion, we will address absolute assignments rather than assignments made as collateral for a loan ("absolute assignments" versus "collateral assignments"). Further, comments on the contents of the assignment itself will be limited to the final document to be signed by the parties, not to executory contracts contemplating a due diligence period followed by a closing. Another assumption made in this chapter is that there is no separate loan agreement that accompanies the note.

Applicable Law

A properly written and endorsed real estate lien note is a negotiable instrument for purposes of Texas Business & Commerce Code Section 3.201 et seq. Specific requirements of negotiability are listed in Section 3.104:

> **Section 3.104. NEGOTIABLE INSTRUMENT. (a) Except as provided in Subsections (c) and (d), "negotiable instrument" means an unconditional promise or order to pay a fixed amount of money, with or without interest or other charges described in the promise or order, if it:**
>
> **(1) is payable to bearer or to order at the time it is**

issued or first comes into possession of a holder;

(2) is payable on demand or at a definite time; and

(3) does not state any other undertaking or instruction by the person promising or ordering payment to do any act in addition to the payment of money, but the promise or order may contain:
   (A) an undertaking or power to give, maintain, or protect collateral to secure payment;
   (B) an authorization or power to the holder to confess judgment or realize on or dispose of collateral; or
   (C) a waiver of the benefit of any law intended for the advantage or protection of an obligor.

A real estate note that does not qualify as a negotiable instrument may still be valid and enforceable, and it may still be sold and assigned, but the usual common law rules relating to the assignment of contracts will apply. Caution is in order, however; the resale value of a note that is non-negotiable will likely be deeply discounted.

Due Diligence by the Assignee

Determining the validity and enforceability of a real estate note is the basic due-diligence duty of anyone considering buying one.

What are issues the assignee should be looking for? Look at the basics. As is the case with any contract, there must be consideration extended (i.e., money loaned) for a note to be valid. *Hughes v. Belman*, 239 S.W.2d 717, 720 (Tex.App.—Austin 1951, writ ref'd n.r.e.); *also* Tex. Bus. & Com. Code Sec. 3.303. The note should identify the parties, recite an unconditional promise to pay a sum certain (the numerical portion must exactly match the written portion), be signed by the debtor and dated, and provide clear terms of repayment (upon demand or at a fixed time). It should not (obviously) contain any provisions that are illegal, such as requiring the payment of usurious interest. The note should be currently performing (no monetary or non-monetary defaults), with no lawsuit or bankruptcy filing anticipated from the debtor, whose payment history should also be examined. If the lien(s) securing the note are against a homestead, both husband and wife must have signed the note and the deed of trust securing its payment. The deed of trust should be filed and otherwise properly do its job.

Clearly, there are many factors that need to be considered, both legal and in terms of risk assessment. Sensible purchasers of real estate notes (and the liens accompanying them) will ask an experienced attorney for assistance in evaluating the validity and enforceability of such documents before committing substantial funds toward their purchase. Accordingly, any executory contract for the purchase and sale of a real estate note should include an adequate due diligence or inspection period before a final closing. The purchase of any note that does not meet the minimum standards of this paragraph should be avoided.

If the parties are registered entities (LLCs, corporations, or limited partnerships), it is important to verify that they are in good standing with the Secretary of State and the Texas Comptroller. If not, they do not have the legal capacity to do business, whether it is transferring notes or anything else.

The Basics of an Absolute Sale and Assignment of Note and Lien(s)

Buying and selling a real estate note involves transferring not only the debt but also the lien(s) that go with it, making it advisable to record any such assignment in the real property records where the security property is located. Two liens are usually involved: the vendor's lien retained in the deed to the payor, and the deed of trust lien granted to a trustee to secure payment.

It goes without saying that the payee on the note should also be given notice of the transfer along with the name of the new payor and the address to which payments will now be sent.

A sale and assignment of note and liens (for the remainder of this chapter we will use the term "assignment") should clearly indicate the parties—the assignor-owner-holder of the note along with the identity of the assignee. Assignment may be made with or with representations, warranty, or recourse, and the instrument should make these variables clear. The assignment should also include the legal description of the security property, exactly tracking the legal description found in the general or special warranty deed. As with all real property instruments, it is useful to also include the property's street address. Both assignee and assignee should sign the assignment in order to indicate unconditional mutual assent to its terms and conditions.

Representations and Warranties ("Reps and Warranties") by Assignor

The assignment may include extensive reps and warranties, limited reps and warranties, or no reps and warranties at all—in which case the assignment is made "as is" and almost always without recourse. It should be obvious that issues like these need to be made clear in the instrument, but often they are left unarticulated or muddled (Internet junk forms are particularly deficient in this respect). A poorly-written assignment can form the basis for later litigation, what lawyers refer to as "an invitation to a lawsuit."

Business & Commerce Code Section 3.416 provides minimal warranties for notes that are negotiable instruments. These are automatically in place unless the assignment disclaims them:

> **Section 3.416. TRANSFER WARRANTIES. (a) A person who transfers an instrument for consideration warrants to the transferee and, if the transfer is by indorsement, to any subsequent transferee that:**
>
> **(1) the warrantor is a person entitled to enforce the instrument;**
>
> **(2) all signatures on the instrument are authentic and authorized;**
>
> **(3) the instrument has not been altered;**
>
> **(4) the instrument is not subject to a defense or claim in recoupment of any party that can be asserted against the warrantor;**
>
> **(5) the warrantor has no knowledge of any insolvency proceeding commenced with respect to the maker....**

What are other examples of reps and warranties? There are many. The core of these would include assurances that the note and liens are legally valid and enforceable; that they are secured by a lawful vendor's lien retained in a general or special warranty deed plus a lawful first-lien deed of trust against the security property; that payments are current and there is no threat of default; and that the assignor is the sole holder and owner of the debt with power to enforce and transfer the note and liens. Many more reps and warranties can (and should, from the buyer's point of view) be included. These can vary and are generally the result of negotiations between the parties. Clearly, the assignor's goal will be to minimize ongoing liability by either transferring the note entirely "as is" or including as few reps and warranties as possible; the assignee will instead want a long and specific list (the inclusion of a couple of dozen reps and warranties is not uncommon). Here's an example of one you might not expect at first: if the assignor was the original payee, and the note was generated from seller financing, the assignee would logically want a specific warranty that the SAFE Act and Dodd Frank were fully complied with in the course of the sale.

From the point of view of the assignee-buyer, due diligence is still required to assure the accuracy of reps and warranties by the seller. The existence of reps and warranties in the assignment does not eliminate this duty. Despite some inroads, the doctrine of "buyer beware" is alive and well in real estate.

Lastly, with respect to reps and warranties, there is the question of how long they will survive—30 days? 90 days? Forever?

"As Is" Assignments

What if the transaction is entirely "as is," with no reps and warranties? There is certainly a market for this, although the sales price of the note or notes will likely be discounted as a result. The key element in the assignment will be an effective "as is" clause, similar to ones found in earnest money contracts and warranty deeds although specifically tailored to the context of promissory notes. Drafting these clauses can be a bit tricky; simplistic, one-liner "as is" clauses simply will not do in this context, since the assignor will want not only to expressly disclaim assurances regarding the transferred note but also any reps or warranties concerning the condition and value of the property pledged as security.

An Indemnity Clause: Additional Protection for the Assignor

If possible, the assignor will want a clause that holds him or her harmless and indemnifies against any issues that may later arise in connection with the legality or collectability of the note. Buyers of anything, however, understandably resist not only taking the heat for defects in what they've purchased but also paying the seller's bills for defending against claims and lawsuits arising from those defects. As with so many issues in real estate, it comes down to price. A seller-assignor may be able to get an indemnity provision included, but it will likely be costly when it comes to the sales price of the note.

Indemnity provisions may be overrated, since they are not self-executing. After all, the terms of an assignment can do nothing to prevent a debtor from suing both assignor and assignee at some later time, resulting in inescapable up-front defense costs. The assignor is then left with a claim against the assignee on the indemnity, often resulting in a second lawsuit.

Recourse

Notes are sold with or without recourse against the assignor. Recourse comes in three varieties: none, full, or limited. "No recourse" means what it says—if the debtor defaults, then the assignee is stuck with a non-performing asset and is solely responsible for pursuing the debtor and foreclosing on the security property.

Full recourse means that the assignee gets to give the note back to the assignor if the debtor defaults. One of two things generally happen: the assignee gets a credit or refund or, alternatively, the assignee can substitute another note that is current and performing. There are quite a few variations on this theme.

Limited recourse is, contractually speaking, all over the place. There are as many different provisions for limited recourse as there are creative attorneys to write them. Limited recourse provisions may state that there will be some sharing of effort and expense in collection or foreclosure, possibly with a reckoning after the foreclosure sale. Remedies may be different when a batch of notes is involved: for example, if 100 notes are sold, the assignment might provide that the first 10 problematic notes will be full recourse, but the remaining 90 will not. In either case, there may be a hard limit on the total monetary amount of recourse available against the assignor.

The availability of recourse—whether none, full, or limited—may also be contained within a specific time period (It seldom lasts forever).

Endorsement of the Note

The note itself should be marked or stamped appropriately and the endorsement (or "indorsement" as it is referred to in the Business & Commerce Code) signed by the assignor. The endorsement should include wording appropriate to the circumstances such as "payable to assignee without representations, warranties, or recourse" and would include the date.

Where does one place the endorsement? "For an instrument to be negotiable, indorsements must be written on the instrument or on a paper so firmly affixed thereto as to become a part thereof [which is sometimes called an allonge]. An allonge is a piece of paper annexed to a negotiable instrument or promissory note, on which to write endorsements for which there is no room on the instrument itself." Failure to properly endorse a note when it is transferred may impair its negotiability, resulting in the recipient being a mere transferee rather than having the superior status of a holder in due course [see Bus. & Com. Code Sec. 3.302]. *"Federal Fin. Co. v. Delgado,* 1 S.W.3d 181, 185-86 (Tex.App.—Corpus Christi 1999, no pet.).

Miscellaneous Clauses in the Assignment

As is the case with most contracts involving the sale of an item, it is advisable for the seller (the assignor, in this case) to insist on an alternative dispute resolution clause that requires a good-faith mediation before the filing of suit. A venue clause, a merger clause, a no-representations clause, and a no-reliance clause are all advisable inclusions, particularly if one is the assignor. Good drafting principles apply, so consult a real estate attorney.

Investor Strategies

Notes are assets and their acquisition can be a part of an investor's long-term buy-and-hold strategy. Like rents, a portfolio of mixed-age performing notes can produce a stream of income; however, unlike realty, there no underlying equity to sell at the end of the rainbow. Value depletes over time, it does not increase, so a note portfolio requires continual management. As notes age and mature, new notes must be acquired in their stead if the income stream is to be maintained.

It is, of course, possible to acquire notes for other reasons. One aggressive strategy is to buy a secured note in default with the specific intention of foreclosing on the security property. A long-term hold is not the objective. The property is the objective. This scenario contemplates more of an "as is" approach to the note, since its price is often heavily discounted. In such cases, it is essential to perform thorough due diligence in order to ensure that both the note and the deed of trust are valid and enforceable, with no obvious defenses available to the debtor.

Chapter 50

Developments in Wholesaling

Still a Wild West Business

Both the legislature and TREC have moved in recent years toward greater regulation of the business of wholesaling. Wholesaling, for those who do not know, is an investor practice of getting a property under contract and then selling that contract to another investor who, after closing, usually does rehab work with the intention of selling the property at a profit, all within a short-term timeframe (usually a year or less). Several statutes now work together to impose a sort of "truth in advertising" disclosure requirement upon those engaged in wholesaling.

Applicable Law

Occupations Code Sec. 1101.002.(A) - Definitions

Do you need a real estate broker's license to engage in wholesaling? Chapter 1101 of the Occupations Code answers this question with a definite *maybe*. As is the case with most statutes, the first part of the law defines relevant terms, including in this case a definition of what constitutes real estate brokerage in the wholesaling context. Chapter 1101 states that a real estate broker "means a person who, in exchange for a commission or other valuable consideration or with the expectation of receiving a commission or other valuable consideration, performs for another person one of the following acts . . . deals in options on real estate, including buying, selling, or offering to buy or sell options on real estate. . . ." Since many earnest money contracts (depending on the stage they are in) can be considered a kind of option to buy real estate, if one is buying or selling such contracts (i.e., wholesaling), and if these contracts are offered and advertised as interests in real estate, then a broker's license is required.

Occupations Code Sec. 1101.0045 - Equitable Interests in Real Property

Again, the Occupations Code focuses on licensing. This section offers a loophole for wholesalers who are working without a broker's license, but only so long as they make express disclosure that what they are selling is merely an "equitable" interest, which generally means an interest that is less tangible, less certain, and more contingent than a solid and present fee simple ownership interest. The statute reads: "(a) A person may acquire an option or an interest in a contract to purchase real property and then sell or offer to sell the option or assign or offer to assign the contract without holding a license issued under this chapter if the person: (1) does not use the option or contract to purchase to engage in real estate brokerage; and (2) discloses the nature of the equitable interest to any potential buyer. (b) A person selling or offering to sell an option or assigning or offering to assign an interest in a contract to purchase real property without disclosing the nature of that interest to a potential buyer is engaging in real estate brokerage."

Section 1101.0045 wants wholesalers to make it clear to buyers of contracts that what is being offered is not the realty itself, but only contract rights to acquire the property in the future (This is what is meant by an "equitable interest."). Accordingly, wholesalers who assign contracts are *not* illegally acting as brokers if they fully disclose the nature of the interest they are selling.

22 Texas Administrative Code Sec. 535.6 - Equitable Interests in Real Property

The Texas Administrative Code contains TREC rules applicable to real estate license holders. Section 535.6 states that a "person may acquire an option or enter into a contract to purchase real property and then sell or offer to sell the option or assign or offer to assign the interest in the contract without having a real estate license if the person: does not use the option or contract to purchase to engage in real estate brokerage; and discloses the nature of their equitable interest to any potential buyer. A person selling or offering to sell an option or assigning or offering to assign an interest in a contract to purchase real property without disclosing the nature of that interest to a potential buyer is engaging in real estate brokerage. A license holder who is engaging in real estate brokerage by selling or buying or offering to sell or buy an option or assigning or offering to assign an interest in a contract to purchase real property must disclose to any potential seller or buyer that the principal is selling or buying an option or assigning an interest in a contract and does not have legal title to the real property. A license holder acting on his or her own behalf or in a capacity described by Section 535.144(a) who is selling an option or assigning an interest in a contract to purchase real property must disclose to any potential buyer that the license holder is selling an option or assigning an interest in a contract and that the license holder does not have legal title to the real property."

This section of the Administrative Code echoes a theme found elsewhere in the TREC rules: a license holder should *disclose, disclose, disclose.*

Property Code Sec. 5.086 - Equitable Interest Disclosure

Mirroring the Occupations Code and Administrative Code, Section 5.086 of the Property Code provides: "Before entering into a contract, a person selling an option or assigning an interest in a contract to purchase real property must disclose to any potential buyer that the person is selling only an option or assigning an interest in a contract and that the person does not have legal title to the real property."

Unlike the Occupations Code or the TAC, the Property Code is not focused on real estate license holders or the requirement of a broker's license. The Property Code applies to everyone, licensed or not.

So even if one could argue that the Occupations Code and the Administrative Code do not apply because one is not a license holder, the Property Code makes it clear that a seller-assignor must still make the required disclosure. Looked at another way: wholesaling without the disclosure gets an investor in double-trouble, both for a violation of the Property Code and for brokering real estate without a license. Note also that the license requirement of Occupations Code Section 1101.002.(A) refers to "dealing" in contracts (selling or buying), while Property Code Section 5.086 appears to only apply to persons selling a contract interest. So does an investor-buyer of a contract need to worry about whether or not the disclosure is present in the document assigning the contract? The prudent and safer answer is *yes.*

Content of Required Disclosure

Our suggestion would be to include the following wording at or near the top of the instrument that assigns the earnest money contract:

EQUITABLE INTEREST DISCLOSURE PURSUANT TO TEXAS PROPERTY CODE SEC. 5.086: THIS INSTRUMENT REPRE-SENTS ONLY AN OPTION OR ASSIGNMENT OF AN INTEREST IN REAL PROPERTY. IT IS NOT A TRANSFER OF TITLE. ASSIGNOR DOES NOT HAVE LEGAL TITLE TO THE

PROPERTY. CONSULT AN ATTORNEY PRIOR TO EXECUTION
IF YOU DO NOT UNDERSTAND THIS DISCLOSURE.

A buyer of an earnest money contract should want the assignment instrument to be recorded in the real property records. Why? As insurance that the contract will not later be sold by an unscrupulous seller to someone else. So the equitable interest disclosure would probably best be inserted just beneath the notice of confidentiality rights that is required by Texas county clerks to be present on filed documents:

NOTICE OF CONFIDENTIALITY RIGHTS: IF YOU ARE A NATURAL PERSON, YOU MAY REMOVE OR STRIKE ANY OR ALL OF THE FOLLOWING INFORMATION FROM ANY INSTRUMENT THAT TRANSFERS AN INTEREST IN REAL PROPERTY BEFORE IT IS FILED FOR RECORD IN THE PUBLIC RECORDS: YOUR SOCIAL SECURITY NUMBER OR YOUR DRIVER'S LICENSE NUMBER.

Assignability of the Contract

It should go without saying that the contract in question should expressly state that it is assignable. This is a suggested way to list the buyer in paragraph 1 of the TREC contract: "Action LLC and/or its assigns without Seller consent." Of course, a careful lawyer would prefer a more comprehensive clause such as "It is expressly agreed that this contract may be assigned at any time by Buyer before closing without prior notice to or consent by Seller. The effect of any such assignment will be to immediately, entirely, and unconditionally relieve any person signing as Buyer of any further obligations under the Contract. Seller unconditionally agrees to accept the assignee as Buyer and timely close without objection according to the terms of this Contract." But the available line is just too short for this (unless a special provisions addendum is being used).

The Assignment Instrument

Transfer of an earnest money contract should be accomplished by means of a "Sale and Assignment of Earnest Money Contract" which shares many of the same features as the note transfer instrument described in the last chapter. The principal difference is that earnest money contracts, unlike notes, are not negotiable instruments subject to the Uniform Commercial Code.

Characteristics shared by these two types of assignments are: (1) the necessity for thorough due diligence by the prospective assignee, which in the case of an assignment of earnest money contract requires not only an examination of the contract terms but also the underlying realty; (2) the general preference on the part of the assignor to make the transfer "as is," to the greatest extent possible; (3) the issue of representations and warranties and, if they are included, the extent to which they may be limited; (4) the period during representations and warranties will survive, if at all; and (5) the requirement that the assignor disclose any material issues, facts, or conditions (pending or threatened) that could reasonably influence the decision of the assignee to buy or not buy the interest being assigned.

Express Consent from the Owner of the Property

It is important—vital, in fact—for the assignee-buyer of an earnest money contract to be sure that the owner of the property consents to the assignment and will honor his or her status as the new buyer. This can be overlooked, and the buyer of the earnest money contract may wind up facing a hostile seller who refuses to accept the assignee as the legitimate buyer and refuses to close. Sellers in typical fix-and-flip contracts are not sophisticated in the real estate business and cannot automatically be counted on to go along with the sale of the contract on "their home" without their consent, even if the contract expressly states that it is assignable by the listed buyer. After all, the assignee of a fix-and-flip contract does not want to be put in the position of being forced to sue the seller for specific performance—an expensive event that could easily destroy the profitability of purchasing the contract in the first place.

Accordingly, the sale and assignment document should include consent wording along the following lines: "I/We, the undersigned, am/are listed as the seller in the Contract which is the subject of this Sale and Assignment. I/We give my/our unconditional consent to the sale and assignment of the Contract to the above-named Assignee, and agree to in all respects henceforth recognize Assignee as the rightful buyer under the Contract to purchase the Property. My/Our consent is effective on the Effective Date of the Sale and Assignment."

The addition of Property Code Section 5.086 requiring an equitable interest disclosure is the beginning of a regulatory scheme for wholesaling. Abuses and mishaps in this area will make the news from time to time, so it is likely that future Texas legislatures will build on Section 5.086 and expand it, just as occurred in the case of executory contracts. The pressure for regulation may also increase as cases inevitably appear that seek to bring wholesaling within the reach of the Deceptive Trade Practices Act.

Made in the USA
Coppell, TX
17 March 2022